Bold numbers refer to chapters in the book

The Orkneys

Inverness

2

2

Aberdeen

Montrose

2

Glasgow **Edinburgh**

Ayr

1

Dumfries

Hawick

1

3 Rothbury

3

Haltwhistle

Newcastle

Whitby

Swaledale

4

4

The Dales

Leeds

York

Blackpool

Hull

Anglesey

Liverpool

Manchester

8

Sheffield

8

8

Wrexham

Buxton

5

Pwllheli

Shrewsbury

Stoke

Nottingham

Aberystwyth

7

Leicester

Norwich

Birmingham

6

St Davids

9

Hereford

Cambridge

Ipswich

9

Swansea

9

10

Cardiff

Cirencester

Oxford

London

Rochester

Bristol

12

11

Exmoor

Salisbury

12

Alton

Canterbury

13

Exeter

Yeovil

Southampton

Rye

Dartmoor

13

Chichester

11

Brighton

11

St Austell

Plymouth

13

13

Penzance

N

100 miles

100 km

The Shell Book of Exploring Britain

Shell UK Limited, while sponsoring this book, would point out that the authors are expressing their own views.

The Shell Book
of
Exploring Britain

Garry Hogg
John Tomes

Second edition published 1985
by A & C Black (Publishers) Ltd

First edition by Gary Hogg published 1971
by John Baker (Publishers) Ltd

Reprinted 1974 and 1977

This edition published 1993 by
The Promotional Reprint Company Limited,
exclusively for Fraser Stewart Book Wholesale Ltd,
Waltham Abbey, Essex, EN9 1DQ

ISBN 1 87472 324 9

Printed in Hungary

Contents

Note: the sections on the Scottish Highlands, the
Yorkshire Moors, Anglesey and The Lleyn,
South-West Wales and Kent were written
by John Tomes

10

List of Maps

Foreword
to First Edition

I am very conscious of the latent objection that, in a country as relatively small as Britain, the term 'exploring' in the title of this book is not easy to justify; that there really is no field of exploration here, let alone of discovery, for light has long since been shed generously on even the remotest places. The objectors certainly have a point: England in particular, and Wales and Scotland to a degree hardly less, have been charted as it were with a fine-tooth comb; nothing, it can be argued, has been left unrevealed. The statement can hardly be challenged.

Nevertheless, even those who profess to know Britain well, who throughout much of their lives have taken pleasure in seeking out its abundant resources, will be among the first to maintain that this inheritance of ours is inexhaustible in its variety and wealth of treasure. This is part of the accepted magic of Britain.

I am one of those whose lifelong pleasure it has been to become intimately acquainted with this country; for half a century, give or take a year or two, I have indulged in this. At first, when little more than a schoolboy, a cycle enabled me (on those then gloriously free and empty highways) to quarter the country between John o'Groats and Land's End, between Thanet and Holyhead, camping solo with a lightweight tent in practically every county in the land. Later I abandoned the bicycle and took to my feet, soon to realise that this is really the only way in which to get to know intimately any stretch of country, whether at home or abroad. In later years, and for inescapable reasons, I had recourse to the internal-combustion engine. Each mode of locomotion has its undeniable points. But travelling by car today would certainly be less rewarding had I not first explored Britain—and the word is used deliberately—in a more intimate if arduous fashion. It is still possible, within definable limits, to combine the two modes.

This book is designed essentially for the motorist who is prepared from time to time to leave his car by the road side and take to his feet in pursuit of some objective that must remain denied to him so long as he stays at the wheel. Because every touring motorist equips himself with a handy road map I have given the Ministry of Transport road numbers throughout the pages that follow. I have added explicit details of direction and distance for the benefit of those motoring readers who are prepared occasionally to venture somewhat off the beaten track—a well-used phrase that might have served as a title for this book. For my book does not deliberately eschew the well-beaten track—save where it is necessary to follow one of these in order, so to speak, to depart from it in due course. Clearly there must be certain areas in which it is more difficult to do this than will be the case in others.

It will certainly be remarked that the Lake District does not appear at all. An inexcusable omission! enthusiasts for that incomparable region will be justifiably tempted to protest. But there is a perfectly sufficient explanation; and indeed this is a case in point. The ratio of car-negotiable roads to fell-walkers' tracks and climbers' routes is demonstrably lower in this district than it is anywhere else in Britain—or at least in England. It would be quite impossible, there, to maintain the basic design of this book; for Lakeland is essentially walkers' and climbers' territory.

As for justifying the twelve choices of region that constitute this book: the responsibility is exclusively mine. I am not so foolish as to expect that everyone will agree with the selection I have made. Indeed, I would agree that anyone who is reasonably knowledgeable about our country could produce alternative areas with an equal or even superior claim to consideration. That, as I have said, is part of the accepted magic of Britain.

At best I can claim—and it is a very modest claim indeed—that those I have selected (out of so many possible alternatives) are regions and areas that I have long known and always loved. I have written here of no place however small, no site however remote, that I have not visited, camera in hand, within the past six months, even though I may have visited them time and time again during previous years; they are all places which I have come to know with some degree of intimacy and, I hope it may be felt, with some degree of understanding. If I have succeeded here in whetting enthusiasm among readers for some at any rate of these, then it is my confident belief that they will derive something at least of the lasting enjoyment they have afforded me in such amplitude over the years since I first went in search of them.

Groombridge, Sussex, 1970   G.H.

For my wife, who for so many weeks during the summer of 1969 remained a 'grass widow', uncomplaining and understanding while I revisited these places.

Foreword to Second Edition

I never knew Garry Hogg, but the further I explored in the company of his book the more I wished I had done so. Here, surely, was a man of boundless enthusiasm, one who loved the far contours of the open countryside yet at the same time had an instinctive eye for things more intimate, whether the set of a thatched roof, the sentiment of a churchyard memorial, the nostalgia of an inn sign or simply a good story; a man, too, who was deeply sensitive to atmosphere, distressed as much by the present melancholy of a redundant church as by the remoter horrors of plague and gibbet.

My tasks have been twofold; to update Garry Hogg's text and to broaden his book's scope by the inclusion of some additional regions. In carrying out the first I have been very conscious of the danger of intrusion. Yet it soon became clear that there was more to updating than simply checking facts and emphasis. Even quite a small correction could sometimes affect subsequent paragraphs, while, of course, a major change such as that necessitated by the opening of Kielder Water in Northumbria could unbalance a significant part of a chapter. Nevertheless I have consistently tried to reconcile the requirements of accuracy and smoothness with minimum alteration.

As to the new chapters, in writing these no attempt has been made to imitate Garry Hogg's very individual style; to have essayed a pastiche would have been as risky as discourteous. I have, though, done my best to write within the kind of framework he always adopted—a general survey, later focusing in on selected detail—and in a style in tune with that of the original.

The preparation of this edition has demanded much skilled use of maps and typewriter, for which, as also for perceptive criticism, I am sincerely indebted to my wife.

Chelsea, London, 1985   J.N.T.

Acknowledgements

All maps were drawn by Tony Garrett, based upon the Ordnance Survey maps with the permission of the Controller of Her Majesty's Stationery Office, Crown copyright reserved.

The publishers would like to thank the following individuals and organisations for permission to reproduce photographs, which are listed by page reference:

Douglas Allen Photography, pp. 351, 357, 362, 375, 393, 395, 398 and colour plate facing p. 352

Barrie Aughton Studio (Woolf/Greenham collection), pp. 390, 407

John Blake Picture Library, p. 259 and colour plate facing p. 257

T. J. Bond, p. 313

J. Butler-Kearney, colour plate facing p. 273

Brecon Beacons National Park Committee, p. 227

Cadw – Welsh Historic Monuments, p. 195

Vic Cleveley, pp. 179, 196, 202

Frank Creese, pp. 81, 85

The Irish Hardwick Library of Photographs, pp. 261, 265, 360 and colour plates facing pp. 209, 256

Heart of England Tourist Board, colour plate facing p. 145

Highlands and Islands Development Board, p. 44

A.F. Kersting, pp. 19, 47, 59, 90, 95, 106, 116, 158, 171, 211, 216, 223, 241, 243, 245, 255, 257, 279, 282, 288, 293, 301, 329, 337, 345, 347, 369 and colour plates facing pp. 48, 49, 64, 65, 192, 208, 272, 273, 337, 353

E. N. Lane, pp. 310, 316 (foot)

Colin Molyneux, colour plate facing p. 193 (top)

The National Trust Photographic Library, by permission of Aerofilms, p. 150 and The National Trust for colour plate facing p. 129

North Yorkshire County Library (from the Bertram Unné Collection), p. 98

Peak Park Joint Planning Board, pp. 127, 133, 139 (photos: Ray Manley) 129, 131 (photos: Mike Williams)

Preseli District Council (photo: Norman Owen), p. 238

Frank Rodgers, pp. 155, 168, 173

The Royal Society for the Protection of Birds (photo: M. W. Williams) colour plate facing p. 144

Scottish Tourist Board, pp. 20, 23, 27, 39, 41, 49, 56, 66, 70, 75

Shropshire Weekly Newspapers, p. 166

South East England Tourist Board and the Romney, Hythe and Dymchurch Railway Ltd, p. 298

Major Raymond Thomas, T.D., F.R.G.S., F.R.S.A., p. 273

Wales Tourist Board, p. 199 and colour plate facing p. 193

George Walsh, pp. 325, 316 (top)

West Sussex Record Office, p. 277

Yorkshire and Humberside Tourist Board, p. 111 and colour plate facing p. 128

About this Book

This book is for those whose pleasure it is to escape from the main roads; to get (to quote from Garry Hogg's Foreword to the first edition) 'somewhat off the beaten track', a phrase which, he suggested, could well have served as his title. This second edition, though expanded to embrace over twenty regions spread across England, Wales and Scotland, remains true to this theme. In each of the regions a broad survey first sets the stage, after which smaller areas are picked out for more intimate attention—usually by way of minor roads which are not only attractive and enticing in themselves but which also more often than not lead to surprising discoveries, some simply visual, some evocative or redolent of legend, some a stimulating challenge to the traveller's imagination.

It is certainly not claimed that the areas picked out are the only ones worthy of leisurely exploration. One has only to glance at the map to see that in most regions this is far from being the case. Essentially, these areas represent the authors' personal choices—byways and corners which the reader is invited to enjoy while at the same time, it is hoped, deriving sufficient encouragement to spread out his maps and plot other courses for himself.

It need hardly be said that good maps are as essential for planning as they are for travelling. Those provided with this book aim to start the reader on his way, but additionally he will need reliable road maps. Shell publish an excellent and comprehensive range, obtainable at filling stations and notable for their accuracy and clarity, while for nationwide planning it would be hard to equal Michelin sheets 401 to 404 inclusive, all to a scale of 1:400 000. For detailed exploration, whether in the car or on foot, the admirable Ordnance Survey 1:50 000 series will surely be found indispensable.

Accommodation need pose no problem in any of the districts described in this book. At the same time it will be obvious that lodging and food will be closer to hand and in greater choice in, say, Sussex or Kent than will be the case up in the Yorkshire Dales or in the remoter corners of the Scottish Highlands. In these latter areas it is only prudent—and doubly so during holiday periods—to book ahead, a telephone call during the afternoon often being sufficient. Accommodation guides of all kinds abound. Travellers with individual requirements—farm-life, for instance, or fishing, self-catering, or simply gourmet—will arm themselves with the appropriate lists. For others, though, the comprehensive if less selective publications of the English, Scottish and Wales Tourist Boards will provide all they wish to know.

J.N.T.

MAP LEGEND

■   Inhabited abbeys, houses, castles

□   Ruined abbeys, houses, castles, hill-forts and other defended places

⊙   Prehistoric sites, crosses, unusual natural features

△   Peaks

●   Towns

•   Villages; sites of interest not included under above categories

- - - - -   Paths

═══   Canals

⌇   Rivers

───   Railways

═══   Bridges or viaducts

⸸   Pass

Roads, as tints, widths according to importance

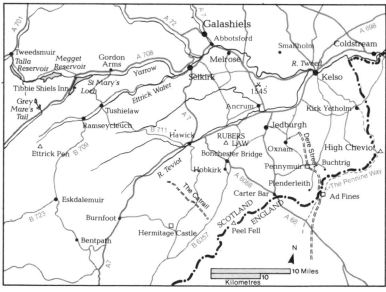

The Scottish Lowlands (East)

I

The Scottish Lowlands

A boldly drawn road spans Britain from Berwick upon Tweed to Gretna Green. Turning its back on the cold grey waters of the North Sea, the A 698 strikes south-west-by-south for twenty-odd miles to Kelso, steering a diplomatic course between the vagaries of Whiteadder and Blackadder Waters to the north and the less spectacular meanders of the River Tweed to the south. Some fifteen miles farther to the north is the skyline of the Lammermuir Hills; about the same distance to the south rise the mightier Cheviots.

Essentially, this is a brisk valley road, one that encourages speed. Momentarily held in check by the tortuosities of Kelso, it is then released, to be carried across the Tweed, reinforced here by the Teviot, on Rennie's noble five-arched bridge. Kelso folk will remind you that Rennie constructed this bridge as a model for the more imposing one that he was later to throw across the Thames, his Waterloo Bridge; his masterpiece has of course long since been replaced by a bridge that is graceful but lacks the dignity of its forerunner.

After Kelso, still a valley road for another twenty miles or more, the A 698 threads Teviotdale all the way to Hawick where it merges with the A 7 road from Carlisle to Edinburgh, a major highway, and swings southwards at Teviothead to Langholm, in the district of Annandale and Eskdale. Some twelve miles beyond, and now briefly back in England, you change to the A 6071 and soon reach Gretna, within a bowman's shot of the head of Solway Firth.

Eighty-odd miles in all. You could well have done the cross-country run in little more than a couple of hours, sea to sea. But at forty miles an hour, and on these main roads, you would have gleaned next to nothing of what these eastern Scottish Lowlands have to offer. Next to nothing, certainly, in those early miles of valley running; just something, perhaps, as the road thrust its way up Teviotdale and the contours changed from a hundred feet or so to the four-figure mark. So, the best way to come to know these Lowlands that lie to the immediate north of the Scottish Border is to abandon the main roads and seek the lesser ones; roads that were carved, may be, by pack-horse trains that were once the only mobile link between one isolated community and another. It is along roads such as these—and there are more of them than you might imagine—that the truest rewards are to be found.

No Border district more lucidly emphasises the contrast between lowland and upland than Roxburgh does. Sloping gently eastwards into Berwickshire, it is a place of many-watered valleys. Teviotdale threads it from its spring-head on the Annan and Eskdale border eastwards for more than thirty miles. The rib-cage, as it were, to this watery spinal column is composed of a score and more euphoniously named becks and burns: the Waters of Bowmont and Kale, Hassendean and Oxnam, Capelhope, Hindhope, Skelfhill, Leap and Flash, Ale, Rule and Jed, Limie Cleuch and Linhope Burn; and there are as many more besides. By no means all of them have a minor road, or even a negotiable farm track, running along their minuscule valleys; but most of them are crossed, at some point or other along their modest, uncertain length, by a road that gives relatively easy access to them, downstream or up.

For the most part low-lying, at least at its eastern end, Roxburgh complacently ignores the frowning mass of the Cheviot Hills that compose its southern flank; even High Cheviot himself, at 2676 feet, fails to dominate entirely its smiling acres of pasture and water-meadow land. The setting, in bygone days, of some of the fiercest Border feuds (and the word is not always adequate for the warfare that obtained in the region) between Scots and English, and some of the bitterest inter-clan and family feuding in the years that followed, today you must look keenly about you to find any substantial reminder of those tempestuous generations.

There are the occasional ruins of the old peles; there are scattered standing-stones, relics of an even older epoch: at Plenderleith, for example, bounded on one side by How Burn and on the other by Kale Water. There are ancient hill-forts, too: notably on the easternmost of the trio of Eildon Hills, which Sir Walter Scott could see from the windows of the spectacular mansion in part pseudo-Gothic style which he built for himself at Abbotsford. If you are historically minded, antiquarian or archaeologically minded, you will find a rewarding hunting-ground in Roxburgh. But the 'feel' of this district induces leisurely rather than purposeful exploration, and not the least engaging of its natural features is the multiplicity of its burns and cleuchs.

A few of these Waters, as they are so often called on this side of the Border, have their origin on the steep north face of the Cheviots themselves, though in fact the greatest area of the Cheviots will be found spreading outwards to the south, into Northumbria. Heatherhope and Kaim and Curr are three of these: all accessible at their lower ends from well made if minor roads and all, incidentally, offering excellent, if strenuous, walking. A fourth has perhaps the added attraction that it accompanies the walker along the last few miles at the northern end of the

Looking eastwards from Carter Bar towards the Cheviot Hills

Pennine Way, whether he is staggering down the last dramatic stretch or setting out southwards, bound for Edale in Derbyshire, and the Nag's Head Inn, two hundred and fifty miles of strenuous walking from the High Cheviots. Its name is Halterburn.

To reach it—and this is well worth doing—take the B 6352 south-eastwards out of Kelso. It is signposted to Town Yetholm and Kirk Yetholm, twin villages that lie on the north-western slope of the Cheviots at a point where the hills have already begun to lose much of the grandeur that has its apotheosis in The Cheviot himself, some six miles to the south-east. Town Yetholm will not delay you; its neighbour, on the other side of sparkling Bowmont Water, deserves something more than a passing glance. Here, the annual gatherings of the Border Gipsy families were held; from time immemorial, or at least for more than a half centuries, this tiny village was the headquarters of the Scottish Gipsies; it was almost certainly from some individual among these Kirk Yetholm based gipsies that Scott evolved the character Meg Merrilies for his novel,

The Eildon Hills

Guy Mannering. Happily, at any rate so far as the villagers themselves are concerned, their trim village is no longer the stamping-ground of the tribes that are still popularly referred to as 'The Egyptians'. But you can still see (in the upper part of the village beside the road to Halterburn mentioned below) a cottage known as the Gipsies' Palace.

Small houses, most of them built of solid stone with stone-slab roofs, line two sides of the spacious green. Two sycamores and a chestnut tree stand in front of the appropriately named Border Hotel, while a notice beside the road that cuts across the green indicates the start, or, if you prefer, the end of the Pennine Way, some ten miles north of the terminal point originally planned for it at Wooler, across the Border in Northumberland.

The road that has brought you as far as the two Yetholms now branches northwards, to cross the Border and nick a corner out of Northumberland before rejoining the Tweed at Coldstream, eight miles away. A lesser road, too insignificant to have been granted a number, climbs briskly away from the village green, passes the Gipsies' Palace, tops a rise, turns sharply to the right, to run exactly parallel with the Border itself for a couple of miles, with the stripling Halterburn burbling and tumbling alongside, and then peters out, as most such roads tend to do, at the small farm appropriately named Burnhead. You are now faced with a choice: either you go back on your tracks or you take to the open road. The term is, admittedly, a misnomer: there is no road beyond Burnhead. But there is a rich variety of narrow tracks lacing the contours that spin their cobweb patterns about Latchly Hill and Windshaw Hill, the ancient hill-fort or camp on the slope of White Law and the less demanding slope of neighbouring Windshaw Hill. For the most part it is true to say that the farther south you penetrate from Burnhead the steeper become the tracks; for the Cheviot Hills rise to their maximum heights between The Cheviot himself and Peel Fell, twenty miles or so to the south and west.

But let us return to the roads; to, for example, the little beauty that runs from the Yetholms and Morebattle to amble its way across lost country below the northern flank of the Cheviots until it meets the A 68 a couple of miles north of Carter Bar, that high-perched border point where the Redeswire Stone commemorates a raid of 1575. As you travel this meandering road the frequent earthworks crowning the bare hills will remind you of earlier peoples who lived and fought here, while streams as lovely as their names—Kale Water, Capehope and Heatherhope burns, How Burn and, finally, the wider Jed Water—provide a contrasting pastoral tranquillity. But it is soon after crossing Kale Water that you are most likely to want to pause and let loose the imagination; at the moorland spot known as Pennymuir where your road meets the Romans' Dere Street, once linking Woden Law on the Cheviots with the Firth of Forth. Northward, this is now a mere track; southward—and it is even unobtrusively signed Dere Street—it is a narrow dead-straight road aiming at Woden Law, distinctive with its encircling Iron Age and Roman earthworks, the latter perhaps representing the labours of the legionaries who once thronged the training camps immediately south of where you are standing and whose pattern can still be traced by a discerning eye.

There is no need to press on as far as the A 68. Better to swing north a mile beyond Pennymuir to round Peg Law and then follow the leisurely descent of Oxnam Water to reach Jedburgh. Astride its own Jed Water, soon to merge with the Tweed to the north, this small town offers enough to keep you interested for a whole day; the dedicated historian would say that seven times as long would not be enough. It is indeed redolent of history: every stone you touch, it would seem, enshrines a story; and the tenor of the story is more often tragic than the reverse.

Looked down upon from above, the older portion of this royal burgh takes the form of a cross: Exchange Street and Canongate strike athwart High Street and Castlegate. Jedburgh has its memories of the '45, for it was in a house in Castlegate that Bonnie Prince Charlie spent a night during his march southwards to Derby. It has earlier memories than that, too. Here you will find a building, now a museum, that is still known as

Queen Mary's House. Within its ancient walls the unhappy Mary, Queen of Scots, lodged awhile before making her memorable cross-country journey on horseback to visit her lover, Bothwell, then lying wounded at Hermitage Castle. It was in October, 1566, that she undertook this ride, over sixty bleak moorland miles, to the bedside of the sick man. It is small wonder that the ride brought her to her own bed of sickness, from which she barely escaped. Jedburgh held memories for her, some of them so sweet that afterwards, in her agony, she was heard to murmur: 'Would God I had died at Jedworth'. That name perhaps strikes oddly on the ear today. But it is only one remarkable number of variants that have been given to the town over its long, tempestuous years. Among these, perhaps the most interesting is 'Jeddart', which came to be used in the phrase 'Jeddart Justice', a euphemism for the well-tried if iniquitous principle of 'hanging first and trying the offender afterwards'.

Jedburgh's (or Jethart's, or Jedworth's) chief claim to attention, however, is probably its abbey, founded by David I of Scotland eight and a half centuries ago and sacked and destroyed four times over by the English and four times restored between one disaster and the next. Today, unhappily, it is largely in ruins: Norman arches intermixed with Gothic and the tower and nave rising at once gracefully and impressively, though shorn of their ancient glory, above the gently flowing waters of the Jed close alongside them. This same river, incidentally, is attractively spanned by a medieval triple-arched stone footbridge that runs from the lower end of Canongate. Little more than a mile to the south of the town, at Hunderlee on the Jed, you will find in a water-meadow a solitary tree, the Capon Tree, so called. Like Queen Mary's House, like Jedburgh Abbey, it is a relic: the sole survivor of the famous Jed Forest that once flourished on these easy slopes between the sprawling valleys of Teviot and Jed.

Just north of the town two main roads intersect: the A 68 running northwards from the Border at Carter Bar to Edinburgh, by way of Lauderdale, and the A 698 from Berwick upon Tweed to Hawick. They are linked by the A 699, which runs from Kelso to Selkirk closely following for much of the way the serpentining loops of the Tweed. Popular guide-books will tell you that this is the most beautiful road in the whole of the Scottish Lowlands. Well, it is every man to his choice! If such guide-books were content with claiming that it is the most beautiful *main* road in the Lowlands then it might not be easy to refute the claim without having explored the region leisurely and, as it were, in depth. You will, however, find other main roads that stand comparison with this one, and some that surpass it on most counts; but it must be borne in mind that the road is hardly more than twelve miles long. Moreover, it is essentially a valley road; and there are many who will say, and with reason, that even the finest of valley roads cannot really compete with a road that winds into and out of hills.

Queen Mary's House, Jedburgh

Northwards from Jedburgh the valley of the Teviot widens. Hitherto, all the burns—the Oxnam and Jed and Kale Waters and their innumerable Cheviot-born tributaries—have flowed into the Teviot to swell its waters until these merged with the more important Tweed to flow eastwards into the North Sea. But now they flow off the hills to the north: Hassendean and Ale and Grindin Beck, for instance; and you find yourself climbing gently towards their sources on the southward slopes of the Eildon Hills and their neighbours.

23

On the hither side, where Ettrick Water joins the Tweed, on B 6360, rise the proud towers of Scott's home, Abbotsford. You may feel that the place is more memorable when seen from a distance, in its riverside setting and to some extent masked by fine stands of trees, than at closer quarters. For this is no integrated noble pile; rather, it is an extraordinary conglomeration of varying architectural styles, not any of them necessarily bad but, let it be frankly admitted, not always appropriately or pleasingly juxtaposed. Clusters of tall chimneys; crow-stepped gables; corbelled turrets that one associates with the *châteaux* in the Loire Valley, for instance, rather than with the Scottish scene or even with 'Scottish Baronial'; towers and turrets, massive bay-windows rising two and more storeys, crenellated walls and ramparts: Scott threw his net wide; he had resolved to build a home for himself that should epitomise the sort of historical romance that is the essence of most of his novels and his narrative poems.

Abbotsford is located some three miles to the west of Melrose, one of Scotland's most mellifluously named towns. It lies just off the road from Melrose taken by Scott when, in the summer of 1832, he returned from Italy to his home for the last time. A tablet records how the great man 'sprang up with a cry of delight', not knowing (though possibly he suspected) that his eyes were dwelling on this well-loved scene almost for the last time. He was then sixty-one years of age. For the past six years he had been working heroically to repay his share of an enormous debt of nearly a quarter of a million pounds incurred by his publishers. He felt himself in honour bound to help them. The concentrated and sustained effort of producing no fewer than six full-length novels, with this end in view, had been too much for him. He had visited the Continent in search of health, and returned a broken man, sick and ill. He died three months after his return along this lovely road from Melrose to Abbotsford; died in his beloved home, in the heart of the Scottish Lowlands that were for him not just a setting for many of his novels but by then a part indeed of himself. An English queen declared that on her death Calais would be found graven on her heart; Abbotsford could as well have been graven on the heart of a great Scottish man of letters.

A quick glance at the map shows clearly that the true lowland area of Roxburgh comes to an end due south of the Eildon Hills. These are the triple outposts of the high ground that lies to the west, immediately over the border in Ettrick and Lauderdale and loftier Tweeddale beyond, and the fine mid-lowlands and mid-uplands of south Roxburgh beyond Teviotdale. Between the A 699 and A 698 a network of minor roads invites; the most distant of these, hardly six miles away, is one that closely follows the Teviot's left bank from Hawick to Roxburgh and Kelso. It is worth a leisurely run, not least because midway along it you will find yourself in the village of Ancrum.

Here you are on historic ground, though you might not think so to glance about you. One of the last of the large-scale battles between Scots and English was fought a mile or two to the north of the village, on a ridge of high ground officially known as Ancrum Moor but traditionally as Lilliard's Edge. Here, in 1545, was fought the bloody Battle of Ancrum Moor, in which the English Borderers, who had recently desecrated Melrose Abbey, were challenged by the Douglases, among whom was a heroic girl named Lilliard, who fought as courageously as any of her fellow-countrymen. That her courage was disproportionate to her size and strength is made clear in a local memorial to her: 'Fair Maiden Lilliard lies under this Stane; Little was her stature, but muckle was her Fame'.

Between the battlefield and the village runs the serpentining Ale Water—a contradiction in terms if ever there was one! On the outskirts of the village, hard by the old bridge that spans the stream, you will find if you look diligently enough a curious congeries of caves hewn out of the friable sandstone of the district and undoubtedly used by the womenfolk and their children while their menfolk were engaged in Border warfare; signs of the hearths on which they cooked their frugal meals may be found to this day.

Whichever one of these valley roads you may have taken, south-westwards from Kelso and bordering the Teviot, they will have merged by the time they reach Hawick. And here too both Slitrig Water and Borthwick Water will have merged with the larger river. You may care to linger in this woollen manufacturing town, for it has much of historical interest, including the monumental 'Mote', now unhappily almost completely engulfed and obliterated by the inevitable modern housing development schemes. If you happen to be there in June you may be privileged to witness the annual 'Common Riding' ceremony, when the young men of Hawick, still referred to as 'Callants', descendants, many of them, of those who defeated the English on a battlefield near by and triumphantly captured their standard, ride round the burgh singing 'The Colour' and chanting the mysterious slogan: 'Teribus ye Teri Odin, Sons of Heroes slain at Flodden!' It matters not to them that the battleground of Flodden Field lies some thirty miles to the east, far over the Scottish Border at Branxton.

Or you may prefer to by-pass Hawick, a busy industrial town today of some sixteen thousand inhabitants. If so, there is an inviting road running southwards from a point midway between Ancrum and Hawick and following the right bank of Rule Water, one of Teviot's major tributaries. After crossing the A 698 this road reaches the B 6357 at improbably named Easter Fodderlee, where you should bear right for Bonchester Bridge on the main A 6088 linking Hawick with the border at Carter Bar. Just one westward mile of this main road must be endured, as far as Hawthornside, before you escape south-westward along a little road which skirts

Stonedge Wood to reach the B 6399. This you now follow south and south-west along Lang Burn and Flosh Burn (another of those improbable names), near the latter crossing at right-angles the Catrail, a mysterious dyke, allegedly dug out by the Picts, which ran for nearly fifty miles before petering out on the western slopes of Peel Fell, almost the highest point of the Cheviot Hills. Beyond, Whitehope Burn is descended to its confluence with Hermitage Water, flowing leisurely down its modest valley. Hermitage Castle stands on its left, or north, bank, utterly detached, clad in its ancient and grim memories. You might not think, from the serene beauty of its setting, that its memories would be grim; nor indeed does its name even suggest this—in fact, quite the contrary, so far as associations are concerned, though these can be deceptive. In fact, Hermitage Castle takes its name from the Hermitage Water that flows idly beneath its enormous walls; and Hermitage Water takes its name from a small community of pious men who established a cell on its banks near by, possibly as long as twelve centuries ago.

The castle itself was built much later, some time in the thirteenth century, and was added to, elaborated and strengthened over the years as it became more and more involved in the tempestuous Border warfare. For all the peaceful associations of its name, it gathered about itself a corpus of legend so sinister that dwellers in the valley and on the hill sides for miles around blenched at any reference made to it; and this long after the Border fighting had receded into the hinterland of memory.

One lord of the castle, Soulis by name, unsuccessfully challenged Robert the Bruce as a claimant to the throne of Scotland. Ballads, which, as always, incorporate the accumulated folk-memory of the region, tell how the wretched man was taken from Hermitage, conveyed to the prehistoric Stone Circle near by, known as Nine Stane Rig, and there boiled alive in a massive cauldron. His screams of agony echoed long among the folded hills; and still, if local legend is to be credited, may be heard among them on windy nights when no prudent man would willingly stir abroad. It was at Hermitage Castle, it will be remembered, that the fourth Earl of Bothwell lay, desperately wounded, to be visited for a fleeting hour or so by Mary, Queen of Scots, who rode to him over the moors from Jedburgh and so nearly died as a result of the hardship and exposure she had to endure on that ride, notably in the great expanse of marshy ground still remembered as 'The Queen's Mire'.

The shell of the castle—its interior having been near-gutted time and again—has been finely restored, so that today, after more than seven hundred years, it is extremely impressive. Sir Walter Scott, who knew the Border castles well, rated it among the finest he had surveyed; and there can have been few, if any, that he had not made it his business to explore as settings for his novels and narrative poems. It may not be generally known that he actually had his portrait painted, with Hermitage Castle portrayed

Abbotsford, home of Sir Walter Scott

in the background. Many miles to the east, of course, and on the Northumbrian side of the Border, is another of his favourite castles, that of Norham, which figures in his best-known narrative poem, *Marmion*. It was in that poem that he wrote of Norham's

> Embattled towers, the donjon keep
> The loophole grates where captives weep.

Here it was not the lord of the castle who challenged Robert the Bruce for the throne of Scotland, but the great Sir William Marmion who defended it, as an Englishman, against the forces of the Bruce. Here, too, the castle stands splendidly above the Tweed, whereas Hermitage stands low on the bank of an altogether more insignificant stream.

The tapestry of legend that had accumulated about Hermitage over the centuries was much to Scott's taste, and he wove further lengths of it on the loom of his vivid story-teller's gift. Most of the material was instinct with evil. But there does appear, just now and then, a gentler thread. For example, the story of the Border giant named the Cowt of Kielder. Kielder, now, is on the Northumbrian side of the Border, if only just.

Determined to take Hermitage Castle by surprise, and without assistance, the giant Cowt of Kielder came down from the hills to challenge the then lord of the castle, the brutal Lord Soulis, who was later to suffer the agonising death in the cauldron. Unhappily for him, the gentle Hermitage Water rallied to the support of the lord of the castle (may be he had not at that time established the reputation he later earned for brutality). As the giant started to climb the castle wall, the water banked up, snatched at his flailing heels and dragged him to a death by drowning. In wry gratitude, Soulis had his retainers bury the giant beneath the stone wall of a church whose foundations date back to the same period of the first building of the castle. You can see to this day the mound they built over the Cowt of Kielder's giant corpse, though all signs of the ancient church have long since vanished, washed away, perhaps, by Hermitage Water when in spate as a result of the melting of the winter snows on Greatmoor and Hermitage Hills immediately to the north of the valley through which it runs. Probably the salient memory that lingers after this part of the Scottish Lowlands has been left behind is the emphatic contrast between the grimness of the castle and the serenity and almost lyric beauty of the countryside in which it is to be found.

From Hermitage Castle the minor road climbs gently up the valley westwards for three or four miles, with hills to the north that do not fall very far short of the 2000-foot mark, matched by hills to the south that are only a few hundred feet less high: Tudhope and Cauldcleuch on your right, as you travel westwards, and Din Fell and Wetherhorn Hill (with its echo of Switzerland's more famous and spectacular mountain) on your left. And then, as though girding its loins for the effort, it springs to the border with Annan and Eskdale and at once begins the easy run down to Burnfoot and the main A 7 road from Carlisle to Edinburgh three miles beyond.

There is no moorland road to carry you westwards, now, into Eskdale, probably your next objective. There is a patterning of fells and peat-bogs, deep-set burns and intervening banks that no road wider than a moorland track for sure-footed ponies could thread. You must inevitably turn south to Langholm, eight miles distant, and then turn sharply north-westwards on B 709. This, you will find, is something better than a B class road, though numbered as such. It runs north-westwards alongside the River Esk, here known as the White Esk, or White Water. The word Esk is simply a modernised version of the Gaelic *uisge*, 'water', from which we derive, etymologically as well as in other respects, the basis at least of the word whisky.

For something like twenty miles the road follows the right bank of the river as far as the point at which the course of the river, now little more than a burn, slants away north-westwards to the border with Ettrick and Lauderdale where its fountain-head is located. The road, too, crosses the border, and at that watershed picks up the little Tima Water, which it follows downhill to its confluence with the Ettrick Water five or six miles distant, at Ramseycleuch. The twenty-odd miles of this road north-westwards from Langholm to the district border and on down into the Ettrick Valley would be hard to equal anywhere in the Scottish Lowlands for sheer sustained beauty. The road from Tushielaw to the Yarrow comes close to this, in quality; but in length it is only one quarter as much. The road from St Mary's Loch, by way of Megget Water and Talla Linn to Tweedsmuir, comes closer to it still; but, once again, in length, and therefore in sheer expanse of excellence, it is considerably less. But then: why even attempt to draw comparisons, when there is sufficient variegated beauty for all to enjoy?

Once clear of Langholm, Eskdale takes possession of you, engrossing your attention in a fashion at once subtle and compelling. Wide at first, and plentifully endowed with trees, it narrows as the waters narrow and the valley sides steepen; yet for a while it remains essentially a pastoral landscape. It is the landscape of which the poet Southey, a West Countryman by birth, was to write: 'Green hills high enough to assume something of a mountainous sweep and swell; green pastures where man has done little, but where little more seems to be wanting; a clear stream, and about that number of cattle which one might suppose belong to the inhabitants for their own use.' A fair comment. If Southey were to return today, more than a hundred and sixty years after the visit which prompted those words, he would find that little was fundamentally different from what it had been in the early nineteenth century. One feature, however, that he would not have seen is the impressive memorial to Thomas Telford, the road and bridge builder and an Eskdale man by birth, that stands beside the B 709 near Bentpath, seven or eight miles up the valley, and looks eastwards across the Esk to the tree-clad hills beyond.

The air of Eskdale has long had a reputation for clarity and cleanliness. As long ago as the first decade of this century an Observatory was built near the isolated village of Eskdalemuir, 'for the observation of atmospheric phenomena', as it was officially explained to those who registered surprise, even astonishment, that such an establishment should be located in so remote a spot. It may be less important than it was, now that 'atmospheric phenomena' include satellites and rockets; but it survives, and you will find temperature readings from Eskdalemuir included in most newspaper records of rain and wind and weather. And the village is a charming oasis in a valley that, from this point onwards and upwards, becomes increasingly spectacular.

Eskdale was inhabited many, many centuries ago, as various groups of standing-stones—notably those on the east bank of the river known respectively as the Girdle Stanes and the Loupin' Stanes—testify. Look carefully at the contours of some of the slanting shoulders of land that are separated by tumbling burns like Harewood, Rae and Moodlaw, and by Windshiel Grain, and you will, if your eye is cunning and the light and shadow co-operate, discern the relics of ancient hill-forts. Among the most impressive of these is romantically named Castle O'er, which stands near a crook in the river between Moodlaw Burn and Rae Burn, a mile north of Eskdalemuir Church.

As you travel farther up the dale—and indeed this is true of the landscapes into which most such dales lead you—the turf is often so thin that it seems to have suffered in being stretched over the moorland skeleton that lies beneath it. Over many acres it has split, in long, parallel cicatrices. It reminds one of a side of pork that has been scored with a giant knife in readiness for basting; or—on a larger scale altogether—of whale-flesh that has been flensed in readiness for cutting up and removing the blubber for the production of oil.

But perhaps this last comparison is a harsh one, for the dominant impression conveyed by this landscape of Eskdale, and the landscape which awaits you beyond the head of the valley when your road picks up the Tima Water, is one of sweetness and light, of graciousness and serenity. It no doubt looks very different indeed when snow borne on northern winds sweeps across it and blankets all beneath it. Then, each of the small, solid and self-contained, self-sufficient farmsteads that are so attractive a scattered feature of this region must become, for a greater or lesser period, a fortress against the foe with knives in his teeth, with none to support it in its annual ordeal. Near where the Esk has its birth rise three summits, Ettrick Pen, Capel Fell and Wind Fell Hill: all three summits exceed by a good deal the 2000-foot mark.

A few paragraphs back, mention was made of St Mary's Loch. This you can reach by staying with the B709 through Tushielaw in the Ettrick Valley as far as the Gordon Arms Inn in the Yarrow Valley, a truly lovely extension of the road that brought you through Eskdale and which now, between the two valleys, carries you through hills rising to 1300, 1400, even 1900 feet. Stand on the roadside looking down on to the quiet waters of the loch and it seems to be the still centre of a heaving, almost tempestuous landscape, a mountainscape that has evolved all about you so gradually, so unobtrusively, as you ascended the well-graded road, that you have in fact only now become truly aware of it.

The twin 'wings' of this boomerang-shaped loch are each a mile and a half in length. Beyond the more distant of the two, beyond the Tibbie Shiel Inn and the memorial (one of several) to James Hogg, the Ettrick Shepherd, there is as it were a loch 'annexe', or appendage, charmingly named Loch o' the Lowes. Skirting it to the west is the road, the A708, that will give you perhaps the first true mountain road of this perambulation of the Scottish Lowlands. It climbs steeply for three miles to the border with Annandale and Eskdale at over 1000 feet, with two summits, each well over twice that height, as architrave to the doorway that leads into Moffat Water. The higher of the two is White Coomb, only a fraction under 2700 feet high and dramatically shaped. Off its southern flanks there flow, or rather tumble, burns that are more waterfall than running water. And of these, the most spectacular by far is the imaginatively named Grey Mare's Tail.

Between White Coomb and neighbouring Lochcraighead, almost equally high at 2625 feet, lies little Loch Skeen. This is the source of the Tail Burn, which flows south-eastwards out of the loch for half a mile or so, increasing in speed as it does so, until suddenly it gives up all pretence of being a burn and projects itself almost vertically downwards over the precipitous crags to splash violently into the head-waters of the River Moffat. It is a truly spectacular fall of some two hundred feet, broken just once or twice by massive chunks of rock that it has not yet been able to carry away with it. Standing at its foot, looking upwards, it is hard to believe that even these mountain sinews will be able much longer to resist the formidable strains to which for aeons past they have been subjected. 'Grey Mare's Tail', with its implicit reminder of Tam o'Shanter's mare, is an apt enough name for this stupendous waterfall; everything about you here was originally cast in the heroic mould, and nothing short of a cataclysm, surely, could ever effect a fundamental change.

If you are wise, you will descend no farther down Moffat Water. For the valley, pleasant as it is, becomes something of an anticlimax, leaving the drama behind and broadening out into something which, by contrast, is almost commonplace. Moffat itself is a wholly delightful small town; but after the wind-swept moorland heights you may well feel that something essential is lacking.

Rather, then, turn about; climb the odd mile or so back to the district border and retrace your steps downhill to St Mary's Loch, beyond Tibbie Shiels Inn; turn left at the first opportunity, in fact just where the main road you have been following for those few miles bears right for Yarrow and Selkirk. You are now literally on the threshold of another mountain road that you may come to think surpasses in beauty and drama even the upper reaches of Eskdale and the approach to Moffat Water that you have so recently explored.

Too unassuming to have been given a name, this very minor road climbs westwards beside Megget Reservoir, between shoulders and flanks of hills that rise to nearly 2000 feet, until, at almost 1500 feet and beside a cattle grid, it reaches the ancient little Megget Stone, marking what was once the border of Peeblesshire but which is now that of Ettrick and Lauderdale to the east and Tweeddale to the west. This spot is in wild, open moorland, but, grand though the view is, better is soon to come as suddenly, dramatically, breathtakingly, the little road falls away beneath your feet, crosses the head-waters of the diminutive Talla Linn, makes a dog's-leg turn, and drops you down to the level of the Talla Reservoir, three miles long and ending within a stone's throw of the hamlet of Tweedsmuir. It is not often that a reservoir controlled by a Water Board so completely and positively retains its natural identity as this one does. Its only near rival in this respect is its close neighbour a couple of miles to the south, Fruid Reservoir, linked to the first by a hidden tunnel.

Having reached Tweedsmuir, you are now committed to a main road, the A701, which runs northwards from Moffat to Edinburgh, for there is no other road in sight. You are in Upper Tweeddale, and the road climbs, close alongside the river, to a point where three regions meet: Tweeddale is a district of Borders region; to your west is Lanark, belonging to Strathclyde; and below to the south waits the Annandale and Eskdale district of Dumfries and Galloway. And it is near this point, too, some eight miles to the south of Tweedsmuir, that this noble river has its birth. You met it first, perhaps, in distant Kelso, where it had recently been swollen by the Teviot; now, among these high hills, you are to say farewell to it, for you are bound westwards for the Nithsdale, Stewartry and Wigtown districts of Dumfries and Galloway.

The Scottish Lowlands (West)

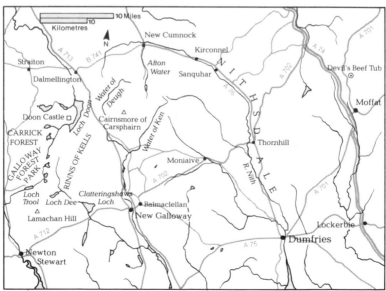

Having crossed the border into Dumfries and Galloway, break your southward run on this finely engineered main road long enough at any rate to look out over what is shown on your map as the Devil's Beef Tub, a strangely shaped hollow carved out of the high hills. 'It looks,' Scott made the Laird of Summertrees say, in his novel, *Redgauntlet*, 'as if four hills were laying their heads together to shut out daylight from the dark, hollow space between them. A deep, black, blackguardly-looking hole of an abyss it is, and goes straight down as perpendicular as it can do. At the bottom there is a small bit of a brook, that you would think could hardly find its way out from the hills that are so closely jammed around it.' Here, Scott tells us, the cattle rustlers who lived in this wild and remote district in which Annan Water has its springs, the 'Annandale loons', as they were often called, used to secrete the stolen cattle. Few other than themselves knew the secret of the entrance; and not many strangers cunning enough to discover the way in ever found their way out again.

It is a grim place, even when the sun shines strongly down upon it, flooding the main valley with light. Shadows fill the hollows, increasing (though hardly exaggerating) the element of depth and mystery that permeates them even in broad daylight. Close beside the road, on the left hand side as you descend the hill and just where there is a sharp double turn, first left and then right, there stands a solitary granite pillar. It bears the name of a Covenanter named John Hunter who, in 1685, was 'shot by Douglas's Dragoons. His grave is in Tweedsmuir Churchyard.' That is all.

No stone, however, marks the spot where, during the Rebellion of '45, a Highlander escaped capture by wrapping himself in his ample plaid and projecting himself down the precipitous slope while the frustrated soldiers fired down upon him from the road side. There is, on the other hand, a stone commemorating the spot where, in the mid-winter of 1831, the Scottish mail-coach ran off the road, the snow-posts having been obliterated by the whirling blizzard, and overturned on the treacherous slope. It was many days later that the mail-coach was discovered, half buried in a snow drift. The driver and mail-guard had died of their injuries and exposure, the mail-guard, as a local newspaper duly reported, 'lying there, dead, wi' a kind o' pleasure on his face'.

Compared with the multiplicity of minor roads to be enjoyed in the eastern Lowlands, those in Dumfries and Galloway are few and far between. Small wonder, either: for the land, albeit referred to as lowland, is really high ground, and the only practicable roads are those that run through the valleys on one side or other of the tumbling burns. These valleys for the most part run north-westwards and north-eastwards; but by some freak of hill distribution they tend to rejoin one another ten, twenty or more miles beyond their points of divergence. From Moffat, for instance, you must go south halfway to Dumfries before finding a negotiable road westwards into the next valley, exchanging Annan Water for Nithsdale, which runs right out into Solway Firth.

The main road, the A 76, northwards out of Dumfries, has relatively
little to offer. But you can pick up a lesser, and more rewarding, road, the
B 729, a few miles to the north of the town, and it will lead you north-
westwards to Moniaive, with its interesting three-centuries-old market
cross. Today Moniaive lies somewhat off the main through-ways—
perhaps not to the contentment of its shop-keepers but certainly to that of
the traveller in search of peace and quiet. It has had its day, though. In the
heyday of the long-distance stage- and mail-coach, Moniaive was a
staging-point for the Craigengillan Coach, one of the far-famed 'Roaring
Dillies', as they came to be known. These coaches did the ninety-odd miles
between Dumfries and Glasgow (a longer route than it is today by the
newer, better-graded road) in under fourteen hours. This may seem slow,
not merely by today's standards but by those of eighteenth-century stage-
coach schedules; but this is not taking into account the sort of terrain over
which these Roaring Dillies had to ply, northwards from the town of
Dumfries.

The boss of the oval shield of high hills to the north of the road carrying
you westwards from Moniaive rises to 2612 feet and is splendidly named
Cairnsmore of Carsphairn. From it, and from its comparable neighbours,
Black Shoulder and Windy Standard (how evocative are such names, how
suggestive of drama and romance!), there tumble countless burns, in
search of the high valley streams such as the Waters of Ken and Deugh.
This is indeed wild country; but there is evidence all about you that it was
not too forbidding for prehistoric man and his immediate descendants to
establish themselves here. Cairns abound; stone circles, too; and isolated
standing-stones, such as those scattered about the Holm of Daltallochan,
near Carsphairn itself.

Now you will have reached the A 713 and your way further westward is
barred by the huge range of hills known as the Rhinns of Kells which are
between two and three thousand feet in altitude. Once again, as so often
already, you must travel either north or south for some miles before
continuing west into the next valley. North is probably the better choice, if
only because it soon offers a detour along a narrow road skirting the shore
of Loch Doon. Here, near the road's end, you will find a curiosity, a
fourteenth-century castle ruin which once stood proudly on an islet—you
can still see it when the water is low—but which was meticulously
dismantled and then re-created on its present site when it was found that
the conversion of the small loch into the present long reservoir would
drown the castle. But there is no escape from here, and you must return to
the A 713 and Dalmellington before you can swing westwards along the
B 741 for Straiton, through which there flows the beautiful Water of
Girvan which now marks your southward route.

It is a mountain road, or at least an uplands, a moorland road, and quite
one of the most beautiful that run through this district; a district,

incidentally, that is consistently overlooked by all save the truly leisurely traveller, for the impulse is always to take the main road north to Glasgow and beyond, or to make for the coast road that leads to Glasgow by way of Ayr and the Firth of Clyde. Now Carrick Forest lies all about you: not the ancient forest, but acres and acres of newly-afforested land replacing what once flourished there and eventually died. The highest hills, neighbours of the Rhinns of Kells, with resounding names like Kirriemore and Shalloch on Minnoch, extend eastwards from the road to the far horizon; in the other direction the landscape falls gently towards the coastline twelve or fifteen miles distant, out of sight and even more positively out of mind; it is difficult in a setting such as this to think in terms of shore-lines and salt water and shipping.

South of Carrick Forest your road, now descending gradually from its higher reaches, brings you to the fringe of Galloway Forest Park. Wild mountain country still, it is true; but with a hint of gentler scenes to come. For now the road begins to dip more steeply as it closes with the Valley of the Water of Minnoch, which is so soon to merge with the Water of Trool. You come suddenly—for trees are now close-set all about you—to Glen Trool Forest Village; and here you turn off sharply among the trees into this, perhaps the loveliest of all the glens of these parts. Indeed, you may well think, when you have penetrated the uttermost confines of this unbelievably beautiful glen, that you can think of no other in Scotland, at any rate in the Lowlands, that can compare with it.

The far end of the loch is compressed between the great heights of Buchan and Bennan Hills to the north and Lamachan Hill to the south. On the steep loch-side slope of Lamachan Hill there is a massive outcrop known as Mulldonach, separated from the higher hill by a saddle called the Nick of the Lochans. We are back to Robert the Bruce, last remembered at Hermitage Castle. Here in the year 1306 he scattered his enemies by hurling down the precipitous hill side an avalanche of boulders that wrought havoc among them as they clawed their way along the twisting track at its foot. A stone, always referred to as the King's Stone, though the king died seven centuries ago, commemorates the site of Bruce's grimly effective strategy.

But perhaps it is a pity to link in the mind the sheer richness of natural splendour that characterises Loch and Glen Trool with old, unhappy far-off things, and battles long ago. The surrounding heights may have a grimness, a starkness that is inescapable; but down in the glen itself, among the birch and beech trees, and on the waters of the loch, you may ignore them and savour to the full the intimate beauty that immediately surrounds you. It will be, and remain, perhaps the dominant memory among all those you have accumulated while exploring the infinite variety of the Lowlands of Scotland.

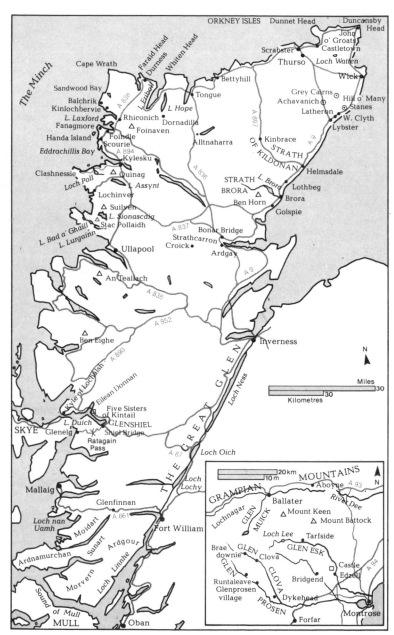

The Scottish Highlands

2

The Scottish Highlands

AN INTRODUCTION

Nothing belittling is intended in the suggestion that there is always something anti-climactic about the term Lowlands. Say Highlands, though, and you have excitement and anticipation. And in few places can this be truer than of Scotland, where Highland is the adjective that brings instant glamour to otherwise run-of-the-mill words such as dance, dress and games, not to mention scenery, clans, whisky and even cattle. Say Highland and you conjure a package, and a highly colourful package at that, of romantic Landseer scenery; of stunning dress based on kilt and tartan; of brawny, ¯kilted clansmen tossing giant cabers; of highly romanticised history and fierce clan loyalty; and of bonnie, wholesome lads and lasses performing their intricate traditional dances to music which cannot fail to thrill. All this, of course, to a background of Gaelic chatter or, at worst, English spoken with an accent as beguiling as the music, whether the stirring accompaniment to a dance or the lament of the bagpipes.

Lament, because there is a latent but insistent melancholy here too; a melancholy nurtured deep in Celtic roots and fuelled by the trauma of Culloden, which ended a Highland way of clan life thought to be immortal, and the shame of the Clearances when both native landowners who no longer cared and alien English drove out a whole people to make way for sheep.

You will not, it need hardly be said, experience all this at one and the same time and place. But you will come close to it if you manage to attend a Gathering, another of those very ordinary English words taken over by the Scots to be given an initial capital and, with it, specific and colourful meaning.

Perhaps it is worth remembering, though—not in any derogatory way, but simply as added background interest—that much of your Highland experience will be a renaissance, and a renaissance which might well never have occurred had it not been for one very determined and very appropriately named man. After Culloden, practically everything that the visitor now regards as the very quintessence of Scotland was forbidden; play your bagpipes or don your kilt and you risked penal transportation for life. But Sir Walter Scott, born less than thirty years after Culloden, would have none of this. He vividly romanticised Scotland's past; he sought and found the lost regalia, the Honours of Scotland; and in 1822 he stage-managed a State Visit by George IV, even persuading that monarch to sport the Royal Stuart tartan. Thus the signal was given, and by the middle of the century a kilted Prince Albert could have been seen striding around his newly-acquired Balmoral.

But where, precisely, are these Highlands? The term has no admini-strative significance, although, confusingly, the area does include the modern local government Highland region; but it also embraces much of Strathclyde, Central, Tayside and Grampian regions. The professional geographer tends to divide mainland Scotland into three; from north to south, the Highlands, the Central Lowlands and the Southern Uplands which in the previous chapter, and following common if loose usage, we dubbed the Scottish Lowlands. But these central and southern divisions need not concern us here. All we have to determine is the southern limit of the Highlands, and on this there does seem to be general agreement on a line between Dumbarton on the Clyde and Stonehaven on the coast just south of Aberdeen. Not only does this line accord with that of a long geological fault known as the Highland Boundary Fault (one place close to this line, Comrie, even experiences the occasional earth tremor), but if you draw this diagonal on a physical map you will see that over most of its course darkening brown predominates to the north-west while lighter colouring shades away to the south-east. This line, then, we can safely accept, as also that the long coast from Stonehaven all the way round to the Mull of Kintyre defines the eastern, northern and western boundaries of the Scottish Highlands.

So you are confronted with a huge, even intimidating, area in which to explore. From Dumbarton to John o' Groats even a crow would have to fly close on two hundred miles, from the shores of the Isle of Skye across to Aberdeen some one hundred and thirty; mileages which could well increase by a factor of up to perhaps a third when the courses of winding and mountainous roads dictate the way. As a start, though, it is fair to rule another line, one from Stonehaven north-westward to Inverness. By doing this we lop off the most populous sector of Grampian region, for that matter of all the Highlands, a sizeable, undulating, pastoral country which, though liberally sprinkled with charming and even historic small towns, not to mention other places of interest, scarcely qualifies as Highland in the popular sense of the term.

Formidable though what is left may still seem, you will readily appreciate from your maps that most of this—the massed barrier of the Grampian Mountains, the long approaches to the jumbled peaks of Wester Ross, the seemingly limitless moorland wilderness of Caithness and Sutherland—is largely empty. Heavier brown shading, spot heights or

Highland games – 'throwing the hammer'

tightening contours all hint at scenic excitement, but across all this there
are relatively few roads and correspondingly few places. The opportun-
ities for exploration, whether by road or on foot, are of course limitless and
hugely challenging, but in large part it is the exploration of scenery rather
than of specific places; of scenery, moreover, which so defies description as
to make it senseless to try. In the main, then, the three later sections of this
chapter will devote themselves to the more incidental periphery.

Geographers sub-divide the Highlands into two more or less equal
parts, north and south of what is variously known as the Great Glen, Glen
More (which means the same thing), Glen Albyn, or, more technically, the
Caledonian Fault. You will find it quickly enough on your map, the clean
split that runs south-west from Inverness, the length of Loch Ness,

followed by Lochs Oich, Lochy and Linnhe and so out to an island-studded sea.

Loch Ness is of course inseparable from its monster, about which no dogmatic pronouncement will be dared here. Nevertheless, those who secretly want to believe in it, yet cannot quite bring themselves to do so, may take encouragement from the fact that the monster was both seen and thwarted by St Columba. On his way to convert Brude, King of the Picts (which he successfully did at Brude's stronghold on Craig Phadrig, just west of Inverness), he ordered a servant to swim across the River Ness and bring back a boat. Once the servant was in the water, however, the monster surfaced and made for him, roaring with mingled rage and anticipation. But Columba had only to make the sign of the Cross, whereupon the monster obeyed the saint's shouted command and turned tail. This is all well told by Columba's biographer, St Adamnan, and surely even the most sceptical must wonder what fire generated this smoke. Anyway that is Adamnan's report, propagandist, for sure, but still a nice example of Scottish bravura.

Large though it is, we can conveniently adopt the geographers' northern sub-division as one of our chapter sections, headed simply 'The North' and the first of the three that follow. But the southern sub-division is less well-ordered, largely on account of the Grampian Mountains, a useful package-name for a sprawled central massif which embraces several famous districts and individual ranges, amongst these Lorn, Breadalbane, Badenoch, Atholl, Monadhliath, Mounth and, best known of all, the Cairngorms. Convenient that name Grampian may be; genuine it is not, for it represents a scribe's error which has been perpetuated over nearly two thousand years. In A.D. 82 the Roman, Agricola, finally defeated the northern tribes at a place recorded by Tacitus as *Mons Graupius*, a word misread by his scribe as *Grampius*. It is ironic that while the site of *Mons Graupius* has never been agreed—opinions range from the region of Inverness to Raedykes above Stonehaven—nevertheless its misspelt name lives on as one of Britain's best-known mountain systems. Tacitus recorded another name, too, that of Calgacus, the tribal leader; defeated in battle he may have been, but nevertheless this Calgacus occupies a uniquely individual niche in history as the first Highlander to have his name in print, or whatever the contemporary equivalent may have been.

Relatively few roads traverse the length or breadth of these Grampian Mountains—three, one may say, from south to north, two from west to east—and even these overlap. All are much travelled, far too much, many would complain, and, being also much documented, are only outlined here.

The A 82 is the westernmost of the south to north roads, and a famous road it is, too, hugging Loch Lomond's shore before climbing between Glenorchy and Breadalbane to top the watershed and drop the length of

Highland cattle

Glen Coe, a name as melancholy and infamous in history as it is famed for breathtaking scenery. Beyond, the A 82 rounds Ben Nevis, at 4406 feet Britain's highest though far from most spectacular mountain, before angling north-east to trace the length of the Great Glen.

Parallel to the southern section of the A 82—the section between Loch Lomond and Glen Coe, that is—some forty miles away to the east beyond moor, marsh, loch and mountain, you will find the A 9, Scotland's principal south to north artery. In part laid out by General Wade in the early eighteenth century (his many roads were an important ingredient in the plans for taming the Highlanders who obstinately preferred the Stuarts to the Hanoverians), and improved by Telford in the nineteenth, the A 9 has never been left alone. Today largely dual-carriageway, this road carries fast and heavy traffic between the Stirling area in the south and Wick and John o' Groats in the far north, on its way passing Perth,

Pitlochry, and the dramatic site of the Battle of Killiecrankie before climbing across the Pass of Drumochter to descend to the lush, generous valley of the Spey. And here you may well choose to stop; at Kingussie, where you will find the admirable Highland Folk Museum as also the ruins of Ruthven Barracks, as visually stark as they are historically poignant. Into these barracks, in 1746, straggled the few survivors of Culloden. Exhausted and wounded but nevertheless prepared to rally, they received neither encouragement nor thanks from their prince; merely a curt and heartbreaking message that each man should seek his safety in the best way he could.

To the east again, two consecutive roads lead you north. First, the A 93, which climbs out of Perth and up Glen Shee to Cairnwell (at 2199 feet claiming to be the highest main road pass in Britain) before dropping down Glen Clunie to Braemar, venue of perhaps the most famous of all the Highland Gatherings, and not only because it is attended by royalty. From here the A 93 will carry you eastward past Balmoral and down Royal Deeside to Aberdeen. But at Ballater another road takes over and points to the north. Officially the A 939, it is, along its steepest part, more interestingly known as the Lecht Road, built by military engineers in 1752 to 1754. Climbing abruptly to 2100 feet, and notorious for its winter snows, this road passes Tomintoul, the highest village in the Highlands (oddly, the highest in Scotland, by a margin of two hundred and twenty feet, is in the Lowlands—a place called Wanlockhead) before falling to Grantown-on-Spey.

The west to east crossings of the Grampians are less confidently defined and also in part merge with sections of the south to north roads. In the north there is the A 86 which will take you out of the Great Glen at Spean Bridge—the place, incidentally, which offers the best view of the grand north face of Ben Nevis—thence ascending gently for some thirty-five miles beside Lochs Moy and Laggan until the River Spey angles in from the west and the trunk A 9 from the south. Across the southern Grampians you have the A 85 which leaves the south to north A 82 at Crianlarich but in twelve miles becomes the A 827 to carry you the length of Loch Tay before you briefly meet the A 9 below Pitlochry. From here a great loop of some twenty miles along the A 924 will complete your eastward progress when you hit the A 93 at Bridge of Cally at the foot of Strathardle.

All the foregoing, a satellite survey of the Grampians one might say, springs clearly enough out of any general map. But more detailed and local maps suggest a fuller story, one which reveals that many a minor road climbs or drops off these major ones. As often as not petering out at the heads of the glens they have been ascending, these minor roads, surprisingly little used, penetrate the real scenic fastnesses of the Grampians, and it is along these, too many for individual mention, that you will venture if you are set on escape and discovery.

So much, then, for a superficial survey of the geographers' southern Highlands. Within this bold, broad region we shall want to focus on two smaller areas for more detailed attention, areas which, for preference, lie on the periphery of the Grampian massif. The first, which we will call The South-West, can be those lands which, at any rate as seen on the map, fall away seaward like a giant's tears; the peninsula of Kintyre and the islands of Jura and Islay (the Cowal peninsula, Bute and Arran are equally part of this geographic pattern, but the spirit here is Lowland and both peninsula and islands look east rather than north). This South-West we will balance with The South-East, here concentrating our attention on the succession of lovely glens which cut purposefully out of the south-eastern Grampian slopes but which, for the most part, the motorist can reach only from the coastal plain.

Thus far this introduction to the Highlands has, if with digressions, largely concentrated on setting the geographic stage. But what of the people, the people who not only lived on this stage but also left such dramatic and ubiquitous evidence of their passage, evidence which is often locally unique, or very nearly so?

Increasingly blurred though the distinction is becoming—a process initiated by the accession of James VI of Scotland to the English throne and hastened by Culloden, the Clearances and this technological twentieth century of ours—true Highlanders and true Lowlanders remain sensitive to their particular origins and identities. Both trace their remote roots to the pattern of tribes which the Romans found when Agricola arrived in A.D. 82 and which, while distinguishing some individually, they tended to lump together as Caledonians, or sometimes Picts (the painted ones)—people, it is revealing to learn, who wore chequered garments and were much given to wild dancing around their up-pointed swords.

During the fifth and sixth centuries, after the Roman departure, the Angles aggressively colonised the vacuum in the eastern Lowlands, while in the distant Highland south-west a Celtic wave, this time Christian and known as Scoti, crossed over from Ireland to Kintyre. Here they founded the kingdom of Dalriada, whose first 'city', Dunadd, survives as one of the most evocative archaeological sites in all Scotland. Over the centuries, Christian Dalriada absorbed the other Highland tribes until by around the tenth an even sharper Highland – Lowland pattern was emerging—the latter Anglian, or Northumbrian; the former, isolated within their mountains, cohesively Celtic, organised in clans and speaking the Gaelic that by now had swamped the ancient Pictish tongue.

But, long before all this, men spanning the Stone, Bronze and Iron Ages were leaving their mark all over the Highlands, building with such skill that even today, eroded and tumbled though they may be, their monuments stand high on any list of Highland sites of tourist interest, commanding not only our curiosity but also our admiration.

Dun Carloway broch, Isle of Lewis

Stone circles and alignments, lone standing stones, chambered cairns (burial chambers), hut circles, hill-forts, brochs and earth-houses; all these, bar the last two, are common to the whole of Britain, representing where ancient man lived and defended himself, where he worshipped and where he was laid to rest. Brochs and earth-houses, though, are almost unique to the Highlands, while chambered cairns may also claim a special category because only in the Highlands have they been so widely and so painstakingly restored that effectively you are seeing, indeed entering, something closely akin to the original. Those dolmens you will surely have come across elsewhere, notably in Wales and Cornwall—naked, capstoned megaliths—are here encased within massive stone mounds which you penetrate by long, low and narrow passages, and if today the inner chamber is lit by a glass skylight then any small detraction there may be

44

from the real thing is amply balanced by our ability to see, study and wonder at our distant ancestors' constructional achievement.

Brochs, intricate and reaching skyward; earth-houses, simple as can be and burrowing into the ground. Stranger structures than these it would be hard to find. Both appear to belong to the Iron Age or thereabouts, starting in, say, 300 B.C. and continuing into the Roman era, and both are still to be found across much of the Highlands.

But just what are, or were, these brochs, and where can you find one that is still recognisable? Drystone in construction and tapering to a height of perhaps fifty feet, they were conical towers, erected probably by local chiefs for the domestic and defensive shelter of their not inconsiderable households. Remarkable enough from the outside, these towers are even more so when studied from within, for only from here can you appreciate why the adjective 'intricate' was used earlier; stand inside and you will see that these brochs are double-walled, the outer and inner being bonded at vertical intervals with slabs so close-set that they form a tier of galleries through which one or more stairs climb to a walkway around the top. Structural strength and stability were probably the prime aims of this design, though doubtless the galleries served also for storage and other purposes. Our next chapter-section, The North, will lead you to the two best-preserved brochs on the mainland, but you will have to journey to remote Mousa in Shetland for anything approaching a complete survival. Meanwhile sites abound on the map, in most cases little more than tell-tale mounds yet each a challenge that may provide a surprise.

Steps, quite steep, down into the ground; a gently descending and curving long narrow passage, stone-walled and stone-roofed; at the end, a similarly walled and roofed chamber, perhaps twelve by six feet and six feet high but in some cases little more than a broadening of the passage. Such is a typical earth-house. What purpose these places served nobody seems to know for certain. Storage or refuge are the favourite explanations, though, if accepting the latter, one must hope that the entrance was well disguised, for were it discovered by an enemy those below would be horribly trapped. Culsh, near Tarland, to the north of the A 93 along the Dee, is a good if rather tidied example, while by contrast one beside Loch Eriboll on the far north coast is far more satisfyingly primitive and adventurous.

To conclude this Highlands introduction, a word of caution. Brochs present no problem, chambered cairns and earth-houses do. These are not places for the frail, the fastidious or those who prize their dignity. Suppleness of body is what counts, together with a willingness to crawl, torch between teeth, across dust and mud, and maybe through water too, and a head sufficiently hard to survive the inevitable encounters with unforgiving rock.

THE NORTH

As we have seen, the Great Glen marks the southern limit of the northern Highlands, the coasts providing the eastern, northern and western confines. So far as one may package a land so large, the pattern is one of a generally unremarkable east coast—flattish to the south, lifting at the centre, flattening off again to the north—from which often featureless moorland rises gently westward to a broken chain of splendidly named peaks (Foinaven, Suilven, Stac Pollaidh, An Teallach, Ben Eighe) which back a strange and spectacular shore, a crazily fretted and islanded wilderness of black water and black rock. Lochs of all shapes and all sizes spatter the scene, some hugged by roads but countless others far out in wild marshland offering a gamut of moods from sunlit sparkle to forbidding gloom.

Some ten main roads link the Great Glen and its linear extension, the east coast, with the western and northern coasts, but if this number perhaps sounds generous, then bear in mind that something approaching two hundred miles separate the Sound of Mull in the south-west from John o' Groats at the north-east and that thus fifteen to twenty Highland miles of moor, peat hag, loch and mountain may lie between each road and its neighbour.

For sheer scenic grandeur the two roads across the south, the two 'Roads to the Isles', are the winners. With their feet in the Great Glen and their heads at the southern and northern approaches to the Isle of Skye, and without the long tedium of moorland preliminary, they plunge quickly into the mountains. The A 830 out of Fort William is the more southern of the two, passing Glenfinnan, the spot where the Young Pretender raised his standard, and skirting the shore of Loch Nan Uamh, scene both of the high hopes of his landing and the ignominy of his departure. This road also offers you the opportunity to explore southward into relatively little-travelled country as scenically stimulating as its districts' names are resounding. Ardgour, Sunart, Moidart, Morvern and Ardnamurchan, rich in associations with the Macdonald Lords of the Isles, are calls hard to resist, whether you meander by road or cruise the length of Loch Shiel.

The other road, the A 87 out of Invergarry, also passes a spot briefly famous in the Jacobite story; Glenshiel (not to be confused with Loch Shiel previously mentioned), where in 1719 Macraes, Mackenzies and three hundred Spaniards, all under the Earl of Seaforth, were defeated in their ill-judged attempt to put the Old Pretender on the throne. A good place, this, for a halt, perhaps to study the skirmish, perhaps just to relax amid glorious scenery, before you continue down the glen below the towering wall of the Five Sisters of Kintail. Approaching Shiel Bridge, you pass the start of the dramatic minor road across Ratagain Pass (about which more below) and finish by skirting Lochs Duich and Alsh, near

The An Teallach range, above Dundonnell, from the east

their meeting being Eilean Donnan, island stronghold of the Macraes and of all the Highland castles probably the most beloved of the poster designers. It also enjoys what must surely be a unique distinction among British castles, that of having been garrisoned, however fleetingly, by Spanish troops.

Travelling these two roads your scenic focus will for the most part be a short one, for the mountains crowd in early while curves and shoulders often block a distant view. But the farther north you go—exploring, let us say, the country between the A 832 to A 897 inclusive—the more this changes. With empty moorland reaching away to either side, your focus lengthens westward, at first searching for those peaks thirty or so miles away, later held by their ever-changing shape as they loom closer until suddenly you find yourself descending some lovely strath between them. Along these roads the peaks provide the promise, the endless moorland approaches, a present sense of solitude. Nowhere is this more the case than driving the length of the remote and very minor road that links Alltnaharra on the A 836 with Loch Hope below the north coast. This surely will be the choice of anybody in search of escape; one, moreover, which passes one of the rare specific sights, or, if you prefer, sites, in these parts, the broch of Dornadilla in lonely Strath More, some four miles south of Loch Hope.

So far we have concerned ourselves only with those roads which will carry us across the empty but always haunting interior of the northern Highlands. But there are of course others, for the most part more incidental, which follow the coastal periphery. The A 9 on the east keeps reasonably close to, if in places well above, an uncomplicated shore, but this is not the case with the succession of smaller roads which define the north and west. Serving a progressively more broken coastline, these roads make little attempt to hug the shore, instead leaving it to the frequent sea lochs to make intermittent and brief contact. Exploring the north and west, you must divert down minor and often improbable-looking byways if you are after a closer and more lasting seashore experience. Such diversions, together with others inland of some scenic or other merit, make up the dozen or so pockets into which you may elect to stray as you round Scotland's far north from Inverness to Kyle of Lochalsh.

The melancholy evidence of depopulation is rarely far away in and around the northern glens and straths. A malady born of Culloden and the Clearances, it is only now, hopefully, being arrested as the rewards of crofting, and whatever else may from time to time crop up (the hope of mineral discovery is always present), find a balance with a modest population prepared to endure rural isolation in what can be a harsh land. Frequently, visitors assume that the drifts of roofless and crumbling stone rectangles fighting a losing battle against encroaching nature represent the homes of those evicted during the Clearances. But this is rarely the case, if only because as often as not the homes of those unfortunates were burned and razed. The ruins you mourn today represent not eviction, but voluntary departure; voluntary, that is, in so far as departure was forced through lack of work, opportunity and modern amenities.

But there does survive one physical reminder of the Clearances, as poignant, if not more so, than any anonymous decaying ruin; the east window of Croick Church which you will find some ten miles west of Bonar Bridge. Quiet roads ascend either side of the Carron, flowing brown and boulder-strewn through a lightly wooded and gentle countryside which was once the home of the Rosses—countryside as gentle now as it was in 1845 and 1854 when the landowner decided that the Rosses must leave to make way for sheep. The Ross women seem to have been of sterner stuff than their men, and at Gruinards, which you will pass if you have chosen the south bank road, seventy or so of them stood resolute against a savage 'police' attack, giving way only when swamped and with twenty of their number wounded.

Three miles farther and you reach a confused junction of minor roads and streams. The Blackwater comes in from the north-west; the Carron

The shores of Loch Duich, looking towards Kintail

Ben Eighe, in the Torridon mountains, Wester Ross

Glenfinnan memorial by Loch Shiel

from the south and west, child and grandchild of Allandale river, of splendidly named Abhainn a' Chlinne Mhoir, of Allt Riabhach, Water of Glencalvie and many another hastening down from the high tarns and bogs. Glencalvie, too, was the home of the Rosses—until 1845 when they were brusquely given notice to quit. Homeless, they straggled, men, women and children, down their glen, across the bridge, then up the broad, open moorland valley of the Blackwater, making their way to the only refuge they could think of, the church at Croick. A modest, white-pebbled little place you will find it to be, built, rather surprisingly, to a plan by Thomas Telford, a name more readily associated with far grander undertakings. But even in their extremity these folk would not actually enter the church. To do so for any reason other than worship would to their God-fearing minds have been sacrilege, so they sheltered in the building's eastern lee, and it was here that they scratched their record on the glass of the window: 'Glencalvie people was in the churchyard here, May 24 1845'; 'This house is needy refuge'; 'Glencalvie people, the wicked generation'—the adjective puzzles and invites speculation. Why did these

49

unfortunates judge themselves wicked? Did they, perhaps, see their plight as some form of punishment?

But these sad scratchings are not all that you can find here, for if you look just outside the western edge of the churchyard you will see the collapsed but unmistakable remains of a broch, a reminder that, perhaps eighteen or twenty centuries earlier, people who may even have been remote forbears of those refugees from Glencalvie also sought safety here. But there was a difference, of course; those who huddled in the lee of the church were the helpless victims of a Highland social system no longer relevant, while those who sheltered in the broch would in all probability have been a chief and his dependants.

Our first formal diversions into prehistory come with a complex between Latheron and Mid Clyth, up the coast beyond Helmsdale. But long before this, at Golspie, you can start out on a scenic inland loop not to be missed by anybody with a sense of adventure and undaunted by sheer wilderness and isolation. Bear hard round St Andrew's Church, as sharply left as sharply upwards, and abruptly you are in another world, the trunk A 9 exchanged for a lane of a road so insignificant that grass flourishes along the centre and the passing places are not always posted. Scrambling out of the town, you soon break clear on to the high moorland shoulder of Ben Horn, cross the infant Golspie Burn just below its escape from Loch Horn, and level out on a marshy plateau marked by a dark lochan, but a lochan with pretensions for this one boasts a name, Farlary. It is an austere and windswept land up here, desolate even in kindly weather, yet one with a strange allure; and not only for the occasional venturing tourist but, it seems, for others too, for the plateau is dotted with scattered homesteads, some of their occupants doubtless here out of necessity, but others surely by choice.

A crossroads appears; up here, surprisingly, if you have been ignoring the map. You bear right and soon you are in yet another world, the upland blacks and heavy browns giving way to what seems every shade of green as you quit the wilderness to find trees and drop the length of a glorious open valley to lovely Loch Brora, a tranquil spot if ever there was one, especially where green peninsulas invite you half-way across the water. The map provides evidence enough that ancient peoples too saw good in this valley, and their cairns, burial chambers, brochs, settlements and field systems abound as a challenge to all with the urge, time, energy and discernment of eye to seek them out. But for those short on these attributes, there is one quite good chambered cairn virtually beside the east-shore road, the one marked opposite Carrol Rock, at nearly seven hundred feet the dominant feature across the water. You may have to search around a bit, but the cairn is there all right, collapsed and overgrown some fifty yards off the road in a copse of dwarf trees.

And so back to the A 9 at Brora, then north-east again above the shore (passing a stone recording the reassuring if paradoxically saddening fact that it was here, near Lothbeg, that the wretched last wolf in Scotland was killed) to reach Helmsdale, where you may well be lured up the Strath of Kildonan and into the wilderness of loch, strath and moor beyond. Prehistoric remains, including no less than three of those mysterious souterrains or earth-houses, are marked in relentless succession all the way from Helmsdale to bleak Kinbrace, but, obvious enough though they may be to the trained eye, they do not readily reveal themselves to the layman who may instead be more tempted to linger beside the Suisgill Burn in the hope of a trace of the gold that was found here a century ago. If prehistoric monuments are your interest, then you will do better to persevere up the A 9 to Latheron, gateway to a clutch of three most remarkable sites, two of them archaeologically rare, the third famous on grounds of restoration and reconstruction.

You start by turning inland off the A 9 here at Latheron, noting standing stones and, most strangely, a hill-top belfry within the north-east angle of the A 9 and your A 895. Standing stones can never be satisfactorily explained; but this belfry can, for had the bells been on the church below the hill their call would never have been heard by the scattered inland homes and hamlets. Five miles of characterless moorland, and then Loch Rangag lies below, insignificant in itself but interesting for a small east-shore promontory bearing the remains of a broch. It all looks like a model, forcing one to conclude that this must surely have been a modest affair; unless, of course, as may well be the case, two thousand years of erosion and shifting drainage have miniaturised this landscape. But it is not for this broch fragment that you have come up here. Your objective is Achavanich Standing Stones, to reach which you hairpin back south-east less than a mile beyond Loch Rangag.

'Standing Stones' is how this site is marked on many maps, but in lay terms this is misleading for this label is more often used for one or two apparently random stones while what we have here are some forty stones (out of an original sixty, we are told) carefully arranged to form an oval. But this oval is (it seems deliberately) incomplete, being open to the south-east, and it is this which gives Achavanich its interest for, with one possible exception (Broubster, to the south-east of Reay), this is the only known site of this arrangement. Why? The perennial question remains unanswered, but we may surely be allowed at least to claim some ritual association with the now collapsed but once large burial cist which you find, open now and empty, just outside the oval's mouth. Today, stone geometry and cist sleep mute, tantalising and seemingly timeless on this desolate moor above bleak little Loch Stemster.

For the second of our archaeologically unusual sites, we leave Achavanich behind us, carrying on south-east to regain the A 9 which we follow through Lybster, four miles beyond which a sign indicates a left turn up to the Hill o' Many Stanes. This affected, tourist-orientated name will not be to everybody's taste, and most will probably prefer the entry Stone Rows which appears on Ordnance Survey maps and in specialist books. But, whichever is preferred, both terms are valid, for here are over two hundred stones painstakingly arranged in twenty-two rows to form a kind of fan. What, one can only helplessly wonder, were the locals of perhaps 3500 years ago seeking to achieve here on this hillside above the sea? At first we are tempted to conclude that it must have been something of purely regional significance, for here in Scotland it is only in this far corner that this arrangement is found. But then one learns that similar if more modest patterns are to be found not only on distant Dartmoor but also across the Channel in Brittany.

So down again to the A 9, back three miles to West Clyth, then arrow-straight north for five or six miles on to the dark, featureless peat bog on which men of long ago sited what we today call the Gray Cairns of Camster; chambered cairns, but chambered cairns with a difference. Chambered cairns, or burial chambers, litter the Highlands and their maps, but whereas the vast majority survive only as naked megaliths or forlorn remnants of the great mounded cairns which once clothed them, these at Camster—of both the round and long types—have been imaginatively restored; imaginatively, because they have been given glass panels in their roofs so that those visitors supple enough to crawl or squat their way along the low passage to the centre are rewarded by being able to see what a cairn was like inside. Indeed, today's visitor is experiencing something almost unique, for hitherto only those who placed the dead here ever saw these interiors.

Nor, even if you cannot achieve the interiors, need you feel cheated. Ignore a discreet Ancient Monuments sign, some planks strategically laid to ease your walk across the springy peat, and the road, small, unfenced, identifiable only by the occasional car, and you are in a timeless landscape, unchanged, surely, since primitive man (but perhaps not so primitive since he could organise the construction of a site such as this) built these huge monuments to shelter his dead, both human and animal, for the cremated remains of both were found here.

At Camster you are well placed to reach the north coast at, say, Castletown or Thurso, on your way passing standing stones and traversing a bleak, black region given over to peat cutting before the scene softens to characterless, sparsely inhabited farming land around Loch Watten. Characterless but for one feature—the distinctive fences made of vertically balanced Caithness stone slabs or flags. Sometimes hailed as the Caithness equivalent of the drystone walling which is such a feature of, for example, the Peak District, the Cotswolds and Cornwall, these fences in fact have none of the homely, crafted orderliness of drystone. Yet in their simple, stark, no-nonsense lines and angles, they are exactly right in what is essentially a harsh setting. Fencing, though, was only one of a number of uses for these magnificent, natural slabs which from 1824 onwards paved towns and cities from Thurso to Paris and even Melbourne in Australia until cheap, drab concrete was poured where polished flags were once skilfully laid. And the fences are going too, so appreciate this unique far-northern feature while you can, and if you have a camera, record it.

The road you join at Castletown or Thurso will carry you the length of the north from John o' Groats (who was, by the way, a Dutch immigrant of the fifteenth or sixteenth century called John de Groot) to Durness. That this road is classified 'A' throughout its length need not deter you, for it falls both far and pleasantly short of what you might fear. Almost as if sensitive to the irrelevance here of speed, this road is unassuming, narrow with passing places, and obsessively undulating, one which offers no encouragement either to those in a hurry or those carrying heavy loads, just a leisurely traverse of this sometimes forbidding far northern landscape.

Nor is this road's physical nature the only reason why the traffic here is rarely heavy. After all, it leads nowhere, *pace* Bettyhill, Tongue, Durness and maybe one or two other small places, and most who drive this way do so for the simple but admirable reason that they want to adventure across the roof of Britain.

Strangely, though, the one element you might most expect is largely missing: the sea. Of this you will find little, for the road keeps cautiously inland, unless you divert down one of the several minor roads and lanes that wander uncertainly seaward. You will brush the sea now and then—at Bettyhill, for instance, and, more intimately, as you cross the Kyle of Tongue—but it is only when you see Loch Eriboll below that you feel that road and sea really accept one another.

It is worth halting a while here, for Eriboll is no ordinary sea loch. Seven miles wide between Faraid and Whiten Heads and very deep, it cuts ten or more narrowing miles into the high brown hills of this remote north-western corner, providing a safe anchorage which, however peaceful today, has over the course of centuries witnessed some stirring scenes.

Breaks in the pattern and colouring of the heather and bracken hint at hut circles, broch and other remains, evidence that men of long ago found both shelter and sustenance here. Then in 1263 the two hundred or more Viking galleys of King Hakon sailed in, assembling for a campaign intended to restore the waning Norse authority around Scotland's coasts and waters. Success came early, but briefly, with an assault on the stronghold of Seanachaisteal, supposed to be guarding the outer western arm of Eriboll (the dun is only a mile's walk from Durness), the garrison apparently fleeing and allowing the enemy to land and burn a score or more villages. But soon the Viking luck turned. Of eleven men (almost incredibly, they were unarmed) sent ashore in search of fresh water, all but two were killed by the Scots who, so the saga tells us, sprang out of the woods—a natural feature wholly absent today. And then, most dread omen of all, there was an eclipse of the sun; interpreted, and all too correctly, as harbinger of disaster, for not long afterwards, far to the south at Largs, Scotland's Alexander III (aided, it must be admitted, by a gale which drove the Viking ships helpless on to the shore) so decisively defeated Hakon that he slunk away to Orkney to die while his Norsemen finally ceded the Hebrides and the Isle of Man.

It is a brave saga, more heroic perhaps than accurate, this one that tells of the Viking fleet in Eriboll. Yet perhaps it is the asides that should most claim our attention, for those references to woods and to a score of villages describe a landscape and a level of population far removed from the depopulated barrenness of today.

Visually less stirring, but certainly no less appreciative of the shelter, were our own century's grey wartime convoys assembled here, while, at the close of the Second World War, victory and defeat confronted one another when German submarines slid in to lower their Nazi emblems in surrender. Was it perhaps this last scene that that respected seventeenth-century prophet, the Brahan Seer, glimpsed when he confidently foretold that a great war would end here at Eriboll?

There is, then, much to exercise the imagination as you round Eriboll, perhaps stopping every now and then to search for those hut circles and cairns so freely marked on the map yet so often elusive to the eye. But there is one stop you really should make; along the west shore by a bridge across a burn just north of the turn down to a jetty pretentiously named Port Nancon. Here, beside the east verge of the road and marked by two cairns so humble that they can easily be missed, you will find a rude, unspoilt earth-house, its entrance waiting behind ferns and undergrowth, its curved stair, passage and rounded chamber all seemingly untouched. Having found the entrance, you may well decide to content yourself with gazing down into the darkness, at the same time asking what sort of people crouched their way along that passage, and when and why? Or were they perhaps so small that a low passage such as this posed no problem? But should you decide to venture in—and this means old clothes, a torch, and the resolve to cope with flooding—then you will hardly fail to draw just a little closer to those who dug and used this place, even though your questions remain unanswered.

The straggling, overgrown and rather characterless village of Durness is your turning point, the place where the A838 anticipates the tidal sandbanks of the Kyle of Durness ahead and swings out of westward into southward. But before obediently following the road, you might well pause here to consider two diversions, one major and one minor.

The major one would be to Cape Wrath, aptly named you might well tell yourself, whether in anticipation or when actually standing at the edge of the precipitous cliffs which rise from what is so often a savage sea. In fact, and disappointingly, the name has nothing to do with anger; in Norse it meant 'place of turning' and this of course is just what it is, the sea equivalent of that road turn you will have to make in Durness. But you cannot go to Cape Wrath in your own car. You must take the Keoldale ferry and then travel by minibus, something you will assuredly try to arrange if you are after splendid coastal scenery, a sea heavy with latent power whatever its mood of the moment, and myriad birds, oblivious of weather and as much at home on a cliff-ledge, on the water or riding the blustering air.

Your minor diversion, this one by car, would be to ruined Durness Old Church, a mile to the north-west. There are two curiosities about this place. The first is intangible and hard to credit, namely that the earlier church which once sanctified this obscure and, one would have thought, wholly unimportant corner, is actually mentioned in Vatican records as being among the contributors to the funding of the Third Crusade (1189–92)—another indication, surely, that in those medieval days this was a region of some consequence and prosperity. The other curiosity, and this one something that can be seen, is a grave incised with a skull and crossbones. This, they say—and though the detail varies the substance of the story remains firm—recalls an arrangement as eminently practical as it was ethically dubious. A notorious but wealthy murderer wanted to be buried here but was excluded on account of his crimes, while the local lord wanted to achieve salvation by rebuilding the church but was thwarted by lack of money. So, it need hardly be recorded, the murderer provided the money and the landowner gave his consent not only to burial here, but also to burial vertically in the wall, thus meeting the murderer's stipulation that his enemies should be denied the satisfaction of walking over him.

The main road winding its way southward below the mountains is as fragmented and exciting as the coast it serves, frequently changing both status and official number over its run from Durness to Kyle of Lochalsh opposite the Isle of Skye. That this main road rarely meets the open sea matters little, for the sea lochs which it touches and fringes are as scenic as any coast, combining, as they do, the best of land and sea. Dark and sheltered, their surface ruffled perhaps but rarely angered, these magical much-islanded inlets creeping in below the rock and heather hills concede just enough hint of the sea—the occasional sandy scoop of a beach, a cluster of kelp-draped humps, even the watchful head of an inquisitive seal—to remind you that these are tidal waters.

It may well be that you are content with what the main road offers. And this is plenty, by any standard. Equally, though, you may decide to plot a more adventurous course, using the main road as a base from which to explore along the choice of smaller roads—and some are very small indeed, and steep too—which wander around the lochs and the promon-

View from Lochinver towards the mountains of Suilven and Canisp

tories that separate them. These detours will carry you to corners at once contrasting and complementary, corners in which the sea lochs are as studded with islands as is the land with countless freshwater lochs.

But, before any of this, you have to cross the forbidding mountain shoulder between Durness and Rhiconich, first fringing the bleak tidal sand flats of Kyle of Durness and then ascending the Dionard before reaching the watershed and dropping to the sea at Loch Inchard. Forbidding, not so much in gradient or height both of which are modest enough, but in sheer landscape, for scenically these must surely be the most hostile fourteen miles in all Scotland. Fourteen or so miles (though rather less if you discount the length of the Kyle) of black and barren wilderness, of wild, rock-littered glen, of sudden, sombre lochs and lochans, and, most remarkable feature of all, of weirdly perched glacial boulders, some lone and individual, others menacingly balanced in rows along precarious ridges. You will not be surprised to be told that this, like that other wilderness on the way to Cape Wrath, was a land notorious for wolves.

Yet, some two-thirds of the way and while still climbing, you will come across something very human; a well with an inscription. Beside the road and dated 1883, it charmingly expresses the gratitude of the surveyor of this road, one Peter Lawson, for the kindness of the local people. How many modern road builders, one cannot help wondering, would experience such kindness (hostility and bitter formal inquiries more probably) or, having experienced it, would go to the trouble and expense of recording their thanks?

You can, if you are impatient, set off on your first diversion as soon as you touch Loch Inchard, whence the B 801 angles high above the loch's north-eastern flank to the small port of Kinlochbervie and, beyond, the trio of hamlets Balchrik, Blairmore and Sheigra. From here you may walk nearly four deserted miles to Sandwood Bay, lovely and lonely yet sad, the scene of many a wreck. Fast rotting now and victim to the restless sand, these wrecks are proof, if ever such was needed, of the value of Cape Wrath lighthouse, for no ship has been cast ashore here since the light was lit in 1828 and the ghosts which haunt this place—so the locals aver—have welcomed no recruit since that date. But the treacherous tidal currents remain unchanged and this is, they warn, no spot for casual swimming. That you must return to Rhiconich along the same road need be no deterrent; in seascape such as this the views homeward can be startlingly different to those enjoyed on the outward journey.

Eight miles farther south and signs tempt you to Foindle, Fanagmore and Tarbet, three points of a diamond in a barren region typical of that mentioned earlier where the seaward views are island-studded while the tightly undulating interior must surely comprise as much freshwater loch as rocky land. The road is tiny—narrow, twisting, blind and in places abruptly steep—but, improbable though it may sound in this seemingly empty corner, you can twice desert your car and take to the water; for a cruise (from Fanagmore) around Loch Laxford with its islands, seals and birds, or for a visit (from Tarbet) to Handa Island, deserted by its few inhabitants in 1845 in favour of America and now a famous bird sanctuary and nature reserve.

If this Foindle-Fanagmore-Tarbet diversion merits, say, one scenic star, then another, farther south and rounding the peninsula below Eddrachillis Bay, surely merits several. The road, which swings off the main A 894 just south of Kylesku Bridge below the dramatic flanks of Sail Gharbh and Sail Gorm (with Spinean Coinich, on the south, the principal components of the gneiss and Torridon sandstone Quinag massif), is as narrow and twisting and in places even steeper than your earlier one, for all that it boasts the classification B 869. But the landscape here is less confined and to a broader scale, more generous with its constantly changing views along the islanded coast and out into Eddrachillis Bay to the north and the waters of The Minch to the south-west. Your road, this B 869, makes the circuit of the peninsula, but it is only rarely, fleetingly at the crests of rises, that you are able to take in the astonishing interior, a virtually impenetrable waste some ten miles long by five or six miles deep in which ten or so scattered spot-heights averaging rather over 500 feet sprout from a confusion of myriad lochs of all sizes ranging from a mile or so in length down to mere ponds. Only from a helicopter, or, more practicably if second best, a detailed map, could you hope to get the true measure of this watery wilderness.

At the far end of this diversion's northern leg you will find yourself bearing south-west beside Clashnessie Bay (whose sandy beach will surely be welcomed by families with children, by now, as likely as not, sated with scenery) to curve into south-east and reach the township of Lochinver where you have to make a choice. You can either desert this coastal region and escape inland along the A 837 to rejoin the main north-south road at Skiag Bridge on Loch Assynt; or you can carry on southward, along the kind of road to which you should by now have become accustomed, to negotiate the western portion of the incomparable Inverpolly National Nature Reserve. Here a belt of trees—rowan seems to predominate—flanking the road provides photographers with a welcome foreground for shots towards the eastern peaks which hang above the reserve's inner fastness of land and loch. Eventually, though, after you cross the river Polly, the trees die away and you are briefly in more open country before you hairpin eastwards, above the dark, overhung lengths of Lochs Bad a' Ghail and Lurgainn and below the 2000 feet of craggy Stac Pollaidh, a Gaelic spelling both more dignified and more musical than the popularised Stack Polly.

A lost valley opposite the Isle of Skye would be no bad choice as a conclusion to your exploration of the Highland North, the principal objective here being the two best brochs surviving on the mainland. The approach is a minor road which leaves the A 87 at Shiel Bridge on the southern tip of Loch Duich; minor in formal classification, but major in achievement, for it hairpins spectacularly from sea level to Ratagain Pass (1116 feet), whence it drops not much less steeply back to sea level. This is a road with something of a story, too, because it was built as a Hanoverian military road and, in fact, is still marked as such on some Ordnance Survey maps. No smooth tarmac, of course, in those days, nor much in the way of verge protection either, if Doctor Johnson is to be believed. He records that as he and Boswell coaxed their weary horses upwards beside a precipitous edge (and Johnson, to quote Boswell, 'was a great weight') his own mount staggered with fatigue so that, fearing for his life, he called out for help. The modern car makes little of this ascent, but as one swings into the fine parking area near the summit one must admit to a sneaking nostalgia for those more demanding days.

In one respect Johnson and Boswell may have had the advantage. When they were up here in 1773 commercial afforestation had scarcely been invented and the view (which, curiously, neither mentions) would have been more generous. Yet today's plantations do their best to compensate, imposing a sombre green geometry on what are still splendid vistas over

Eilean Donnan Castle on Loch Duich

the fastnesses of Glenshiel and across to the barren cliff massif of the National Trust's Five Sisters of Kintail.

Glen More, a giant of a valley as its name implies, takes you firmly but soberly down its northern wall until you reach sea level at the village of Glenelg. Here you can hardly miss the drab ruins of Bernera Barracks, built in about 1722 and the original reason for the engineering of this road across Ratagain.

Already, as you dropped down Glen More, you will have sighted the mountains of Skye. Now the island is just across the water, a mile and a half distant yet in a strange way insisting that it is much closer. There are many who assume, and reasonably enough, that it was across this strait that Bonnie Prince Charlie sailed 'over the sea to Skye'. In fact his wanderings first took him to the Outer Hebrides and it was from Benbecula that he sailed with Flora Macdonald to Kilbride Bay on Skye's north-western coast. You, too, though for a different reason, may debate whether to visit this island which on first consideration you may feel inclined to dismiss as over-advertised and tourist-ridden. And these it certainly is if you are thinking in terms of the town of Portree or the popular MacLeod castle of Dunvegan. But think again, study the map, venture a little, and you will find many a rewarding corner—scenic, interesting or merely remote—reached only by minor roads, forbidden to coaches and caravans and, to a surprising extent, spurned by the average motorist.

But Skye, should you elect to go there, must be for later. Your present objectives, those two brochs, await two miles or so south and east, beside a little, wooded road which turns away from the sea to ascend Glen Beag. Suddenly, as you emerge from the trees, they are there, Dun Telve on the right, Dun Troddan a short way farther on the left. Both, needless to say, are sadly ruined, but their walls, over thirteen feet thick at the base, rise to thirty-three and twenty-five feet respectively and preserve more than enough to enable you to appreciate the complex construction of these drystone towers which once rose in such strange profusion over so much of the Highlands.

Most people will be content with what they have found here, especially since this is about as far as you can get by car. But with its stream, woods and heights, all lifting and narrowing to a half-hidden pass, Glen Beag is as lovely as any of its kind and on a fine day the path towards those upper reaches can be tempting. And not only for scenery, because if by now your eye is attuned you may already have spotted a fort on a bluff above the east side of the gorge. Called Grugaig and probably representing an earlier period, this dun may not compete in structural preservation with those below (it is largely debris and its walls stand only a few feet high) but, perched defensively here on the very rim of a precipitous drop, the depths lost in trees and undergrowth, it has an excitement of its own and, at worst, serves as a satisfying objective for a not over-arduous climb.

THE SOUTH-WEST

Look at any map of Scotland with half-closed eyes and you will surely sense that the whole weight of the Highlands seems to be bearing down inexorably against the south-west; that the entire territory is sliding helplessly in that direction, at the extremity shedding fragments as islands or peninsulas. Even the scenery conforms. High Jura and Arran stand guard on the flanks, but down the mainland the fine array of peaks from lofty Cruachan to the great cluster of Argyll Forest Park shades obediently down to the modest hills and moorland of the south. Kintyre is the spine. Pendant, long and narrow, the peninsula falls away towards Ireland, its north-west epitomising the slide effect with a land and waterscape in which every feature—whether contour, forest, loch, island and islet even—is streaked and stretched relentlessly downward. Beyond, one after the other, the islands drop off; Seil, Luing and Scarba; Colonsay, Jura and Islay. To the east, the contrastingly fat peninsula of Cowal clutches the island of Bute, with the Cumbraes and Arran not far beyond.

This land of Kintyre, together with its northern approaches, has for centuries been Argyll. Meaning the 'Coast of the Gaels' (in the misty legends that tell of Ireland's origins the Gaels appear as a Celtic tribe which came from Spain), the name encapsulates the early local story, reminding you that the land you are about to explore was the very cradle of modern Scotland—of its kings and many kingdoms, of its clans, of its Gaelic language, of its Christianity, and even of its very name. Put differently, it was here in Argyll that the watershed was crossed between prehistoric and historic Scotland, and as you journey the length of Kintyre and out to the islands you will find evidence in plenty of both sides of this divide.

So how did all this come about? Briefly, it started in the late fifth century A.D. when a Gael called Fergus MacErc, a shadowy figure but almost

Jura, Islay and Kintyre

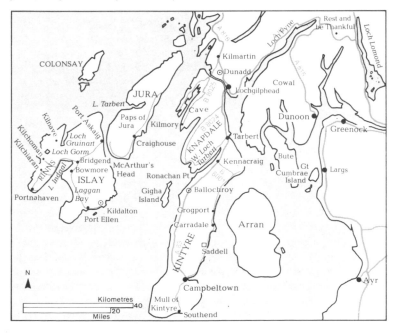

certainly a scion of the royal house of Ireland, crossed what we today call the North Channel and settled in Kintyre with a following of his fellow Scoti, a Celtic word appropriately enough meaning 'raiders'. No more is heard until the second half of the sixth century when the more substantial Aidan and Columba appeared, a prince and a priest who together established the Kingdom of Dalriada (a sort of overseas extension of the kingdom of the same name already flourishing at the north-east tip of Ireland) around the hill-fort settlement of Dunadd, where, we may perhaps allow ourselves to surmise, Columba gave formal Christian sanction to Aidan's kingship.

Over the centuries two closely linked streams, the Christian and the secular, crept across what we now know as Scotland. St Columba, building on foundations already laid in Galloway a century earlier by St Ninian, personally brought Christianity to much of the north, while a succession of Dalriadic and later kings persistently extended their sway, the two most notable steps being the merger in the ninth century of the kingdoms of the Scoti and the Picts into a single Scotia and, in 1034, the emergence under Duncan I of a unified Kingdom of Scotland, embracing Scots and Picts in the Highlands, Angles in the south-east, and Brythons (Welsh) in what is now southern Strathclyde and Dumfries and Galloway. With both these streams, the Christian and the kingly, came the Gaelic language, giving little quarter as it swamped the native Pictish but irrelevant in the Anglian speaking Lowlands.

The small town of Lochgilphead is the gateway to Kintyre. At the head of Loch Gilp, it is also beside the Crinan Canal which loops across to Loch Crinan and has, since its opening in 1801, more or less made Kintyre into an island. From the north only two roads reach Lochgilphead; the A816 from Oban and the A83 from Loch Lomond, and which of these you use will of course depend on where you find yourself when you take your decision to head for Kintyre.

Breasting high across the splendid mountain country of Argyll Forest Park, the A83 is incomparably the more scenic, its culmination being the pass between Glen Croe and Glen Kinglas, curiously but most aptly known as 'Rest and be Thankful'. It is a name familiar to most who cross here—and this can be a busy road, at any rate as far as Inveraray—but of the stream of motorists who draw into the simple but attractively arranged parking area few seem aware of the origins of this name and even fewer bother to seek out the stone on which the words were cut by eighteenth-century army engineers. The poet Wordsworth and his sister Dorothy knew this stone, though, and its words. But the injunction was of course a great deal more relevant in 1803 when the Wordsworths not only had to ascend on horseback but also had to use the far steeper military road. Wordsworth's climb, 'Doubling and doubling with laborious walk', can have had little in common with today's smooth motorised experience. But the stone is still there, beside the old road, an evocative if minor historical marker well worth the effort of a minute's search.

There is another equally evocative and even less noticed spot a few miles farther on near the foot of Glen Kinglas. Take the A 815 westward and you will soon reach the junction with the B 839. Here, on the surface of the old road, you may trace white stones set in the shape of a heart; they mark the traditional wedding site of the Argyll tinkers.

If the A 816 from Oban can hardly compare scenically with the A 83, it certainly wins when it comes to places of interest. The star, one need hardly say, is Dunadd, a rough and conspicuous hump and natural fortress erupting nearly two hundred feet out of the marshy flats beside the River Add to the west of the A 816 some five miles short of Lochgilphead. You already know Dunadd's story. Now you can clamber up its bouldered slopes, noting the skilled use that was made of the native rock, searching for traces of walls and in imagination clothing this place with the perched assemblage of huts which would have represented Aidan's settlement; reminding yourself, at the same time, that although you came here by car or on foot, Aidan and Columba in all probability had to use boats since the surrounding Mhoine More, or Great Moss, would not then have been drained and their Dunadd may well have been an island. Scramble to the very top and you will be rewarded by ancient carvings—a boar, a footprint, a small scooped hollow—relics perhaps of far-distant royal rituals which may even have centred on the Stone of Destiny, now in London's Westminster Abbey but, tradition insists, originally brought from Ireland to Dunadd.

Those who built Dunadd—Aidan, or perhaps Fergus MacErc before him—can scarcely have failed to be aware that they were settling on the very edge of, if not well within, a district that had already long been of profound religious significance, one which, indeed, was perhaps still regarded as such by the natives. From where they performed their royal and Christian ceremonies on Dunadd's crest, Aidan and Columba would easily have seen those standing stones less than a mile to the south-east; and they had only to move two miles north to find themselves in a modest valley filled with more standing stones, burial cairns, a stone circle and several of those baffling cup-and-ring clusters, cut not only into cist slabs and standing stones but also, and even more mysteriously, covering random flat rocks. The vague word 'ritual', coupled with a tentative reference to the sun, represents about the limit of expert cup-and-ring opinion, leaving you free to speculate as you will on the meaning of a design and activity which, to judge by the profusion, must have given continual if repetitive occupation to countless prehistoric masons.

The valley is easily reached; just west of the A 816, beyond the B 8025 and the Kilmartin Burn. It is a place you should not pass by. For all the long intervening centuries, despite the cynicism and sophistication of our times, despite, even, the admirable Ancient Monuments signs, a sense of mystery still broods here.

The southern edge of Mhoine Mhor surrounding Dunadd is defined by the Crinan Canal and the B 841, beyond which spreads the Forestry Commission's remote Knapdale Forest, a part of that north-west corner of Kintyre which, at any rate on a physical map, seems so ruthlessly etched southward. With time to spare this is a rare and lovely countryside well worth exploring—perhaps for the forest walks, many of which fringe unexpected lochs; perhaps to travel the northern length of Loch Sween as far as Keills where you will find a roofless medieval chapel, guardian of several carved graveslabs. Or you may prefer to try Loch Sween's southern shore, the road along which will bring you to Castle Sween, built in the eleventh or twelfth century and claiming to be Scotland's oldest stone castle. Considering this place's age there is still a surprising amount to be seen—keep, kitchen complete with oven, a tower with a very practical-looking rubbish or drainage chute—but, confronted with a caravan site, the imagination has to work overtime here. Beyond, you come to Kilmory Knap Chapel, a thirteenth-century skeleton roofed now with glass and housing a collection of elaborately inscribed Celtic and later stones. But wherever you venture here you must be prepared to return by the same long north-eastward road, for in this stretched and watery country you will find nothing lateral.

The message at Dunadd is strictly secular; that this was the defended base of a conqueror chief. Of Christianity there is no hint, unless you accept the suggestion that the purpose of that scooped hollow beside the boar and the footprint was to hold holy water used at the coronation of kings. But even if you accept this, and it is both convenient and not unreasonable to do so, the association with Christianity remains pretty suspect. For harder—and humbler—evidence you must look some ten direct miles to the south, to St Columba's Cave near the head of Loch Caolisport, reached by B 8024 and then three miles round the loch-head by a minor road signed to Ellary.

Whatever your religious belief, and even if you lack any, there are some early Christian sites—St Govan's Chapel in South Wales is one, St Seiriol's Well in Anglesey another—which through sheer humble simplicity reflect such an unquestioning piety that even the most sceptical of visitors cannot fail to be moved. In this company St Columba's Cave ranks high. There are in fact two caves and, whether or not Columba personally worshipped here, there can be little doubt that they were in use as chapels at or very soon after his time. The larger is the more interesting, with a stone altar, crude carved crosses above, and a basin which may have been a Stone Age mortar put to use as a font—a suggestion not as far-fetched as it may sound since archaeological evidence indicates that these caves sheltered prehistoric man. The second and smaller cave is more of a

View of Sutherland coastline

Looking southwards over the Loch of the Lowes, near Selkirk, in the Scottish Lowlands

Northumbria – looking towards Wooler and the snow-clad Cheviot Hills

challenge, but if you have a sharp enough eye and are lucky with the light you may succeed in identifying a faint cross on the rear wall.

To continue south you have the choice of either returning to the A 83 below Lochgilphead or, more interestingly if probably slower, of rounding the Knapdale bulge on the B 8024. Whichever you choose you cannot avoid finishing up in Tarbert, overlooked by a ruined castle once a home of Scotland's kings. The word 'tarbert' means isthmus and that is just what you will find here, a mile-long neck of land separating the eastern and western lochs, the former little more than a glorified harbour but the latter running out for all of ten narrow miles before reaching open sea. Today, in your car, you will cross the isthmus in perhaps a couple of minutes. In 1198 King Magnus Barfud took rather longer. After raiding the coast he negotiated a treaty which gave him all the land he could sail around, a wording which his enemies doubtless judged safe enough but which was no deterrent to the wily Viking who, taking the tiller of one of his galleys, had himself hauled across, and on arrival at the other end claimed that southern Kintyre was an island. He set a precedent, too. Robert Bruce ordered his ships dragged across prior to his attack on Castle Sween in about 1308 and, indeed, though with more peaceful intent, local fishermen could have been seen doing the same thing right up to 1801 when the opening of the Crinan Canal made such a labour no longer necessary.

You could easily miss the ordinary-looking parking area behind Ronachan Point, twelve miles south of Tarbert on the A 83 at the entrance to West Loch Tarbert. But it would be a pity to do so; unless, of course, you have no interest in seascapes and seals, in which case, though, there is little point in your having come to Kintyre. You don't have to stay in the car park. Take the path (and your binoculars) down to the shore, gaze at all those seals (some of them grey Atlantic seals, Britain's biggest wild animal) basking out there on the rocks or swimming around, and then, should you tire of this, drop your eyes and fossick around the sea-pinks for lumps of dazzling white quartz. And the view seems infinite; given dimension, if you are lucky, by a car ferry moving purposefully in or out of the loch. Across the water switchback the Paps of Jura, a reassurance that you are still in the Highlands and a lure to which you should surrender if you possibly can; to the south stretches the lower, humped length of Gigha, with the promise of Islay beyond; and to the north your view is broken by mainland Knapdale which you may recently have rounded on your way south from St Columba's Cave.

Nor is this all; not, at any rate, if you are prepared for more ancient sites, of which there are at least three within two miles north and south of Ronachan. Dunskeig requires no finding; rising to over four hundred feet less than two miles to your north-east (it is splendidly seen from the boat), this guardian of the loch's entrance rewards the climber with twin forts, one with a vitrified wall, and a cup-marked rock. The so-called

The Paps of Jura

Corriechrevie cairn, overlooking the road just south of Ronachan, is easier to reach but less satisfying even if it does rank as the largest in Kintyre. But the Ballochroy group, just over a mile farther south, can hardly disappoint with its three standing stones, a burial cist, and, nearby to the east, a boulder showing cup markings.

Now, once again, you have to face a decision. The A 83 will carry you southward to Campbeltown swiftly enough, but, and even more so as the island views fall behind, this is not a road of character. Better by far to retrace the six or so miles to Kennacraig (if you plan to cross to Islay and Jura you are going to have to come here anyway to board the ferry) and then bear off on the B 8001, becoming the B 842 as it takes you down the east coast. Slow and narrow though it is, and in places quite steep too, this is an agreeably incidental road, rarely out of sight of the peaks of Arran and threading a succession of peaceful and very individual hamlets and villages. One of these, Grogport, is not what its name might imply. No distilleries here, no bonded warehouse. Disappointingly perhaps, 'grog' is simply a shortening of 'grogach' meaning difficult or awkward, though why this apparently harmless little place should have been so christened must remain something of a mystery. Carradale follows, with its Forest Centre and walks, and then Saddell.

Here, at Saddell, you may well decide to visit the abbey ruins, not so much to view the ruins, for they are scanty, but rather to admire the collection of carved graveslabs, officially suggested as the finest in Argyll. Certainly, the hounds, stags, galleys, warriors and their weapons and much else, all survive in astonishing clarity. But there is more to Saddell than material remains. As you stand here it is worth reflecting that this deserted, tranquil corner was once a rich and busy Cistercian house, in these western Highlands second only to Iona in esteem; that, furthermore, this house may have been founded in the twelfth century by the redoubtable Somerled, a Scots–Norse nobleman who defeated the Norse rulers of Argyll's mainland and islands, became ruler of Morvern and king of all the islands south of the Sound of Mull, and through his three sons founded the many lines which still bear the name Macdonald.

Tucked almost smugly around the head of its own small loch and with an inviting waterfront, Campbeltown is one of those places which insist that you stop and look around. And while you do so—perhaps as you are admiring the famous and elaborate Cross; perhaps as you are trying to picture the scene here in 1774 when the Jacobite heroine Flora Macdonald and her family set sail for Carolina—you may also remind yourself that Campbeltown was not always Campbeltown. Whether or not, as is sometimes claimed, this place was antecedent to Dunadd is something which can safely be left to the visitor's individual judgement. What is certain is that prior to the mid-seventeenth century this was Ceann Loch Cille Chiarain (Head of the Loch of the Church of St Kieran), usually abbreviated and corrupted down to simple Kilkerran or Church of St Kieran, a name establishing a link to an Irish saint who was contemporary with Columba and Aidan. By the early seventeenth century, though, the end of the long strife between the Campbells, since 1457 Earls of Argyll, and the Macdonalds of Kintyre was in sight and the latter's lands were granted to Archibald Campbell, Seventh Earl of Argyll, who soon substituted his own family name for that of the saint.

A few years later, in 1647 and a few miles farther south, the Macdonald story in Kintyre came to its treacherous and bloody end. Catholic and supporters of the Marquess of Montrose (who had sided with Charles I against Parliament) the Kintyre Macdonalds, some three hundred of them, were hunted the length of the peninsula by the Covenanter general, David Leslie, making their last stand when they reached the sea at Dunaverty, a battered erstwhile stronghold of the Lords of the Isles which you can see just beyond Southend. Without water, and led to believe their lives would be spared, they surrendered. They should have known better and sailed away with their Irish comrades, because only two years earlier, after his victory at Philiphaugh in the Lowlands, Leslie had shot over a hundred of his prisoners in cold blood. And here at Dunaverty, just where you may now be standing, he did the same, sparing only one lad.

As only to be expected after a lapse of some fourteen hundred years, more opinion than fact governs any discussion on where it may have been that St Columba first set foot in Scotland. Some scholars suggest that he sailed direct to Iona (where he founded his monastery in about 563), either before or after this perhaps accompanying Aidan to Dunadd. Others, knowledgeable about the tidal races between Ireland and Kintyre, think that the Gaels would have made for Cowal, thence finding their way either around or across Loch Fyne. And, if you go to Islay, you may be told that Kilchiaran was the place. But at Kintyre's extremity, at Keil Point just west of Southend, no doubts are entertained. A sign near the ancient roofless chapel and well bearing the saint's name confidently directs you up a hillock to St Columba's Footsteps.

Here is another of those occasions on which you are safely at liberty to make your own judgement—on what these footmarks are, on whether the ruined chapel is successor to one founded perhaps six centuries earlier by Columba, on what link there may be between Columba, the well and the cross cut into the rock above it. But at least one official opinion accepts that one of these imprints dates back to Bronze or Iron Age times and that then or later it may have served as the sacred spot in which chiefs set their right feet when taking their oaths. So might not the newly arrived Columba have followed the same tradition? And might not that footprint at Dunadd have served a similar purpose? There is no limit for the imagination and this foot-printed hillock, beside the ancient chapel and well and with Ireland in sight, is just the place to fire it.

It will take you two hours to cross to Islay, which you should pronounce Isle-lǎ; by ferry from Kennacraig, down the length of West Loch Tarbert whose rocks are so favoured by seals, below fortified Dunskeig, and on to Port Askaig or, more probably, Port Ellen. Two hours and a ferry which will carry you to a different world. Those small places you have left behind, places such as Tarbert and Campbeltown, are recalled as sophisticated urban centres as you meet Islay's almost toy townships and

villages in which any building over two storeys high at once catches the
eye. Haste seems indecent here; nor, if you are a motorist, is it even
possible along the island's small roads. History comes through as strictly
local, or at any rate as Hebridean. And the landscape is as undemanding as
it is varied; moorland hill, salt and freshwater lochs, arable and pasture,
black peat and sparse turf, all combining as a restful whole at one with the
sea which is never more than a mile or two away.

Historically, Islay is inseparable from Somerled and his descendant,
John of Islay. After his victories over the Norse rulers, the former in 1156
became King of the Islands, making Islay his principal base. John of Islay
married a daughter of his suzerain Robert II, the first Stuart king of
Scotland, and assumed the title of Lord of the Isles, which, splendid
though it may sound, was in fact a voluntary demotion made as a gesture to
his father-in-law. Had these Kings and Lords of the Isles been content
with islands, their sway might have lasted longer than it did. But you will
find the ruins of their arrogant castles all the way from Mingary and
Ardtornish on the Sound of Mull down to Dunaverty at the foot of
Kintyre, and by the end of the fifteenth century the Scottish kings had had
enough, James IV subduing the island chiefs and abolishing their title.
During the seventeenth century the Campbell-Macdonald feud in
Kintyre was repeated in Islay, the ownership of which James VI
transferred to the Campbells, the family name which from now on would
govern island events.

So much for the past. Today, whatever other activities there may be—
farming and fishing for instance—as a visitor you will probably conclude
that the three things which really count here are whisky, cheese and birds;
in fact you may find yourself in a hotel which keeps a special book in which
guests competitively record their ornithological sightings.

The chances are that you will land at Port Ellen, a trim, snug little
harbour backed by a crescent of nineteenth-century stone cottages and
named after the first wife of William Campbell who started to rebuild here
in about 1821. Should ferry timings allow, there are two short excursions
you can make straightaway, the first being along the coast for seven miles
to the famous Kildalton Cross.

On the way, though, there are places where you may care to stop, the
first being on the very edge of Port Ellen where a minor road angles up to
the farm of Kilbride. Here, if you feel like a few minutes' gentle exercise,
you can walk up to an unusually tall standing stone which you will find
within the north-east angle of the two roads. Less easily found is the chapel
marked on the map as being two or three hundred yards beyond the stone.
It is there, nevertheless, two fields away, though you may not readily
recognise it as such because today it is no more than a hollow in the turf
surrounded by a tumble of rough stones. But two of these stones are
upright, serving both to identify the chapel but also to puzzle, for they

Kildalton Cross, Islay

have holes through them. One is tempted into all sorts of speculation—
recalling perhaps a stone at Trumpan, on Skye, known as the Trial Stone
(suspects were blindfolded and, to prove innocence, had to insert a finger
cleanly into the hole) or at unexplained Maen-an-tol at Cornwall's tip—
but probably these holes served only some prosaic building purpose.
Surprisingly, this remnant of a place enjoys a name, Cil Lasarach, perhaps
a dedication to an obscure sixth-century Irish nun, St Lasar.

Lagavulin Bay, a couple of miles farther on, offers both speculation and
certainty; speculation that it may have been into this bay that the
victorious Somerled sailed his galleys, near certainty that the castle beyond
today's distillery was built by his grandson.

Beyond, and now on a minor road, you fringe the rock and island-
studded shore of Loch an t-Sailean, the Loch of the Seals—and there are
plenty of these, though they tend to bask some way out and binoculars are
a help—before heading some three miles north-east for Kildalton Cross,
the star among Islay's many Celtic and later crosses and by many
authorities judged to be the finest in Scotland. As you marvel at the
elaborate patterns, animals and biblical scenes still so sharply clear in the
lovely greeny grey of the local stone, you will surely find it hard to credit
that the craftsman who achieved this, an unknown but probably from
Iona, completed his task all of eleven hundred or more years ago. And
while you are here, do not fail at least to glance around the churchyard and
into the ruined chapel; you will be rewarded by a wealth of carved stones,
spanning from medieval times to the eighteenth century.

Nor do you have to turn back at Kildalton. The road will carry you a
good two miles farther, after which you can follow a footpath to
McArthur's Head and lighthouse, the latter's surrounds so brilliantly
splashed with white that seafarers can pick out this corner of Islay from far
out in the Sound of Jura.

The other excursion from Port Ellen, a mere three miles to the north-
west, is, to be honest, only for those with an empathy for ancient stones
and for that shadowy world where legend and history meet. Druim an
Stuin (you will find it on the left of the road just before Kintra) is not even
much of a stone, but it takes on stature if you accept that it marks the grave
of Godred Crovan, a Norse chieftain who drove Fingal out of the Isle of
Man, made himself ruler of the islands and died here in Islay in 1095.

You may wonder why the road to Bowmore, the island's capital, arrows
so straight for over six miles across the desolate expanse of flat marsh and
peat which backs the great curve of Laggan Bay. The explanation, it
seems, is that this was originally intended to be the course of a railway
which, however, was never built. Bar the airfield, which like so much else
on this island seems not quite real, peat stacks are about the only feature
along this stretch. Even the grandly named 'rivers' you cross—they work
out at about one a mile—would rank no higher than burns elsewhere. It is

far from being the most inspiring part of Islay, this, and you will probably
be glad to reach Bowmore. This you will find to be a planned nineteenth-
century township of broad streets and homely character, known best for its
round church, a design architecturally discordant but, because of the lack
of corners in which to hide, effective in baffling the Devil.

From Bridgend, just beyond Bowmore, you can fan out into the
hammer-head of lonely countryside around Loch Gruinart and Loch
Gorm and down the spine of the Rinns, the name given to the peninsula
which falls away southward to the point of the same name; lonely—and
remote too, though this latter adjective must define atmosphere rather
than distance, for in the opinion of many it is in these western hills and
flats, and around the two large lochs, one salt and one fresh, that the true
soul of Islay is to be found. What you have seen so far—Port Ellen and
Bowmore, perhaps also Port Charlotte and Portnahaven—has been
essentially eighteenth and nineteenth century; charming, quietly confident, homely, and doubly so within an island frame. But where you are
now going there is a different feel altogether, something you will surely
sense as soon as you bear north or west off Loch Indaal's A 847. There will
be modern, or at any rate comparatively modern, pockets—the occasional
hamlet and farm, a Coastguard Station, even here and there a picnic site—
but what really count here are the prehistoric enigma of the Cultoon circle,
the evocative evidence of early Christian faith, and, by contrast, that cross-
sworded entry on the map at the head of Loch Gruinart, 'Battle 1598'.

As to the battle, what happened was that James VI granted lands in
Islay to Sir Lachlan Maclean of Duart, on the Isle of Mull. Needless to
say, the local Macdonalds did not take kindly to this, so, led by their chief,
four hundred Macleans sailed in ready to give battle—only to suffer a
defeat so crushing that all but a handful were killed. Today, even if little
can have changed scenically, you must call heavily on your imagination to
people this site. All the same there are two places where that imagination
may receive a little help. One is a stone near the road junction just west of
the head of the loch; identified on the map as Clach Mhic-illean it marks
the spot where the Maclean chief was killed. The other is Kilnave Chapel,
beside the loch two or three miles along its west shore. Long closed and
now a sad ruin across a field, in 1598 this chapel beckoned as a welcome
refuge to a group of the defeated Macleans, fated, though, to die beneath
its blazing thatch. Today, an eight-century Celtic cross can be your excuse
for crossing the field. Broken and badly weathered it cannot stand
comparison with many; yet, rooted by this desolate ruin and perhaps a
witness of what happened here in 1598, it seems to carry a message of its
own.

Rounding Loch Gorm, you should look out for two islands, both off the
south shore. One is an example of a crannog, a type of Iron Age site you
may not yet have come across. They are man-made defensive islets,

reached either by boat or along a sunken causeway, in this case the latter, and if you are lucky and the water is low you should be able to make out the approach. On the other island are the last fragments of a once powerful Macdonald castle, the objective in all probability of the unfortunate Macleans.

Beyond, your last objective before you move on to the Rinns may be Kilchoman churchyard. Sadly, what has been a Christian site since perhaps the sixth century is no longer in active use. It is of historical interest because of the claims made for a graveslab and a cross. Look around and you will find a number of tombs bearing figures of what seem to be pygmies, strange little people believed to represent priests of late medieval times. One figure, you will notice, is larger than the others, the grave, some will tell you, of Sir Lachlan Maclean. Here, too, there is a fine cross, several hundred years younger than that of Kildalton but nonetheless remarkable for its elaborate design. But was this erected by John of Islay in memory of his Scottish princess, the lady who was the indirect cause of his giving up the title of King of the Isles for the lesser one of Lord? In both cases legend seems stronger than hard evidence, but the choice is yours.

Kilchiaran Chapel is a mere two miles south of Kilchoman, but you will have to drive all of twelve miles by way of Port Charlotte to get there. But it is a drive you are unlikely to regret, because this little chapel on a turf rise above an inviting bay, ruined and long unused though it is, somehow comes closer to simple, unquestioning Christianity than does many a proud cathedral. Yet there is little enough here—a slab bearing one of those pygmy figures you found at Kilchoman, an aumbrey and a stoup, a font, and, outside but close by, a fragment of a cross-shaft and (but surely not Christian?) a cup-indented stone. They say that Columba landed here on his way to Iona, perhaps founding a chapel on this site seven hundred or so years before the present one was built and dedicated to St Kieran. It is a claim you will be happy enough to accept if you draw a line on the map and then look down at that sandy, sheltered bay.

That cup-marked stone prompts the sobering thought that that slope above Kilchiaran Bay may have been a religious site untold centuries before Christianity was born. Certainly the stone circle of Cultoon a couple of miles farther along this most minor of roads was such. Or was it? The rough, weathered stones lie mostly prone and the theory has been advanced that they were never raised, that the project, whatever its purpose may have been, was abandoned before completion. Probably we shall never know the answer. What can be said is that of all the stone circles you may have met, there can have been very few as forlorn or in such a windswept and desolate landscape as this, and that, paradoxically, this is just why you will surely wish to visit Cultoon and ponder its riddle.

Beyond, you drop sharply off Cultoon's breezy, unprotected upland into the utter contrast of the twin village-ports of Port Wemyss and Portnahaven, cosy, sheltered and picturesque either side of their burn. There is something curiously miniature and unreal about this place; more than a touch of sadness, too, if you picture the jostle of fishing boats which once crowded in behind those islands. The cottages reach tentatively up the turf slopes towards the nineteenth-century church, characterless but for one feature. It has two doors, one for each village, imposing a sense of order decidedly out of tune with this otherwise rather haphazard corner.

It would be a pity to return to the mainland without at least sampling the island of Jura, as close to Islay geographically (a short ten minutes by ferry) as it is dramatically distant in character. Noble Highland scenery, ever-changing seascapes, and deer are what matter here. Apart from the patches to which man clings along the east coast, the entire island is a largely trackless wilderness of mountain and loch, the principal features being the Paps, a group of peaks lifting to around 2500 feet, and the deep gash of Loch Tarbert, carving erratically in from the west coast and failing by little more than a mile to make two islands out of one. That man was here millenia ago is proven by the occasional standing stone, but, at any rate numerically, he now seems in retreat, the fifteen hundred or so inhabitants of the early nineteenth century now down to about two hundred, the cattle grazing superseded by estates given over to rod and gun. It is to the deer in their thousands that this island naturally belongs, and, appropriately, it is they who have given it its name, Jura being a corruption of the Norse for Deer Island.

Unless some walking is planned, Jura can be comfortably enjoyed as a day's diversion from Islay, though if time does not press you will find a pleasant hotel at Craighouse, the island's hamlet-capital. Armed with your binoculars—for although the deer keep largely to the central and western fastnesses, you would be unlucky not to spot some in the east—you simply drive up the island's only road for as far as you feel inclined, and then back again.

THE SOUTH-EAST

The Grampian massif ends in the south-east as a range of peaks defining the south side of the Dee valley. From Lochnagar, towering 3738 feet above Balmoral, heights such as Mount Keen, Mount Battock, Cairn o' Mount and Leachie Hill shade down to coastal levels in the neighbour-hood of Aberdeen and Stonehaven. Although on most maps included under that omnibus entry Grampian, more properly this range is the Mounth, a name as improperly corrupted to Mount as *Graupius* was to *Grampius* (as you read in the Introduction to this chapter). However the correct name does survive in those of some of the roads and tracks across

Glen Clova

the passes: Capel Mounth ascending Glen Muick from Ballater to reach
Braedownie in Glen Clova; Fir Mounth, a track crossing from Aboyne
into Glen Esk; and, nearer the coast, Elsick Mounth which as B 979 links
Stonehaven with Deeside.

The Mounth's southern flank is distinguished by three glens, Esk,
Clova and Prosen, the first two of which can be reached from the north by
the fit and experienced walker but all of which require the motorist to
approach from the south. Each glen fulfils the promise of its own
character. But there is nevertheless a common pattern; an alliance of
forest, pasture and moorland ascending either side of a Highland stream
until blocked by a lofty mountain wall, as often as not patched by snow
even in summer. There is grandeur here too, but welcoming and rarely
forbidding. Add gorse, broom, rhododendron, orchis, wild violets and a
profusion of other flowers; add oyster catchers, curlews, buzzards and
what must surely be some of Britain's plumpest pheasants; add rabbits in
their hundreds and the occasional deer—and you have glens as lovely as
any in Scotland.

Elegant Edzell Castle would be a good start to your drive up Glen Esk,
not only because it was the home of the Lindsays, the lords of this glen, but
also for its unique and most attractive feature, a seventeenth-century

Pleasance, or walled garden, notable for some strange symbolic sculpture. From here the road enters the glen proper, a point at which you can add interest to your drive by reflecting that in all probability you are, if more comfortably, following in the footsteps of Macbeth, King of Scotland from 1040 to 1051, who fled up this glen after his defeat by Malcolm at Dunsinane, near Perth, crossing the mountains by the Fir Mounth to meet final defeat and death at Lumphanan, beyond north Deeside.

From now on scenery will be your main interest, all the way to the glen's head. But there is one place which may tempt you to stop, namely Colmealie Stone Circle, some six miles out of Edzell beside some farm buildings a few yards up a track from where the road touches the river. It is only a very small, rough, unsophisticated circle, this, tumbled, ignored and overgrown, the home of sheep and rabbits, yet for this very reason it must provoke thought. Those glen people of so long ago who assembled these stones may not have had the resources of those able to build an Avebury or a Cultoon, but they surely had their own humbler vision and motivation.

The road ends at Invermark Castle. A typical shell of a tall tower-house of the sixteenth century, with its equally typical corner turret and garderobe, it perches within the confluence of the Water of Mark and Water of Lee, encircled by the bare, brown mountains out of any of whose several passes might appear raiders tempted by the rich glen and Edzell beyond. You cannot get in—the entrances are high and barred as they always were—but what you can glimpse through the windows shows clearly enough that this was a place for security rather than comfort. And if by now you are in sufficiently reflective mood you may like to walk on to Loch Lee, where a ruined church and its forlorn graveyard will remind you that you stand where once was a village community.

A pleasant small ridge-road will lead you from Edzell to Cortachy and Dykehead, at the feet of Glen Clova and Glen Prosen. But first, under four miles out of Edzell, you will come to a crossroads where a sign points north to the White and Brown Caterthuns, and, whether you are interested in hill-forts or not, this is a sign worth following because it quickly brings you to a hillside parking area offering really superb views inland across the moors and southward down to the coastal levels. Given the weather, the walks up to the forts may well seem inviting, especially that to the White Caterthun, only an easy few hundred yards away and claiming one of the most impressive stone and earthwork defensive complexes in Britain. This White Caterthun, so-called because of its stonework, is the younger of the two, dating from about the first century A.D. and perhaps not even started until after its fellow across the road had been abandoned. Climb up to the Brown Caterthun, then, and you will find yourself on a rather older site but one still imposing with its several defensive surrounds.

In Glen Esk you may have felt some sympathy for Macbeth; in Glen Clova you will surely feel plenty for another monarch. In 1650 the exiled Charles II, then aged twenty, landed in Scotland, making his way to Perth where he fell into the hands of fanatical Presbyterian Covenanters who forced him to deny his Catholic mother, forbade him the pleasure of a game of cards, battered him with interminable declamatory sermons and made Sunday even more of a hell than the rest of the week. Deciding that he had had as much as he could take, Charles fled, making for the more sympathetic Highlands and resting at Cortachy Castle (now, as doubtless then, a gracious oasis amid splendid trees) before heading up the glen. But to no avail, for he only got as far as Clova before he was recaptured. The wretched lad had been free of sermons for just two days.

Glen Clova has the merit of two roads, one on either side for most of its length. In its lower part it is wider and more open than the other glens, but beyond Clova, where the roads join, the mountains abruptly close in, forcing a high-walled approach to Braedownie where the road ends and the South Esk is fed by head-streams tumbling in through the Forestry Commission's Glendoll Forest.

As far as its village, neighbouring and heavily wooded Glen Prosen also has roads along both sides, that on the west being by far the higher, steeper and more incidental. Although without the royal associations of Esk and Clova, Prosen does its best since it was here that Captain Scott and Dr Wilson planned the bitter-sweet Antarctic expedition of 1910–1911; bitter-sweet because although they succeeded in their aim of reaching the South Pole, they failed to be the first to get there (Roald Amundsen forestalled them) and all the expedition's members perished on the return journey. A memorial fountain was placed beside the east bank road, but this was damaged when a car ran into it in 1949 and it has been replaced by a cairn.

3

Northumbria

It is an odd fact that, while still in England, you can find yourself farther to the north in the county of Northumberland than in the Lowlands of Scotland. For this county thrusts its wedge-shaped tip northwards to a point just beyond Berwick upon Tweed, before giving way to Scottish territory: small wonder that this erratically drawn Border has always been a subject of bitter and sustained controversy. The Percys and the Douglases are only two of the great clan names of those whose warlike deeds crowd the Border Ballads.

Today you may cross that Border into Scotland by a number of roads that fan out northwards from Newcastle upon Tyne. Oldest and best-known, of course, is the Great North Road, the A 1, that keeps within a few miles of the coastline as it passes through Morpeth and Alnwick to Belford

The Border

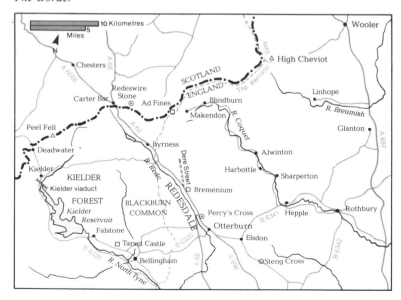

and Berwick, sixty-odd miles distant. It is being changed almost beyond recognition these days, thanks to road-widening projects and dual carriageways. It never was a beautiful road, and now it never will be; only the traveller northwards-bound in a hurry and the long-distance haulier would think of using it.

A much pleasanter, and much less congested, road, the A 697, branches away from it just to the north of Morpeth and makes for Wooler (the originally designated northern terminus of the Pennine Way) and Branxton. Here it bends left-handedly round Flodden Field, as though reluctant to trespass where so many gallant men fought and died over four and a half centuries ago. You can just see the great cross on its three-tier plinth, commemorating the battle, as you follow this road northwards out of the village. It stands on a mound overlooking a saucer-like plain, with low hills beyond. Here, on September 9th, 1513, still remembered by all Scots loyalists as 'Black Friday', an English army commanded by the Earl of Surrey defeated the Scottish army and slew, if records are to be credited, ten thousand of them. James IV of Scotland was with his army, and was slain on the battlefield; it is remembered by Scotsmen the world over as one of the most disastrous events in the whole of Scottish history. Sir Walter Scott immortalised the battle in *Marmion*. But the fine memorial stone is of recent date, having been erected no earlier than the year 1910. And since then, every year, there is a cavalcade of horsemen who, in early August, make their pilgrimage to the site; a wreath is laid on the mound that supports the memorial stone of hewn granite, and a service is held, with an address which, by tradition, pays tribute to the valour of the fighting-men of both sides who died in the battle.

The road crosses the Border, marked there by the River Tweed, at Coldstream. Though it skirts the foothills of the Cheviots for more than half of its forty-odd miles, and High Cheviot himself a bare eight miles away as it passes through Wooler, it never once touches high ground. For all that, it is incomparably finer than the main road to the north, the A 1, even though that highway does bear the evocative name, Great North Road, on which Frank Morley wrote a memorable volume some years ago, wisely using the name as his title.

The third main highway to the Border begins its career as the A 696 at Newcastle, merges with the A 68 just to the north of Otterburn, and crosses the Border at Carter Bar at 1400 feet. This is a nobler route into Scotland than either of the others; it is finer, too, than the road leading northwards out of Carlisle, far to the west, by way of Gretna Green, for this road runs through some dreary low-lying country for many miles before lifting on to the uplands. However, it is a trunk road, over which lorries and long-distance coaches thunder their way from England into Scotland and back again by day and by night.

All the approaches to Scotland so far mentioned have been along main roads. But for those who trouble to seek them out there are several others, quieter, more adventurous and infinitely more satisfying. One such (about which more below) is by way of Kielder Water, a little crossing especially to be recommended to anyone aiming for grim and historic Hermitage Castle. Another—though this involves taking to your feet—could choose the village of Alwinton as its starting point. From here a minor road leads north and then south-west to the farmsteads of Blindburn and Makendon, and it is a mile or so beyond the latter, at the point where the road swings sharply southward, that you must don boots, or heavy shoes, and head northwards under your own steam.

It is not far: a matter of perhaps half a mile in all. And the exact route? Alongside the Coquet, now shrunk to a mere trickle; it rises exactly on the Border, on Harden Edge. If you are there in unusually dry weather the tiny rivulet may have vanished altogether. But you need not despair because your last clue to direction has gone; for here, seventeen or eighteen hundred years ago, the Romans laid out one of their most spectacularly sited camps. On some maps it is named Ad Fines. Having regard to its setting, you could loosely translate this, echoing generations of frustrated legionaries exiled to this bleak spot from their own warm land, 'The Limit'; and you would not be far wrong.

Clearly there must have been means of access to this remote camp, either from the south or, across the Border, from the north. In fact, it was from both directions, for Ad Fines, today on the Pennine Way, once stood on Dere Street, a more northern section of which you may have met if, while touring the Scottish Lowlands, you explored the small road dropping east off the A 68 below Carter Bar, a meandering way which will have led you to Pennymuir and its Roman camps. Clear-cut, the straight uncompromising lines of Ad Fines stand out boldly on their slope of turf, but if from here you want to explore northward in the footsteps of the legionaries you would be well advised to carry a detailed map and a compass and at the same time be prepared for a few miles of turf that, even in dry weather, can be spongy and treacherous.

Southward, though, you can follow the Romans more easily. Until a few years ago the track that climbed the Cheviot Hills from Alwinton and on through Blindburn and Makendon ended short of the hill top just beyond this lowly farm. But one good thing has come out of the present-day army's possession and exploitation of this magnificent stretch of country: the track has been turned into a well-metalled road, and the road has been extended westwards and then southwards, sheer across the open, windswept moorland; and a dramatic piece of road engineering it is, too. As the larger-scale map clearly shows, the army engineers who surveyed this new section utilised a good many miles of the original Roman road, the continuation southwards of Dere Street. This is evidence that the Roman surveyors all those centuries ago had as good an eye for layout and the

The River Coquet at Warkworth

utilisation of natural contours as any of their army counterparts today. Incidentally, it is from the first rise of this new section of the road that, looking northwards, you will obtain the most impressive panoramic view of Ad Fines. The last three miles of this road, once again bearing the proud name, Dere Street, and ending at Redesdale Camp, near the Roman base of Bremenium on the A 68, runs die-straight, just as the Roman surveyors laid it out for their own purposes, almost identical with those of the army today.

What a tragedy it is that so much of the mapped area of the Cheviot Hills immediately to the south of the Border should carry the forbidding words, DANGER ZONE. A rectangle some eighty square miles in extent, bounded on the west by the main road, the A 68, on its north side by a line drawn from Coquethead to Windy Knowe, on its east side by Coquetdale, and on its south side by the road from Otterburn to Harehaugh, is, and has for long been, a loosely-defined firing-range. On all its summits red flags fly when artillery practice is the order of the day. You follow these roads, if those flags are flying, literally and inevitably, at your peril. Certainly the guns are aimed eastwards from the main road that flanks this area to the west: but the very road you are most likely to choose, if you are bent on a leisurely exploration of this magnificent terrain, is the one that climbs the beautiful Coquet to Coquethead, on the north-east and northern fringe.

Strangely, you do not actually hear much of the firing: perhaps the swampy turf and the deep tracts of peat-bog do something to muffle all but the loudest reverberations. But the sight of the red flags, the awareness of what they symbolise, spells discomfort, unease. It is as well to ascertain in advance on what days, and between what hours, those flags will be flying, to proclaim that the army is in command of this particular area of the Northumberland National Park.

Perhaps, though, it is somewhat churlish to speak so harshly of what the army has done, and is doing, to the Cheviots. The danger zone is, in fact, only a relatively small proportion of these apparently limitless square miles of high and open moorland. The Cheviot himself dominates the landscape for miles in all directions: a triangular plateau well above the 2500-foot mark just on the Northumbrian side of the Scottish Border. But you cannot approach this, even within several miles, save laboriously (if rewardingly) on foot. True, there are a few roads that make half-hearted attempts to lead you to it. There is one that branches westwards off the A 697 a few miles south of Wooler and climbs gently alongside the River Breamish as far as Linhope. But there the road ends, and if you want to explore the foothills, or even The Cheviot that dominates them, you must do so the hard way. You leave the Breamish and take first Linhope Burn and then Standrop Burn. They will lead you to the 1700-foot contour; but you will still have two miles, and another thousand or so feet, to climb if you are to attain your final objective.

By branching off the same main road, within a mile or two of Wooler, you can pick up another of these alluring minor roads. This one makes almost directly for The Cheviot, passing a small place charmingly named Shining Pool and then for two or three miles ascending Harthope Burn. Then once again the road becomes too narrow for anything other than a biped or—if he can ride and is fortunate enough to have the use of one—a quadruped. But still that high plateau remains remote: three miles distant, this time, and some 1500 feet above the highest point on the marked track. You may think it better on the whole to leave the High Cheviot unattained; just one more of those consummations devoutly to be wished!

Instead, this seems a good point at which to swing our attention westward, to explore a road already hinted at, the one up the North Tyne valley and skirting the length of the south shore of Kielder reservoir, or, more pleasingly, Kielder Water. Anybody who travelled between the village of Falstone and the Scottish Border before and up to the early 1970s would be hard pressed to recognise now very much of what he saw then. Then the emphasis was on the great complex of man–made forests which distinguished, and indeed still distinguish, this wide tract of remote country; forests traversed by a minor road which, after Falstone, ascended the right bank of the ever-diminishing North Tyne river and could honestly enough be described as carrying virtually no traffic and as perhaps the most rewarding of all the border approaches. But when they built the Kielder Dam that riverside forest road drowned beneath the reservoir, and in 1977 a superb new road, the one we enjoy today, was opened along the water's south shore. And the emphasis shifted from forest to water; or, more accurately perhaps, to an outdoor scenario combining all that is best of both.

Needless to say—at any rate between spring and autumn—that phrase 'virtually no traffic' no longer applies, something to be deplored by those who, selfishly perhaps if understandably, prefer not to share nature. But the compensations have been immense—Britain's largest reservoir set in Europe's largest man-made forest, water enough for the whole Tyne-Tees district until well into the twenty-first century, a land of more open, more spacious and more varied beauty than the earlier closer-set afforestation and one moreover which offers to thousands a generous choice of forest, moorland and water recreation. Yet, despite the summer crowds, this is a huge area so plentifully and skilfully provided with secluded parking sites that the claim that Kielder is the most rewarding of all border approaches remains as valid today as was the case in the pre-reservoir past.

Bellingham, which you should pronounce with a soft 'g', can be regarded as the outer gateway to Kielder, the best road westward from here being the one along the North Tyne's right bank; however, so long as you are prepared to cope with gates, you may prefer the much smaller road along the left or north side, generally tracing the course of the dismantled railway and taking you as far as Falstone where you have no choice but to cross the river.

Falstone lies just below the reservoir's dam; Tower Knowe Information Centre just above it is an unobtrusive yet superbly sited facility where you can find out all you want to know, whether technical or recreational. Recreations include cruising, fishing, water sports, pony trekking and wildlife, to mention but a few of the possibilities.

Some eight scenic miles farther on you reach Kielder village, built for Forestry Commission workers and their families and marking the western limit of the reservoir. It is not an attractive spot, this—scattered groupings of uniformly characterless houses—but you may nevertheless decide to linger here, perhaps for purely practical reasons such as a need for petrol, perhaps to visit the Information Centre, perhaps even to have a look at Kielder Viaduct, an achievement of modest fame which you will find between village and reservoir not far from Bakethin Fishermen's Car Park. Until the 1950s this viaduct carried the railway linking Hexham with Hawick in Scotland; today, stretches of the abandoned and dismantled track provide pleasure for walkers, while the viaduct attracts visitors with a specialist interest or simply intrigued by the striking and unusual design. Consisting of seven arches, all shapely, no two identical, but all cut at a curious angle to the main axis, this is recognised as a rare and possibly the finest example surviving of the 'skew' form of construction. Each stone in the arches had to be individually shaped, in accordance with the method evolved by Peter Nicholson of Newcastle-upon-Tyne, a pioneer geometrician in this field.

There are of course many other 'skew' bridges. There is a fine specimen on the outskirts of Harpenden, a small township in Hertfordshire, carrying what was the old Midland Railway north from St Pancras. But this bridge is constructed of brick and is wholly different in design, consisting of what is in effect a skew-built tunnel through a huge embankment. What is impressive about the Kielder Viaduct—quite apart from its design and construction—is the fact that when the railway was abandoned and the threat was uttered that, like so many of the smaller bridges along the route, it would be blown up to prevent illegal use, the Forestry Commission donated the sum of £1000 for its preservation and maintenance. The gesture was made in sympathy with the strong feeling of people living in North Tynedale, and even farther afield, that so noble a viaduct should be preserved from demolition. The Northumberland & Newcastle Society sponsored an appeal to preserve 'this notable example of Victorian engineering, constructed in 1862 to carry the North Tyne Railway'. The response to the appeal was widespread and generous, and the viaduct today is in a splendid state of repair more than a century after it was built.

Northumbria incidentally can offer another abandoned railway-line for the pleasure of the walker. This runs northwards from Alnwick by way of Glanton and Wooler, following pretty closely the line of the A697. North-westwards of Wooler it enters the valley of the River Glen and, soon afterwards, that of Bowmont Water. At Mindrum it leaves the eastern Cheviots which it has been skirting for several miles and runs due north to Cornhill on Tweed, on the hither side of the river that separates this township from better-known Coldstream. There is excellent and easy walking here, though in a less dramatic key than that which is offered by the abandoned track of the old North Tyne Railway.

But to return to Kielder. Having, so to speak, reached the end of the road—of the new road, that is—you now have to consider how best to extricate yourself. You may, of course, simply decide to retrace your steps, but, should this not appeal, you still have two choices, both scenically rewarding. One choice is to carry on through the village, beyond it slipping on to a narrow road with passing-places, two miles along which a sign informs you that you are in Scotland; stop here a moment and look back and you will see that a distinctly more grandiose sign announces England. It is on this watershed in a patch of swamp spread over the lower slopes of Deadwater Moor that both North Tyne and Liddel Water are born, the latter tipping northward into Scotland, the former southward until, fed by burns such as Deadwater, Bells and Kielder, it swells to the size sufficient

Kielder Viaduct

to fill the great reservoir that now straddles the once modest valley. Your other choice—the one if your touring plans lean towards the north-east— is to pay a small toll and set out along the Forest Drive which after twelve miles of forest and moor will bring you to Byrness on the A 68, only a mile short of Catcleugh Reservoir, itself only a short distance below the border at Carter Bar.

Should you, though, opt to retrace your steps you need not necessarily do so all the way to Bellingham. Instead, if you study a detailed map, you may well be tempted to explore the network of roads and tracks snaking across the open moorland extending north of the river and east of the forest

between Falstone and Otterburn (beyond the A 68 on the A 696). Cross
the river at Falstone, if you wish, but remember that you will meet gates;
better, probably, to cross farther east to Lanehead and then plot your way
to Otterburn across what on the map are called 'Commons'—Hareshaw,
Troughend, Blackburn, Corsenside—but which in fact are nothing so
homely but, rather, bleak expanses of bare and often windswept moor.

A mile outside Otterburn, to the north-west, hidden in a copse but still
just visible from the road, is the simple but shapely stone that
commemorates the fierce Battle of Otterburn in 1388 and known as the
Percy Cross though today only the upright survives. But more interesting
than this, perhaps surprisingly, is the former vicarage in Elsdon, three
miles or so to the east.

Elsdon is one of Northumbria's most charming and peaceful villages. It
has a particularly spacious green; it has its ancient church of St Cuthbert,
almost entirely embowered in trees; and above this, above a succession of
terraces of turf, is Elsdon's unique possession, the 'pele-vicarage', a
vicarage embodying a pele tower, a fortified home that was originally a
stronghold designed to protect its owner-occupiers against the worst that
the Border fighting-men could do in their savagery.

Unlike so many of these Border peles which have been cannibalised for
the building of farms and byres, and even walls, as at Tosson, near
Rothbury, and Duddo and Doddington, near the Berwickshire border,
this pele has been miraculously preserved. Its preservation is due almost
entirely to the fact that the original edifice was incorporated in medieval
times within a larger, if less massively conceived structure, designed for
the incumbent of the church it overlooks at its feet. For many generations,
even centuries, it constituted the rectory, or vicarage. Today it is a private
house set amid beautiful grounds, surrounded by velvet lawns shadowed
by graceful trees. Looking at it, it is hard to believe that the place was
originally built as a stronghold against raiders, that strife in any form could
have taken place hereabouts. What was added to the original pele has long
since blended so perfectly with the fabric that it takes a knowledgeable eye
to discern where the union took place.

Two miles south-east of Elsdon, on a minor road leading eastward
below Harwood Forest, you will arrive at a point marked on your map as
Steng Cross. There is, in fact, no Cross here at all; not even the stump of
one such as is to be found in the unlikeliest corners of, for example,
Cornwall. But on this 1000-foot hill brow there stands an eighteen-foot
gibbet, its arm pointing northwards to the Cheviots. Two pack-horse train
routes intersect just here; less than two hundred years ago, passing pack-
horse drivers would have seen the corpse of one William Winter, hanged in
the year 1791 at West Gate, Newcastle-upon-Tyne and conveyed here to
be suspended until only his skeleton was left to remind people of what was
once a man.

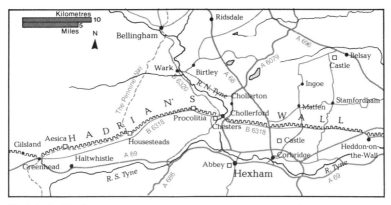

Hadrian's Wall

Winter was hanged for the murder of an old woman named Margaret Crozier. According to an old guide-book to the district, this desperate character, who had only recently returned to England after a long spell of transportation for an earlier grave crime, teamed up with two vagabond women, Jane and Eleanor Clark, itinerant vendors of crocks and tinware. The two women had been befriended one cold and stormy night by Margaret Crozier. They took the opportunity, while enjoying her hospitality, of assessing what might be her wealth. On the night of August 29th, 1791, they encouraged Winter to break into the old woman's humble cottage and murder her. They then ransacked the place and loaded on to the donkey that ordinarily carried their crocks and tinware such possessions as they felt it worth their while to take.

But the night before this dastardly deed it happened that they had rested and eaten a frugal meal in a sheepfold on nearby Whiskershield Common, the two evil-minded women and the man they were associating with. Unknown to them, a shepherd boy had watched them through a cranny in the wall, and was sharp-witted enough to suspect that they were up to no good. He particularly noticed the pattern of nails in the soles of William Winter's boots, and a sinister looking butcher's knife with which he was equipped. And he was struck by the savage fashion in which the man wielded the knife, even though it was only to hack through some coarse bread and meat the three were sharing among them. It was, in fact, the shepherd boy's sharp-wittedness that brought Winter to the gallows. He was brought from Newcastle to this grim site, high on the moor, surrounded by hills such as Simonside, Hindhope Law and Ottercops Moss, and there hung in chains. The gibbet is known to this day by his name. Curiously, no mention is made by the teller of this grisly tale of the fate of the two evil women, Jane and Eleanor Clark, who were the instigators of Winter's crime. There is no other gibbet surviving in the country that is comparable with this one in its sinister setting, its power to evoke the days of harsh justice meted out to malefactors in such a way that passers-by could see for themselves and be duly warned as to possible retribution.

This same minor road will take you a few miles farther eastwards to a point known as Gallows Hill, though no gallows will be found there today. Here the road turns sharply south and brings you in due course to Chollerford, on the North Tyne, the river you last saw when you turned away from it, many miles to the north and west below Kielder's dam. Now a mature stream, it is spanned by a stately bridge only a few hundred yards above that other bridge which the Romans threw across to serve their fort of Cilurnum, to us known as Chesters and the place where at last you touch Hadrian's Wall, the noblest and most splendid of all relics of the Roman occupation of Britain and comparable with the finest to be found anywhere in Europe outside Italy itself.

This is not the place to write in any detail about this most remarkable feature of South Northumberland. Not only brochures and guide-books have been written about it, in their scores and long-hundreds, but full-length volumes too, and by expert archaeologists and others who write with authority and deep knowledge. Suffice it for the present that the Roman Wall was built, between the years A.D. 122 and 128, on the orders of Emperor Hadrian to demarcate Roman-occupied England from territory to the north along a seventy-mile line stretching from Wallsend in the east to Solway in the west. Not all of that length was completed; and not all of the scores of miles of this magnificent conception, originally completed, survive to this day. But a great deal of it does, with its *vallum* and Military Way running close behind it, on the 'English' side, and its forts and intermediate mile-castles spaced out methodically and strategically along its length, notably where the actual wall is carried on the crest of the northward-facing basaltic formation known to geologists as Great Whin Sill.

Immediately to the south of the Wall runs the fine road, the B 6318, sometimes inaccurately known as General Wade's road. Its width, grading and surfacing are so admirable that it is difficult to understand why it has not been promoted into the 'A' category. For much of its length this road, undulating easily over the north-to-south ridges of South Northumberland, runs within a hundred yards or less of the Wall; it is rarely more than a mile to the south of it at most. This means that anyone wishing to explore the Wall and its camps, forts and mile-castles on foot—the only way, really, to come to terms with it—has innumerable points of easy access among which to choose.

The finest section to explore is between Gilsland, on the border common to Northumberland and Cumbria, and Chesters at Chollerford.

In this length of some twenty miles and more the Wall rises to 1230 feet above sea level, westwards of Housesteads, where it frowns down northwards from Hotbank Crags on to Broomlee, Crag and Greenlee Loughs. Carrawburgh Camp and Procolitia, Sewingshields and Housesteads, Aesica and the Nine Nicks of Thirlwall are all to be found within these twenty-odd historic miles.

You can be within touch of them, on a fine, well-metalled road, the whole way along. Or you can actually 'walk the Wall', mile after glorious mile, westwards or eastwards according to your fancy and the direction of the sun and prevailing wind. Then, the soles of your shoes (or, better, boots) will be in direct contact with the stones that were hewn by quarrymen who were also Roman legionaries, conveyed to the site by impressed labour, and set in place by Roman master masons, specialists from the ranks of the three picked legions, the *Victrix Pax Fidelis* from York, the *Valeria Victrix* from Chester, and the *Augusta* from far-away Caerleon-on-Usk.

There is no need to be particularly knowledgeable about Roman history, or even Romano–British history, to appreciate this superb memorial to a great people who governed wisely, and though sometimes of necessity harshly yet often much more leniently than is commonly supposed by those who imagine that the North Britons were slaves beneath the Roman overseers' lash. An hour or two spent at, for example, the great fortress-camp, Housesteads—Borcovicium to the men who designed and built and garrisoned it more than eighteen centuries ago—will afford you countless intimate glimpses into the garrison's way of life to complement the factual information that fills the guide-books.

Take that great stone water-trough, for example—only one of quite a number to be found on the site, as elsewhere. Why should the upturned edges of thick stone all round it be 'scalloped' as they are? And why so extraordinarily smooth? Is it an example of deliberate, though unasked-for, ornamentation by the mason and his mate with time on their hands in the early years of the second century A.D.? Not a bit of it! It was on this stone edge, with water (ostensibly of course for drinking purposes) readily to hand, that the legionaries honed their short-bladed two-edged swords in readiness for service in the next foray they might be called upon to make among the wild men north of this arbitrary line of demarcation. Those concave curves, those uniform scallops, were worn gradually into the tough stone, while the swordsmen gossiped and grumbled about Northumbrian weather and thanked whatever gods they worshipped at the time that their lot was not yet cast far to the north, in the windswept Border camp known officially as Ad Fines and to them by more viciously descriptive names. It is touches such as these—and you will find many of them along the line of Hadrian's Wall—that bring to life, and so into the forefront of your consciousness, the men who lived and fought and died

Hadrian's Wall, Housesteads

here not much less than two thousand years ago. Men who, as excavation here at Housesteads has revealed, worshipped Mithras, the Sun God. And can they be blamed for becoming involved in the cult of such a god when they were exiled for so long in what must have seemed to them a god-forsaken land?

You reached Hadrian's Wall at Chollerford. Here, as you stand on today's graceful bridge, and whether or not you have time and inclination to divert westward along the wall's length, you will surely wish to see where the Romans crossed. All you have to do is follow the easy, signed path leading from the southern end of Chollerford bridge, a path which in about ten minutes brings you to the massive approach causeway, the bridge abutments and the pier bases strewn beside and across the shallow river—great, tumbled blocks (on many you can still see the lewis holes by which they were coaxed into position), which seem to have an evocative quality of their own—such that it does not demand too much imagination to rebuild this bridge and conjure back the soldiers, serfs, traders and others who made their way across it.

Those lewis holes tell us that two thousand years ago the Romans knew of a principle commonplace today. Set this fragment of trivial discovery alongside the scalloped edge of that trough at Housesteads, and chalk it up as one more example of an unconsidered trifle that somehow lingers in the memory.

Another such trifle, with a somewhat macabre element in it, will come your way as you browse around Hexham Abbey, on the south bank of the Tyne four miles down the road. Strictly, the abbey should be called the Church of the Priory of Augustinian Canons. It was founded by St Wilfred who, in the year A.D. 674, made a solemn vow to build 'the largest and most magnificent church this side of the Alps'. Not much of what you look at today is St Wilfred's handiwork; but it does contain the crypt which he had built—out of stones taken from Corbridge near by, the Roman base of Corstopitum, from which the garrison and camp-followers had departed a century or two before, leaving the way clear for any vandal to get to work upon it for his own purposes. Sadly it must be admitted that, in this respect at least, St Wilfred must be marked down as a vandal.

He would not, of course, have agreed. Was he not building to the greater glory of the God whose Faith he had brought to this country? And what better material to hand for such a purpose than that so ably quarried by the Romans five centuries before, men who bowed down and worshipped before the pagan god, Mithras? But it is not this particular aspect that strikes one as macabre. Rather, it is the belief, firmly held by many who should be qualified to know, that the plaster used as a base for the murals painted on it in medieval times and earlier was given its extraordinary lasting qualities by being mixed with animal, and even human, blood as well as hair. A hint here, then, of the macabre, but no more than a hint. Make your way, though, a couple or so miles north-west, to the churchyard of the hamlet of Warden, and you will find something both visibly and tangibly macabre. Here, just inside the gate and beneath a yew, lie three graves, side by side, one of them smaller than the other two. All three of them are protected by a number of blacksmith-made wrought-iron hoops, installed with the aim of foiling the activities of the body-snatchers, whose grisly trade a century and more ago was digging up corpses and selling them to unscrupulous anatomists for dissection in their laboratories. The family of the Rev. W.T. Shields were taking no chances with his corpse and those of his wife and their eighteen-months-old child.

Nearly as much could be written about the glories of Hexham Abbey as about the Roman Wall that pre-dates it by so many centuries. Again, the advice must be given, at any rate to those for whom ecclesiastical architecture and tradition is of importance, to look up the authoritative guide-books and learned volumes that have over the years been written by experts in their subject.

Though Northumbrians born-and-bred may challenge the statement, the fact has to be accepted by those of us at least who come from softer, gentler regions that there is a haunted element in this landscape, in the very air that lies over the vast moorland and mountain expanse of this county. Here and there it seems to absent itself for a while. In the Coquet Valley, at least in its lower reaches, fairly well removed from the Artillery Range established in the higher Cheviots, it is not so pronounced. Indeed, the whole way from Warkworth, on the coast, with its fine castle, inland as far as Rothbury and a few miles farther than that, Coquetdale is a smiling valley. It remains open and smiling at least as far as Hepple and West Hepple.

As it approaches Sharperton and Harbottle, with its impressive relic of a castle, one of the finest earthworks in the county, perhaps in the country as a whole, it begins to narrow and deepen. Yet it was a sufficiently gentle valley for a nunnery of Augustinian canonesses to have been founded there centuries ago; you can still see the remains of their church, and the Holy Well of St Ninian, blessed by the saint, from which the canonesses abstemiously drank, persuaded that virtue was communicated to them as they did so. Only beyond Alwinton, that remote and isolated stone-built Northumbrian hamlet 'at the end of the line', does the Coquet begin to take on its slightly sinister, even menacing, aspect—an aspect that could hardly be less in keeping with the implication of its dainty name. Follow my course, it seems to say; but do not dare to question whither I may lead you into the distant hills from which I came.

For the most part, then, Northumbria throws out a challenge. Its scattered peles and ruined castles, like that of Norham, overlooking the Tweed's southern bank, are a constant reminder that warfare and feud were its customary way of life. Its 'cup-and-ring' incised stones, such as the mammoth specimen at Routinlinn, are the relics of prehistoric peoples who lived harsh and uncertain lives in a forbidding and menacing land because they had no option, though there is no evidence that they continuously fought among themselves as the later Borderers, those dedicated warmongers, chose to do. There is too, of course, the grim grandeur of Hadrian's magnificent Wall, built on the very ribs of the country through which it so arrogantly passes.

And there are the innumerable deep-scoured cleuchs that pattern the moorland slopes. Not once but many times over, if you explore these, you will find the skeletons of sheep that have fallen on their backs in their tight folds and, unable to right themselves and undiscovered by shepherd or dog, have died there and rotted as time passed over them. Where, as here, there is grandeur, there exists also the hint of latent, implicit evil. But there is no gainsaying the fact that the grandeur and beauty of Northumbria as a whole far outweigh the other characteristics of this most northerly and impressive of England's counties.

4

The Yorkshire Dales and Moors

THE DALES

The Pennine Hills, which run northwards from Derbyshire's High Peak to the Cheviots, are often referred to as the Pennine Range, or Pennine Chain. The term is a misnomer, for the Pennines are not in fact a continuous range, or even a chain; rather, they are a succession of folded, or interlocked, hills of varying altitude, the highest being Cross Fell, in eastern Cumbria, which rises to 2930 feet. Colloquially, the Pennines are often called the backbone, or spine, of England; if this were the case, then it would be a sadly dislocated system of vertebrae that they represented! This succession of hills and foothills is frequently interrupted. The North and the South Tyne rivers both cross them: the first as the hills slant downwards to merge with the southern Cheviots, the second more completely severing them from their northernmost outliers by running directly across them from west to east, between Alston and Newcastle upon Tyne. Farther to the south, Teesdale slants across their track, from its source below Cross Fell to Barnard Castle and beyond, incidentally forming the border between County Durham and North Yorkshire.

Through North Yorkshire there run two major valleys (or three, if you include that of the Tees, on its northern boundary). These are Swaledale and Wensleydale, the 'true' Yorkshire Dales as ordinarily understood by those who regard them as unmatched throughout the length and breadth of England. Both rivers—the Swale, and the Ure (there is no 'Wensley') that runs down Wensleydale—have their head-waters close to the border. From these head-waters to the points where, roughly at Richmond and at Masham, they run off the eastern slopes of the Pennines into the flat Vale of York, their valleys are some thirty miles long. Not comparable in length with, for example, the valley of the South Tyne; but incomparably richer in character and 'feel'.

The two dales are linked, across the intervening fells, by the minimum number of minor roads; it is as though they have never had the wish to become easier neighbours. And that may well be a fact; for those who are true dalesmen, and inordinately proud of the term, make it very clear that, though geographically so close, and both carved out of the same good Yordale limestone, they are two distinct types of dale, and of dalesmen too.

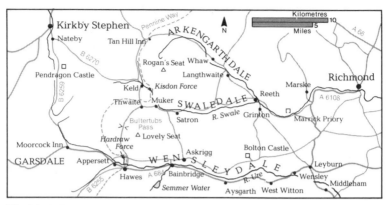

The Yorkshire Dales (North)

They always have been so, and fully intend to remain so. As far as mere topography is concerned, the most cursory glance at the map reveals that while Wensleydale is wide open, and much of it low lying, its neighbour five miles to the north across the fells is, right through to the stupendous gorge that carries it below the massive walls of Richmond Castle, close-set, hemmed in on either bank by craggy, steep, often precipitous moorland slopes that tumble headlong into the dark yet sparkling water. Melbecks Moor and Gunnerside Moor, with the latter's summit at Rogan's Seat, topping the 2000-foot mark, loom over it to the north, with flanking moors to east and west only just less high and stark. And to the south, between Swaledale and Wensleydale, there are heights only a hundred or so feet less, though oddly enough they are noted on the map as 'Commons'. Rogan's Seat to the north is closely matched by Lovely Seat to the south: two summits just six miles apart as the curlew flies and with only nine feet difference in their altitudes.

Is a valley better appreciated by being ascended from its foot to the head-waters of the river that has been running through it ever since the glacier that originally carved it out melted and vanished from the scene? Or by descending from its head-waters to the point at which the grown river flows out into open water-meadows? Swaledale and Wensleydale offer the opportunity to ask and answer the question, to reach a conclusion; a conclusion, anyway, that will apply to these two particular dales, if not as a general ruling, for each can be entered from either end.

You may enter Swaledale from Kirkby Stephen, just over the Cumbria border, and thence trace it eastwards to Richmond and the Vale of York. If you do enter it from this direction, you will not find it marked immediately as Swaledale. For the Swale itself derives from a network of named gills

The course of the former road from Kirkby Stephen to Hawes by Hell Gill Beck

and becks that flow down off the moors on the Yorkshire side of the border. The most important of these named becks is Birkdale, which itself is augmented by the steeply falling Whitsun and Uldale Gills and by Great and Little Sled Gills. Not until they have all merged with the beck that flows down West Stonesdale to the hamlet of Keld does Birkdale Beck take on its new, and final, name, Swale.

Alternatively, you may prefer to enter Swaledale at Richmond itself. There is the danger that if you do this, great as may be your desire to ascend the dale, the little town, which has been well described as being 'not quite English, a fairytale town depicted by a French artist'; or again as 'an illuminated manuscript, the work of an English artist trained in the monastic schools of Northern France, a fragment of the Middle Ages at their twelfth-century zenith of achievement, dignified without pomposity', may well induce in you that mood of contentment that invades those who find themselves in Lisbon, Siena or Venice, and subtly dissuades them from ever moving on to pastures new.

Perhaps in this particular case the deciding factor had better be that the road which tortuously links the head of one valley with that of the other has more to commend it than the somewhat commonplace one that links Richmond with Masham, the small market town at the eastern end of Wensleydale. But before setting off up Swaledale there is much to be seen in Richmond itself, even though you may be primarily interested in exploring the dale rather than the pavements of the towns scattered about it; above all, of course, the castle.

The site was superbly chosen. Like Durham Cathedral, towering above the cliff whose feet are laved by the River Wear, the giant walls of Richmond Castle give the impression—and a not wholly unjustifiable one either—of being a continuation of the precipitous hundred-foot rock face above the gorge of the Swale on which it is poised.

Built by the son of the first Constable of Dover Castle when he was granted the Earldom of Richmond by William the Conqueror in appreciation of his valour at the Battle of Hastings, the castle dates back to the second half of the eleventh century. Unlike most castles of the period, it is, strangely, triangular in plan; but like so many of its contemporaries and immediate successors it shows all too clearly the effects of the ravages of time and weather. The barbican is a ruin; but the magnificent keep, rising as high above ground level as the Swale lies below the cliff, has walls eleven feet thick. So, like the splendid curtain-walls, where so much else has collapsed and disintegrated, the keep survives.

You will not have lingered long inside these containing walls before you become conscious of the haunting quality of this lofty castle that dominates the cobbled market square sloping townwards away from it. Such is the atmosphere inside the walls that if some local man or woman should chance to tell you that beneath the massive bulk of the keep the legendary King Arthur and his Knights of the Round Table sleep their 'ancient, dreamless, uninvaded sleep', awaiting a call to arms, you may not find it altogether easy to preserve an attitude of legitimate scepticism.

Out of Richmond, when you have succeeded in tearing yourself away, you have a choice of roads along Swaledale, both of them on the left, or north, bank of the river. The one which most closely accompanies the Swale is the larger of the two, the A 6108 (becoming the B 6270) to Grinton and Reeth. So closely does it follow the river, crossing it once from the north bank to the south a mile or so beyond the outskirts of the town, that it barely reaches four hundred feet above sea level and is still less than six hundred feet above as it approaches Reeth, known as the capital of Swaledale. But though it lies low for so much of its length, prettily named Halfpenny House Moor and Downholme Moor rise steeply against it to a thousand feet or so just where road and river in harness take a bold swing southwards and then westwards again, to be close-squeezed between Marrick and Stainton Moors.

The more rewarding, however, of the two roads westwards-bound out of Richmond is the smaller unnumbered one, which swiftly spurns the valley and climbs the fells to clamber along the 1000-foot contour until it is forced to descend by way of Clapgate Gill to the hamlet of Marske, where the clints are of such outstanding quality that they actually rate a specific mention on the map. You may feel that they are not comparable with the extraordinary terrace of clints to be seen at Malham Cove, in North Yorkshire's district of Craven; nevertheless, clints are always fascinating to study, whether extensively distributed or concentrated in one limited area.

Here, then, is the visual evidence of the astonishing action of rain-water, and the chemicals carried in its individual droplets, and of frost, on the carboniferous limestone of the region spread over aeons of time. It is a ramification of miniature crevasses, their width to be measured in inches only, their depth in feet, running hither and yon, cicatrices in off-white stone whose face has been presented to the elements for two hundred million years, since that period, unimaginably remote, when this whole vast landscape was up-thrust from the original sea-bed that was its origin. There is infinite variety in the whorls and convolutions into which the resistant stone has been magically sculptured. Here are exotic flower-petals, broad and delicately curled leaves, fairy-like foliage, prototypes, imagination might suggest, of the fanciful work of medieval stone masons giving free rein to their inspiration as they chiselled away at the white Caen stone of the cathedrals. The poet Francis Thompson wrote of 'The hammer of wind, and graver of frost': the metaphor could hardly be bettered.

You can pick up the main road, just below Marske, if you want a change from the minor road; indeed, you will have to do so anyway, some five miles farther on, just short of Reeth, and this south bank main road offers the added advantage of views of, in turn, ruined Ellerton Priory, on your side of the river, and then of Marrick Priory on the other.

Marrick Priory can be reached from Grinton. Built in the middle of the twelfth century by Roger de Aske, its remains seem now to have been almost completely incorporated in what is evidently a prosperous farmstead whose pastureland dips to the very water's edge. Until the Dissolution this priory housed a community of devout nuns, and in nothing is their devotion to their faith, their piety and—it must be said— their masochism better revealed than in the extraordinary 'flight' of no fewer than 375 stone steps, undoubtedly the longest and severest in the country.

Oddly enough, the church used by the occupants of the priory was not in the precincts at all, but in the hamlet of Marrick on the top of a hill immediately to the north. Between the priory and Marrick there was, and still remains, a wood composed of close-set, stunted and gnarled and

Limestone weatherings or 'clints'

twisted trees. To climb to the top of the hill must at all times have called for stamina and sureness of foot as well as for resolution, for at this point the Swale has entered one of the narrowest stretches of the valley and the enclosing sides lift almost precipitously from its banks. At the bidding of their prioress the nuns set to and laid nearly four hundred slabs of stone, many of them weighing little short of a hundred-weight, step-wise up this slope from bottom to top.

They did their work well. It is not unreasonable to guess that many of their number, in the laborious years that this task must have occupied them, became incapacitated by exposure and by the unaccustomed use of back and shoulder muscles, and perhaps ended their days half-crippled as a result. Today, after many centuries, the great majority of these stone slabs lie just as they were laid, not far off true level, for the most part, though a number of them have been tilted or even dislodged by the remorseless growth of roots beneath and among them.

It is certainly a strenuous climb from the level of the priory to the field in which the track levels out as it approaches Marrick and the church. It is no less strenuous in the descent, for the upper thigh muscles are continuously at stretch to prevent one from descending too swiftly or tripping over the occasional broken slab or protruding root. What must it have been like in those far-off days, gathering stone from the outcrops among the trees, carrying them—perhaps two or three frail nuns to each heavy and cumbersome stone—and setting them one by one in the beds prepared for them, securely so that they would stand up to generations and, in the event, centuries of regular use? If *Laborare est Orare*, then surely those pious women earned a place at the foot of the throne of the God to whom their prayers were said, both in their cells and within the walls of the church to which this flight of steps led them. And equally during the long self-imposed labour of quarrying and laying those stepping-stones to higher things. Even at that, it is said, there were members of the community who ascended those tortuous steps, not on bare or sandalled feet but on their knees. The same harrowing sight may be seen, even today, at places of pilgrimage such as the Basilica of Nossa Senhora at Fatima, in Portugal, and on the monstrous flight of ornate stone steps leading up to the Sanctuary of the Bom Jesus at Braga, in the Province of Minho in the same country.

Grinton itself is no more than a small village, curious, however, for the size of its church: out of all proportion, you would say, to the community it serves today or served even a century ago when lead-mining was a major occupation in the region and the local smelting-mills gave work for the forbears of the men who now graze sheep on the lonely fells.

If you have a taste for the macabre you may like to don boots or heavy shoes and follow a narrow track westwards out of Grinton on the south bank of the river and close beneath the frowning mass of Harkerside Moor.

It has a traditional and evocative name, not shown save on the larger-scale maps: the Corpseway. Why the name? Because in olden times the only means by which the body of a man or woman or child who had died in one of the fell-side farms or in one of the isolated cottages could be fittingly buried was to place it in a pannier and have it conveyed on horse-back or mule-back to Grinton, for burial in the churchyard. And the route was this lonely and uneven and often treacherous track. It runs for some eight miles, crossing Crackpot Beck and continuing westwards as far as Satron, where it joins the road that runs up Swaledale after changing to the south bank of the river at Gunnerside. But here there was no church to greet and accommodate the burial procession from the Corpseway. There is, incidentally, another such track, at the western end of Wensleydale, running down off the hills just behind the famous Moor Cock Inn. Along this, too, corpses were carried from their remote death-beds to the nearest valley churchyard.

At Reeth, just above Grinton, Arkengarthdale, the valley of the Arkle, merges with Swaledale. Here anyone with an impulse to depart from the beaten track is faced with a difficult decision. Should he continue on his way along Swaledale, or should he take that most tempting minor road north-westwards out of Reeth that climbs between Reeth High Moor and Fremlington Edge and on to Arkengarthdale and, in due course, to Tan Hill Inn, the self-styled and truly 'highest inn in England'?

In fact, though the terrain is magnificent the overall distances are not great, whichever choice he makes. So, he can climb to Tan Hill and regain Swaledale in its upper reaches by taking the tortuous road down West Stonesdale, with its hairpin-bend at the bottom; or he can continue along the Swale to Keld and then turn northwards up West Stonesdale to Tan Hill and return down Arkengarthdale to Reeth. In any case these dales, the major and the minor ones, are so beautiful, the smaller ones so awe-inspiring, that they deserve to be travelled both up and down if their character is to be fully appreciated.

Take then, first, the steeper and narrower road out of Reeth, following the right bank of the Arkle. It descends steeply, between close-set banks, falling rather than merely running where its bed has been scoured out of the softer stone so that a miniature 'force', or *foss*—the word is common in these dales, where so much of Scandinavian origins persists: Hardraw Force, in Wensleydale, for instance, and Kisdon Force in Upper Swaledale—has resulted. All this is former lead-mining territory.

Lead was certainly mined here during the Roman occupation eighteen hundred years ago, as it was in Derbyshire to the south. Archaeologists maintain that the first lead mining here may well have pre-dated that of the Romans. Lead continued to be mined throughout medieval times and well into the nineteenth century. With a sharp eye, and given good light, it is not difficult to spot here and there the small spoil-banks and even the cave-like entrances to some of these old mines, often worked by no more than a handful of men and the most rudimentary of tools. Among these 'tools' was the moorland water itself: a gang of men would dam up a small, steeply-flowing beck until it contained a good head of water; then they would pierce the dam, thus releasing the water suddenly, so that it swept down in unnatural spate and scoured the peat and sub-soil from the surface of the rock which their instinct told them most probably contained veins of the mineral they were after.

Lead abounded in sufficient quantity in Arkengarthdale for there to have been a smelting-mill on the fell side a mile north of Langthwaite. You will find, as you continue beyond this dale hamlet, that the minor road you are following once again divides. The one that branches off due northwards climbs steeply up and over East Arkengarthdale Moor and Hope Moor, making for Barnard Castle on the Durham side of Teesdale. If you follow it you can picture in your mind's eye the long, slow-moving trains of what were then known as 'jagger' ponies, carrying the lead ingots northwards to the nearest port from which they could be shipped to their various destinations.

Whichever of these roads you take you will deem yourself 'on top of the world'. You will be imbued with a sense of splendid isolation, for your only company will be that of the Swaledale black-faces grazing these inhospitable looking moors and fells. Even on the roads, the heights hereabouts do not fall far short of the 1700-foot mark. You may, high up on Arkengarthdale Moor, feel inclined to wonder whether anything as low-lying as Swaledale can belong to this lofty, remote world of lonely summits. The first building that you will see, and the last for some miles to come, will be the Tan Hill Inn. It stands four-square, unprepossessing in the extreme, on the 1700-foot contour-line. One claim for it is that it is 1707 feet above sea level; the other, probably more accurate, makes it twenty-five feet higher than that. Its nearest rival is the Cat & Fiddle, alias *Caton Fidéle*, on Axe Edge, between Buxton and Macclesfield. The map indicates a difference of only twenty feet in altitude between the two. But what is twenty feet in so many hundreds, and especially in terrain so similar?

The Tan Hill Inn must rank among the most unprepossessing looking inns to be found anywhere in the country. The exterior, indeed, has little to commend it. But the tally of travellers down the centuries that it has stood there who have found it a haven when caught in the blizzards that so frequently blot out this grim plateau in winter and early spring must be immense. The writer remembers to this day the sense of blessed relief he experienced when, many years ago, he tumbled into a vast feather-bed lately occupied by a shepherd who had gone home down the dale the day before, after nearly thirty miles of foot-slogging up the then little-known Pennine Way; and this was late August, not mid-winter or early spring.

Was it his imagination, or did that billowing feather-bed still retain something of the warmth imparted to it the night before by the shepherd? Whether or no, he gratefully murmured as he fell asleep, 'For this relief, much thanks'. When Shakespeare wrote 'Now spurs the 'lated traveller apace, To gain the timely inn' he was thinking in terms of Scotland; but there cannot be many inns in that country, even in the vicinity of Glamis, which stand more remote, more blizzard-swept, which have been more eagerly sought by the benighted traveller, than the inn at Tan Hill.

It is only twelve miles or so back down Arkengarthdale to Reeth where you first joined it. Such a landscape merits something more than a backward glance, so you will be well advised to turn about at Tan Hill and follow the stripling Arkle as it tumbles south-eastwards through Whaw and Langthwaite, after which the gorge down which it has been cascading widens into a small valley that makes a graceful ogee-curve before joining the Swale. And now, it will seem to you after the dramatic heights of Arkengarthdale Moor, you are once again on familiar ground as you turn due westwards up the dale, heading for Muker. Here the Swale descends from the north down a gorge too steep for a road and you are forced to curve round through Thwaite and below Hocker Mill Scar to rejoin the river at Keld, where you should go in search of Kisdon Force, undoubtedly the finest in Swaledale though it cannot compare with the finest of them all, Hardraw Force in Wensleydale.

At Keld the road divides once more. Before following the continuation of the Swaledale road north-westwards to Nateby and Kirkby Stephen (these '-by' suffixes are all reminders of former Scandinavian influence, found also down the east coast of Yorkshire, Humberside and Lincolnshire in their hundreds, of which perhaps Grimsby is the most obvious specimen), across the border into Cumbria it is well worth taking the road northwards, up West Stonesdale, to Tan Hill. It is a true minor dales road, twisting and turning, leaping from one hairpin-bend to the next, almost from one outcrop of limestone to another. Desolate country in the extreme. High Rogan's Seat dominates it to the east, at well over 2000 feet, and Robert's Seat, not so much lower, to the west.

Look keenly over to your right and you may be able to descry, in a tight fold of the fells, the entrance to what has come to be known as Tan Hill Mine, or 'Peacock's Mine'. It gave access to a miniature coalmine that was developed single-handed by the one-time owner of Tan Hill Inn, the very man who took in an early explorer of the Pennine Way and let him use a shepherd's bed for the night. The man died many years ago, and the mine has not been worked since. So much the better, too, for it was a deathly place to approach, let alone enter. Rusting rails that once carried his two small-scale iron tubs into the hillside lay there abandoned, disused, for many years, tinting the peat-stained water a yet deeper tone with their scaling rust. One would think fuel must have been expensive indeed for a man to think it worth his while risking his life daily to extract a hundredweight or so of inferior coal for his hearth; especially when for the most part the hearths in these dales have always burned locally-dug peat. Perhaps he was seeking isolation in the dank passage that led to his dubious coal seam, as a change from the company that frequented the inn which afforded him his livelihood. Isolation it may have been; but it was not the 'splendid isolation' that comes with finding oneself on the bracing expanse of Arkengarth and its neighbouring moors.

Now turn about and look back down the dale to where the beck threads its way between Raven Seat and Black Moor. Just short of Keld, where you temporarily left Swaledale, you find again the westwards run of the dale, though now it calls itself Birkdale. It climbs, and climbs more steeply than any other of the roads you have so far taken, save perhaps the 'jagger' ponies' track over the moor. In six miles it has climbed to a road summit that comes to within a couple of feet of the 1700-foot mark. Even if there were no sign to inform you that you were there passing out of North Yorkshire into neighbouring Cumbria, you could guess that this was so. For this is a watershed; Birkdale Beck gives place to westwards-running Kitchen Gill—and gill, or ghyll, is a word seen more often on Lakeland maps than on those of Yorkshire.

A downhill run of two or three miles to Nateby lies ahead of you. There you turn south, along the B6259, a glorious Cumbria-Yorkshire border road that skirts Pendragon Castle—a haunted ruin if ever there was one— to cross a succession of little gills tumbling off the valley sides and then re-cross into Yorkshire just north of the Moor Cock Inn. Near this county border, somewhere on marshy Abbotside Common to the east, Ure Head marks the source of the river which runs down widening Wensleydale to Leyburn and beyond, to Middleham and Masham, to Ripon and so eventually into the Yorkshire Ouse near Boroughbridge.

To begin with, say for the first four or five miles eastwards from the Moor Cock Inn, Wensleydale promises to be as tight and concentrated a dale as its sister on the north side of Abbotside and Angram Commons. But at Appersett, a valley hamlet a mile or so short of Hawes, 'capital' of Wensleydale though in fact it is little more than a stone-built village straggling along its one wide street, the constriction is almost dramatically released. The road you have been following, the A684, takes a sharp turn, first right then left over old Yore Bridge, crossing the Ure to make for Hawes itself, on the right bank. And in doing so it leaves behind it what appears to be its original continuation eastwards, certainly the more rewarding of the two near-parallel valley roads which eventually merge a mile or two short of Leyburn, some fifteen miles farther on.

And yet—and yet! Is it ever safe to make so categorical a statement in such a context? Has this road that runs along the foothills of Abbotside and Askrigg Commons, Woodhall and Carperby Moors, through the endearing tortuosities of little Askrigg and almost through the shadow of Bolton Castle, really so much more to commend it than the one on the other side of the valley that runs through Hawes and Bainbridge and Aysgarth and West Witton, to rejoin its fellow in the village of Wensley itself? It is hard to say. Again the recommendation might be offered: trace the valley of the Ure westwards along one bank of the river and then eastwards along the other, thus obtaining the best of both worlds.

Admittedly it is the upper road of the two that will take you to Hardraw Force, which you must approach by way of the inn by the road side. It is immensely impressive: a plunging cascade of milk-white water that drops sheer some ninety-odd feet from a lofty lip of rock into a boulder-filled maelstrom of water that has changed colour as it were in reverse. Instead of having turned white from sheer vertigo as it leapt over the precipice, it has darkened to a lead-coloured hue. The enterprising visitor may take a curved ledge of rock that passes actually behind the tumbling water and emerges on the far side; it is an ordeal to be attempted, at least in times other than those of rare drought, only by the footsure; and even then one must be acutely conscious of the latent treachery of water-worn, spray-strewn limestone.

The map shows clearly that the two dales are linked across the intervening fells by five minor roads, with a sixth at the eastern end linking Leyburn with Richmond. Moorland roads, of course, all of them; and each worth exploring in its own right, quite apart from the fact that it is a means of access between one dale and another. The first of them is certainly the best known, for it is the only one of the quintet to have been given a name: the Buttertubs Pass. It lifts spectacularly off the valley floor just behind Hardraw Force, climbs to seventeen hundred feet on the western-falling slope of Lovely Seat, and serpentines downwards into Swaledale between Muker and Thwaite. Of all the views northwards down into and across this dale this is the most breath-taking and perfect.

The Buttertubs which give their name to this high moorland road are, like the clints and swallet-holes and other rock formations for which so much of North Yorkshire is noted, evidence of the effect of rain-borne acids on limestone over immense periods of time. It is not difficult to miss them, especially if your eye has been caught by the splendour of the moors rising towards you out of Swaledale and the even greater splendours of Kisdon and Rogan's Seat beyond.

They are grouped together by the road side, to your left as you travel northwards: a small cluster of unevenly shaped well-mouths, partly screened by ferns and approached over tumbled boulders among which it is easy enough to twist an ankle. Some are deep, others quite shallow; their sides are near vertical, but sprout maiden hair and other ferns so amply that it is not always easy to estimate their dimensions. Here and there a ledge gives the impression that these 'tubs' are man-made. They are not, of course; it is just that a stratum of more resistant rock has held its own against the action of water and acid combined where other strata have succumbed. You might think that with a powerful torch you could plumb their depths. But you could not. The dank stone seems to have a curious deadening effect on even the brightest shaft of light directed upon it, and the torch seems hardly more effective than a candle on the end of a string.

Five miles eastwards along the valley is Askrigg, a valley-fell-side village that might well be chosen as the epitome of such. The single street winds upwards, taking a dog's-leg turn here and there, and you are through it almost before you are aware of having entered it. The market cross stands on a curious cobbled triangle just outside the church gate, the site, they say, of what was, in harsher times than these, a bear-pit.

North of Askrigg two minor roads lift high on to the moors before dropping to Swaledale. Both cross Askrigg Common, one then flanking Oxnop Scar to reach Swaledale at Crow Trees, the other choosing a more north-easterly course, to descend split either side of Summer Lodge Beck.

Or you may prefer, before continuing down Wensleydale, to cross the river and spend a little while in Bainbridge, on the south side of the valley. It would be difficult to name two villages in any county, let alone in North Yorkshire, at once so close and yet so strongly contrasted in layout and in atmosphere. Bainbridge is built along the sides of a huge sloping triangle of turf, on which the villagers, young and old alike, enjoy themselves. If Askrigg gives the impression (quite possibly erroneous, of course) of being introverted, Bainridge is, by contrast, the extrovert. On the green are the stocks, a pair of massive beams inset in the groove of two stone pillars, while at its foot is the Rose & Crown, repository for the famous Bainbridge horn which, from time immemorial, must be sounded at nine o'clock every evening between Michaelmas and Shrovetide: three blasts each, to north, south, east and west of the inn. The purpose of the horn sounding is to enable shepherds and others on the adjacent fells to obtain their bearings in relation to the village. When mist as well as darkness has fallen upon the valley and the uplands to either side of it, a man may well lose his way entirely, even though he may have been born and bred in Bainbridge. With the sound of the horn still ringing in his ears there is a good chance that he will find his way home safely.

But there are older traditions than this, by far, in the bloodstream of Bainbridge folk. They may not attach much importance to the fact that a mere eighteen centuries or so ago the Romans established and garrisoned a fort here, the remains of which can still be seen. But they certainly believe that those strange marks which you can see for yourself any day, inset in a huge boulder on the edge of Semmer Water on the outskirts of the village, are the palm and fingerprints of Old Nick. None but a true Yorkshireman, of course (they maintain), would dare to challenge the Devil. But a Bainbridge man would, and did. And the Devil was so enraged at his

Bolton Castle from the east

impudence that, tradition has it locally, he plucked a stone still molten from the flames of Hell and hurled it at him. The stone fell short, and solidified on the edge of Scmmer Water; the Yorkshire man thumbed his nose at the Devil and walked leisurely back to Bainbridge and a cup of strong tea, mocking as he went.

Eastwards again lies Aysgarth. If, as is natural, you wish to see anything of this village you must for the time being remain on the right bank of the river, for the one bridge linking the two roads crosses the river some way beyond the village and takes you almost directly to Aysgarth Force, a lesser waterfall than Hardraw but well worth a visit all the same. Here the valley has noticeably widened, and as it were softened too. Beyond Aysgarth Force the two roads are more than a mile apart, which would have been impossible farther up the valley. As you look northwards you can see the grey mass of Bolton Castle on the hillside immediately to the west of the hamlet which shares its name in reverse: Castle Bolton.

It should be emphasised that Bolton Castle is not, in the true sense of the word, a castle at all. Set beside Alnwick and Raby, Arundel and Hermitage, for example, it would at once be shown up for what it was: a fortified manor house. You could compare it, for instance, with Hever Castle, in Kent. True, it is ancient: it was built towards the end of the fourteenth century, when the then Lord Chancellor of England obtained a Royal Licence to crenellate his manor house.

But it did not, as so many other and more specifically castles did, enter the lists of war. For three hundred years and more it remained a fortified manor house, under a succession of owners, though from time to time it served as a prison as well as home. The most famous person to have been incarcerated there was Mary, Queen of Scots, who spent six weary months there in 1568 after her transfer from Carlisle Gaol. A hundred years later, when standards of comfort and amenity had improved, Bolton Castle was virtually abandoned as a residence, and so inevitably fell into disrepair. Today, perhaps its greatest asset is the magnificent view it commands over the valley, and the contrast it unwittingly provides between its own grimness and the smiling landscape at its feet.

Another minor road scrambles over Bolton Moor, behind the castle, into Swaledale at Grinton. Yet another crosses Leyburn and Stainton Moors from Leyburn, at the lower end of Wensleydale, diagonally towards Grinton. These are almost certainly old pack-horse train routes. They invite exploration; but by now you will have a pretty good idea as to what to anticipate in the miles that intervene between valley and valley. If you have now reached Leyburn and want to cross over northwards to Swaledale you would do better to take the road marked A 6108 to Richmond, and take new bearings from there.

There are those who maintain that the best way to approach the main Yorkshire dales is neither from the western head-waters nor from the low-lying eastern extremities where they debouch into the Vale of York. They declare that the true threshold to the dales lies to the south: the border, that is to say, between North Yorkshire and either West Yorkshire or Lancashire.

Certainly this approach is an impressive and memorable one. It involves, for example, the long moorland climb northwards from, say, Skipton by way of Grassington and Kettlewell; or from Settle by way of Horton in Ribblesdale, followed by the long descent into Wensleydale. The summits that rise all about you include several that comfortably top the 2000-foot mark: Great Whernside, Fountains Fell, Pen-y-Ghent and Ingleborough among them. And there are others that come well up to the shoulders of those named. Indeed, it almost seems as though Nature sought to persuade you to approach the major dales by this route; for the waterways, and the narrow roads hammered out alongside them, run from the north southwards rather than, as in the North, from west to east. But if you have in fact now worked your way downwards from Swaledale and Arkengarthdale to Wensleydale, then logic suggests that you should continue on your way southwards; and this logic will be wholly acceptable. So, let the great mass of Yorkshire moorland astride this part of the Pennines be explored a little farther southwards yet—if only to see the best of its most characteristic feature, its drystone walling.

All this region is of course limestone and millstone grit. As a glance at a geological map will speedily show, the two types of stone are closely associated: a layer of one upon a layer of the other, though there is a general tendency for the millstone grit, commonly referred to for convenience as

The Yorkshire Dales (South)

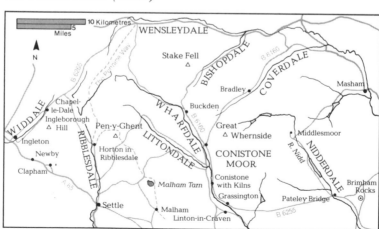

'gritstone', to come out on top of the carboniferous limestone on the higher plateaux. Because the one weathers dark while the other remains greyish or off-white, a Pennine landscape such as that of Yorkshire and North Derbyshire too, for that matter, alternates in a criss-crossing pattern of dark walls and lighter walls. The otherwise 'faceless' moorland, so hard to photograph with any degree of success, takes on 'shape' when outcrops of these rocks, in natural formation, or in the form of walls built by men who have quarried among them, are superimposed upon them.

To most visitors, especially first-timers from the south of the country, the endless miles of gritstone or limestone walls, sometimes intermixed, rank among the most memorable impressions that they take away with them. Not many of them, surely, will feel sympathy with the well-known landscape photographer from Kent who was recommended, for a complete change of scenery, to turn his camera lens on the Pennine scene as exemplified particularly in what was then the West Riding. He returned to his native county after a week of frustration, with the acid comment: 'Impossible to take pictures anywhere in those counties. The damned stone walls got in the way every time!'

A region builds in the materials that come most readily to hand, and nowhere is this better seen than in the south-western, or Craven, district of North Yorkshire, where limestone and millstone abound in such quantities and so close beneath the thin top-soil. It does not require a trained geologist's eye to assess whether the predominant stone of any one district, or even parish, is limestone or gritstone: if the houses and barns and shippons, the bridge parapets and footings and boundary walls, are sombre in tone—indeed, sometimes almost black—then this is an area in which millstone grit is more readily accessible than the carboniferous limestone beneath it. When the whole landscape seems lighter in tone, the buildings of a paler hue, less immediately forbidding in their presentation, then it is the limestone that has been easiest to quarry.

As you run down any one of the main southward-flowing dales out of Wensleydale—Bishopdale, for instance, the exit from Aysgarth, or the Stake Fell road south of Bainbridge that picks up Cragdale Water, or the road south of Hawes which takes you to Oughtershaw Beck and Langstrothdale and the River Wharfe—you are penetrating an area which presents these fine walls, these alternating building-materials, at their most impressive.

These beck-side roads merge near Kettlewell, in Wharfedale. Pause, as you enter this attractive moorland-valley village and look back, north-eastwards. One of the finest 'green roads'—pack-horse-train roads, drove roads—to be found anywhere in the Pennines curves up over the moors between parallel limestone walls that stand out brilliantly against the sombre grey-green of the turf between them and stretching out to the horizon on either side. There is another such 'green road' many miles to the south, running between Peak Forest and Castleton, in Derbyshire; and of course there are many others still to be located in various parts of the country, notably among the Pennines, some of which call for a large-scale map if they are to be positively identified.

The buildings in Kettlewell itself are for the most part of this same fine off-white limestone. And south of Kettlewell, to the east of the point where Littondale joins Upper Wharfedale, there is a magnificent limestone scarp that looks, from a distance, as though it is the father-and-mother of all man-made limestone walls, though it is in fact a major outcropping of this stone high on Conistone Moor, while the criss-crossing chequer-board patterns of drystone walling on its lower slopes are of course the handiwork of man.

Buckden village, a few miles to the north, and the hamlet of Conistone-with-Kilns, a few miles to the south, offer you a blend of the two types of stone: the off-white limestone is counterbalanced by buildings of the more sombre gritstone; you will see the same thing in many of the valley farms, such as that near Hubberholme. As you reach farther south, however, you will note a change of emphasis on the face of the moors. Where, not so far back, the flowing lines of the walls looked bright and clean, now they give the impression, the more distant ones at least, of having been drawn across the rough turf with some giant felt-nibbed pen soaked in indigo ink.

There is an impressive example of this to the north of the moorland hamlet of Slack; and on Widdop Moor, a few miles farther north, the outcrops on the skyline are of gritstone, and so stand out more boldly—even menacingly, you would find, in certain conditions of light—against the sky. Hereabouts, the cottages and shippons are all built of this millstone grit, its sombre hue contrasting strongly with the whiteness of the mortar laid between the courses of hewn stone. Yet only a few miles away, on the other side of the Wharfe, is the captivating village of Linton-in-Craven, which presents a very different picture indeed.

Linton-in-Craven lies close to the B 6265, some eight miles to the north of Skipton. Almost completely tree surrounded, its stone is so mellow that it might almost be a modest outcrop of virgin rock. The centre of the hamlet is a sloping green set with a tree or two, a tall flagpole, and a stone column carrying an astrolabe. At the foot of the green there are three different types of bridge, side by side: the stone road bridge, a gracefully proportioned pack-horse bridge, and, oldest by far of the trio, though sadly deprived of character by a modern surface and handrail, a clapper-bridge of massive stone slabs laid on massive stone piers that carry it only a foot or two above the surface of the water.

Facing the green on its higher side is the homely Fountaine Inn, overhung by fine trees. Down the right-hand side of the green as you face the running water at its foot there is an impressive and perhaps unexpected stone building that looks more like a ducal seat than a block of almshouses

View across the Yorkshire Dales

for aged pensioners. They were built as a token of gratitude for recovery from the Great Plague by a village carpenter who went to London three centuries ago to seek his fortune, succeeded, was knighted, and returned gratefully to his native village. His name is commemorated in that of the inn.

As for millstone grit: it still lurks beneath the surface, to crop out, often unexpectedly and in the unlikeliest of places. To the south-east of Pateley Bridge, hardly a dozen miles from Linton-in-Craven, it does so with a vengeance. Here, if once again you are prepared to take a very minor road, too minor to have yet been granted an official letter and number, and rising to nearly a thousand feet, you will come upon some sixty acres of millstone grit outcropping on a high plateau, almost every individual stone and group of stones having a formation that lends itself readily to name or nickname. Here are Druids' Altars, the Devil's Anvils, prehistoric monsters and—beloved of all children and like-minded adults—the famous Dancing Bear. Wind-eroded, carved by blizzards both of snow and of blown abrasive sand, these survivors of what was once a submarine plateau, a veritable sea bed, now raise their grotesque shapes to the sky, challenging the imagination for appropriate nicknames. Seen in broad daylight—and they are visible, though not individually identifiable, from many miles away—they invite exploration; seen in the half-light, or with swirling grey mist about them, they could, and undoubtedly do, strike fear rather than wonder in the heart.

It is certainly a far cry from the lonely heights of Swaledale and Arkengarthdale, Birkdale and West Stonesdale and their fellows in the far north of North Yorkshire to the monstrosities of the Brimham Rocks, near Pateley Bridge. But the stone that lies so near the surface, that gives to fell and moor and valley slope alike their formation and character, is stone common to them all. And this, whether they were carved in the first instance as Swaledale and Wensleydale were carved, by the inexorable passage of glaciers during the last ice age, say ten thousand years ago, or by the winds which still sweep, as they have always swept, across the moors, carrying grit in their teeth snatched from one outcrop to abrade and shape another perhaps fifty miles away. You will leave this North Country more conscious, perhaps, of what went in to its fashioning than will be the case in any other part of Britain save, may be, the softer limestone, the oolitic limestone, of the Cotswolds and the iron-hard granite of the West Country.

THE MOORS

You may well have pondered why it is that the long broken mass of lonely upland lining the western flank of the narrow neck of the northern Yorkshire plain is known as The Dales, while the more compact but not dissimilar region to the east, sandwiched between the plain and the sea, enjoys the title of The Moors. After all, both terms are common to both east and west.

The most probable answer lies in the simple geography of length, breadth and height. The dales of the west may cut and twist their way down twenty or thirty miles, either broad-bottomed as in the case of Wensleydale, or tight below cliffs and high-perched eroded scars as in the case of much of Swaledale. In the east, though, the dales are altogether more modest and pastoral, and ten miles would be a generous average length. Hence there is quite a difference of emphasis, scenically at any rate, as between west and east. In the former it is the valleys that matter. Visitors come here for the promise of long-famed valley names—Wensley, Swale, Arkengarth, Wharfe and Nidder—while the moors from which these dales are born, for all the lure of their peat-blackened loneliness, are traversed not for themselves but rather as unavoidable barriers on the way to the more varied and more obvious attractions of the next dale. The eastern moors, on the other hand—more flattened, less daunting with their glorious colour contrasts of summer's heather or autumn's tawny bracken

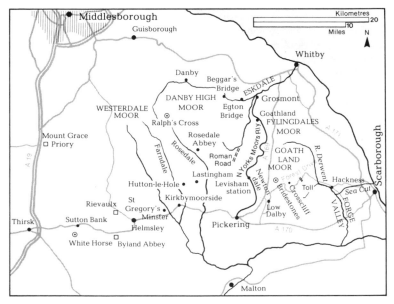

The Yorkshire Moors

matched against interruptions of brightest green—are sought out for themselves, for the sense of freedom they convey and for the panoramic vistas they offer; the dales here, cosier and more intimate than their counterparts in the west, take second place, though only just and certainly not in everybody's book.

Let us define more precisely this eastern upland tract now claiming our attention. Most of it now designated a National Park, it lifts unequivocal and almost sheer out of the plain some twenty miles to the north and north-east of the city of York. It measures thirty-five to forty miles from east to west, and, at its longest, some twenty-five from north to south. And it is contained within precise and even spectacular confines—some of the most dramatic cliffs in England along the east; the Cleveland Hills embracing the north and north-west; the Hambledon Hills defining the south-west, springing, as we have seen, precipitously out of the plain; and, by contrast along the south, the lush, broad Vale of Pickering, watered by Rye, Dove and Derwent, and Kyle, Seven and Foss, a gentle country which separates the Moors from what are still called the Yorkshire Wolds even though they now occupy the northern limits of the county of Humberside.

On the map it all looks nicely compact, even small, an easy day's pleasure. But relatively short though the measured distances are, they are far from such in achievement, as you will speedily find as you explore the generous network of minor roads—mere narrow, gated threads, many of them—sometimes ribboning away unfenced over miles of open upland, just as often confined within grassy banks and plunging as suddenly as steeply into some pretty dale. Plunging down—but climbing just as steeply out; for gradients of 1:4 and even 1:3, with the road's width allowing little scope for error on the hairpins, are commonplace here and this is no country for the tyro driver or a car of capricious performance.

But you do have an alternative, and an adventurous one too. For if the railways in Northumbria and the Peak District have been dismantled, reduced now to little more than sad traces of a romantic past, here across the Moors a real steam (or diesel) railway still prospers. Called the North Yorkshire Moors Railway, it will carry you along a line built by George Stephenson in the 1830s; all the way from Pickering in the south, up afforested Newtondale, out on to airy Goathland Moor and down into Goathland itself, before descending close to the Murk (or, as some write it, Mirk) Esk to Grosmont. Five stations in all, and a spring to autumn service of sufficient frequency to enable you to stop and enjoy the surrounds of each, whether the way-marked trails of Newtondale Forest, Levisham, which doubled as Melton Carbury in the television offering of *Brideshead Revisited*, the delights of green-turfed and straggling Goathland with its becks and fosses and spout, not to mention the ubiquitous sheep, or, finally, Grosmont, where the technically-minded can watch the maintenance and restoration of veteran locomotives. Using the railway you will of course have seen but a fraction of the Yorkshire Moors, but it will have been a splendid cross-section and one you will have savoured without hassle and under nostalgic circumstances.

The moors and dales apart, it is perhaps the forests and the religious houses that stand out as the principal other attributes of this region. These, and the many unexpected villages which, as often as not set with lush meadows and ancestral trees, nestle below the slopes in strange and total contrast to the featureless moorland pressing so close above.

As to religious houses, you can if you are ingenious assemble, if no longer see, something like a dozen in all. Do this, and you will find that they range from Cistercian aristocrats such as Rievaulx and Byland, through the Carthusian masochism of Mount Grace down to Rosedale and Hackness which preserve only a few stones.

But of them all you will surely decide that it is Whitby which most stirs the imagination—for its site, for its early foundation, as a mixed house, for its historical importance, as a place of learning (no fewer than five bishops received their training here), and as the home of a most remarkable lady. Whether you visit the actual site, or whether you are content with a far view from the moorland heights to the west, must be a personal choice.

What can be said is that this abbey, despite its unequalled associations, is relatively small and lacking the visual architectural impact of many, and that for this reason you may well opt for the distant view, reinforced by your own reflections on the Dark Ages past. But whether you experience Whitby close to or from afar, you can hardly fail to be struck by its siting. Almost every other abbey you visit—and not just here on these moors but throughout the kingdom—you will find comfortable and serene in a rich, well-favoured valley. Not so Whitby; it stands on a barren clifftop at the mercy of every wind that blows.

This abbey is almost synonymous with St Hilda, born in 614 and a lady of the royal houses of both Northumbria and East Anglia. Soon after passing the age of thirty she took formally to religion, in the year 657 founding (some say refounding) Whitby as a house for both monks and Benedictine nuns, but with herself, needless to say, as undisputed ruler. So wide was her learning, and so deep her wisdom, that her advice was sought far and wide and it was only six or seven years later that she hosted (some say convened) that famous Synod of Whitby which, seemingly remarkably amicably, reconciled the differences of the Celtic and Roman Churches, largely in favour of the latter, so that from now on Catholic observances became the rule over much of England.

Sadly, it is not of course the abbey in which the Synod disputed that you see today. Probably this was not even of stone, and in any event whatever its structure it was destroyed by Vikings in about 867. The ruins you wander around today, or maybe gaze at from far afield, are essentially twelfth- or thirteenth-century work, the result of a refounding for Benedictine monks in 1078. But, whatever their architectural period, these stones recall a Dark Ages sectarian reconciliation the like of which is apparently beyond our grasp today, and an example of feminine freedom and achievement unrepeatable, save in rare and privileged cases, until the emancipation of our own times.

There is something else, too, for which Whitby is known; the stone called jet, a word which has become synonymous with the colour black. Like that other semi-precious stone you may have come across in the Peak District, Blue John (*bleu-jaune*), the name has its origins in French, or, rather, in old French, the word being *jaiet*, itself derived from the Latin name of a place in Asia Minor where jet was once found. To see a Blue John seam you must descend deep into one of the Peak District caverns. Jet, though—a form of compressed lignite—is embedded in coastal lias, and a search for it, whether successful or not, can provide an original beach ploy and one, moreover, seemingly practised by our prehistoric ancestors since they have left us quite a legacy of jet beads and ornaments.

Abbeys, monasteries and priories are by no means the only evidence of religious compulsion on and around these moors. You have only to glance at a large-scale map to appreciate the rich sprinkle of standing stones,

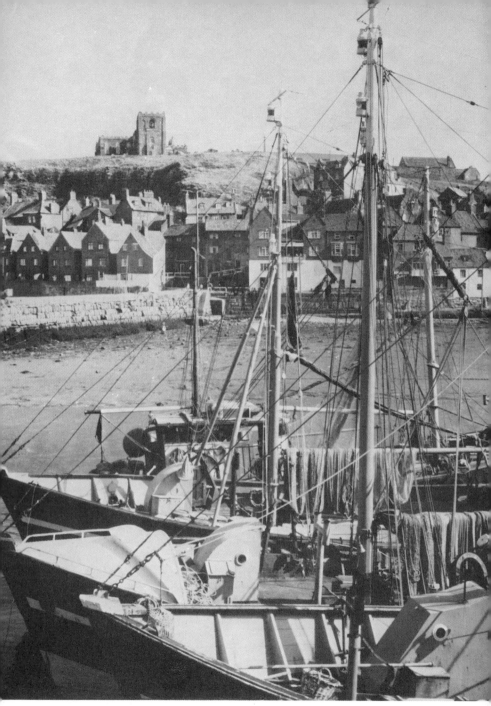

Whitby Harbour

tumuli, howes and cairns still here to remind us of strange rituals, their nature long forgotten, while, more evocative perhaps and certainly closer to our understanding, there are the many simple crosses. Ralph's Cross (he was, it seems, a loyal servant of a prioress of Rosedale), at a junction of minor roads where Westerdale meets Danby High Moor, is the best known, if only because it serves as the symbol of the National Park. But you will find many others—complete or mere stumps, standing alone, grey and weathered against a skyline or looming briefly out of a mist— Christian stones to mark a route or a boundary or at which to offer up a prayer while journeying through a hostile landscape.

Where to go? Indeed, where to start? This is the insistent problem posed by the combination of a large area and, all too frequently, insufficient time. But in the case of the North Yorkshire Moors simple geography indicates an answer, for most (though by no means all) places of specific interest lie within the dales and the great majority of these dales work their way southwards. Many-armed Eskdale dropping west to east across the north and meeting the sea at Whitby is the only significant exception. Your emphasis, then, while not ignoring Eskdale, could well focus on the central moorland core and the dales which break its southside slopes.

Scarborough is, and has long been, a resort of style and refinement as also one which tends to boost itself as 'The Gateway to the Yorkshire Moors'. Nevertheless, with your sights set on those moors you are unlikely to choose to tarry here, unless perhaps to see the ruined castle in which Edward II's unpleasant favourite, Piers Gaveston, was besieged and taken in 1322, or maybe to pay your respects at the grave of Anne Brontë who with her sisters Charlotte and Emily so darkly portrayed those other moors around their bleak parsonage home in what is now the county of West Yorkshire. But a mere four miles west of central Scarborough, sneaking off the A170 between East and West Ayton, you can slip into as unexpected and lost an approach to the uplands as you could wish for. It is called Forge Valley, too harsh a name by far for this leafy two miles imperceptibly climbing through Ruston Cliff, Searwell and Raincliffe woods, splendid trees which, so a notice informs us, represent a 'remnant of that forest which covered much of Britain in prehistoric times'.

Rather over halfway along this short valley you will find, on your left between road and river, what is called a 'Bird Feeding Station', an absurdly ponderous name, but an enchanting spot. It is a cleared crescent around which stand short, simple posts topped by arms, boxes or miniature platforms, all provided with whatever food is known to appeal to the many birds native to these unspoilt woods. Alongside, an illustrated board lists and describes the birds you may see, ranging from woodpeckers to tits, from finches to nuthatches.

Not much farther and you break out of the woods as the valley eases and broadens, carrying the trees, now increasingly conifer plantations, away to the upper ridges while green pasture slopes down to the small kinked bridge beside which you will probably have stopped. This bridge crosses the canalised waterway known as the Sea Cut, with its tended turf, bricked banks and unnatural straightness strangely out of place here so close to its parent Derwent whose erratic course you can make out only a few yards away. But, demure though it now seems, the Derwent when fed by the rains and snows sweeping across its source on high Fylingdales Moor once regularly flooded that Forge Valley up which you have just driven. So in the nineteenth century they dug this Sea Cut to divert the flood water down a north-eastern dale and into the sea to the north of Scarborough. Nor is this the only place where the Derwent suffers interference. Uninterrupted down Forge Valley and out into the Vale of Pickering, its natural course is eventually absorbed into man-made channels.

Another mile and a half and you are back with the Derwent, in more enclosed country, where a sign at a T-junction offers you Forest Drive to the left and Hackness to the right. Hackness will probably be your first village, a haphazard kind of a place as welcome for itself as for its park-like setting in a wooded bowl at the foot of a complex of dales. Stone and water are the first impressions here, where, beside the church, the road passes below a long, high, stone wall at whose foot a narrow, channelled brook trickles along its stony runnel.

Many might rate the approach to Dalby Forest Drive—the official entrance to which is all of five miles from that signpost at the T-junction on the edge of Hackness—above that of the Forest Drive itself. At first ascending the Derwent, and less darkly enclosed than when in the forest proper, the small narrow road wanders and switchbacks past banked meadows, half-hidden dales and ever-increasing patches of formal woodland. The Derwent is crossed, and deserted, below its long descent between Langdale and Broxa forests; then the Black Beck, soon after which a sharp left turn across Bickley Dale brings you to the Forest Drive toll, where the sum asked is modest enough, you will surely agree, when you see the work that has been done here, and which of course requires constant maintenance. Here, too, you can pick up a map and guide to the many picnic areas, forest walks and other facilities, these last including an information centre and museum at the Forestry Commission's village of Low Dalby, seven miles away and the conclusion of the Drive. Admittedly the forest is largely conifer, but it is also liberally dotted with other trees—pools of fresh green in spring, flashes of red and gold in autumn—and surely nobody will be disappointed by the spectacular vista of moorland, forest and dale offered by Crosscliff.

There is Bridestones Moor, too, abutting the north-western edge of the forest and owned by the National Trust, a place to tempt anybody whose interests embrace geology as also those who simply appreciate strangely shaped rocks. Here you will find a nature trail, laid out by the Yorkshire Naturalists Trust, and the Bridestones themselves, contorted gritstone outcrops similar to, though more modest than, those Brimham Rocks you may have found while exploring in the Dales near Pateley Bridge.

To the west of Low Dalby the A 169 will speed you up on to the moors, across Lockton Low, Saltergate and Lockton High to Goathland Moor, to the east of which rises Fylingdales, famous or infamous, according to your viewpoint, for the weird white 'golf-balls' and searching dishes of the Early Warning complex.

Turning your back now on both Fylingdales and the main A 169, you can drop westwards across the track of the North Yorkshire Moors Railway and down into the green, rural peace of Goathland. This is a village you have met already when the railway was described, and there is nothing that need be added, except perhaps to stress that when you come to the T-junction by the church you should be sure to bear right to have a look at the village before picking up the signs and heading south for the Roman Road.

One of the best preserved lengths in Britain, and by many visitors held to be by far the most exciting place in the National Park, the Roman Road is reached across several miles of as lonely and typical moorland as you could ever wish for; narrow, unfenced and negotiating a watersplash before climbing on to Wheeldale Moor, your road traverses a spacious land of gently rolling heather, bracken and peat, its long, smooth skylines broken only by the occasional unhappy tree or the low humps that mark the tumulus-graves of others who passed this way millenia ago. Then, quite suddenly beyond a rise, you glimpse your objective, angling in rather vaguely from your left but soon crossing your road and becoming anything but vague as it descends to a beck rounding a plantation. Ignore the plantation and the modern road, repair the Roman surface, and you are back two thousand years, so little can this landscape have changed.

This, remember, was primarily a military road, one which in the first and second centuries linked Eboracum (York) and Derventio (Malton) in the Vale of Pickering, with a coastal signal station on Kettle Ness to the north of Whitby, and as such it would have been narrower than the main highways. Yet the width seems generous enough, and the road impressively measured and skilfully drained too. What strikes one most, perhaps, is its roughness. But this of course is the result of centuries of weathering and centuries of service as a handy quarry for local drystone walling, and before we waste too much sympathy on the soldiers who trudged along here we should remind ourselves that all we are seeing is the foundation and that this would have been covered by a surfacing, possibly of sandstone slabs and gravel.

Stonework of a very different kind will be found close to Glaisdale, a few miles to the north in Eskdale, reached by retracing your steps and then

bearing left to leave Goathland to your east while you head first for Egton
Bridge, which is a village as much as a bridge. And a village of character
this is, too, a pattern of stone homes set within a park-like frame of steep
hills, green meadows and trees to match. There are even stepping stones.
It is not easy to reconcile the almost unreal quality of this place with what
happened here only just over three hundred years ago when, in 1679, a
local priest, Nicholas Postgate, was dragged away to York and put to
death, his offence being that he baptised a child into the Roman faith. One
can but regret that his persecutors can never know that Postgate's parish
still flourishes with a fine new church, built in 1866, and that their victim's
name is perpetuated in that of an inn.

At Glaisdale, though—at the foot of a very steep hill a short way up
Eskdale—there is a happier, if perhaps less well authenticated story,
associated with the Beggar's Bridge, the packhorse bridge of 1619 you have
come here to see. Thomas Ferris was probably never an actual beggar, but
as a lad he was desperately poor, and although he waded repeatedly across
the Esk to woo the squire's daughter the girl's father gave no encouragement to one so impecunious. So off he went to seek adventure and wealth,
in both of which ventures he was successful, fighting the Spanish and
amassing a fortune on the Main. Returning to Glaisdale he married his
girl—who must surely have been quite a mature lady by now—and
presented the village and future generations with this perfect stonework
arch with its neat side-walls. Today it shares this leafy corner with ugly
metal road- and rail-bridges encroaching on three sides, but traffic over
these is light and it is Thomas Ferris's Beggar's Bridge that shames the
others.

Your peripatetic course might head next for the village of Rosedale
Abbey; in a straight line—which of course you have no chance whatever of
achieving—seven miles to the south-west across the high moors. But you
have a choice of routes. One is to continue to ascend the Esk for seven or so
miles to Danby, a choice you will certainly favour if you feel you want to
absorb more about the National Park, for Danby Lodge, with its acres of
gardens, woodland and riverside, houses the principal information centre.
You then turn southward to pursue moorland roads past Ralph's Cross,
already mentioned as the best known among the moors' ancient crosses
and the one chosen as the symbol of the National Park. Otherwise your
best route is to turn round and climb back out of Glaisdale, returning to
Egton Bridge whence a minor road—very similar to the one which took
you from Goathland to the Roman Road but more lined by shooting butts,
both square and round—will eventually drop you precipitously into
Rosedale Abbey. A trim, isolated, grey little place, you will find this to be,
deep in its own narrow glacier-cut dale (the river is the Seven, not, as you
might expect, the Rose) and really too modest for its rather grand name.
Nor was there even an abbey here; it was a Cistercian nunnery, founded in

the twelfth century but, even in this remote corner, unable to escape Henry VIII's Dissolution, so that a couple of corner-buttresses and a bit of a turret stairway are all you will find today.

The climb westward out of Rosedale Abbey seems, and maybe is, even more precipitous than was the descent from the north-east. But it can also be rewarding with, first, long views down the pastoral dale spread out below with its farms, glimpses of the Seven and backdrops of forest, and then, as you level out at Bank Top, the abrupt change to upland moor and marsh. Here, rooted into a low ridge to the left of the road, stands one of those crosses, a mute yet insistent reminder of earlier wayfarers without benefit of metalled road or car. Then, almost at once, you are at the watershed, ready to quit the moors in company with Hole Beck and Loskey Beck, now, with several others, well set on their descent to lose themselves in the many waters of the Vale of Pickering.

Hutton-le-Hole, the first place you will reach, is one of those villages which attract adjectives such as charming, pretty, picturesque, curious, individual; they all fit, but the last two probably best. The Hutton Beck, hurrying and even cascading southward below broad grassy banks, is the key here, yet one which almost seems to ignore the village whose sturdy stone houses have had to distance themselves in an opportunist scatter above. Mentioned in the Domesday Book, and in the seventeenth century a refuge for Quakers, Hutton-le-Hole is a place with a story in a district with a story; a story well told in the Ryedale Folk Museum.

At Lastingham, the village a couple of miles to the east, you meet St Cedd, second only to St Hilda in local early Christian fame and her Celtic colleague at the Synod of Whitby. A monk from Lindisfarne who later enjoyed the resounding title of Bishop to the East Saxons, he founded a monastery here in 654 (three years before St Hilda founded Whitby), apparently because King Ethelwald wanted a place at which to pray. That Lastingham was in fact this place was disputed, not very convincingly, by a nineteenth-century scholar who favoured St Gregory's Minster (about which more below), but the evidence in favour of Lastingham seems overwhelming, even if one only refers to the Venerable Bede who records that Cedd fasted for forty days and then built at 'Laestingau'. In any event, Cedd died here of the plague immediately after the Synod—some maintained that he was only getting his deserts for so meekly accepting the Roman view at Whitby—and, like so many other religious houses including Whitby itself, his foundation seems to have been destroyed by the Vikings two centuries later.

Another two centuries would pass before (in 1078) Abbot Stephen of Whitby began to rebuild here, his motive being a shrine above Cedd's tomb and possibly also above that of King Ethelwald. From the contemporary local point of view—pious doubtless, but nevertheless well aware that shrines brought pilgrims and pilgrims brought commerical pickings—the venture must have been disappointing because less than ten years later the monks abandoned Lastingham and moved to York. However, within those few years they completed much of the new church, including the now much admired crypt, a place which, whatever its failures in the past, now attracts plenty of modern pilgrims, most of them here to wonder at the sheer simplicity of the pure Norman architecture—rows of vaulted low compartments supported and divided by sturdy, squat piers—but a few, one hopes, sparing a thought for Cedd and his master, Ethelwald.

Here in Lastingham and Hutton-le-Hole you are in pleasant enough but indecisive countryside, neither real moor nor real dale nor yet the flat, elongated bowl of Pickering's vale. On the ground your geography is not easy to work out, impeded as your vision must be by trees and rises, but it becomes clear enough on the right kind of physical map. From this you will see that you are on a kind of intermediate shelf into which Rosedale and Farndale have debouched and the southern limit of which is the A 170. Should it be spring you will surely not fail to drive up Farndale (in company, it must be said, with hundreds of others) to marvel at the daffodils along the Dove. Otherwise your next objective awaits to the south-west; that of St Gregory's Minster, also known as Kirkdale Minster, which a century and a half ago put in its claim to be the site of St Cedd's monastery.

You will find St Gregory's just north off the A 170 rather over a mile west of Kirkbymoorside, the approach to it along leafy lanes and across a ford being everything it should be. Here, in a hidden dell close-crowded with trees, and with no other buildings in sight, sits the neat little church which, basically Saxon, is one of the oldest and by a long way the most interesting in the whole Moors district.

The first thing to do here is to ignore that tower; it was added in 1827, to replace a wooden belfry, and although restrained and inoffensive enough it really has no business to be here, either architecturally or aesthetically. Inside the church it is even more incongruous, for here a strangely tall but very narrow eleventh-century arch, once the church's west door, serves as your access to the base of a tower of eight centuries later.

But what is the story of this place? The claim that it started as a Dark Ages monastery we can surely accept. The status of Minster which, as we shall see below, it certainly enjoyed well before the eleventh century, is evidence enough; minsters were nearly always associated with monastic communities. And this evidence can be reinforced by the suggestion, intriguing in more senses than one, that the dedication to St Gregory (the pope who sent St Augustine to England) may well have been a diplomatic gesture underlining a sincere acceptance of the swing to Rome signalled by the Synod of Whitby. The claim, mentioned earlier, that St Gregory's, rather than Lastingham, was the monastery recorded as having been founded by St Cedd we can probably just as surely dismiss as a nice try by a Victorian scholar indulging his wishful thinking. His 'evidence' will be found within the church; two large graveslabs, originally built into the west wall but at the beginning of this century brought under cover. Examining these in 1846 our scholar concluded that one bore the words 'Cyning Aethilwald', that the slabs must therefore be those of Ethelwald and Cedd, and that it followed that St Gregory's must be the site of Cedd's monastery. The local guide's dry comment that this theory has had few supporters is one we would be wise to accept, but at the same time we may allow ourselves to romanticise over those intricately incised and enigmatic coffin slabs.

But all this dissolves into little more than academic speculation once you stand below the church's greatest treasure, the Saxon sundial which you will find over the old south door, now sheltered by a nineteenth-century porch bearing a modern dial. There are inscribed panels to either side, and it is quickly obvious that the masons who carved these, and presumably also the sundial, were no lay-out artists, for they unashamedly ran out of space; confident and generous in the left-hand panel, they began to panic and compress in the right. Even their signature (Hawarth and Brand wrought me) went wrong, the information that the pair were priests being forced on to an upper line. It is all as humanly endearing as the gentle conceit of the message left by the lord of the Manor of Orm. Put into modern shape, it reads: 'Orm, the son of Gamal, bought St Gregory's Minster when it was all broken and fallen in and he caused it to be built anew from the ground up in the name of Christ and St Gregory. This was in the days of King Edward and Earl Tostig.'

So what we have here is the sobering information that the church we are looking at, nine centuries old though it is (the reference to Edward and Tostig establishes a date somewhere between 1050 and 1065), is in fact a restoration. But a restoration of what? Of, it is surely reasonable to assume, a small church, probably that of a monastery, built and dedicated to St Gregory at about the time of the Synod of Whitby and, like so many, destroyed two centuries later by Vikings.

All this may seem a very long time ago. But as you leave this place you can if you wish cast your mind even farther back in time. Millenia farther back in fact, for, near the ford, your map marks a cave and it was here, in 1821, that the bones were found of lion, bear, mammoth, rhinoceros and other animals, among them something like three hundred hyenas.

Rosedale, Lastingham and St Gregory's were modest enough religious houses. Even Whitby is hardly pretentious, while in the north-west Guisborough's ruins are scanty. But understandably, at any rate in tourist terms, it is for the more spectacular foundations that the North Yorkshire Moors are best known; for the great Cistercian complexes of Rievaulx and Byland, places which, though piety was doubtless still paramount, in a sense served as commercial centres and which were built in an era that sought its God through magnificence rather than simplicity. Mount Grace Priory, below the western slopes of the Cleveland Hills, is, though, in a class of its own, a Carthusian house designed around its monks' regimen of isolation and silence. All these are much visited and well documented, requiring no elaboration here.

You may have started your North Yorkshire Moors experience high on the eastern escarpment above Whitby, and you could do worse than close it at Sutton Bank, high on the precipitous western escarpment and famous for its views across the plain to the shadowy brown and green hills that mark the entries to the Dales. Gliding, an information centre, a nature trail, medieval and earlier earthworks and, far below, a bottomless lake are among the attractions here. And a White Horse with a difference; different because it was cut only in 1857; different, too, in not having a base of chalk. To Thomas Taylor, fired with enthusiasm by the white horses he had seen in the south, it must have seemed a splendid idea, but it was succeeding generations who inherited the problem of keeping his animal white.

5

The Peak District

Sandwiched as it is between two vast conurbations, those of Manchester and Stockport to the west and Sheffield and Chesterfield to the east, it is small wonder that, compared with Yorkshire, north Derbyshire is moor-and-dale country writ small.

Small in area, that is; but, for all that, often comparable in altitude. For this part of Derbyshire contains a considerable number of moorland summits that easily top the 2000 foot mark, and thus join the league represented by Fountains Fell and Whernside and Pen-y-Ghent. Its dales, however, are diminutive compared with the major ones in the north. Monsal and Chee, Millers and Dove, Lathkill and Wye, Taddington, Cressbrook and charmingly-named Water-cum-Jolly: these are but miniatures when contrasted with Wharfe and Wensley and Swale, Langstroth and Arkengarth. Nevertheless, like so many things conceived and designed on the Lilliputian scale—whether repeater-watches, Victorian dolls-house furniture or the modern 'match-box' model or the miniature dwarf trees that the Japanese call *bonsai*—they have a beauty, an ability to please and satisfy some innate instinct within us that is more subtly potent than apparent.

It is to the north of these little dales, however, that the most dramatic scenery is to be found, for the Peak District of Derbyshire is in fact the southern bastion of the Pennines. And the term bastion is fairly chosen. For the Pennines do not start gradually and build up slowly; they begin not with a whimper but a bang, and reach their first great climax within a very short distance of their southern terminus; there is nothing tentative about it. From the start they launch themselves on their long and lofty sequence that ends only when they merge with the distant Cheviots, even if interrupted once or twice by river valleys such as that of the South Tyne. Two thousand feet high, above Hope Valley and the Vale of Edale, there spreads the star-shaped group of lofty summits compositely referred to as The Peak. The tough climb up Jacob's Ladder takes you to Edale Head, at 2088 feet. Look ahead and to your right, and half a dozen cairns mark summits like Kinder Scout and Kinder Low, which are only a few feet less high. If you have done the climb, or a similar one up Grinds Brook or

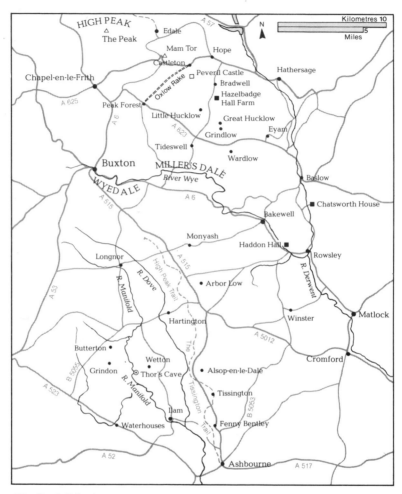

The Peak District

Crowden Brook, you well deserve the keen sense of accomplishment with which you will be imbued.

It is up one of these cloughs—Grinds Brook, in fact—just behind the Nag's Head Inn, Edale, that the arduous 250-mile tramp northwards along the Pennine Way to Kirk Yetholm actually begins. The Chinese have a saying, older by many centuries than the 'thoughts' of Chairman Mao, and likely, one would think, to survive a great deal longer than the contents of those little note-books: 'The longest journey begins with but a single step'. It is one of those simple utterances that are profounder than

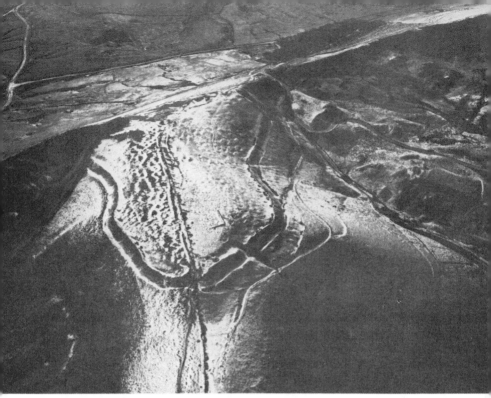

Aerial view of Mam Tor – 'Shivering Mountain'

they appear, whether taken figuratively or literally. Certainly it is a thought to bear in mind as you stand there, looking up at the first of a long sequence of unobtrusive signposts, and contemplate what lies ahead of the walker with his face turned to the north. Not for you, perhaps, this marathon 'over the tops' ordeal; but others have done it, and the sense of achievement that lights those last few miles down the northern slopes of the Cheviots proves ample compensation for the sustained rigours of the journey.

Since so many of these pages have hitherto concerned themselves in the main with the exploration of moorlands and the raised valleys that intersect them, perhaps now a descent from the sublime—not to the ridiculous but to the less dramatic—might be fitting. So, southwards then to the proliferation of little dales of north Derbyshire short of the actual Peak, and what is to be found amongst them. Yet, not immediately; for there is more than a little to be seen in the folds of the hills threaded so delightfully by Hope Valley, by Bradwell Dale, by Highlow Brook and Abney Clough—the last with its unexpected echo of Shropshire and the poet A.E. Housman.

There is, for example, that strange sliced mountain which so distinctively breaks the view to the west of Castleton by way of the steep defile of Winnats ('Wind-gates') Pass; marked Mam Tor on your map, it is colloquially known as 'Shivering Mountain'. And for a very good reason. Is it fact, or is it merely an optical illusion, that persuades you as you stand there contemplating it that the face of Mam Tor is in motion? Is this—momentarily you almost hesitate to voice the words—an incipient Aberfan? Will this monstrous hill side, that looks curiously as though man had something to do with its creation, suddenly begin to slide down into the valley at its feet, carrying all before it? It has not done so—yet; at least, not to any real extent. But this is shale; and shale is unstable. The face of Mam Tor is one to be contemplated not merely with curiosity but with a justifiable degree of apprehension.

Quite close to Shivering Mountain are the famous Speedwell, Treak Cliff and Blue John Mines. They are magnets to all who enjoy caving the easy way, along well-lit subterranean paths originally hewn out of the rock by the men who quarried for this exquisite fluor-spar, peculiar to this part of Derbyshire and ranking among the most beautiful crystalline substances to have come from any mine in any country in the world. Why is this fluor-spar known as 'blue-john'? The story goes that it was first sought after by French connoisseurs, who noted its predominant colours, blue and yellow; so, they called it, for want of an immediate better name, *bleu-jaune*—later Anglicised as 'blue-john'. It is as good, and as likely, a derivation as any other.

There is, too, not far from here, Peak Cavern, Mecca of several generations of speleologists, its ultimate secrets as yet almost certainly unrevealed though lives are risked unceasingly by those enthusiasts to whom claustrophobia, if recognised by them at all, is just a naughty word. So, while barely three miles to the north, across the valley, tough moorland walkers seek the heights and treachery of Kinder Scout and Kinder Low, the challenging scramble up Jacob's Ladder or Crowden Brook, their fellows, preferring to burrow like moles in the darkness, penetrate ever more deeply beneath the rock mass just south of Castleton that carries on its 1000 foot summit the ruins of Peveril Castle.

Sir Walter Scott knew of this castle—there cannot have been many, at least in the north, with which he was not familiar; he wrote of it as having been 'built upon principles on which the eagle selects her eyrie'. The comment is apt, for to reach it—a labour that earns an ample reward—involves a really stiff climb.

Alternatively known as Peak Castle, Peveril was built soon after the Norman Conquest and given by William of Normandy to his natural son, William. Most castles built in the eleventh century started as timber forts, their timber being replaced by the more enduring stone as the years went by. Peveril, however, was an exception: there was, and is to this day, very

West Stonesdale Moor – the route of the Pennine Way near Tan Hill, Swaledale

Dovedale, in the Peak District

Treak cavern

little suitable timber for building in this area, but excellent building stone
has always been abundant. The Romans had discovered this eight or nine
centuries before, when they built their fortress of Anavio, a mile or two
down the Hope Valley and known today as Brough.

Perhaps because of the severe weather in this region, among other
factors, Peveril Castle suffered less at the hands of enemies than most
others did. As a result, its noble keep, built almost exactly eight hundred
years ago, still stands, forty feet square and almost to its original height.
Visitors interested in both ancient and medieval architecture may here
spot an unusual and striking feature: in the walls of the round tower
located at the eastern end of the enclosure on the hill top there are to be
found some reddish tiles, almost though not quite as thick as bricks. Close
examination of these by experts has revealed that they are Roman brick-
tiles, almost certainly taken from the Roman fortress by the builders of
Peveril Castle. The Romans, incidentally, mined lead in these parts, and
for centuries after their departure the mineral continued to be mined here,
as farther north in the region of Swaledale and Arkengarthdale. So it is
quite possible that the main function of both castles in this district was to
protect the interests of the owners of these valuable mines against the

continuous threat of encroachment and seizure by aliens who sought the valuable commodity in their own interests.

Castleton itself is a fine example of a Derbyshire dales township, or overgrown village, picturesque in a somewhat stark fashion, if the apparent paradox can be accepted. It comes into its own, perhaps above all, on the 29th of May, which to most of the county, and to other regions of England too, is traditionally known as Oak Apple Day. In the early evening, a procession of villagers makes its way leisurely through the narrow street, flanked by stone houses and cottages and shops, headed by the 'Garland King' and the 'Garland Queen'. It is these garlanded figures that account for the fact that here in Castleton Oak Apple Day is specifically 'Garland Day'.

Eventually the procession comes to the gates of the church, and the high spot of the whole ceremony is about to take place. The King rides through the gateway into the churchyard, and there the Queen Posy is ceremoniously removed from the top of his massive 'garland'. The garland itself, of which he is doubtless very glad to be rid, is carried ceremoniously to the top of the church tower. There it is carefully draped over one of the eight stone pinnacles, the other seven of which have already been decked with sprays of oak leaves. In olden times the garland was allowed to hang from the pinnacle throughout the whole of the following year, until the next 29th of May. More recently, however, it has been removed at the end of the first week, to be stored along with the Restoration costumes of the Garland King and Queen until Oak Apple Day, Castleton's own Garland Day, comes round once more.

Eastwards from Castleton the valley widens, and correspondingly, inevitably, declines in picturesqueness. Sheffield now lies only a dozen or so miles away, and already the hot breath of the steel industry may be felt in the air. And also that most important Derbyshire industry: the quarrying and processing of limestone. Lime is all too essential a commodity for mere beauty and remoteness to be considered of greater importance; hereabouts, quarries and lime works begin to develop into a major and, to the lover of silent, unspoiled nature, disastrous menace.

But you can in fact escape this, threatening as it is. The secret is to branch off this Hope Valley road southwards, on B 6049, leading up one of the less-sung dales, Bradwell: this dale road runs almost due south of the A 625, between Bradwell Moor to the west and Abney Moor to the east. You enter it through a magnificent limestone portal, best appreciated if you turn round, soon after you have passed through it, and consider it from the south side; the crag on your right is particularly impressive. Immediately beyond you will come to a farmhouse on your left which is a farmhouse with a difference. This is Hazlebadge Hall Farm, the main fabric of which dates back well over four hundred years, actually to 1549. But its very prominent gable is of much more recent date, though it has some beautifully proportioned mullioned windows of an earlier time, above which you can see the carved stone crest of Lady Dorothy Vernon, romantic heroine of Haddon Hall, far to the south in Derbyshire, near Bakewell.

Much farther up the valley lies that gem among Derbyshire dale villages, Little Hucklow, sheltering beneath the 'Edge' from which the gliders take off, soaring into the Derbyshire sky from which their fortunate occupants can look down upon the pattern of hill and dale, 'green road' and stone outcrop, that lies far beneath and to the south of them, to Ashbourne and beyond. From Little Hucklow you can take minor roads, as yet unnamed and unnumbered, between drystone walls, through Great Hucklow (which, in fact, is not all that much larger than its more unassuming neighbour), Grindlow and Foolow, to the memorable village of Eyam, lying low beneath the slopes of its jostling hills.

You have been surprised, even puzzled, at the number of villages and hamlets hereabouts that carry the suffix '-low'; it is, of course, the 'law' of

Little Hucklow village

country farther to the north, to the Border and the other side of the Cheviots: the word denoting summit, or hill. Countless villages and smaller congeries of stone-built homes, groupings too small to be given a composite style, have been given names that end with this common suffix: Wardlow and Arbor Low, Bee Low and Low Foot (the suffix reversed), Cowlow (an unconscious happy juxtaposition), Woolow and Bleaklow; the list is endless.

Entering Eyam from the west, at a crook of the road and well into the village, you pass a diminutive green on which a pair of somewhat dilapidated stocks tacitly reminds you that unsocial behaviour formerly merited punishment; in that age there was a less permissive society than obtains today. A hundred yards farther on, on the other side of the road, is a much rarer object: a mechanically-operated sheep-roasting spit. It is not an object of beauty; but it is one that is very rarely seen; indeed the Eyam folk might tell you that theirs is the only one in the whole country. It stands rather more than head-high, with a canopy sheltering from the weather the somewhat crude mechanism that enables a whole sheep to be slowly turned, while vertically hung over the fire. This sheep-roasting ceremony, a milder form of the older traditional ox-roasting ceremonies held in various parts of the country, takes place annually at the end of August or at the very beginning of September.

Just beyond the small, narrow green in which the spit stands there is the row of stone cottages, the second of which is ominously named 'Plague Cottage'; and this is the more the pity because the cottages are so charming in themselves. But the name is one of very long standing, and successive occupants have had no desire to change it for something less ominous. For it was within the stone walls, behind the small windows of this very cottage that, in the year 1665, the Great Plague that was already decimating London broke out in Eyam.

It was brought, so it is believed, in a parcel of clothing despatched from a London tailor to a client in the village. In October 1665 twenty-three of Eyam's small population died in hideous agony of the plague and, as a result, the Reverend William Mompesson, rector in Eyam, whose 'Plague Church' is on the same side of the road a hundred yards farther on, 'closed' the village to the outside world. He was a man of courage, a man who exercised a strong influence over his flock. His parishioners, aghast at what had already happened and fearful of what was yet to come, agreed to this self-imposed isolation in the belief that the inhabitants of neighbouring villages might thereby be spared a similar dread experience. They had to agree to live as best they might on their own resources until the plague had completed its deadly work among them.

So, a rough circle was marked out around Eyam. Provisions that were essential, such as flour and salt, were brought from neighbouring villages and deposited on certain designated stones. They were paid for with

Eyam village stocks

money left alongside, in troughs kept filled with water in the pathetic belief that this would sterilise the coins and prevent the disease from being transmitted to those generous enough to bring the provisions. Mompesson gave orders that every villager, man, woman and even young child, should smoke as much tobacco as could be obtained; it was, he told them, a prophylactic.

No one can say whether it really helped; certainly it was no guarantee of immunity. In the month of August alone, ten months after this period of voluntary isolation had begun and the small community had so deliberately cut themselves off from the outside world, seventy deaths were recorded. By the end of the full twelve months no fewer than two hundred and fifty-nine men, women and children, from seventy-six families, had fallen victims to the horror of the plague. This was worse than decimation, for Eyam was only a very small community. But Mompesson and those of his parishioners who survived had the consolation of knowing that they had kept its ravages to themselves, that none of the other communities scattered about the Derbyshire moors and valleys had fallen victim to the plague on their account.

Today Eyam sleeps betweeen its limestone slopes. Wander about the churchyard and you will come upon innumerable reminders of the plague that struck the village three hundred years ago; the gravestones bear the names of so many of the inhabitants who lived and died within that charmed circle. But not all the gravestones have this melancholy element in their partly defaced inscriptions. There is one that offers a strong contrast. You will find it beyond the north-east corner of the church, beneath an overshadowing tree. It is the grave of a man who was a dedicated cricketer for more than half of his three-score-years-and-ten, one Harry Bagshaw, who represented Derbyshire in county matches and then graduated to membership of the M.C.C. His highly polished tombstone carries the words 'Well Played', and one thinks instantly of Newbolt's cricketing poem and the 'Breathless hush in the Close'. Four lines of verse appear beneath the salute:

> For when the one Great Scorer comes
> To write against your name,
> He writes—not that you won or lost
> But how you played the game.

(The author was one Grantland Rice.) And beneath the quatrain there is—just to bring the point home—a carved reproduction of three scattered stumps, two flying bails, a cricket-ball with the stitched seams well in evidence, and a bat tilted at an odd angle beside them. No one holds the bat; it was, presumably, the final over of the game—a game which, it is made abundantly clear, he had played well, and to the end.

Nor are gravestones the only things of interest in this well-tended churchyard. A magnificent eighth-century Celtic Cross combining pagan and Christian symbols recalls those days, nine centuries before William Mompesson, when Christianity was far less firmly established, while a nearby elaborate eighteenth-century sundial well repays study.

If you care to walk a short distance out of the village, or to drive up what is at first a steep and twisting road, you will come upon 'Mompesson's Well'. This is a rough stone trough on the north side of the village, one of several in which coins were expectantly laid and beside which provisions were placed for the people of Eyam so far as it was in the power of neighbouring villagers to come to their aid. Not far from here, on the other side of the village, there is a small horseshoe curve of turf and limestone and small trees known as Cucklet Dell.

It was in Cucklet Dell that the Reverend William Mompesson gathered those who remained of his flock, a number that diminished sadly with every passing week, Sunday by Sunday, throughout those twelve grim months, to lead them in prayer and praise, fortifying them for their continuing ordeal with words of comfort as well as of command. You cannot linger anywhere within that half-mile radius of the village drawn by Mompesson and marked out with stones and stone troughs without becoming, even after three hundred years, acutely conscious of the history that was enacted here. It is a tale that has been told countless times, and at greater length than is possible here; but it is one that should not be allowed to die.

Just to the south of Eyam, beyond Cucklet Dell, a somewhat larger road runs east-west along Middleton Dale to Tideswell and beyond, and so on to Chapel en le Frith and industrial Cheshire. You will probably not wish to follow it to its end; but in Tideswell, a village of less than two thousand inhabitants, you will find a church so large that once again it seems out of all proportion to the community it serves. Not surprisingly, it has long been known as the 'Cathedral of the Peak', though of course this is something of an exaggeration. Locals will tell you, in illustration of the size of their church, that if you were to run a map-marker along the length of its walls from the south porch right round again to your starting-point it would have registered a distance of no less than 1760 yards. The great church has, however, its own beauty, and to put such a suggestion to the test would somehow be a desecration in itself.

North-westwards of Tideswell, at a point just north-east of the valley hamlet somewhat grandiosely called Peak Forest (though trees here are today few and far between, mere scattered survivors of a medieval forest in which records clearly state that wolves abounded), a magnificent specimen of a 'green road' runs north-eastwards to the far horizon. On the map it is shown as Oxlow Rake, deriving its name from Oxlow Moor, which it tops on its way to Castleton. It zigzags to nearly 1400 feet before dropping down into Hope Valley between Peveril Castle and Peak Cavern. Three or four miles at the most, from start to finish, when measured on the map; but it seems a good deal more than that when you set foot on its thin, sparse grey-green turf, dodging the outcrops of limestone that tend to trip the walker, though the pack-horses for which it was designed, perhaps in the late seventeenth or early eighteenth century, will have passed over them unscathed, whether in clear sunshine, gathering dusk, or the swirling mists that are so frequent in the region. It is impossible to stray unwittingly from this long-beaten track: the limestone walls rise to breast height for almost the whole of the way, fifteen feet or so apart and as solidly constructed as any you have seen among the dales of Yorkshire.

From the A 623, near Peak Forest, there is a southward running minor road that will take you by way of Hargatewall to the junction of two, or even three, of Derbyshire's most attractive dales: Millers Dale, with Tideswell Dale hard by, and Chee Dale. Parallel to this road, and less than a mile to the east, a curious succession of truly miniature dales will be found, each one giving place after a mile or so to the next: Dam Dale, Hay Dale, Peter Dale and Monks Dale; it sounds like some family gathering that might almost have been recorded in 'Mrs. Dale's Diary'. But there is no motorist's road here, only a twisting track.

As already stated, these dales are all unassuming in their proportions, hardly deserving comparison, at least in so far as dimensions are concerned, with the giants far to the north. But they make up for their lack of stature by the ingenuity with which they interlock—or perhaps interweave is a more appropriate word, for there is a flowing rather than an abrupt element in their association. The four dale-lets close to which you have come down from Peak Forest flow one after the other into Millers Dale; westwards of the height named Chee Tor, Millers Dale gives place to Chee Dale; Chee Dale becomes Wye Dale; Wye Dale becomes Ashwood Dale as it comes close to the eastern outskirts of Buxton. It is all a little confusing—but pleasurably so, for all that. And these dales, small as they are, are themselves fed by even smaller dales that flow down into them from the northern slopes: Great Rocks Dale (which, it must be admitted, hardly lives up to the promise of its high-flown name); Woo Dale; and, as though admitting the soft impeachment, finally Cunning Dale itself.

South again from Millers Dale this proliferation continues. You pays your money (but of course entry to each and every one of them is quite free) and you takes your choice. This is all limestone country; none of it is millstone grit. There are great outcrops, miles of drystone walls, quarries and quarry faces—all too many of these, unhappily, the nearer you come to Buxton from east and south, though you will soon be leaving the quarries behind you. There are buildings large and small. There are the sheer side of the dales, some of these so small that you wonder how they ever came to be allocated names at all. Everything hereabouts has the quality of brightness that immediately attracts, the 'shining morning face' that persists throughout the day and retains something faintly incandescent even after the evening light has begun to fail. No two people will exactly agree as to which is the loveliest of these dales, the one that will remain longest in the memory; but many will say that the claims of Lathkill are hard to challenge.

Two major roads cross this part of north Derbyshire: the A 6 from Buxton and points north down to Bakewell, the Matlocks, Derby and points south; and the A 515 Buxton south to Ashbourne, the first section of which is, as its forthrightness suggests, exactly on what was once a Roman road. Of the two roads, the latter is by far the more inviting, though it is true that with the coming of the M 6 motorway traffic has been largely drained off the old A 6 trunk road and you can now travel along it without too much jostling and take in the fine contours that swirl about you, with a glimpse here and there of some hill-fort topping one of the summits. But for all that, it is the A 515 that you should take, southwards from the main Derbyshire dales. It possesses an element of invitation that is not immediately apparent to the eye or indeed explicable in normal terms, to begin with at any rate. In fact, you must turn to the map and study this with some concentration to probe its secret.

You will find that, particularly in its southern section, say from near Hartington to Fenny Bentley and Ashbourne, this road is criss-crossed time and again by a meandering black line. This, of course, represents a single-track railway-line. But the important thing about this interweaving of road and rail is that the railway is now disused; its rails and sleepers and signal wires have been removed, its crossing-gates and few wayside halts dismantled. So now it presents a serpentining track, grass- and weed-grown, lit by clumps of broom, picked out by young sycamores and a wide variety of free-growing shrubs.

Perhaps the most attractive stretch of the whole of this former railway is that which can be picked up at the point where the road and abandoned track both together come closest to the Staffordshire border, at the former station of Alsop-en-le-Dale. This particular length, running southwards, passes in due course through the 'model' village of Tissington, and has in fact been dubbed the 'Tissington Trail'. As a contrast to the headier atmosphere of the Derbyshire Peak and the moorland generally to the north of Millers Dale this less dramatic countryside is quite perfect.

The track will of course take you to Tissington, one of mid-Derbyshire's loveliest and least-spoiled villages. You can approach the village through open parkland by way of a seemingly private road that branches off the A 515 between three and four miles north of Ashbourne. You can also approach it from the B 5056 road that links Rowsley with Ashbourne, though this involves negotiating a water-splash that, in wet weather, can defeat any vehicle other than a milk-float or other high-axled lorry. But whichever mode of approach you adopt, you will surely find that Tissington amply rewards the slight effort made to attain it. It is a village of one wide street, flanked by trees topping the sloping grass verges. The church is almost hidden by trees, and trees embower also the fine building, Tissington Hall, on the opposite side. Grey stone abounds, and there is a suggestion of unity, of integrity, about the whole assembly of small stone cottages that cluster at the foot of the hill, occupied in the main, one would say, by retainers currently working for or pensioned off by the owners of the Hall. Little traffic passes through Tissington; indeed, there is no real road through the village: you come upon it virtually unaware, from whichever direction you approach it.

There is, however, one period in every year, Ascension time, in which traffic does abound here. For it happens that Tissington provides one of the finest examples of the traditional Derbyshire ceremony of 'Well Dressing', and not surprisingly people flock into the quiet village from much farther afield than the county itself to take part in it and see what there is to be seen. If you want to linger in the quietude of Tissington, as it is for fifty-one weeks of every year, then do not go during this one week when it comes into its glory.

The ceremony of Well Dressing takes place in many small towns and villages in the county: Tideswell is one of these; Youlgreave, Barlow and Wirksworth are others, and this handful is only a small proportion of them. Well blessing, of course, dates back far into the pre-Christian era: a mass gesture to ensure the vital supply of water, and closely associated, as so many of these pagan ceremonies were, with the all-important matter of fertility in man, beast and crop. But in Derbyshire, whether or not its origin can be traced back to prehistoric times, for many centuries the ceremony has been a religious one: a form of pious thanksgiving to God for His gift of that most vital commodity, water. It may be that the tradition took root and flourished so consistently here in Derbyshire because this once again is carboniferous limestone country, and where this stone predominates the predictability of a regular water supply reaches its nadir. Water appears—and disappears; it cannot be relied upon—or at least could not until piped water through the mains supply was fully organised so as to reach even the most isolated parts.

One theory is that the tradition of Well Dressing, and of course the closely associated aspect, well blessing, dates from the period of the so-called Black Death which, in the year 1348 (it must not, of course, be confused with the Great Plague of three centuries and more later), decimated the population of the whole country. During the period while the Black Death raged, the wells of Tissington, and some other Derbyshire villages, remained consistently pure and undefiled. People came from considerable distances in all directions to drink from them and carry the rare water back with them to their homes. Astonishingly, in spite of this contact, not one single Black Death casualty was recorded here. So, the ceremony of dressing and blessing the wells came to be instituted.

Another theory is that the origin of Well Dressing dates from the year 1615, when the whole of Derbyshire and neighbouring counties suffered a drought that lasted for almost five months without a break. But Tissington's well, and those of some neighbouring villages, remained full and flowing throughout the whole of that grim period.

Whichever may be the true origin—and in all probability both origins, so to speak, may be accepted without real contradiction, for the basic element of needs fulfilled is common to them both—these wells are 'dressed' for Ascension Day each year. The dressing is most elaborate, and

Well-Dressing in Tissington village

calls for skills peculiar to the villages concerned and practised by old and young alike, for there is hardly anybody, save the too-young or the bed-ridden and infirm, who does not play his or her part in preparing for the occasion, and there is a very strong element of competition, not only between one village and the next, but among those responsible for the dressing of each of the wells in any one village. Tissington has no fewer than five wells, named by tradition Town Well, Hall Well, Yew Tree Well, Hands Well and (somewhat ominously) Coffin Well.

Behind and to either side of each well a large wooden frame, perhaps ten feet high and more, is erected, after being first plastered very smoothly with soft and ultra-plastic clay prepared by means that are a closely-guarded secret. Meanwhile, the children of the village, and often their mothers too, have been collecting a vast quantity of 'natural substances': flower petals, fragments of the local fluorite quartz, berries, fir-cones, pieces of vari-coloured moss, birds' feathers, and so on. These, in their hundreds of thousands, often no larger than a child's finger-nail, are laid and pressed into the surface of the soft clay in such a fashion as to result in a bold yet subtly 'painted' picture. The subject will vary, but of course there is always a strong traditional biblical element to be seen, and the picture, which may take the form of a triptych, is customarily surmounted by a carefully selected and relevant text.

There seems no limit to the ingenuity, the artistry and the craftsman-ship displayed in these well dressings, all of them the work, the loving work, of amateurs drawn from among the villagers themselves. Those responsible for the actual designs may continue their work year after year, having established themselves among their neighbours as possessed of outstanding individual ability. But this is matched by the patience and perseverance with which old and young alike seek out, find, collect and assemble the basic raw materials that go to the making of the finished article. And the competitive spirit that informs all concerned has yet another facet: not only must each well be more beautiful than any of the others; not only must all the village wells be dressed better than those in any other village; but the Well Dressing in any one year must be more beautiful, more ambitious, than it was last year or in any previous year. The standard of creative excellence must not merely be maintained but be improved upon with every passing year.

The climax of the whole festival of Well Dressing is of course reached on Ascension Day itself. At eleven o'clock in the morning a service is held in the village church. After this, there is the procession of parishioners and clergy. It passes from the first well to the second, the second to the third, and so on to the fifth and last; each well is 'blessed'. The blessing takes the form of an expression of thanksgiving for the service they rendered so generously and unstintingly all those years ago, when disaster threatened. Whether this was in 1348 or in 1615, few if any of those present bother to speculate; thanksgiving is all. Today, Tissington, like Tideswell, where the preliminary service is held in the 'Cathedral of the Peak', and Youlgreave and a dozen and more other centres of Well Dressing, has piped water. But the five wells still contain bright, sparkling, cool and eminently drinkable water, and there are many who prefer that water to the water that flows so readily, today, from the taps in every cottage.

Beyond Ashbourne, four miles south of Tissington, the railway-line curves away, south by west, closely following the valley of the Dove— pronounced Doave by older Ashburnians and those who live along its length. The river marks the border between Derbyshire and Staffordshire for most of the way until, at Burton, it flows into the Trent. You may well be tempted to follow this exquisitely beautiful river, especially where it flows through the best part of Dove Dale, between Alstonefield and Thorpe Cloud. But if you once step westwards over the county boundary at this point you will be still more tempted to explore that strange 'vanishing' river, the Manifold, with its caves and gorges, its precipitous cliffs and contorted limestone strata. Could a river with such tortuosities in its channel conceivably be better named than this?

And why 'vanishing'? Because it does, quite literally, vanish from time to time, abandoning its stony bed completely and, presumably, for good and all!

This borderland of Derbyshire and Staffordshire, like Yorkshire farther to the north (and the Mendips, too, far to the south and west), is essentially carboniferous limestone country; and where such stone is predominant, the water is made to perform some very curious acrobatic feats. The feats are to be seen on a giant scale, of course, in similar if more spectacular limestone country such as that of south-west France and the Franco-Spanish border. Famous speleologists like Norbert Casteret have given vivid accounts of the quite extraordinary vagaries of subterranean streams in these limestone masses, and they have been seen at their most dramatic in such world-famous cavern systems as the Puits Berger and the Gouffre Pierre Saint-Martin, where brave lives have been lost in the desperate attempt to solve some of Nature's hydraulic mysteries.

In Yorkshire, of course, there is that strange 'dry' river bed to the north of Malham Cove. Water flows out from a tarn to the south of Malham Tarn House and almost immediately vanishes from sight. The course it originally took is indicated by the stony bed that makes for the great horseshoe curve of Malham Cove, and it may well be that the water still flows along a course roughly beneath it, though this has yet to be established. What has been established, however, is that the trickle of water that flows out beneath the base of the limestone precipice known as Malham Cove, with the magnificent plateau of clints on the top, is the same water as that which leaves Malham Tarn several miles to the north. The insertion of dyes into the water of the tarn proves this conclusively.

But the strange thing about this is that when the tarn water re-appears at the foot of the precipice after its subterranean journey it is several degrees colder than it was when it left the tarn.

The same phenomenon may be noted here, in the Manifold Valley. At a point near Wetton Mill, just above that astonishing cavern so evocatively named Thor's Cave, the Manifold vanishes into a fissure in its bed. Thereafter its bed remains bone dry: a stony wasteland such as you may see during periods of drought in many parts of Spain and other countries that suffer from prolonged dry and hot weather. During periods of excessive rain, water may flow for a short while along this bed, but for the most part the river, now wholly lost to view, follows a subterranean channel that serpentines about in the lower strata of the limestone, not necessarily beneath its original bed, to emerge some four or five miles to the south in the grounds of a National Trust country park near the tiny village of Ilam. It has been calculated that though only four or five miles separate the point where it disappears from the point where it re-appears, in fact the water has travelled underground anything up to twice that distance.

The Manifold Valley is at its narrowest, loveliest and, for the motorist, most accessible, along the three or four miles above Thor's Cave. Meet the river at, say, Hulme End on the B 5054 and from here you can enjoy a little winding lane of a road, sometimes clinging to the left bank, sometimes to the right, and at one spot plunging through a dank and gloomy tunnel. But, whichever bank you find yourself following, you will be close-hemmed within a few yards of the sauntering stream finding its gentle way below darkly wooded slopes which now and then break to reveal exciting cliff faces and high caves. And when you are tired of the valley, when perhaps you begin to sense a need for release, then you can climb out—as indeed you have to do in any case from Thor's Cave to Wetton—and explore the rises and dips of the small upland roads which link the many typical villages and hamlets on either side of the river—Butterton and Grindon, for example, to the west; Wetton, Hopedale and Alstonefield to the east. They run, these roads, for the most part, between drystone walls, and the walls reach out and over the grey-green pastures where small flocks of sheep graze, out of sight of the scattered farms where their owners live. An occasional clump of trees offers a skyline landmark—useful in rough weather. When winter blizzards sweep across these uplands—and not only in winter, either: the writer recalls heavy snow in this region in June many years ago—these walls offer welcome protection to the traveller obliged by business to be away from his own hearth; he must walk, if he is on foot, with head bent, to gain the advantage of this protection, for most of these walls are little more than breast or shoulder high.

It may be that you finish your exploration somewhere near Hopedale or Alstonefield and that the A 515 to the east represents your pressing if unwelcome 'escape' road. Should this be so, then you can plot your way below Sunny Bank to Milldale on the Dove, glimpsing the timeless weir and crossing the river below Shining Tor—a farewell two miles of pretty names and entrancing valleys which will seem like toys beside so much else that you will have seen.

In former times a little railway, used almost exclusively for freight, meandered along the upper reaches of the Manifold Valley, from near Hartington. It twisted westwards by way of Waterhouses and Ipstones, to merge with the more important line to the south of Leek, in Staffordshire. But this little line was closed to all traffic many years before that which linked Buxton with Ashbourne. Of the two, it is the line that includes the Tissington Trail in Derbyshire that you will be wiser to choose. Derbyshire, and Staffordshire too, for that matter, must rank among the smaller of the English counties; but they contain more that is worth the effort of search and discovery than might, from their mere statistics of area, be supposed.

6

East Anglia

Geographers may tell us that East Anglia is composed of the counties of Norfolk, Suffolk and Cambridge, together with a part of Essex; historians that it was a kingdom in its own right, along with Mercia, Wessex and Northumbria, in the early seventh century. For the majority of holiday-makers it consists simply of a hundred-and-fifty-mile coastline of attractive seaside resorts from, say, Felixstowe by way of Southwold and Lowestoft, Great Yarmouth, Cromer and Sheringham, to the Wash, together with the Broads to the north-east of Norwich for those whose pleasure lies in sailing on inland waterways. But these places are no more than the fringes of two only of the four named counties, Suffolk and Norfolk.

There is some justification for thinking of East Anglia in terms of these two counties (whatever Essex and Cambridge folk may say), for the two stand out above those that lie to the south and west of them; they literally *are* East Anglia. But also they are very much more than a mere string of coastline holiday resorts. They are some three thousand or so square miles of open countryside, in which are to be found only two towns of more than a hundred thousand inhabitants and only two others that reach even half that figure. Topographically, the counties comprise a countryside that only once tops the four-hundred-foot mark; a countryside that, perhaps more than any other in Britain, gently persuades you to accept the even tenor of its way, to relax, to take the foot off the accelerator, to tune-in to its unhurried wavelength. Perhaps the catch-phrase 'Silly Suffolk' echoes somewhere in the depths of memory? May be so; but the origin of the word dates back to the Anglo-Saxon *selig*, and that word means simple, innocent, blessed. It has, it is true, been used also of Sussex; but it is pre-eminently of Suffolk that the epithet seems so just.

Saints and pious men who dedicated their lives to prayer and good works and may well have merited canonisation after death are well represented on the map of East Anglia. What is more, they are frequently commemorated in pairs, in trios, even in quartets. Weasenham St Peter, in the north of Norfolk, is neighbour to Weasenham All Saints; Pulham St Mary Magdalene in Suffolk has for neighbour Pulham St Mary the Virgin,

The Royal Society for the Protection of Birds reserve at Minsmere, Suffolk

Roman remains at Wroxeter (Viroconium) in Shropshire

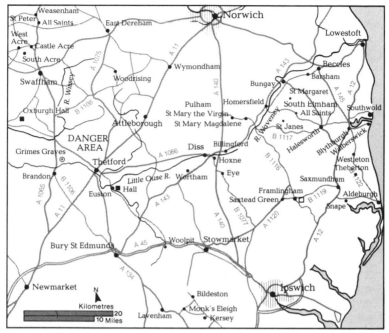

East Anglia

just north of the River Waveney that forms the border between Norfolk and Suffolk; just to the south of the river the hamlets of Ilketshall St John and Ilketshall St Lawrence have Ilketshall St Margaret for near neighbour; and a brief way to the west lies a cluster of hamlets all named South Elmham, but distinguished among themselves by the patronage respectively of Saints Margaret and Michael and Cross, Nicholas, James and Peter, and, for good measure, as elsewhere, All Saints. There are also the good men of the monasteries, of course: Monks Eleigh, for example. It is small wonder, surely, that the term *selig* should have become attached in particular to Suffolk.

You could do worse than make these saintly villages and hamlets the pin-points among which your roving itinerary led you. The choice would be wider, more rewarding, than you might expect; certainly if you had hitherto supposed that all that Norfolk and Suffolk had to offer was a smooth, if sadly crumbling, coastline with its string of popular seaside resorts. Unhappily, however, you will not, even in so rural a district, find yourself completely free to pick your itinerary as you will. What the army has done on the southern slopes of the Cheviots it has also done here. You may draw on your map of East Anglia a heart-shaped outline that has

Castle Acre for its northern limit, Bury St Edmunds for its southern limit, and stretches from Lakeneheath and Mildenhall in the west across to Attleborough in the east. This outline will contain Thetford, and Thetford Heath; it is named Breckland. Breckland is the strangest and certainly the most anciently-occupied portion of all East Anglia.

But, in the very heart of Breckland is a huge expanse uncompromisingly marked DANGER AREA. It was thus designated many years ago, by the then War Department. Promises have been given that the villages that for the purposes of battle training had to be depopulated, the vast forest areas that had to be cleared to accommodate the straggling camps, the hideous hutments of concrete slab and corrugated-iron, all the harsh and ugly signs of war-time occupation, in fact, would be duly cleared away, once the war was over and the land could be returned to peaceful occupations. But today you will still find quite unexpectedly that your road, a minor road that seemed so innocently promising when you set out along it, is suddenly blocked by painted poles, by a manned or padlocked gate, by formidable rolls of rusted barbed-wire, by an uncompromising order to turn about, because you are now on 'holy' ground, though not in the *selig* sense.

To be fair, though, the percentage of acreage, of square-mileage, of the two counties that is sacrosanct to the army is small indeed in comparison with what is still abundantly free. And in a way it is perhaps as well that if any one area had to be thus denied to us it should be this forested part of Breckland; for what the eye does not see does not grieve the heart; it is in fact possible to come quite close to this Danger Area, and from any direction, without becoming unduly aware of it. Anyway, there remain so many blissful square miles through which to wander: miles of open countryside characterised by noble flint-built churches, by thatched and half-timbered houses and cottages, farmsteads and barns, by winding lanes bounded not by drystone walling but by flowergrown hedgerows. There are idly-flowing streams, often so shallow that no one has ever felt the need to build a bridge over them, so that you still make close contact with them as you splash cautiously through a ford that elsewhere, surely, would have long since been replaced by a bridge, however modest in size.

And of course, though in a different, more imposing vein, there are castles such as those of Framlingham and Orford; churches exhibiting that unique East Anglian feature, the flint 'round tower', such as may be seen at Theberton and Little Snoring and, above all, at Wortham, right on the border of Suffolk with Norfolk; fortified manor houses such as that of Little Wenham, said by experts to be the best preserved of all thirteenth-century non-ecclesiastical buildings, and the earliest to have been built in brick. Nor should one omit to mention in this catalogue the living symbol of the true tempo of this open and lovely countryside, the windmills, of which the tower mill at Billingford and the post mill at Saxtead Green are perhaps the most outstanding and memorable examples.

North of Breckland and its enclosed Danger Area is Castle Acre. It is famous, of course, for the noble outer bailey of locally quarried flint, whose massive pointed archway leads you straight into Bailey Street. Look closely, and you can still see the grooves cut in the stonework to accommodate the portcullis. Virtually nothing remains of this gateway above a height of about twenty feet. If you examine the cottages that line the sloping street immediately behind it you will realise why this should be so. Cannibalisation is a word that does not apply solely to the consumption of human flesh. The builders of these old cottages did not have to go to the trouble, labour and expense of opening quarries in the environs of Castle Acre: there was quarried stone for the taking, literally on their doorstep, stone quarried centuries earlier and cut to shape to form this bailey. The builders of the cottages and larger houses in Castle Acre did to the castle on its doorstep very much what the builders of Peveril Castle in Derbyshire did to the Roman fortress of Anavio, which we know today as Brough. It was handier, more economical in time and effort, to filch stone thus than to go out in search of it.

A notice by the gateway informs you that it was built in the thirteenth century 'to defend the northern entrance to a large outer enclosure, fortified by earthworks, that adjoined the west side of the Castle of the Warennes'. The castle is still there, though of course as ruins, while in the other direction you will find the glorious Cluniac Priory that dominates the southward slope to the west of the village, without question the finest survivor of its kind in all East Anglia. Like the castle, it is, unhappily, largely in ruins today. And once more—quite apart from what must be termed natural causes—the reason lies partly in this element of cannibalisation. Take a second look at some of the small domestic buildings in Bailey Street and elsewhere, and you will spot without much difficulty massive stones of such unusual shape and size that they must have come from the more ornate masonry of the priory rather than from the purely functional stonework of the de Warennes' bailey.

For all its charm, there is a curious 'blind', or 'dying' feel in the heart of Castle Acre. From the bailey westwards, an unusually broad and empty, lime-tree-shaded open place, neither quite street nor park, contains a shop or two, two inns, oddly named Albert Victor and Ostrich, and a diminutive post office. At the far end of it is the church, beyond which a lane drops to the remains of the medieval priory.

It is not easy to explain, even to assess, this curious negative feeling with which the whole place is imbued, but it does make itself noticeable. Strangely enough, there is a more pronounced feeling of life and the living amid the majesty of the columnar walls and eyeless windows of the priory than there is in the brief length of Bailey Street. Perhaps this is in part explained by the number of windows in its cottages that were bricked in and sealed at the time of the notorious Window Act and, for some reason, presumably expense, have never since been thrown open to the air and light. These blanked-off windows, black-painted and sometimes lined in white rectangles to simulate woodwork, are somehow more sightless and therefore depressing than the great empty sockets of the priory high in its medieval walls.

One small but memorable feature of Castle Acre, however, is its carved and painted sign. If you are approaching from the north, it confronts you as you turn into the place, with the bailey on your left and the street dipping downwards from the massive stonework of the arch that frames it. Norfolk and Suffolk alike, though not unique in the country, are notable for this feature. There is a fine carved and painted ornamental town sign on the boundary of, for instance, Beccles and Bungay; such signs may be found also on the outskirts of villages so small that you would hardly expect to find them there. An obvious example is the one at charmingly named Woodrising, south of Swaffham.

Castle Acre is one of a trio of hamlets, the others being West Acre and South Acre. You can try to approach the latter by a lane that descends beside Castle Acre's church. But this soon reaches a sign reading Unsuitable for Motors, a few yards short of a ford across the little River Nar, so if you have a car you would do better to choose other roads around the east and south.

West Acre, smaller by a good deal even than Castle Acre, consists of a sloping triangular village green on the upper side of which stands the fourteenth-century church of All Saints, hard by the ruined entrance to a foundation of Augustinian Canons established here in the twelfth century. The church's fine clock face carries, in place of the customary twelve numerals, the twelve letters forming the sober admonishment, WATCH AND PRAY. If you care to look closely enough, you will find inset in a niche in the wall of the massive porch a diminutive stone figurine, doll size, no more; carved in the thirteenth century it represents a seated Madonna and is almost certainly a relic from the religious house alongside, piously removed when it fell into decay and placed in the church porch for safe keeping.

Southwards from the trio of Acres, just outside the village of Oxborough, on the south side of the A 1122, but on a road that has as yet no official designation, is the fifteenth-century masterpiece in mellow brickwork, moated Oxburgh Hall. Though it is moated, as Bodiam Castle in Sussex is moated, it is not, and never was, a castle; it is a medieval hall, the home of a family that can trace its ancestry back to the year of the Norman Conquest. Its proudest feature, one of many, is its gate tower. This rises to seven storeys from the bridge over the moat at its feet that now replaces the original drawbridge that enabled the occupants to seal themselves off at need from potential assault. East Anglia is not essentially a region in which brickwork predominates; flint and oak constitute its basic raw material for building. But here brickwork is to be seen triumphant; the only brick-built towers that can really be compared with that of Oxburgh Hall are those at Kirtling, a few miles to the south of Newmarket and at Layer Marney, Essex.

You must here keep to the west side of the area of heath and conifers—those extraordinary, ancient-looking gnarled and contorted pines that are so prevalent in the area known as Breckland, comparable in their tortuosities with the ancient olive trees of the north Majorcan hills, or the tree-fantasies of the late Arthur Rackham. Otherwise you will be repeatedly and frustratingly checked in your movements by reminders of the proximity of the Danger Area. But you can approach without let or hindrance that unique feature of the Norfolk-Suffolk border, where the Little Ouse separates the two counties a few miles short of Cambridgeshire, the prehistoric flint-workings known as Grimes Graves, just to the north-east of Brandon.

Breckland not only looks old—as though it is a survival, somehow, of a prehistoric landscape—it *is* old; indeed, ancient. Archaeologists, ecologists and anthropologists assert positively that it ranks as inhabited territory among the oldest in Britain, where we tend to think of the Berkshire Downs and parts of Wiltshire and Dorset as the home of the earliest inhabitants of these islands. Certainly prehistoric man was settled here in pre-neolithic if not actually in palaeolithic times. Here he found, as rarely elsewhere in Britain apart from the chalk downland of West Sussex, an abundance of flint so suitable for his purposes, whether domestic or warlike.

Here and there in this region, near Brandon and Weeting for example, you will come upon saucer-like depressions in the ground. A few of these have been excavated. Careful examination revealed that beneath the infilling of earth and turf there were well-like shafts in the chalk from which, over not merely hundreds but literally thousands of years, the prized 'black flint' has been extracted for processing by the method long known as 'knapping'—the highly skilled and specialised art of reducing shapeless lumps of flint to slivers suitable for fitting into the mechanism of flintlock guns. One of these shafts is in a zone now under the care of the Historic Buildings and Monuments Commission and it is possible to descend by ladder and see for yourself the cramped galleries in which neolithic men—admittedly smaller people than we are—worked four thousand or more years ago. Sadly, for safety reasons, it is no longer possible to crawl through the galleries and you must be content with what you can see from the foot of the pit—reminding yourself that the neolithic miners did not enjoy the good lighting provided today but had to make do with primitive lamps.

Though Breckland has chalk on its periphery, notably in the region of Grimes Graves, it consists largely of a sandy soil, ideal for the growing of

Aerial view of the fifteenth-century Oxburgh Hall

the Forestry Commission's conifers, here found in their millions, in various stages of development. It is ideal, too, for heather, furze and bracken, and for plants which the dedicated botanist recognises as being rare in other parts of the country, if indeed they are to be found anywhere else at all. Though Breckland is not officially designated a National Park, it certainly deserves to be, if only for the outstanding nature of its flora and fauna. Perhaps when the Ministry of Defence can at last be persuaded to release its iron grip on the heart of this fine area it will come into its own.

East Anglia is comparatively rich in designated National Park areas. In addition to the coastal nature reserves and bird sanctuaries such as those at or near Wells and Blakeney Point, Cley Marshes, the Broads, Blyth Estuary, Minsmere and Orfordness—to name only a few of them—there are Thetford Heath, Westleton Heath and Cavenham Heath, and many more. They are mentioned here, without amplification, to emphasise the variety of natural amenity that East Anglia has to offer. The enthusiast will equip himself with some of the many expertly compiled guides to the individual areas that are available to him, and make for the object of his choice without lingering unduly on his way.

Even on the fringe of this lonely and secretive region known as

Breckland there are villages and hamlets that amply repay looking for. Euston, for instance, on the A 1088 just south of Thetford and still just inside the periphery, is a dreamlike village. Perhaps village is too grandiose a term, for the impression gained as you enter it is that it consists of little more than a row of beautifully maintained thatched cottages, each with its own shelving slope of turf. The immense cedars come perhaps unexpectedly on the eye: certainly they lend distinction to an essentially rural scene.

These cottages, of mingled flint and mellow brick and whitewashed cob beneath their spreading thatch, are most of them almshouses, built in the first instance no doubt for the retainers of the early Dukes of Grafton. The Great House, with its fine gardens, is near to but not quite visible from the village itself, being enclosed by a long flint-and-brick wall shaded by well-spaced and full-grown lime trees. A curious feature of this wall, which separates house and gardens from a field and ends at the church, once the private chapel of the Great House, is a series of stone plaques marking the graves of fox-hounds that died nearly two hundred years ago, and one that died as comparatively recently as the year 1813. One of these, beneath which Trouncer was buried, reads: 'Foxes Rejoice! Here Buried Lies Your Foe'. Its fellow hound, one Garland, who died eleven years later, is referred to as 'This Spotless Rival of her Grandsire's Fame'. Her grandpa (presumably Trouncer) would doubtless have been proud of the tribute.

A few miles farther down the same road you will come to the little village of Woolpit. In a county once famed for its wool, as is constantly emphasised by the magnificent 'wool' churches in such places as Lavenham and Kersey—the latter of which has given us the word for a particular type of coarse, long-ribbed and narrow cloth—you would feel justified in supposing that the village took its name from wool. But you would in fact be wrong. The name comes from the word wolf. Having seen something of Breckland and Thetford Chase, it is not difficult to accept the established fact that wolves once roamed at large in this part of East Anglia. The last of the wolves were trapped in a pit dug for the purpose in this very district, surprisingly, only a matter of six hundred years ago.

It is a peaceful village. Its triangular green, in sight of the church with its splendid spire, is overlooked by houses of brick, of freestone, of half-timbering and of weather-boarding, some of them dating from the sixteenth century. But Woolpit's fame—if that is not too extravagant a word for a place so unpretentious—lies in the story of the 'Green Children', a strange, indeed unique story that smacks of magic and myth.

Eight hundred years ago (it is said), two small children, a boy and a girl, emerged one sunny day from a furrow in a ploughed field in which the corn was just beginning to spring. Hand in hand they stood there in silence, green as the shoots of corn at their feet. They were taken in by a goodwife in the village and to begin with fed exclusively on greenstuffs. After a while this diet was gradually changed to one of milk and eggs and cheese, and eventually to meat. The children, though still silent, throve on the diet; and as their diet changed, so, basically, did their colour, until eventually they came to resemble in this regard at any rate the other children of the village.

But they remained incapable of speaking any language other than their own, which consisted of nothing more than a few quite incomprehensible sounds exchanged between brother and sister. They grew to adulthood. Or at least, the girl did. The other died as he reached his teens. But the girl, to the astonishment of the good folk of Woolpit, was wooed and won by 'a man from King's Lynn', and taken away by him for a new life in a new setting. Eight centuries ago, King's Lynn, not fifty miles from Woolpit, might as well have been a town in some other planet altogether; it is not known, in Woolpit at any rate, what became of the 'Green Child' after her marriage to the stranger from those distant parts.

If you had journeyed south from Castle Acre on the other flank of Breckland you might have found your way to a diminutive hamlet named Woodrising. No numbered road leads to it; it simply stands in the heart of the triangle formed by the A 1075, B 1108 and B 1135 roads and accessible from any one of these by a twisting lane so unassuming that you might well suppose that it goes nowhere at all but simply ends at a field gate. Follow this, however, and it will lead you past the charming sign that announces with modest pride the name of the hamlet and, in due course, a matter of yards, no more, to a glimpse of its sequestered church, the collapsed fourteenth-century tower standing sadly at its west end.

Well to the south of Woodrising you will come to the borders of Norfolk and Suffolk. A few miles to the west of Diss, the River Waveney, which has marked the border between the two counties all the way inland from the point where it flows into the River Yare, close to Yarmouth, cedes its responsibility to the newly-born Little Ouse; this river here flows westward and then northwards to King's Lynn and its channelled outflow into the Wash.

You are now approaching what many would tell you (and this is no place to deny it) is the most delectable region of all *selig* Suffolk. Here are names such as Wortham and Hoxne (to be pronounced 'Hoxen' if you are not to evoke the hint of a smile from a Suffolk man), Saxtead· Green and Framlingham, Saxmundham and Blythburgh, Kersey, Bildeston and Lavenham, Little Wenham and Snape and—but the tally must be brought to an end some-when!

At Wortham, on the A 143 just below Diss, you will come upon what is by far the finest of Suffolk's famous church round towers built of flint. There are, as will be seen, many others, in Norfolk as well as in Suffolk; some are more ornate, some taller, some perhaps better proportionate to the churches to whose western ends they are attached or which they actually form. But not one of them, in either county, is as impressive as that which dominates Wortham's Church of St Mary the Virgin.

It is no less than a hundred feet in girth and still, after some ten centuries, more than sixty feet in height. It looms among the trees. Its cylindrical wall is three feet thick in its lower courses. It does not actually taper, but, like a gas-holder, is 'built telescopic', which is to say that each successive upward stage is slightly less in diameter than the one immediately below it. This, of course, is one of its unique features.

These towers were built cylindrically rather than square for a perfectly simple—if not immediately obvious—reason. Whereas flint in much of East Anglia is abundant, good building-stone is not; thus stone suitable for quoins was relatively hard to come by, and reserved for the major churches, the 'wool' churches, which all date from long after the period of the churches built with round towers. But flint can be used as building material without recourse to the use of quoins to reinforce, indeed to make, the corners of a structure. Flint could be utilised in the round; it could provide a uniform, cylindrical wall, equally strong at every 'point'; and a cylindrical tower was likely to be as enduring as any.

These round towers were built in part as a main feature of the fabric of the church and in part as look-out stations. Navigable rivers like the Yare and the Waveney offered easy access from the North Sea to the interior of East Anglia, and those who manned the Viking ships were quick to realise this. Where a church stood close to such a river, as does Wortham's Church of St Mary the Virgin, such a tower would be constantly in use, so that the earliest possible warning could be given when the first signs of Viking rovers were descried, and steps could be taken to prevent the ravaging on which they were so consistently bent.

This aspect of history accounts, in part at least, for the proliferation and frequent distinction of these virtually unique church towers. The nearest parallel to them, and it is not an exact one, for the towers are rarely if ever set close to a church, are the Round Towers in the Republic of Ireland, such as the famous one at Ardmore, in Co. Waterford or the beauty known as the Rattoo Round Tower in Co. Kerry, which surely ranks equal with the best-known of them all, at Glendalough. Known in Eire as *clochteachs*, they were usually associated with isolated monasteries and served as places of refuge and hiding-places for such valuables, and saints' relics, as the monks might possess and wish to preserve from the ravages—again of the ubiquitous Vikings of the tenth century and after. Their entrances (unlike those in East Anglia) were ordinarily set ten feet or so above ground. They could be easily barricaded and offered a very real obstacle to the marauding Norseman.

If you care to go in search of them, there are no fewer than forty round towers in East Anglia, each with some individual quality to distinguish it from its nearest neighbour. Basically, for the reason given, they are all flint built; as opposed to the *clochteachs* of Southern Ireland, for which good building-stone was available. Many of them are still in excellent condition; indeed, in very much better condition than the huge one at Wortham. And this is all the more remarkable for the fact that so many of them date from the twelfth, and even from the eleventh century. Flint is an almost indestructible stone, and the cylindrical form of building is an excellent one—until a breach is made in it; after which there is a tendency for such a structure to disintegrate simply because it has no really strong and individual buttress to support it.

At Haddiscoe, for instance, on the A 143 a few miles north of Beccles, there is the church of St Mary, standing high above a shallow valley and dominating the whole landscape to the east. Its sixty-foot round tower was built primarily as a look-out post. The North Sea is not five miles away to the east, and the Yare and Waveney rivers offer easy access from the north, the latter to within no more than a few hundred yards of the place, where it describes a bold curve right round the low hill on which it stands. The wall of this round tower is so thick that when, five centuries after it was built, it was decided to install a peal of bells in the top of the tower, a spiral staircase could be carved out of it and there was still sufficient 'shell' to support the weight of the upper part of the tower, swinging bells included. Several centuries after the round tower itself was built, too, a circular crenellated top 'storey' was added. For this, knapped flint alternated with freestone, and the effect is extraordinarily satisfying to the beholder, so beautifully proportioned is the whole conception.

Much farther to the north and west, off the A 148 Cromer road, you will find the church of St Andrew, at improbably-named Little Snoring. Here the round tower is most unusual, unique, in that it is wholly detached from the church. Like the very much larger tower at Wortham, that of Little Snoring is 'stepped' inwards, part way up. Unlike Wortham, however, and indeed most of the others, it has a few courses of freestone, at about head height; this suggests that it may have been built somewhat later than the majority of the others. Nevertheless, the fact that its first rector was inducted in the year 1292 makes it clear that the church and its tower cannot be less than seven hundred years old, and the tower at least could be older by a good deal than that. It is capped by a neat cone-shaped roof—in which it closely resembles the Irish *clochteachs*, most of which were so capped, whereas it is not known how the original East Anglian round towers were topped. This neat cone-shaped roof has four miniature dormer windows in it, each accurately orientated to one of the four major compass points.

Back again to the south, and you will come to St Peter's church at Theberton, on the B 1122 a few miles to the north of Aldeburgh and very nearly right on the coast. This is an altogether larger church than either Wortham or Little Snoring. It has an immensely long nave, thatched for

Church of St Andrew, Little Snoring

the whole of its length. The particularly interesting feature of its round tower is that from a point level with the ridge of the thatch a fine crenellated top section was added, as at Haddiscoe. But this top section, unlike the one at Haddiscoe, is octagonal, instead of continuing the upward lines of the original flint tower. A certain proportion of this section consists of freestone, notably in the framing of the fine Gothic louvred windows; the whole effect is one of dignity coupled with beauty and originality.

Parts of this church are Norman in origin, but there is one thing of interest here which is of much more recent date. In the south porch you will find a macabre relic, a fragment of a zeppelin shot down in flames near here during the 1914–18 war; it recalls the burial here of the zeppelin's crew, though their bodies were subsequently exhumed and buried elsewhere.

Another of these thatched churches is to be found at Barsham, some three miles west of Beccles on the A 1116. Or rather, it lies just off that road. You must look out for it, on your right-hand side if you are travelling westwards, for it is to be found on the far side of a large stretch of pastureland by way of a drive that in fact leads to the adjoining rectory with its fine and unexpected columned portico. The church of the Most

Holy Trinity, Barsham, is an altogether smaller one than that at Theberton. Flint and freestone, roofed with thatch, the upper section of which has been particularly attractively fashioned in scallops and sharp points.

The west end of the church consists of a round tower of slender proportions, rising some sixty feet. Considering that the main fabric of the tower, at least for its lower half, dates from the Saxon era, the whole is in a remarkable state of preservation. The upper portion, with its large windows pointing north, south, east and west, is Norman. The lych-gate, incidentally, is one of the most attractive features of this small church, matching it well in its rustic simplicity. Like the church, it is roofed with thatch. The timber framing above the lintel has been in-filled with plasterwork, and the centre post carries a charming effigy in carved oak of some saint unnamed who frowns downwards on those who pass beneath his feet—and at the Friesians that graze imperturbably in the field immediately outside the gate.

But the true glory of East Anglian churches is of course to be found, not in these tiny rural examples but in the great 'wool' churches such as those already mentioned, at Lavenham and Kersey and Blythburgh and elsewhere. They were, as the saying goes, 'built on wool'. Built, that is to say, at the expense of, and at the instigation of, pious merchants whose fortunes had been founded on the wool and clothing trade that here reached its peak during the second half of the fourteenth century and lasted for a hundred and fifty years and more. These men, then, gave due thanks to their Maker in this most practical fashion; and we have become their debtors. For to visit them, and examine them in detail is to be imbued with a deep sense of wonder, and awe.

Lavenham's enormous flint-built tower, for instance, rises to over a hundred and forty feet; the church itself stands on a slight rise to the west of the lovely village of incomparable half-timbered houses, dominating not only the village but the countryside for miles around. It is not, of course, a flint round tower but a square-built tower, like those of all the churches that succeeded the early ones. It is quite extraordinarily gracious and even graceful, considering its massiveness and the fact that it is shouldered by monumental tapering buttresses of freestone and flint. In this church, and in some others, notably the glorious one at Blythburgh, you will be less conscious of the flintwork than of the fine use made of the freestone, which here constitutes not merely the quoins but so much of the main fabric itself.

This is not, however, the case at Kersey, a few miles to the south and east of Lavenham. The village is a much smaller one, and infinitely less self-conscious than its famous neighbour across the low hills to the north and west. It must also be admitted that it is very much less beautiful than Lavenham, its half-timbered buildings fewer and less impressive. On the other hand its single street has a beauty of its own, and drops to the famous water-splash at its foot, tree-shadowed, beyond which the road takes a sudden and unexpected leap upwards—one of the few steepish hills in the county. And it is at the top of this hill that the church most splendidly stands, even more impressively sited, perhaps, than that at Lavenham.

Here, the flintwork is incomparable. Here you will see, at its noble best, the so-called 'flush-work' for which the best of the East Anglian churches (and others, too, in regions where good flint is abundant, such as parts of Hampshire and Wiltshire) are famous. Only at Blythburgh, perhaps, will you find flush-work as fine as that at Kersey.

It is to be seen here at its best in the fabric of the South Porch. (As it happens, it is Blythburgh's South Porch that contains the best examples of the craft to be seen in that church.) The term 'flush-work' becomes self-explanatory as you examine the flat-faced black flint, square-knapped and inset panel-wise in framings of freestone. The contrast of black and off-white, the balance and ratio of 'picture' and 'frame', strike the eye at once. There is a living quality about it. The face of the stonework, its very texture, seems to vary according to the angle at which the light strikes upon it, and the quality of that light, whether of high noon or early morning or early evening.

There are, however, homelier aspects of East Anglia than its fine churches; aspects homelier even than the tiny ancient churches with their round towers to remind us of the remote days when these eastern counties lived in fear of the invaders' long-ships sweeping up the estuaries that so deeply indent the coastline. The windmills, for example.

Few of them are in operation today, more's the pity. We no longer enjoy bread made from stone-ground flour such as came from the countless windmills of Essex and Suffolk, Norfolk and the county of Lincoln beyond the Wash.

A very few tower windmills, and rather more post and smock windmills, however, have survived, and are a notable feature of this most agreeable landscape. In some cases this is because their well-being and maintenance has been taken over by archaeological and other public-spirited societies; in others because they have become the property, by purchase, of right-minded citizens.

There is a magnificent example of a tower mill, one of the very few and possibly the finest to be found in any windmill-owning county in England, at Billingford, on the A 143 a few miles to the east of Diss and on the very border between Norfolk and Suffolk. It stands like a lighthouse in the heart of open, level, gently undulating country and when its sails turn shadows curve lovingly about its rounded side, as though seeking to enfold them in some dark, close-clinging material. Far to the north, in Lincolnshire, on the outskirts of the village of Heckington, a few miles to the east of Sleaford on the B 1394, there is a tower windmill that is in fact

Post mill, Saxtead Green

unique. Less beautifully proportioned by far than that at Billingford, and far less notably sited, for it rises from a coal-merchant's yard, it possesses one feature that singles it out from every other windmill in the country: it is equipped with no fewer than eight sails. Four is the norm, though there do exist in Lincolnshire and elsewhere a few windmills equipped with the odd number of five.

Back again in Suffolk you will find a wide choice. Among the most memorable of these is the post mill at Saxtead Green, on the A1120 a few miles to the north-west of Framlingham. Connoisseurs of windmills rate this one, with the famous Union Mill at Cranbrook, in Kent (another county in which, once, windmills abounded), and the mill at Outwood, in Surrey, as among the half-dozen finest survivors in the country. It is not surprising that it has been taken under the wing of the Historic Buildings and Monuments Commission, so that its survival is now ensured.

Nowhere in Britain, either, is better thatch to be found than the reed or straw thatching of East Anglia—and this is not to ignore the claims of the West Country, whose partisans will naturally challenge such a statement. Reed thatching is enormously expensive; but it is infinitely more durable than thatching done in straw, however good its quality. It is a melancholy fact that the craft of reed-thatching now rests in the hands of an ever-dwindling number of men. Just occasionally, however, one learns of some young man who plans to follow in his father's and grandfather's footsteps; this craft, like that of the Pennine dry-wallers and the Brandon flint-knappers, tends to run in families.

Much of the thatch that you will see in East Anglia (as elsewhere in the country, of course) is already old. That on the nave of Theberton's parish church, for example, looks as though it has been there almost as long as the church itself. This of course is not the case, for the life span of thatch, even of the best-laid and cared-for reed thatch, must be measured in decades at best, whereas these flint-and-stone churches date back six, seven, eight hundred years and more.

Now and then you will come upon thatch that is obviously new—only a few years old at most, that is. There is an outstanding example of this modern thatching on a range of almshouses in the hamlet of Homersfield, overlooking the Waveney, on the B1062. Here, as is happily so often the case, the thatcher has exercised artistry as well as craftsmanship, notably in the way he has worked his thatch round the chimneys and down the eaves. An additional pleasing touch is the thatched roof to the well-house in the garden that fills the concavity of this horseshoe-shaped row of low-pitched almshouses: it perfectly matches the greater expanse of roofscape that constitutes its back-cloth. It is not surprising that this little unit has won much-coveted prizes for the trimness and perfection of its appearance.

The area of East Anglia on which emphasis has been laid was an arbitrary choice; it could have been matched by others no less rich in rewarding material. For example, much space could have been devoted to that quiet corner along the Waveney between Bungay and Homersfield (mentioned just above for its thatched almshouses) where the admirable Otter Trust seeks not only to conserve these appealing creatures but also to release them back into the wild. Waterfowl, herons and deer also enjoy these pleasant surroundings. Nor has anything been said of the less familiar aspects of the coastline, those sections that have not been wholly taken over by the tourist and catering industries. There is the 'lost city' of Dunwich, for example: a former township of some size, alleged to have contained no fewer than nine splendid and well-filled churches, which fell victim to the merciless erosion of this coastline that is so distressing a feature today, but was already at work seven hundred years ago. Nothing has been said of neighbouring Aldeburgh, another example of a former township, a seaport of some note five hundred years ago, which also has fallen victim to the capricious movements of the tides up and down this tortured coast; today it is known almost solely for its Music Festival.

Just inland from this coastline, however, in the estuary of the River Blyth behind Walberswick, the naturalist will find a breeding-ground and refuge for waders and waterfowl generally; and a little to the south of this, near the charming and so-far unexploited and unspoiled hamlet of Westleton, on Westleton Heath in fact, there has long been a National Nature Reserve that matches in its potential that of Orfordness yet farther to the south. Indeed, to do anything like justice even to so relatively constricted a region of Britain as East Anglia really demands writing at full-volume length. And this, of course, is just what has been done, primarily by men, and women too, who are natives of the region and so write with intimate and exhaustive knowledge of what others know, as it were, only from the touch-line.

7

Shropshire

From Whitchurch, on its northern border with Cheshire, to Ludlow, on its southern border with Hereford and Worcester, Shropshire is fifty miles in length. North of the Severn, which cuts across it, it is so flat that it seems just a continuation of the flat Cheshire plain. Once clear of Shrewsbury, however, the terrain seems to shrug its ancient shoulders and reach for the skies.

The main road to the south, the A 49 from Whitchurch to Ludlow and on to Ross-on-Wye, which ordinarily you would choose only if you were intent on getting clear of the county with the least possible delay, does in fact enable you to see, with hardly more than a sideways glance to left and right, just what the southern half of the county is about. The roads runs straight, like the spine of a book whose opened pages are tilted and curved upwards on either side as it rests in the hand. And what pages they are! Pages scattered with place-names so many of which echo with words that arc half remembered, words perhaps even set to half-remembered music.

That long, narrow ridge slanting north-eastwards from Craven Arms, for instance: Wenlock Edge. What is that faint but moving echo of words possessing a mellowness of both sound and colour?

> Wenlock Edge was umbered,
> And bright was Abdon Burf . . .

So sang the poet. Why? Abdon is just on the other side of Corve Dale from Wenlock Edge, and would capture the slanting rays of the sun while the ridge itself had become shadowed.

And Hughley, on the north side of Wenlock Edge:

> The vane on Hughley steeple
> Veers bright, a far-known sign . . .

He sang of the lads who came 'home from labour at Abdon-under-Clee': that village is tucked into the lower slopes of Brown Clee Hill, on the opposite side of the valley from the Edge. Beyond, farther up the valley, is Wenlock Town, near which, he tells us, 'the golden broom should blow'.

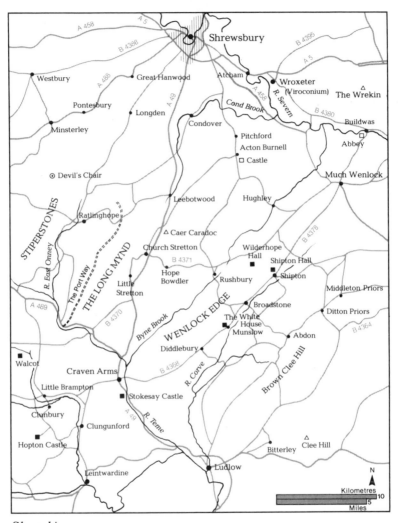

Shropshire

He looks farther north, to where 'His forest fleece the Wrekin heaves'. And he looks south and west, where:

> Clunton and Clunbury,
> Clungunford and Clun,
> Are the quietest places
> Under the sun.

Housman country, of course: the country of A. E. Housman's *The Shropshire Lad* and *Last Poems*.

The phrase was used of this southern part of Shropshire 'shrugging its ancient shoulders'. All terrain, of course, is ancient, in that the origin of our planet goes back to so astronomically remote a time. Current expert opinion dates it as 4500 million years old—give or take a handful of expendable millions. In any case, some regions are more ancient than others. You might, for instance, suppose that the Alps are ancient. By certain standards they are, for petrologists and geologists consider that they were 'born'—to use a hardly applicable term—some thirty-eight million years ago. But the limestones of the Cotswolds date back five times as far in geological time, to some 200 million years ago. The figure is breath-taking. But it is nothing compared with the age of the terrain that characterises much of Shropshire, to which the date 435 million is authoritatively given—more than twice as far back in geological time as the Cotswolds, and more than ten times as remote as the Alps!

If one's notion of geological antiquity is of jagged peaks and summits far exceeding the 1800-foot mark, at which figure a hill officially becomes a mountain, then it may be difficult to think of this region of southern Shropshire as truly ancient. For here, the Wrekin apart, there are virtually no summits, as such. In fact, of course, generally speaking the more rugged a landscape, the more jagged its summits, the 'younger' (again the term is relative) it is. The peaks of the Alps that challenge every mountaineer worth his salt are infinitely less ancient than the smoothly-rounded whale-back ridge of the Malverns, which offers a leisurely walk for the family, including its older members. For the most part, the uplands of Shropshire date from roughly the same geological period; call it, to be precise, the Silurian period. But figures running into millions, let alone hundreds of millions, virtually cease to have meaning for those of us who are not astronomers or actuaries.

Geologists have established that the heights which now survive for the most part as elongated Edges, such as that named Wenlock, and as rolling and lonely moorland such as the Long Mynd, are only the shadow, barely even the skeleton, of their original, Silurian, selves. There is in fact, no summit in Shropshire that quite reaches 1800 feet, at which it would be entitled to call itself mountain. Brown Clee Hill, at 1790 feet, comes closest to that figure; far away to the west, on the Welsh border, the highest point on the Stiperstones Ridge, known of course as the Devil's Chair because for once such a summit has a clear and even menacing outline where almost all else is smoothed and rounded, comes not far short of it at 1731 feet.

The Wrekin, south of the A 5, appears at first sight to top them all. But this is only because it is an isolated hill that leaps skyward out of the Severn Valley, well up the county and, being so isolated, and of spectacular shape, it gives a totally false impression. In fact, it is little more than 1300 feet high—a hundred feet less than, for example, Porlock Hill in Somerset, which carries a road over the top. No, it is not the actual heights that impress, here in southern Shropshire; it is the subtle interlocking of hill and valley and the perfect attunement of one to the other, attained over more than four hundred million years, an unimaginable time of evolution. It is the distribution of the small, gracious villages and hamlets in the valleys and on the lower slopes of their intervening hills. Here, as a poet who lived and died many years before A. E. Housman noted, 'every prospect pleases'.

For the first few miles southwards from Shrewsbury much of the stonework has the warm, russet-red tinge familiar to all who know Cheshire, to the north, the red sandstone of a geological age later than the Silurian. Looking across the wide Severn near Atcham, you will see it well represented in the lovely chestnut tree-embowered church of St Eata, the footings of whose western tower are almost washed by the river when, as so often, it is in spate. Before entering the church itself you should stand and consider it remotely, from the parapet of John Gwynn's beautiful eighteenth-century bridge, now happily spared the thunder of east- and west-bound traffic along the A 5 by the timely building of a wider, if much less graceful, replacement. The warm pink of its stonework is perfectly set off by the heavy green foliage that enshrouds it.

Entering Shropshire at this point, with the Romano-British town of Viroconium just over your left shoulder and the splendid mass of the Wrekin—itself a corruption of this Roman word—rising magnificently behind it, you are now on the threshold of a sequence of valleys, in each of which a hamlet, with its little church and a shop or two intermingled with the cottages, awaits you at every turn. The low-lying terrain between the A 458 and the trunk road, A 49, offers you a wide choice of these, all of them happily remote from the busy traffic on those roads. And as you continue southwards, the pink-hued stonework of the churches and lesser buildings gives place gradually to a soft stone that has something of the colour of the skin that lies over clotted cream.

Yet the tradition of russet-red stone dies hard. Outcrops of this stone, in worked or unworked form, persist. You will find, in the charming hamlet of Acton Burnell, for instance, a few miles south of Atcham, a curious companionate marriage of the two stones. The thirteenth-century church (whose tower alone is modern) is built entirely of the yellow-grey stone of the district. Admittedly this is a cliché, but it is not inapposite to call this beautifully built church a 'poem in stone'. Connoisseurs will note how very much finer the workmanship is than is usually the case in these very small country churches. There is, as it happens, a perfect explanation for this: the village of Acton—one of the many Saxon 'oak-tuns'—took the second half of its name from the Burnell family, of which Robert was Lord Chancellor of England under Edward I and so obviously could command the services and skills of masons of the first rank to do his building for him.

Robert Burnell built also a fortified manor house, always referred to locally as The Castle. It stands close alongside the church, a little behind it. And it is here that this companionship-in-stone is to be seen: whereas the church was built of the yellow-grey stone, much of the manor house was built of the warmer stone, flushed with pink, that belongs more truly to the northern part of Shropshire. The contrast is not harsh, for the two types of stone, very similar in their texture, blend happily enough with another; indeed, here and there the effect is almost as though the russet had 'stained' the paler stone adjacent to it by gentle contact.

As you leave Acton Burnell you see ahead of you the northern foothills of the uplands that are, generally speaking, Shropshire's most impressive and memorable feature. You can branch right-handedly, taking a short stretch of rule-straight road which is, as you may have already guessed, a survivor from Roman road-building days: it points directly towards Viroconium, behind you, and towards Leebotwood, where it merges with the main road to the south. Or you can branch left-handedly, taking a road that, in its tortuosities, is an emphatic contrast with that length of former Roman road. It climbs a hill and drops soon afterwards into a valley, the valley of Hughley Brook; and here is the minuscule hamlet of Hughley itself, snug beneath the steep northward slope of Wenlock Edge beyond.

Housman wrote of Hughley's church that its vane is a 'far-known sign', and that its tall tower 'divides the shade and sun'. Poetic licence, it must be assumed; or could it be that in his day, in the latter part of last century, this diminutive church, dedicated to St John, possessed such a tower? Certainly it does not possess one today, over three-quarters of a century later. At the west end of the church the tower, so called, consists of a squat red-brick and oak-framed structure topped by an oak finial and carrying a black-faced clock with gold hands. And such a church, in such a valley setting, is perhaps better thus: an upward-thrusting stone tower such as those that dominate so many of the churches of East Anglia, of Somerset and Dorset and elsewhere, would surely not be in true keeping here.

You can climb steeply from the valley in which Hughley is sequestered to the heights of Wenlock Edge at not far short of the 1000-foot contour. Better, though, to turn your back on the village for the time being and approach the Edge from its western end, beyond Leebotwood. Here the

View of Wenlock Edge

thirteenth-century church of the Virgin Mary, with its interesting and unusual 'Priest's Door', though much less characterful than that of Acton Burnell, and curiously remote from the village community it serves, is worth more than a mere passing glance. You are now almost on the outskirts of Church Stretton to the south. Though you can of course climb on to the Edge from Wenlock also, at its north-eastern tip, it is better to do so from Church Stretton; for one thing, the sun will be over your shoulder or behind your back, rather than in your eyes, and this will enable you to see the beauties of Wenlock Edge at their best.

You will climb steadily, beyond Hope Bowdler, to where a lane leads off righthandedly to Rushbury. Connoisseurs of the Shropshire scene maintain that this is the most perfect of all the county's isolated villages, and certainly a strong case can be made out for it. But there are others with a case as strong, and Hughley itself, a few miles farther along on the other side, is one of these. There are others, too, on the far side of the Long Mynd, close to Shropshire's border with Powys.

The farther eastwards it goes the more the Edge narrows, tapering indeed to quite a fine point as it approaches Much Wenlock, with its impressive ruins of the eleventh-century priory, and then broadening out for a while before terminating almost suddenly at Broseley, just short of the Severn where it is spanned by the Iron Bridge at the township which derives its name from that remarkable feature. Fifteen miles in length, and running consistently along a contour not far below the 1000-foot mark,

Wenlock Edge invites walking rather than driving, though this is wholly practicable.

A 'ridge walk', or walk along an Edge such as this, is infinitely alluring to the true walker. There is a comparable walk north-southwards along the rounded crest of the Malvern Hills, thirty miles to the south. There is another, somewhat more spectacular and challenging, from North Barrule south-westwards to Bradda Head in the Isle of Man. But both of those are turf walks, whereas on Wenlock Edge there is a good made road. Three miles before you come to the end of it you can look almost sheer down its steep north face on to the roof tops of Hughley, nestling unobtrusively in its little hollow. This bird's-eye view of valley villages is one known to and relished by everyone who enjoys such ridge walks, whether they are on the Cotswolds, on the various Edges to the west and north of Sheffield, or anywhere else: they induce in one a curious and not unpleasing sense of topographical omniscience.

Another advantage of exploring Wenlock Edge first from Church Stretton is that you can then swing about and take an almost exactly parallel ridge road running south-westwards to Craven Arms. The turning-point is at Much Wenlock itself. From there, if it were not for the hill that rises on the other side of the A 458 road linking Shrewsbury with Bridgnorth, you would be able to descry in the distance that remarkable bridge that gave its name to the little township close by, Ironbridge. This too, though it can hardly claim to be truly off the beaten track, or something to be discovered, deserves a leisurely inspection.

Spanning the Severn where it runs through a spectacular gorge a hundred feet wide, it is the first bridge ever to have been built in the country wholly of cast iron. It is over two hundred years old, having been designed and constructed by two of the early iron-masters, Abraham Darby and John Wilkinson of Coalbrookdale, in 1779. The bridge consists of five semi-circular cast-iron girders with a span of 140 feet, sprung from the iron bed-plates set in the stone abutments of both banks. These five main arches are reinforced by secondary arches braced against one another in such a way as to spread the load of the carriageway above, which slopes upwards from each side to meet on a well-estimated curve immediately above the highest point of the arches.

The Iron Bridge was a remarkable achievement for its period; all the more so in that no bolts and nuts or rivets were used, only skilfully contrived dovetail-joints strengthened by pegs and keys. This was the only concession to the original design of the bridge, which was to have been of timber until the progressive-minded Darby and Wilkinson showed what could be done with a material that had never before been tried out on such a scale. The bridge fulfilled its function without lapse for a century and a half; but in 1934, traffic having increased so prodigiously over the previous decade or two, it was wisely closed to all wheeled traffic other than

Ruins of eleventh-century priory at Much Wenlock

bicycles and perambulators and, quite properly, designated an Ancient Monument.

It must be said that the ridge road that runs along the south-east side of Wenlock Edge is less remarkable than its counterpart on the north-western side. The reason of course is that the Edge slopes more gently on the latter side, as Edges, wherever they are found in the country, generally tend to do. The western escarpment of the Cotswolds is a case in point, and there are others in Yorkshire and in Derbyshire and elsewhere. At Sutton Bank, for example, in Yorkshire, and at Hucklow in Derbyshire, it is the existence of these Edges that makes the growing sport of gliding possible. Nearer to hand, and germane to the present county, the western-facing flank of the Long Mynd, overlooking Wales, is another example.

Nevertheless, this second ridge road is beautiful in its own right; memorable even though less dramatic. It passes through a succession of attractive villages such as Bourton (not to be confused with the two Bourtons in the Cotswolds, far to the south), Brockton, Broadstone and Munslow. There are naturally more villages on this side of the Edge than on the other, for Corve Dale offers a plentiful supply of readily available water, and the sun lingers longer on this side than it does on the opposite

168

one. This flank of the ridge, too, offers the traveller a magnificent view across Corve Dale to the Clee Hills beyond.

And near Munslow, just a mile south-west at Aston Munslow, there is a bonus over and above the beauty of the region. This is the beautiful fourteenth-century manor house, The White House as it is named, which in itself constitutes a Museum of Country Life. Cruck-built houses are rare today; they are to be found almost exclusively in areas where oak trees once grew in abundance, for the 'crucks' were formed of whole tree-trunks or major oak boughs split (not sawn) down the middle and set up, tip to tip, to constitute the gable-ends that between them supported the ridge-pole. There are examples of this style of building at Lacock, in Wiltshire, and in Pewsey in that county too.

Most such examples of medieval house-building, as here at Munslow, date from the fourteenth century. At The White House the cruck construction can still be well seen, though superimposed upon and about it is the more easily recognisable and familiar traditional mode of half-timbering, including the 'cross-wing' principle. Externally it may not seem to have much more to commend it than a hundred other houses of its period in Cheshire and Shropshire generally, in Herefordshire and Worcestershire and Gloucestershire, and on the other side of the Welsh border too. You must go inside to savour its unique riches.

For here, lovingly over the years, the house has been as it were gradually revealed to itself. Its great hearths and chimney-breasts have been laid bare, its floors have been cleared of deposits, its beams stripped of plaster, its famous 'hanging staircase', an eighteenth-century addition, opened up. In and around the main building there is a display of domestic and farm implements of many kinds, from many periods, and these are to be seen in the type of setting of which for so many years they formed a natural and integral element. A museum, it is true; and one that can be entered only on payment of a nominal sum. But how much more rewarding than the type of museum that is filled with glass-enclosed cabinets and near-illegible printed cards and reference-numbers. Here at The White House, Munslow, is a living museum, one so natural that, having entered it, you find yourself transported back through the years and into a world that has been long forgotten by most of us in this second half of an ever-increasingly industrialised century.

Road and rail alike thread the valley that runs between Leebotwood and Ludlow. You drop off Wenlock Edge at Church Stretton, or at some other point to the north of Craven Arms, and the vast expanse of the Long Mynd rises in front of you, challenging your step. It is a challenge that ought to be taken up, whether on narrow, tortuous, uneven road or (better still!) on winding path. It is what you will almost certainly find most memorable in this southern half, indeed in the whole of Shropshire.

'Our most ancient ancient monument,' wrote a man who had known the shire intimately the whole of his life. 'A thing that has watched out not merely the reigns of kings and the turmoils of peoples but all the known ages of the world.' Perhaps the word 'thing' is an ill-chosen term to describe the Long Mynd; and he may be an epoch or two out of reckoning so far as geological time is concerned. But basically of course he is right in his reference to this zone having 'watched out all the known ages of the world', for its origin indeed lies in the 'far backward and abysm of time.' And he goes on to observe that this region of Shropshire is 'not spectacular; it is notable for its completely uneventful outline and its smoothness'.

Not spectacular? You may be inclined to disagree; especially if you come from one of the lower-lying regions of the country: from the Home Counties, from East Anglia, from Sussex or Hampshire or Kent. And as to its 'smoothness': this is the smoothness of rough, untamed turf land, of a shaggy coat, of apparel that has weathered and must always weather every kind of storm. What you come upon today, as you climb (necessarily on foot) the stony path that follows the tortuous, narrow cleft of the Cardingmill or Ashes Hollow Valley, or thread your way, by car, along the Burway and Portway, soaring above the roofs of Church and Little Stretton, is honest-to-God moorland, undulating to the far horizon on contours midway between 1000 and the 2000-foot marks.

It has a brooding air about it. 'The face of the heath,' Thomas Hardy wrote long ago, 'by its mere complexion added half an hour to evening; it could in like manner retard the dawn, sadden noon, anticipate the frowning of storms scarcely generated, and intensify the opacity of a moonless night to a cause of shaking and dread. It could best be felt when it could not clearly be seen. When night showed itself, the sombre stretch of rounds and hollows seemed to rise and meet the evening gloom, the heath exhaling darkness as rapidly as the heavens precipitated it, a black fraternisation towards which each advanced half way.' He was writing of Egdon Heath, in Dorset; but he might equally well have been writing of these limitless upland acres of the Long Mynd, west of Church and Little Stretton.

It is not, of course, always thus. In bright sunshine there is colour and warmth in the texture of its surface; the twisting moorland pack-horse tracks laid out over much older pathways gleam off-white between their constricting borders. But there remains always the dominating impression that at any time, and without any warning, the sun's light may be withheld; and then this ancient, this primeval 'thing', this aeons-eroded mountain (for Mynd is the Welsh word *mynydd*, mountain, subtly contracted), will take on a wholly different and forbidding personality. Even an extensive cloud shadow sweeping across it as a bank of cumulus is swept across the sky overhead can do something more to this strange landscape than merely drop the air temperature above it by a degree or two.

Ironbridge

Yet, as always in such terrain, a sense of exhilaration, even of exaltation, is communicated. You find yourself, here, in splendid isolation; you are, in the hackneyed phrase, but literally rather than figuratively for once, 'on top of the world'. The Portway is narrow; few vehicles use it. The exceptions will be those making their way to and from the glider base immediately above the Edge that drops almost sheer down into the valley of the Onney and the gently inviting landscape of northern Powys spread out beyond it, a chess-board pattern of fields on which the glider pilot gazes down from his lofty and silent perch as he spirals about in search of thermals to sustain his fragile wings and give him impetus for flight.

Look back over your shoulder, eastwards, from almost any point on the vast Long Mynd plateau and you will see Caer Caradoc, the 1500-foot high hill fortress defended by one known to every schoolboy as Caractacus rather than by the Celtic form of his name; at least, legend and tradition hereabouts declare that this lofty earth-contained fortress was defended by him. Whether or no, it is an imposing and even moving feature of this high landscape, dominating the valley that lies between the Long Mynd and Wenlock Edge.

Then look westwards, to the far side of the gentle, dreamlike Onney Valley; if visibility is good you will see that lofty spur of moorland hills beyond, known as the Stiperstones Ridge, a striking outcrop of quartzite that has not been eroded, thanks to its extreme hardness, to the same extent as most of the *mynydd* all about it. It gives the impression of having broken through the skin of shaggy turf that has contained the rest. If you are prepared to follow a very minor road that becomes progressively narrower and steeper at every turn, and threatens at any moment to come to an absolute stop, you can get quite close to the ridge without taking to your feet. But you should compromise, and cover the last few hundred yards of rough turf and outcropping rock to achieve your objective and, incidentally, obtain possibly the finest and most unforgettable impression of the Long Mynd as a whole that could be obtained from any point, save perhaps from a hovering aircraft.

Take now a snake-like road that spirals back down into the valley and climbs again, steeply as ever, by way of Ratlinghope. This is little more than a cluster of farm buildings. Beyond Ratlinghope, when you have perhaps begun to suspect that you never will find your way back to your starting-point, you will come to one of the very few finger-posts on these windswept uplands: you are back once again on the Portway. Whether or not you made the effort actually to seat yourself in the so-called Devil's Chair (and it is not inappropriately named by any means), it will be a long while before the memory of this particular expedition fades.

You began your exploration of this part of Shropshire among the small valley hamlets; you left these for the uplands. It might be no bad thing, finally, to go in search of Housman's 'quietest places under the sun'. Take, then, the B 4368 road westwards out of Craven Arms, leaving behind you on your left the remarkable stone obelisk at the junction of this road with the main A 49. The stone is worth a glance before you set off. It stands not far short of twenty feet high, beautifully tapered, and carries three dozen place-names and their mileages, ranging from 'Ludlow 7½ Miles' to 'Edinburgh 295 Miles'.

These 'quietest places' all lie in or very close to the Clun Valley. The smallest of the quartet, Clun, is some eight miles west of the obelisk; Clunton is a mile or two short of Clun; Clunbury is right in the valley; Clungunford is just beyond, where the River Clun takes a southerly turn, heading for Leintwardine. A bare six miles separate Clungunford from Clun.

They were quiet places when Housman was writing about them, and they are quiet places still. 'Dear God, the very houses seem asleep,' wrote Wordsworth of the Thames at Westminster Bridge; here the whole valley seems asleep: the river itself, the water-meadows, the hillsides sloping gently down towards them, the houses and farmsteads and cottages and bridges and walls and every man-made object too. They are epitomised by

The Feathers Hotel, Ludlow

the stillness of the second Lord Clive's beautiful stone finger-post at Little Brampton, pointing down the valley to Clungunford, the very weight of whose name somehow induces somnolence. Here Rip Van Winkle might fall asleep, and wake a hundred years hence—to find that nothing at all had changed.

Beyond the quiet villages lies Clun Forest. Threading this region, north and south, runs by far the finest surviving portion of that ancient boundary-line established by Offa, King of Mercia, between his kingdom and that of the wild men of Wales. Known for some twelve hundred years as Offa's Dyke, it is a hundred-and-fifty miles of earth-and-turf wall with a ditch to the westward side running from south of Chepstow northwards all the way to near Prestatyn. As with that other famous boundary-wall, that built in Northumberland by the Emperor Hadrian, you can walk much of Offa's Dyke even today, and you certainly should not leave Shropshire without seeing for yourself something of this astonishing man-made landmark that in facts looks so very much more natural than anything man might have designed and made. It is not, of course, 'our most ancient ancient monument': that epithet was given, and rightly, to the Long Mynd. But in purely historic terms, as opposed to geological terms, it is ancient enough; and in its sheer impact it is something that you may well remember as vividly as anything that impressed you on the Long Mynd, the Stiperstones Ridge or lovely Wenlock Edge.

8

North Wales

CLWYD AND EASTERN GWYNEDD

Close to Chirk Castle, six miles north of Oswestry, the A 5 trunk road from London to Holyhead lifts out of the flat north Shropshire plain and enters the Vale of Llangollen, with some eighty miles still to go. As far as Corwen, some seventeen miles or so, it follows the valley of the Dee; then, as the Dee turns south for Bala Lake, the road, now much shrunken in stature, lifts more emphatically for the hills to the west and north. Past Pentre Foelas it runs, to Betws-y-Coed and Capel Curig; then up the Afon Llugwy to Llyn Ogwen and down the Nant Ffrancon Pass to Bangor and the Menai Strait. Before reaching sea level it has cut its way across Snowdonia, forcing a hard passage between the huge mass of Carnedd Dafydd and Carnedd Llewelyn to the north and the Glyders Fawr and Fach to the south, with Snowdon itself looming only a mile or two beyond.

Two northward-running valleys have their point of origin close to the flanks of this major road. The smaller of them, that of the Conway, runs for some fifteen miles from Betws-y-Coed through Llanrwst to the sea at Deganwy. The other, that of the Clwyd, parallel with it some fifteen miles to the east, runs from Derwen, just north of Corwen, by way of Ruthin, Denbigh and St Asaph, to its entry into the sea at Rhyl, twenty and more winding miles away.

Look at any map in which the contours are represented in colour and you will see at a glance the basic difference between the two valleys. The River Conway has cut its channel down a relatively narrow valley, the sides of which, particularly to the west, slope upwards to the high ranges of Aberconwy and Arfon beyond. The River Clwyd, however, runs down a more leisurely-cut valley, one which is three or four times the width of the Conway and opens out into a triangle of low-lying terrain which, if it had been only twenty or so feet nearer to sea level, might long since have been metamorphosed into a delta such as that of the Bouches-du-Rhône.

Between the two valleys the irregularly shaped uplands rise to twelve hundred feet, with an occasional surge to three or four hundred feet higher still. But eastwards of the Clwyd the hills assume a more positive shape: a great whale-back perhaps five miles across and running for some twenty-five miles from Prestatyn south-eastwards until it merges with the

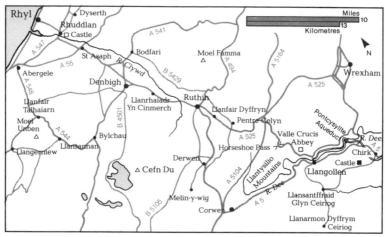

Clwyd and Eastern Gwynedd

Llantysilio and Ruabon Mountains just north of Llangollen. Though generally less high than those that separate the two valleys, the Clwydian Hills have one summit, Moel Famma, which succeeds by twenty feet in entering into the category of 'mountain'. It is a landmark for miles in every direction; and it dominates from the east, as the other hill-massif does from the west, this smiling Vale of Clwyd that runs so unassumingly between them.

Unassuming, perhaps; but how warmly that vale, and the associated range, invite you! An open valley, it is true, and with a good main road running from Rhyl in the north to Ruthin and beyond in the south. But now turn your back on the sea-coast town and the teeming coastline itself, and go in leisurely search of what the valley and the valley slopes hold in store for you.

There is no absolute need to keep to the main road, though you will certainly wish to use it if your interests lie in the direction of castles and ecclesiastical architecture, for Rhuddlan boasts an exceptional and historic castle while St Asaph Cathedral is the smallest in Britain, smaller by far than many a parish church. But there is a minor road that by-passes these towns on the east, starting at Dyserth, which is a place in which you may well choose to linger because the tiny church here has a curious and relatively rare 'Jesse' window: a window setting out the alleged genealogy of Christ. Dyserth also has an eleventh-century churchyard cross, older by more than three hundred years than the very fine one that you will later see at Derwen, at the very head of this valley.

Leaving Dyserth you will travel for some seven miles before reaching the hamlet of Bodfari where you may be tempted by the A 541 which will take you up on to the crest of the Clwydian Hills. But, once here, you must either be lured into industrial eastern Clwyd and Cheshire beyond, or take to your feet – no bad alternative in a terrain so inviting. Certainly this alternative offers you one of the finest of the less demanding ridge walks to be found in all North Wales. Moel Famma, so beautifully proportioned and shaped, looms ahead of you, eight winding ridge-miles distant, and eighteen hundred feet and more in height. From its summit there is a superlative view north-eastwards over the estuary of the Dee and the Wirral Peninsula, and indeed in every other direction north, south, east and west.

From the ridge itself you look westwards across the smiling Clwyd Vale to the uplands beyond, seemingly of uniform elevation right to the horizon, but holding the promise of nobler heights beyond as Clwyd cedes place to Gwynedd and its dramatic apotheosis in Snowdonia itself. Down in the valley beneath you lies Denbigh, part-encircled by its thirteenth-century walls, with its ruined castle, the gate of which is still surprisingly intact though so many long centuries have passed over it. You may well feel the urge to abandon the small road along the foothills, on your ridge walk, to descend and inspect this lovely little township nestling in the vale.

Denbigh of course lies astride the main road through the valley. Pause here, therefore, awhile before considering your next move; or rather, before returning to the minor road that continues along the vale near the lower edge of the foot-hills, by-passing Ruthin, to the village with the disproportionate name, Llanfair Dyffryn Clwyd, where Clwyd and Hesbin's waters mingle. The choice may be hard. For the upper reaches of the vale itself call temptingly; and, no less temptingly, the uplands on its western side which extend the whole way to the Conway valley, threshold to the giants beyond. There are not many roads reaching out their tentacles in that direction, across the heights; but one that does will more than repay you for the brief strain of coming to a decision as you stand looking about you in Denbigh's spacious main street.

It bears the number A 543, and wriggles its way westwards out of the town for a mile or two and then at once begins to climb. Not steeply, for these foot-hills, like those that you left on the other side of the valley, take no sudden decisions but slope gently, almost hesitantly, at first at any rate, as though in two minds whether to leave the valley or not. But soon the road begins to twist and turn, sure sign that the terrain over which it is passing has tilted upwards. Within three miles it has climbed to nearly seven hundred feet; at Bylchau, three miles farther on, it has topped the 1000-foot mark. And here it divides: the A 543 branches south-westwards and, within ten miles or so, has joined the A 5 trunk road now thrusting up the valley to Betws-y-Coed; but there is a more tempting road branching off to the right, the A 544, which will take you north-westwards to Llansannan, a hamlet in a valley to which you must drop down five hundred feet before again climbing on to the 1000-foot contour you so recently left.

Here yet again you have a choice of upland roads, and indeed there is little to choose between them. Both of them run along this exhilarating contour: the first almost due north, to splendidly named Llanfair Tal-haiarn, on the beautiful little Elwy; the other, north-west, to Llangerniew, on the upper reaches of the same stream. These two roads, together with the main road, the A 548, that unites them, form an almost perfect equilateral triangle enclosing a lovely area of upland rising to Moel Unben at its centre. The southward-running road from Bylchau, it is true, would have taken you over higher ground; but the thought that it was so soon to merge with a main trunk road is sufficient to deter any motorist unless his objective is to get to Holyhead from these uplands by the most direct route.

Not, of course, that he must necessarily go from this point, shown on the map as Pentre Foelas, all the way to Holyhead. Let us consider, for a while, before continuing up Clwyd Vale, what alternatives await him if he now turns his face truly westwards to the far horizon. Only a mile or so beyond the merging of the A 543 with the A 5 a south-west-running minor road, the B 4407, enters the valley of the upper Conway and follows the dwindling stream towards its birthplace in remote Llyn Conway. This is the water-shed. Now the road runs downhill all the way, through once busy slate quarries and into the Vale of Ffestiniog, through which the little Afon Dwyryd, fed by a multiplicity of mountain streams, trickles its leisurely way past Penrhyndeudraeth and so, by way of the Traeth Bach estuary, out into Tremadoc Bay.

To the south of the estuary, now, the splendid mass of Harlech Castle dominates the flat expanse of Morfa Harlech, while to the north awaits that fantastic 'dream-town' conceived and executed by architect Clough Williams-Ellis and named by him Portmeirion. It stands on a peninsula of its own, jutting southwards into Traeth Bach, and is unlike anything you ever saw before—in one place, that is.

For here the architect has assembled a hybrid township that incorporates the most variegated and diversified types of architecture and 'atmosphere'. Here Cape Dutch and Cape Cod rub shoulders with Italian Renaissance; Jacobean Town Halls stand beside elegant eighteenth-century colonnades; campaniles are paired with mosque-like domes; gun-emplacements are screened by umbrella-pines. The variety is as wide as its impact on the first-timer is hammer-like. You will approve—or violently disapprove: you can hardly declare yourself unaffected, neutral. The site, at any rate, is magnificent; it has to be said that the architect has most skilfully utilised its natural features to incorporate and frame his startling fantasies.

It is possible that in order to recover somewhat from the forcible impact

Harlech Castle

of Portmeirion at close quarters you may care to cross the Traeth Bach to Llanfihangel-y-Traethau, close to Harlech Point; there, steadying yourself with a deliberate effort, look due northwards across the intervening water. On a still night, when its surface is unruffled by an onshore wind, or a breeze coming down off the high hills to the north and east, the reflection of Portmeirion may be seen, upside-down in the blue-glass mirror; then, and perhaps only then does Clough Williams-Ellis's dreamworld become real.

Now, if only to see how man has made use of nature for his own purposes, and with no driving-force of architectural whimsy this time, turn south along the A 496, with Harlech Castle straight ahead of you. Just beyond the castle is the village of Llanfair; and just beyond this, the even smaller village of Llanbedr. In the heart of this village, so inconspicuous that you will overshoot it entirely if you are not on the alert, a narrow road branches sharply off to the left, away from the sea. This is the road that will lead you, ultimately, to the so-called 'Roman Steps'. This objective, once reached, will more than compensate for the time and expenditure of effort that will be involved in threading your way up this ever-narrowing and wall-constricted track.

It is a road, to begin with; a road that follows pretty closely the course of the diminutive Afon Artro for something like six miles. To your left, the hills rise to a thousand feet and more. There are Stone Circles and Standing Stones to be found there by anyone who cares to don heavy shoes or boots and go in search of them on the south slopes of Moel Goedog. On your right-hand side, across the Artro, the contours are set closer, and you can climb in half the distance to twice the height, by way of the escarpments of Cerig Ddu to the summit of Rhinog Fawr. But this would involve a major expedition and could present hazards at any rate for the inexperienced.

The narrow valley, however, winds on, and on, and on. Or so at least it seems, for its course is so tortuous, so narrow, so cramped between rough stone walls, so set about with odd boulders only just clear of the track itself, that progress can only be, almost literally, at a snail's pace. The stunted trees are reminiscent of those in the Doone Valley on Exmoor; the scrub seems to be filling in every possible space between tree and tree and at the same time reaching out sideways in a maleficent endeavour to obliterate the track, such as it is. Passing-places become rarer, less and less negotiable. Nevertheless, you should not lose heart; for you are now within hail of one of the least known and most remarkable features to be found in this corner of Wales, the 'Roman Steps'.

Eventually the trees thin out and the track, still surfaced but as narrow as ever, balances beside the mountain tarn of Llyn Cwm-Bychan before petering out at a farm, close to which there is a field in which you must park before taking to your feet along a path signed 'Roman Steps'. The walk is steep in part, and also rough, but this is glorious countryside and for this alone the effort is worthwhile. The steps—an early length of which you will reach in what can seem a very long mile—turn out to be a series of laid and fashioned rock slabs which lead up towards and eventually across Bwlch Tyddiad on the north side of Rhinog Fawr. As to what the steps are, and as to their possible Roman origin, expert opinion remains non-committal, agreeing only that this must be a very ancient route which served at one comparatively recent period as a packhorse trail. But we have departed a long way from the delights of Clwyd and must return thither in order to work our way southwards to our next main objective.

There are few houses, indeed few farms, on this plateau between Clwyd and Conway, save on the lower slopes reaching down into the valleys. But signs of man's presence and activities are not wanting. There are small reservoirs, most of them happily conforming to the contours which nature, not the mechanical shovel, gave them. More rigid, however, are the acres and acres of afforestation among which these small, lost reservoirs glint in the sun like semi-precious stones and catch the reflection of the occasional wandering cloud.

It takes time, and patience, to accustom oneself to this bold signature of the Forestry Commission, which is on so wide and ample a scale. In the remote north of the country, south of the Scottish Border, the vast extent of the Kielder Forest was perhaps easier to accept and assimilate. Here, where dimensions are smaller, proportions more restricted, this cramming of straight-lined plantations into every hollow, on to every promising slope, over the shoulder-blades of almost every hill, seems an offence to eye and spirit alike. The beautiful curves of interlocking hill and cwm are harshly, even violently, assaulted by the rule-straight lines of planted trees and intersecting fire-breaks. Where such lines are horizontal or vertical they can sometimes be accepted by the eye, if only just; it is the crude diagonals that really affront.

What a relief it is after a surfeit of such arrogant signatures to drop down into a narrow valley where a brown yet sparkling stream, its surface broken here and there by tumbled boulders that have learned their place, is spanned by a grey stone single-arched bridge with close-set parapets that enforce circumspection as you cross from one side to the other. It may even be with something of relief that you return, now, from these conifer-infested uplands to the open Clwyd Vale, narrower now by a good deal than it was when you first entered it, ten miles and more to the north of Denbigh, to see what the upper reaches of the vale and its enclosing hills yet have to offer.

Now turn south to Ruthin, and from here take the B 5105 which is signposted to Cerrigydrudion. Within about five miles a minor road on your left brings you to the hill-top hamlet of Derwen, from where a very steep, winding and constricted road—hardly more than a hill track, in fact—turns westwards and then northwards, encircling the hill on which the village stands. But before you return to Ruthin, pause by the plinth of the churchyard cross, a magnificent specimen. Look now straight over the town of Ruthin at the long Clwydian Range and the summit of Moel Famma on the distant skyline: a superb view.

The other 'horn' of the Vale is that of the Hesbin, which runs into it from the south. You can follow this for a short distance, as far as Pentre Celyn; after this you must again choose between delectable alternatives. One is to take the obvious roads, the A 525 and the A 542, which will bring you in due course to Llangollen; the other is to pick up the A 5104, which will lead you along the beautiful Afon Morwynion (and could a river name be more tempting than that?) to a point just north of Corwen, where your eye will be caught and held by the Iron Age hill-fort of Caer Drewyn, and you will join the minor road, the B 5436, which runs parallel with the A 5 Holyhead road, but on the left, or north, bank of the Dee the whole way to Llangollen. This is a longer route than the other, but infinitely to be preferred; and this not simply because it enables you to approach Llangollen without becoming involved in the trunk-road traffic.

Your road is certainly one that must be negotiated with care, for often it is so narrow that if you are unlucky enough to meet another vehicle you may have to back some distance to the nearest possible passing-place. But the effort is well worth while. For this small road winds among trees, dipping and rising where tiny streams cut across its line, past the occasional half-hidden farmstead and cottage—whitewashed, glossy-black painted like the generality of these isolated buildings—to debouch on to the main road, the A 542, at Llantysilio, close to the now ruined Valle Crucis Abbey at the foot of the notorious Horseshoe Pass.

Llantysilio is as picturesque and haunting a Welsh hamlet as you are ever likely to discover. The abbey nearby ranks among the most impressive and beautiful monastic remains, certainly in North Wales, perhaps in the whole of the Principality. It was a Cistercian abbey, the first stones of which were laid as early as 1202. Not surprisingly, so many centuries having passed over it, even in this delectable valley it shows the scars of time. The chapter house and sacristy, built a hundred or so years later than the earliest portions of the main fabric, survive in fairly good condition, and there are other remains that are not difficult even for the non-expert to identify: the *dortoir*, or dormitory, for instance, on an upper floor. Of the focal point, however, the church itself, sadly there is little more to be seen today than what remains of its west end, in which the most impressive individual feature is the fine rose-window.

But it may well be that what you remember best from Valle Crucis Abbey when you have left is not so much the quality of the masonry itself as the sheer beauty and appropriateness of the abbey's setting in this valley, between the great mass of the Ruabon Mountains on one side and the Llantysilio Mountains on the other: truly a haunt of peace in a dramatic landscape. Yet even here there are echoes of harsher times. A few hundred yards to the north of the abbey there stands a broken shaft of stone, Eliseg's Pillar. It was erected nearly twelve centuries ago—four hundred years before the first of the abbey's stones were laid—by a Welsh princeling in pious memory of a remote forbear, a Prince of Powis named Eliseg, who had been slain in battle not many miles away. And a mile or two to the south and east there rises the imposing hill-top fort with its battle-cry of a name: Castell Dinas Bran. It looms above the lovely little township of Llangollen in the vale below; a dark and silent threat to its serenity that, in fact, it has never disturbed, at least since historic records were first kept.

As you come close to Llangollen from the foot of the Horseshoe Pass, leaving behind you first the Valle Crucis Abbey and then charming Llantysilio, you will come upon the western terminus of the Llangollen Canal. It skirts Llangollen, keeping to the higher ground on the north side of the River Dee, following an eastward-flowing contour line that matches the one on which the A 5 runs along the opposite bank. To leave Clwyd without having explored at least a few miles of this man-made waterway, so 'natural' seeming for much of its course that it is hard to believe that it is not in fact the work of Nature herself, would be to miss an experience that would be hard to parallel anywhere else in the country—even among the reaches of the abandoned Kennet & Avon Canal in Wiltshire.

A few miles east of Llangollen the Vale of the same name begins noticeably to open out, and it is here that you will find a man-made feature often, and appropriately enough, referred to as a 'waterway in the sky'. It was necessary for the Llangollen Canal to cross the broad valley of the Dee, the wide mouth of the Vale of Llangollen, from north to south, for its objective was to merge with the Shropshire Union Canal by way of Chirk and Ellesmere and thence to the 'wich', or salt, towns of the Cheshire Plain, such as Northwich and Middlewich. To carry a canal from one contour to another of equal level across a valley bottom a hundred and twenty feet below involved, of course, an aqueduct. Nothing unusual about that: had not the Romans, those masterly civil as well as military engineers, accomplished that very feat two thousand years or so ago with such triumphant achievements as the Pont du Gard, in Provence? But this aqueduct, named from the hamlet near by, Pontcysyllte, is unique in that, like Darby and Wilkinson's famous bridge over the Severn fifty miles away on the far side of Shropshire, it is an aqueduct of cast-iron carried on towering piers of stone, a masterpiece from the brain of that giant among early civil engineers, Thomas Telford, whose memorial stands by the roadside in distant Eskdalemuir.

A much older bridge spans the Dee a few hundred yards up stream: arches of stone close to the running water. Stand on this, leaning against the parapet, and look upwards. There, striding across the sky on its sturdy yet graceful stilt-like piers, is Telford's splendid 'vision in cast-iron'. The term may strike you as self-contradictory: could anything, you may want to protest, be more prosaic, more pedestrian, more brutally commonplace, than cast-iron? Perhaps not; though there are fire-backs in this hard, brittle substance that are poems in metal sufficiently explicit to contradict this. Looking upwards from the sparkling river and its tree-clad banks, you will have to agree that this achievement of Telford's has an aerial, almost an ethereal quality that is breath-taking to contemplate.

And now, leave the valley bottom and climb up to the level of the canal, a hundred and twenty-one feet above the river. A towpath runs alongside the canal, on its east side, and you can walk along this the full length of the aqueduct, one thousand and seven feet, to be precise, from one side of the valley to the other, with the water in its square-section cast-iron bed glinting in the sun just as that of the Dee sparkles far below. It still seems to glint, as a matter of fact, when it passes into the shadow of the overhanging trees on the far side, as though determined to give the lie to the foolish supposition that a cast-iron channel must be nothing other than functional, utilitarian to a degree. From your aerial viewpoint, with still water close beside you crossing the lively waters of the Dee so far beneath you, the stone bridge has diminished to a child's model, and a car crossing it, circumspectly because of the closeness of the parapets on either side, must have come, you tell yourself, out of a matchbox.

It took Telford's men eight years and more to build this masterpiece, this filigree-work in stone and cast-iron that, in spite of its eighteen massive yet gracefully-proportioned stone piers, seems to hang from the sky rather than stand with its eighteen feet firmly planted on the valley floor and sides. It was officially opened to canal traffic in 1805, the year of Trafalgar, and it was Telford's boast that only one man had died during the course of its construction—a dramatic contrast to the battle that took place in the same year. It may seem strange, in a land that has neolithic remains galore, Roman relics and medieval castles unnumbered, that the Pontcysyllte Aqueduct should be scheduled as an 'Ancient Monument': it is, after all, not much more than a hundred and fifty years old. But the designation is absolute, not relative; the important aspect of the matter is that this noble and imaginatively conceived structure is in the care of authorities who will maintain it as such a memorial to a man's faith and vision and workmanship deserves to be maintained.

You can walk for miles along the towpath of this lovely canal, on the north and on the south side of the aqueduct; every mile you walk is more rewarding and memorable than the last. Small, solid stone canal bridges, semi-circular or otherwise shaped, carry lanes and farm tracks from one side of the water to the other; brief straight lengths are followed by curved lengths so continuous that you would suppose that the contour followed by Telford's surveyors took the form of a spiral. Open stretches give you a clear view across the Vale of Llangollen from one side to the other, with the stripling Dee meandering between its banks. There are stretches where the towpath plunges deep into overhanging trees and close-set under-growth. There are stretches from which you can obtain the occasional rare vista, such as that which focuses the eye on distant and dominating Castell Dinas Bran. There are—but there is hardly a limit to what this sort of leisurely, easy walking has to offer. So many people pass briskly through Clwyd, westwards-bound for the admittedly alluring coastline of Cardigan Bay or the mountains and National Park of Snowdonia, overlooking entirely the delights to be enjoyed in this north-eastern corner of Wales; it is not only churlish but indeed self-punishing to decline a gift so generously yet so unobtrusively offered.

ANGLESEY AND THE LLEYN

Far to the west, across and beyond the massed peaks of Snowdonia, Wales runs out as two arms somewhat half-heartedly embracing the wide yawn of Caernarvon Bay. The northern is the island of Anglesey, the southern the peninsula known as The Lleyn.

Scenically different, if only because The Lleyn boasts a mountain massif denied to generally pastoral and low-lying Anglesey, both these arms are largely Welsh speaking and both are exceptionally rich in prehistoric sites testifying to man's presence here over millenia. Of the two, though, it is Anglesey that has always been the closer to mainstream history. As was the case in Wales's south-west, across Presely and on St David's peninsula, so, also, Anglesey reached out towards Ireland and was thus transit land along the important if ill-defined net of ancient trade routes—as indeed it still is along the sometimes all-too-clearly defined road and rail approaches to the modern port of Holyhead. Later, it was Anglesey that took the bloody brunt of the Roman onslaught: Anglesey that became a part of the heartland of the powerful princes of Gwynedd; Anglesey that was overrun by the Norman Marcher Lord, Hugo d'Avranches; Anglesey that had to suffer Edward I's great castle and alien

Anglesey

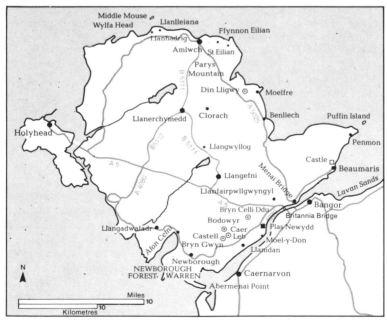

English Borough of Beaumaris, and Anglesey that by historical irony nurtured the Tudors, destined eventually to mount England's throne. The Lleyn, by contrast, has always distanced itself, although thanks to the holy island of Bardsey lying conveniently off its tip its early Christian associations are strong.

Anglesey first, then; a main thread in the story of Wales and a place instantly intriguing for the generous choice it enjoys both of names and of their etymology. *Ey* we know to be Anglo-Saxon for 'island', so it seems reasonable, especially since the Anglo-Saxons did find their way across Menai during the Dark Age centuries, to accept that it is the Island of the Angles that you are about to explore. Other experts, though, point out that the Norsemen too were here; the old Norse for a fiord, they say, was *öngull*, so this could be the Island beyond the Fiord. Then there is that other name, the one favoured by the Welsh today, Ynys Môn. About *Ynys* there is no dispute—it is Welsh for 'island'—but whence Môn? That it derives from a Celtic word meaning 'end' seems not only the most authoritative verdict but also one that makes geographical sense; in which case Tacitus, writing at roughly the time of the Roman conquest, was adapting a native name when he referred to Anglesey as Mona. But this is not all, for Ynys Môn is often elaborated by the words Mam Cymru, meaning Mother of Wales, a picturesque and nostalgic touch with its roots in the fact that Anglesey with its equable climate was once so rich in grain that it was able to feed all Wales.

You have a choice of two rather special bridges to carry you across Menai, both impressive and each with its story. One is Telford's famous suspension bridge opened in 1826, though it has to be admitted that it was so-to-speak updated in 1938–41; but a forward-looker such as Telford would surely have approved, though he might well have expressed some astonishment that it had been found possible to simplify so much his cradle of chains. As you drive across it is hard to conjure back the emotions aroused by the mere proposal to build this bridge; the bitter opposition of all whose livelihood depended on the many ferries, the insistence by ship owners that the passage of their tall ships should not be impeded— magnates to whom we should be grateful for it is because of their insistence that we cross at a height of 100 feet and thus enjoy such a view. With luck you will get across in a minute or less, but spare a thought for those travellers of less than two centuries ago who, making for Beaumaris, had to trudge far out on to the Lavan Sands to find their boat and then, in dark or foggy weather, had to rely on the tolling of a church bell for navigational success. And if, maybe, you are slowed down by a lorry filled with cattle, it may divert you to reflect that prior to the building of this bridge these beasts, urged by a drover with skills very different to those of his modern successor driving that lorry, would have had to swim the strait.

Some twenty-five years after Telford, another famous engineer had the satisfaction of seeing his bridge here, or, rather, a short distance to the south. This was Robert Stephenson whose Britannia railway bridge in 1850 carried its first train through its strange tube, the start of over a century of service sadly and abruptly ended by a fire in 1970. But Anglesey is now served by a fine new combined rail and road bridge, resting on the stonework of its predecessor and still carrying its proud name and that of its distinguished first engineer. Nor need the bridge buff feel too thwarted, for he has only to drive the few miles along the coast to Conway where he will find Stephenson's slightly earlier tubular railway bridge still in use alongside Telford's now superseded road bridge.

Excepting Beaumaris, the A 5 to Holyhead, and Holyhead itself with its surrounds, it is fair to say that most of Anglesey is off the beaten track. True, there are some unpretentious little resorts—places such as Moelfre and Benllech on the north coast—true also that fine weather and school holidays can attract modest crowds to Newborough's national nature reserve at the island's southern tip, but these seem to reinforce the general impression of remoteness. So, ignoring the A 5 and a broad swathe to either side, and with prehistory, history and nature in mind, you are unlikely to be disappointed if you aim for Anglesey's northern and southern thirds. Yet, having said this, Holyhead cannot simply be dismissed, for here there is an example of that rare occurrence, a Christian church within the walls of a Roman fort, the former the medieval successor to a chapel built here in the sixth century by St Gybi, who ranks as one of Anglesey's two leading saints, the other being his friend Seiriol. It is to this marriage of Roman and Christian that Holyhead owes its Welsh name of Caer Gybi – an association, one suspects, that would hardly have appealed to the holy man of peace who would doubtless have preferred the prefix 'llan', meaning a sacred enclosure. However, a modest village in The Lleyn does bear this name. Nor is this the only feature of interest in and around Holyhead, for the remainder of Holy Island, of which the port forms the north-eastern tip, boasts several groups of easily accessible hut circles, a hill-fort, three standing stones and a burial chamber. However, all this is within or close to built-up areas and you will find as many and better sites, and in far pleasanter surroundings, scattered around the northern and southern thirds suggested as your objectives.

To reach Anglesey's southern district you should bear south-west off the A5 just before reaching Llanfairpwllgwyngyllgogerychwyrndro-bwllllantysiliogogogoch, a place which, willy-nilly, has to be mentioned by anybody writing about Anglesey, even if much of the last part of the name (it means St Mary's Church in a hollow by a white hazel near the rapid whirlpool by the red cave of St Tysilio) was probably tacked on in the nineteenth century by a tourist-conscious local. And, whoever he was, it has to be said that he was not unsuccessful, for if most maps stop at 'pwll', or even content themselves with 'Llanfair P.G.', the whole fifty-eight letters obstinately remain a part of local folklore and the station will happily sell you the world's longest platform ticket.

The A 4080 which you now follow south-west is, despite its classification, an unhurried road which soon passes the National Trust's elegant Plas Newydd (long the home of the Marquesses of Anglesey), a place you will certainly choose to visit if your interests embrace fields as diverse as stately homes, the trompe l'oeil art of Rex Whistler, and the activities of that flamboyant character Lord Uxbridge, Marquis of Anglesey, who in his eighty-four years commanded the cavalry at Waterloo, lost his leg there, eloped with the Duke of Wellington's sister-in-law and sired eighteen children. This, of course, is all nineteenth- and twentieth-century history, but if you drive on for less than a mile you will reach an infinitely older spot, no more than a modest crossroads, admittedly, yet one which you can legitimately picture in use by both prehistoric people and, later, their Roman conquerors.

First, those prehistoric people. For these you should turn right to find the well-known burial chamber of Bryn Celli Ddu, or, if you prefer, the Hill of the Black Grove, a name strongly suggestive of Druidical associations although this place was in fact built maybe 1500 or more years before anybody had heard of Druids. To be honest this site is somewhat artificial: the mound, which is the first thing you will see across the field, is no more than a modern protection and considerably smaller than the original would have been; the lone inscribed stone at the rear is a replica of an original now in Cardiff's National Museum of Wales; and the interior has been shored up. Yet none of this really matters. Without support the interior would have collapsed, whereas now the modern work points to rather than detracts from the megalithic achievement; the replica stone is a good one and in fact, had he not been told, the average visitor would readily enough presume it to be original; and the mound, especially if in imagination you inflate it to cover the whole site, does clothe great stones which elsewhere stand misleadingly naked beside the eroded traces of their mounds.

From Bryn Celli Ddu you may be tempted to take the opposing arm of the crossroads down to Menai Strait, to the hamlet of Moel-y-Don, strongest claimant to be the landing place of Suetonius Paulinus in A.D. 61 and of Agricola in A.D. 78. Here, with a caravan site close by and modern housing spilling down to the water's edge on the southern shore, you have to call heavily on your imaginative powers, aided perhaps, if you are a classicist, by the lurid descriptions of Tacitus who, as much propagandist as historian—after all, Agricola was his father-in-law—was perhaps less than fair to the Celts who stood massed and defiant where you are now parked. The Romans won, of course, and at once set about exterminating the Druids, some of whose centres – Brynsiencyn and Llanddaniel for instance – were concentrated in this corner of Anglesey.

But who or what were these Druids? Probably one should reject the received picture of bearded, bardic, white-robed priests, waving mistletoe, making abstruse mathematical and astronomical calculations from the alignment of stones, and at the revealed moment sacrificing garlanded virgins. Elements of truth there may of course well be in this, and Tacitus may have had reason for his accusation of obscene rites, but it does seem that the Druids were something more than just the ignorant priests of a crude contemporary Celtic religion. Such evidence as there is suggests that they formed a powerful oligarchy, rulers in practice if not in name, who provided the tribes with their teachers (in religious but more importantly also in agricultural matters), their administrators and even their judges. In any event the Romans took the realistic view that such people were more likely to hinder than further their plans to subjugate the island and plunder its grain and copper. So the Druids had to go, a process commenced by Suetonius and completed by Agricola.

Some two miles south-west of here you can immerse yourself in a very different ambience. Here at Llanidan old church medieval Christian faith and simplicity rule undisputed. And this despite the total neglect; or, one is tempted to write, because of it. To get here you should bear south off the A 4080 at a small crossroads half-a-mile short of Brynsiencyn, following a lane the entrance to which is marked by stone gate-supports, in fact an approach to Llanidan House. At the lane's foot, deep among trees, you reach a rather vague T-junction and you may well wonder where the church is, because behind the trees and undergrowth it is virtually invisible. Yet it is there, beyond the narrower of two iron gates, a part-ruined, primitive and even eerie place in which a crude reliquary dumped casually in an old cupboard shelters some dusty bones, reputedly those of St Nidan who was said to have founded a church here in 616 (one report, suggesting that the bones are female, is probably best ignored). But, thought-provoking though it is, the reliquary is not why you have come here. What you have come to see, in the rear porch, is a miraculous stoup that never dries up. Never? Well, the writer can only testify that when last he was here it was well into a prolonged very hot and rainless spell and that the stoup held at least four inches of clear, cool water. Whether you accept this as a miracle or merely as an unexplained natural phenomenon makes little difference. This simple little stone stoup remains something over which to ponder. Believers will readily accept their miracle; sceptics will go round to the back, find ferns and other symbols of damp, and rationally conclude that there must be some form of seepage.

Nor are the stoup and the reliquary the only things in this haunted place. Fight your way through the long grass and undergrowth and you will find a beautiful ruined arcade, probably of the fifteenth century and a reminder of the time when this was a larger and thriving church, its arches part Gothic and part, it seems, Norman, though surely more by weathering than origin; you will find ancient cracked slabs, some intriguingly inscribed if you take the trouble to puzzle out their message; and you will find massive tombs, once proud and inviolate behind their iron rails but now half lost beneath grass, bramble and nettles. One day, maybe, somebody will tidy up this place; maybe the site will be cleared, the tombs exposed, their inscriptions restored to a legibility their occupants doubtless assumed was for all time. But, should some of this happen, one's feelings will be very mixed. The preservation would be welcome, as recognition that a pious past deserves a more caring present. Yet something unique would have gone, a simple, holy place slowly and gently being absorbed by nature.

Brynsiencyn was, as we have already noted, a Druid centre. But of this you will find nothing today, although records show that fragments of a temple survived into the eighteenth century. What you will find, though, and within less than two miles to the west and north-west, is a group of three ancient sites, two prehistoric and one belonging to the earliest centuries of our era, the names of which alone should be sufficient to draw you to them: Bodowyr, Caer Leb and Castell Bryn Gwyn. The first, if you have already seen many such, you might dismiss as just another burial chamber. And this of course is what it is, although the huge capstone is perhaps more spectacularly balanced on its three uprights than some and thus once again commands admiration for the strength, skill – and, indeed, motivation – of the men of so very long ago who not only raised it into this position but did it so successfully that it has stayed there for perhaps more than three thousand years, long surviving the stone and turf barrow that once covered it. Bodowyr, and the many other similar tombs scattered the length and breadth of Britain, commemorate the ancient dead far more effectively than do many of the (by comparison) modern tombs now sinking below the soft turf and encroaching undergrowth of so many untended Christian churchyards.

Caer Leb, beside a minor road halfway between Brynsiencyn and Bodowyr and younger by perhaps two thousand years, is a fortified enclosure of around the third century A.D. By this date the distinction between Celt and Roman was blurring—the Roman presence as far west as Anglesey was never a colonising one anyway—and one can reasonably look at these earthworks as having been built by locals for defence against raids by other locals taking advantage of the increasingly unsettled times.

Castell Bryn Gwyn, half-a-mile to the south-west of Caer Leb, is a more challenging and more rewarding site because it seems to have been a defended place—yet one which perhaps grew out of a ritual monument— over a long period spanning from neolithic to Roman times. And there are two surprising things here. One is why such low ground should ever have been chosen. The other, that there appear to have been only two significant structural changes over the whole period—one involving the broadening of the original neolithic rampart across its ditch; the other, the building of a new rampart atop most of the earlier site and the digging of a new ditch. But you need both archaeological knowledge and a trained eye to follow this story and most people will probably gain more satisfaction from finding the two standing stones about four hundred yards to the south-west. Traces of earthworks and a ditch suggest that these stones once formed part of a circle, evidence to reinforce the view that Castell Bryn Gwyn may first have been conceived as a religious rather than a fortified place.

The many and varied elements of Newborough's nature reserve together fill a fat, bulbous peninsula hanging below the A 4080 and with spindly, untidy arms dropping south into Caernarvon Bay and reaching east across Menai's tidal sands. You may find quite a crowd of people here, and there is a large car park for the use of which you will probably have to pay, so you could be forgiven some doubts about this as a place for exploration. Yet the area is so extensive—from its extremes it is around four miles in length and breadth—that even at peak holiday times you can escape, and so varied, too, that you can in fact explore as many places as you can themes.

There is, for example, the Malltraeth Pool at the reserve's north-west corner, formed when Telford built a protective cob and today a bird sanctuary. There are salt marshes along the Cefni, rich in sea plants, birds and crustacea. There is Newborough Forest, beneath whose 2000 sandy acres there rests, tradition tells us, a village buried by fearful storms in the fourteenth century. There is that contrasting rocky projection, Ynys Llanddwyn, a place inviting geologists and lovers, the former for the pre-Cambrian rocks, the latter because in the fifth century this was the retreat of their patron lady, St Dwynwen. And finally there is the extensive Newborough Warren, tapering out across the tides and sands to lonely Abermenai Point. As you follow the paths across the warren's marram grass, it will surely add to your interest to reflect that until those storms of the fourteenth century swept in the blanketing sand, this was a rich, agricultural land, and that, even after this disaster, the marram which then took over provided the raw material for an industry which produced mats, baskets and suchlike over some four centuries until it was ended by the last war. Abermenai Point is not only a rival claimant to Moel-y-Don as the crossing-point of the Romans, but also, in the tales of the *Mabinogion*, the place from which Bronwen, daughter of Llyr and 'fairest maiden in the world', and her new lord, Matholwch, King of Ireland, set sail with thirteen ships after their feast and bedding at Aberffraw—a small town north-west along the coast which, sadly, today preserves no touch of its glittering past as the palace of the Princes of Gwynedd.

However, if you go just a mile east to Llangadwaladr, to the thirteenth-century church here, you will find a famous stone commemorating Cadfan as the wisest and most renowned of all kings. He was a Prince (or even it seems King) of Gwynedd who died in about 625 and the stone was erected by his obviously admiring grandson Cadwaladr, a man far less wise and renowned and notorious for a crushing defeat he suffered in 634 at the hands of the Northumbrian Angles.

Soon, now, you may begin to feel the pull of the other side of Anglesey, and, when you do, you could do worse than route yourself past the little church of Llangwyllog which, so far as such a position is measurable, is just about at the island's centre, off the B 5111 between Llangefni and Llanerchymedd. The sign is to a sixth-century church, but this is somewhat misleading, for even if this church was perhaps founded at about that time, the building now here dates only from the fifteenth or sixteenth century. But one should not feel too deceived by the sign. After all, the blessed Gwyllog did live in the sixth century, and in any event this is an appealing low, long, stone and slate-roofed little place on a hillside at the end of a grass-centred lane; a lost place where there is space to park your car and perhaps enjoy a picnic. The church may well be open, too, and if you go in you will be rewarded by a simple font of *c.* 1200, some gleaming dark eighteenth-century woodwork and a large Welsh bible.

You should now aim north towards Amlwch, at Llanerchymedd perhaps diverting east for a couple of miles to where the road crosses a stream at a spot called Clorach, traditionally the place where Anglesey's two leading saints, Gybi and Seiriol, journeying respectively from Holyhead and Penmon, used frequently to meet. Above Amlwch your road (assuming you are on the B 5111) skirts the western flank of strangely-named Parys Mountain, where copper was extracted from Roman times until the late nineteenth century. This, surely, is a landscape you never expected to experience in pastoral Anglesey; a tumbled, hostile, burnt-out craggy upland, often described as lunar, although the moon is dusty, grey and pale whereas Parys is hard, black and ochre. There is something strangely tempting about these cooked stones of all shapes and sizes, and knowing that copper was for long so successfully mined here the urge is to search, not so much in the hope of finding something of value, but out of simple curiosity. But this temptation must be resisted because the many notice boards warning of dangerous shafts are not crying wolf and even what may look like a firm, wide track can suddenly gape with fissures or dip into ominous subsidence.

Better, then, to look the other way and enjoy the view across the north-west of this island—towards Wylfa nuclear power station and the contrasting nature trail which rounds its head; towards Llanlleiana, Anglesey's northernmost point, seemingly chosen by a female recluse of the sixth century as the place to build a chapel, now long disappeared (if indeed it was ever here at all); or towards the rocks of Middle Mouse on which, they say, St Patrick was wrecked, later in gratitude for his survival founding the church at nearby Llanbadrig. Were he to return today he

The Fairy Glen, near Betws-y-Coed, North Wales

View from Yr Eifl, in the Lleyn
Castell Dinas Bran, near Llangollen, north Wales

would be as taken aback as you may well be should you visit here, for much of the interior is Islamic in style, a condition imposed by the Muslim Lord Stanley in 1884 when, broadmindedly, he paid for the restoration of the church. And there is another church you may like to discover while you are near Amlwch, one dedicated to St Eilean. It is a long mile to the east of Amlwch, but, if you are lucky enough to gain entry, you will find quite a number of curiosities, including dog tongs (used for removing unwanted dogs from the church) and, in a chapel, a challenging piece of furnishing which will bring you good luck if you can turn within it without touching the sides. But if in any doubt, leave well alone, for failure is said to bring disaster. From here, if your mood is still one of faith, you can make your way on foot to the saint's well near the shore where, if there is any water in it, you can both cure your ills and curse your enemies.

Your next objective, some six miles to the south-east and not far from Moelfre, is a group of three ancient sites—a burial chamber, a fortified settlement and a ruined chapel—which between them span perhaps 3000 years of human occupation of this corner.

The fortified settlement, Din Lligwy, at the centre of the time-span, is by far the most interesting of the three and a place you are likely to want to reach (it involves a pleasant half-mile walk) however sated you may be with archaeological experiences. It may also compensate you for all those Hut Circles so tantalisingly marked on your large-scale maps, but so hard to find and often disappointing if found. Here is something in all probability very different from any other site you have ever come across— a place in which families lived rather than, as all too frequently, one in which they were buried or, maybe, worshipped. For a change this is a homely world, not a mysterious one; one of ordinary men, women and children rather than of shadowy priests and ghosts. Nevertheless, with the Roman withdrawal around the fourth century and the spreading lawlessness that filled the vacuum, the occupants of Din Lligwy decided that they would be wise to fortify their home. So walls were built, or existing ones perhaps strengthened, to enclose the half-acre domestic complex of rectangular and circular buildings, several of which survive today, some still with walls up to six feet high, some still with massive doorway posts, some still showing traces of drainage systems along the floor and through the walls. Notice, too, the imaginative and labour-saving use of the natural rock which over so much of Anglesey is close beneath the turf surface. Turn your back on the nearby farm (not that it is unattractive, the contrary in fact), and, if you are lucky enough to be here on your own, it is not too difficult to heighten the walls, clothe the huts with roofs of skin stretched taut over posts, and then not only to people this place but also to admire the physical effort and the organisation which went into its building. But there is one feature today that is almost certainly different. The site is surrounded on three sides by a screen of bushes and trees, something, one cannot help feeling, that would have been kept cleared by a community whose survival would have depended on all possible warning of an approaching enemy. But for how long did these people survive? The strange thing is that there is no archaeological evidence of occupation into the fifth century. So what happened? Perhaps these defences were stormed, perhaps the crops failed and there was enforced migration elsewhere, perhaps the chieftain died leaving no heir and his people simply drifted away, perhaps epidemic struck. There seems no limit to speculation.

As you walk back you will pass the ruin of a chapel built by whatever people lived here some eight hundred years after Din Lligwy flourished. It is a sad, roofless place, with a simple Norman-arched doorway, a crude hollowed stone which was presumably a font and a chapel with a crypt added in the sixteenth century. Finally, beside the road just south of where you left your car, you will find a monument that preceded Din Lligwy by perhaps 2000 years. But we are back with the dead here, for the remains of some thirty people were found when this burial chamber was excavated in 1908. Some were buried in neolithic times, others, it seems, during the Bronze Age. This—the long continuity of use—is one uncommon feature. Another is that this burial chamber boasts one of the largest and heaviest capstones in all Britain, and one with no less than eight supports. Confronted with such a mountain of a stone, it is, as you can well see, hardly surprising that this monument's builders were content with low supports and dug down below to hollow out the actual chamber in which the dead were laid.

There is one other corner of Anglesey you could well take in if you can find the time. For every hundred visitors to Beaumaris and its great castle—and they crowd in by car and coach—maybe less than ten press on beyond. Yet these extra four or five miles to Penmon bring you to yet another collection of sites, all of real interest, all within a few yards of one another, and all but one descendant from a priory founded here in the sixth century by St Seiriol. Follow the short path signed to St Seiriol's Well—the first and by a long way the most interesting of the four sites here—and it may be that you are treading in the steps of the saint himself for some authorities suggest that this was where the original priory stood, that the lower courses of the well-structure may at least in part be those of its chapel, and even that the adjacent oval foundations could be those of Seiriol's humble cell. It can be overwhelming, this transition within a few yards, from twentieth-century car park to sixth-century piety, but in a place such as this doubt and cynicism scarce dare to show themselves.

As to the other sites here, the church dates from the twelfth century and contains an unusual Norman pillar-piscina as well as a font gouged from the plinth of a pre-Norman cross; the surviving priory domestic buildings—refectory, dormitory and cellar—are a century or so younger;

Beaumaris Castle

Puffin Island and lighthouse, Anglesey

and, to complete the scene, there is a large seventeenth-century dovecot, that essential source of fresh meat for rich men during the centuries before the introduction of turnips and swedes made it possible to feed livestock throughout the winter.

It is free if you walk, but you have to pay a modest charge to drive the last, very narrow, mile out to the point, along a road still used by the quarries from which Edward I's military architect, James of St George, extracted the stone for Beaumaris and which centuries later provided footings and piers for Telford's and Stephenson's Menai bridges. This is no wild headland; just a modest termination of shingle, sand and black rock backed by the gently humped turf on which you leave your car. Some cottages, a disused lifeboat station, an automatic lighthouse and a bell-buoy which manages to sound foggy and mournful even in bright weather are about all you will find here. You look across the strait to an island – tantalisingly just too distant for detailed study – with no less than three names. Ynys Seiriol and Priestholm are explained by the fact that St Seiriol founded a hermit settlement here, of which the remains of later buildings still survive. As to Puffin Island, these birds were once numerous. Rats escaping from a stranded ship are usually blamed for their decline, but man is just as much the culprit because in the nineteenth century young pickled puffin was a fashionable delicacy on both English and Continental tables.

The Lleyn can conveniently be defined as the whole long, narrow peninsula which drops away south-westward from the A 487 linking Caernarvon with Porthmadog. Scenically its most distinctive feature is the precipitous massif of Yr Eifl, piling up sheer to nearly 2000 feet to hang dark and scarred by giant quarries above the central part of the north coast. Through and beyond this massif, unpretentious roads dawdle vaguely south-westwards to bring you eventually to Aberdaron and the cliffs from which you can see Bardsey's sainted island. The southern shore, one you will likely wish to avoid, could scarcely be more different. Here main road and railway parallel one another to link a series of popular family resorts: Porthmadog, Criccieth with its castle, unusual for being native Welsh in origin though strengthened by Edward I, Pwllheli, and the yachting centre of Abersoch. In between, there waits a quiet, little-touched countryside – part hilly, part gently undulating pasture and woodland—dotted with very Welsh villages and hamlets. Near quite a number of these your map may indicate a well, a reminder of the tens of thousands of pilgrims who, spanning the fifth century to the Reformation, found their way down The Lleyn to cross to Bardsey, three visits to which counted as one to Rome.

Caernarvon is a sizeable town, well documented and attracting crowds throughout the year. Not, one could be forgiven for judging, the kind of place likely to reveal anything new.

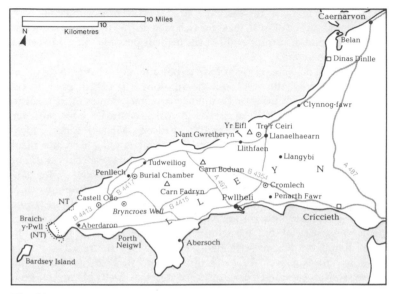

The Lleyn

Yet many visitors are unaware that in order to man and service the castles he built Edward I established and chartered associated towns which came to be known as English Boroughs. English traders and artisans were invited to settle and in return for privileges, not the least of which was that the Welsh were excluded and thus provided no competition, they were obliged to meet the governor's calls for garrison and other duties. From Edward I's point of view this was an admirable system which not only ensured manpower for the castle, but also provided prosperous English enclaves within what had long been treated as hostile territory. It led too to the growth of English-run administrative centres, and the dispersal of the Welsh around unimportant country areas where, in theory anyway, they could not easily conspire. Few of these boroughs have survived in their original rectangular plan, within town walls integral with those of the parent castle, but Caernarvon certainly has. So if you ascend the castle's Eagle Tower, by all means study the weathered stone eagles and other detail, but also let your eye roam farther to appreciate how castle and walled town would have formed a single effective unit.

In Wales, hill-forts are never far away and you will surely see a particularly fine, isolated shape beside the shore only five or so miles out of Caernarvon. It is called Dinas Dinlle and features in the *Mabinogion* as the fortress where the youth, Lleu Llaw Gyffer, destined to become Lord of Gwynedd, 'was reared till he could ride every horse, and till he was

Caernarvon Castle

perfected in feature, growth and stature'. A splendid picture, but one conjurable only from a distance; approach closer, and indifferent modern holiday housing takes over. However, should you nevertheless have decided to drive down here, perhaps you would choose to continue north across the flats for the three miles necessary to reach isolated Fort Belan, looking out across the narrow western end of the straits, defined on the north by Abermenai Point to which you may have walked if you visited Anglesey's Newborough nature reserve. The fort—not open to the public—is of course interesting in itself. As a light on the social conditions and attitudes of the eighteenth century, it is even more so. For this place was not only built (at the time of the French wars) as a patriotic duty by the 1st Baron Newborough, but it was also garrisoned by his specially raised private regiment of 400 men, the Royal Caernarvonshire Grenadiers.

Not much farther south along the A 499, and you are in the village of Clynnog-fawr, a place much associated with St Beuno who founded the church here in 616, a church which together with the adjacent holy well soon became one of the first and most important stages along the pilgrimage trail to Bardsey. As to be expected, there is no trace now of Beuno's original structure—probably it was a primitive affair of wattle and daub—but if you walk through today's large church, along a passageway which once served as the village lock-up, and into the early sixteenth-century chapel you will be in the place which housed the saint's miracle-working shrine until it perished in a fire in 1856. Here you will also find the outline of an earlier church, picked out in grey stone on the floor, and a stone bearing a cross, traditionally the actual stone set up to mark the land given to Beuno by the Prince of Gwynedd but more probably either a medieval boundary marker or perhaps a pilgrim's prayer-stone.

Beuno is said to have been uncle of St Winefride. And a useful one he was, too, because when his niece's head was struck off by a thwarted lover he not only successfully replaced it but caused a healing well to gush from the spot where the head had fallen. This was at Holywell in Clwyd, where you can still enter the water and kneel in prayer on the Stone of St Beuno. Here at Clynnog-fawr you will find Beuno's more modest well in which the sick were expected to bathe before seeking a cure at the shrine.

At Llanaelhaearn, four miles on and approaching Yr Eifl (the name means The Forks, from the triple peaks, but an anglicised corruption, The Rivals, appears on some maps) there is a church, fascinating for being entirely furnished with box pews, as also another well, that of course of St Aelhaearn, which however forms a part of the local water system. This too is the place where you leave the A 499 which is heading for Pwllheli, choosing instead the B 4417 to climb across the massif between Mynydd Carnguwch to the south and Yr Eifl to the north. But well before you get to the watershed, less than a mile out of Llanaelhaearn in fact, you should decide whether you have the stamina and the interest to park beside the road and take to a steep public footpath. It can seem a long climb (it is at least a mile) as false summit succeeds false summit. It can be rough and ankle-twisting too, but eventually, at some 1500 feet, the path reaches the dramatic hill-fort of Tre'r Ceiri, a fortified Celtic village of the early centuries of our era. With its virtually intact walls and hut traces of varying design and different periods, it is interesting to compare Tre'r Ceiri with Anglesey's not dissimilar if much smaller Din Lligwy. But the inhabitants of this high-perched place must surely have been a tougher breed.

Back on the B 4417 you soon reach Llithfaen whence a track leads seaward into Nant Gwretheryn (Nant meaning Valley), sandwiched between high mountain quarries and with a 'village' once busy with the stone. This place is also known as Vortigern's Valley, and really by now, if one has come across this ill-starred bungler elsewhere, one cannot but begin to feel some sympathy. Harried by Picts and Scots, thrown out of Kent by his father-in-law (if we accept Geoffrey of Monmouth's fanciful assertion that he married Hengest's daughter), confronted by a pool of dragons when he tried to build a tower at Dinas Emrys, he eventually, it seems, finished up in this dark valley, only to have his castle split asunder by lightning and to drown when forced to leap into the wild sea.

You probably now feel the pull to go deeper into this increasingly rural Lleyn, as far perhaps as Aberdaron and the hammerhead peninsula from which, standing on National Trust land, you can look across to Bardsey. Lost and rural much of this country may be, but nevertheless there is a generous network of minor lanes and roads along which to plot a peripatetic course past whatever places appeal. Perhaps your choice would simply be for scenery, in which case you would be well advised to head for one or more of the glorious National Trust coastal properties which cluster beyond Aberdaron or wait high above either side of Porth Neigwl, that great sandy arc scooped so cleanly out of The Lleyn's south coast. Nefyn, the only resort along the northern shore, you may well wish to avoid; on the other hand this small town has something of a prim Victorian charm and offers accommodation, food and splendid beaches sweeping away east and west, the latter ending at Porth Dinllaen. And it's worth more than just a glance, this hamlet, for, but for a single vote in Parliament, this could have been chosen as the port for the Irish steam packets. Or—it matters not whether on religious, historical or simply nostalgic grounds—you may enjoy seeking out the holy wells, now often quite hard to find but in the pilgrim centuries doubtless well publicised. You will, for example, find one marked on the map at Bryncroes, the Hillock of the Cross, off the B4413 some five miles short of Aberdaron; another, rarely marked, near a ruined chapel on the National Trust's Braich-y-Pwll estate overlooking Bardsey Sound. If you are fit, energetic and one of those incapable of resisting the promise of heights, you have a choice of at least three well-known hill-forts. Garn Boduan, lifting through woodland just south of Nefyn, is one, a large fort once sheltering well over a hundred huts. Carn Fadryn, three miles south-west, is another, but one imposing a very steep climb and not a place for everybody; walls, hut remains, a well and a superb view are the reward here. Castell Odo, beside the B4413 two miles short of Aberdaron and a much smaller fort, could be a third and less demanding choice. There is even a burial chamber for those in search of the prehistoric; off a minor road, itself off the B4417 just east of Penllech, it enjoys the resounding name of Mynydd Cefn Amwlch.

Whatever route you follow, the B4417 and B4415, merging to become the B4413, will be your axis, one that ends at Aberdaron as emphatically as did the pilgrim tracks of old. Today, as probably always, a cramped and twisted little place, Aberdaron is not one the imagination can easily populate with the pilgrims of many centuries. Nor, though occupying an old building and arguably providing continuity of a bizarre kind, does a café-cum-souvenir shop help to improve the atmosphere. The largely

Ruin of Fynnon Cybi with the Parish Church of Llangybi in the background

twelfth-century church, hard by the sea and surely a gathering place, is the best spot for atmosphere. From here the pilgrims made their short way to Braich-y-Pwll, there perhaps to bathe in its well and pray at the chapel before embarking for Bardsey, where, it is to be hoped, they found whatever they were seeking even if, statistically, each stood a good chance of becoming one of the 20 000 saints reputed to be buried on the island. You too may be able to cross, from Aberdaron, though your purpose is more likely to be nature than piety.

The last two paragraphs assumed time and inclination to explore deep into The Lleyn. But there may well be many who have neither and look instead for a short-cut, from, say, Nefyn. Such is admirably provided by the B 4354, rounding the wooded southern foot of Garn Boduan to run six miles east to cross the A 499, at which point, within the south-east angle of the crossroads by a spot appropriately marked Cromlech, you can find both a small burial chamber and two standing stones.

The little village of Llangybi, two miles north-east of here, recalls that Anglesey saint whose name has come down the centuries as founder of a Christian church within the Roman fort at Holyhead, or Caer Cybi. Here, in more modest Llangybi, an easy footpath starting from the church will bring you in about a quarter of a mile to a peaceful spot beside a stream watering a gentle green valley. Here you will find Fynnon Cybi, or the Well of Cybi, sheltered within a building generally accepted as being at least in part early Christian in date. The well's shelter is next to another roofless building which, although it does not look very different, is in fact an eighteenth-century cottage. But it is worth a glance all the same, if only for the fireplace and chimney, the latter cleverly twisted to serve an upper floor. How, you may also ask yourself, was that huge stone lintel ever raised into position? Nor is this all, for round at the back, immediately below the hillside and hard against the well shelter's wall, you have another pool, an open-air one complete with surrounding stone walk and steps down to the astonishingly clear water.

There is one more Lleyn spot you should try not to miss. Called Penarth Fawr and about two miles south of Llangybi by small roads, this is the single-room home of a late-medieval family of some substance. Or, more technically, a fifteenth-century hall-house. From the outside the place looks no more inviting than a Victorian schoolhouse, but inside it is astonishingly different. Today, it is difficult to appreciate that this single room, even allowing for the raised platform at one end, was sufficient not only for the doubtless numerous family but also for its servants. But properly to picture those fifteenth-century days your imagination must first do a little scene-shifting. A tall screen must be placed along the open passage below the platform, the lord and his family being on one side, the servants on the other; and the seventeenth-century's elegant windows and fireplaces must be ripped out and replaced by slits and an open hearth.

9

South Wales and Herefordshire

THE BORDER LANDS

One of the most pleasurable of occupations for a dark and dismal winter's day, even if spring happens not to be too far behind, is the revisiting in retrospect of some region of the countryside explored in the not-too-distant past. This is best done, of course, with the relevant map outspread upon your knee. Who was it who observed, 'I delight in a map'? Whoever it was who uttered that simple, unadorned statement spoke for many of us for whom a map, of reasonable scale, is, as someone once said of a book, 'A jolly good thing whereon to look, And better to me than gold.'

Map-contemplation takes on an added piquancy when it is possible to compare notes with others, whose views and opinions may support or conflict with your own. You might, for instance, take a purely arbitrary area of, say, three hundred square miles – an area, that is, of about twenty miles by fifteen, one spacious enough to offer variety and yet limited enough to be held as it were in the grasp of one hand. Which, given these arbitrary conditions, out of all Britain would you designate as *primus inter pares*?

For the purposes of discussion, specialist interests would of course have to be discounted. For the dedicated climber would naturally plump for the Cairngorms, the English Lake District, or Snowdonia. The pot-holing enthusiast would plump for the carboniferous limestone of Lancashire and Yorkshire, north Derbyshire or the Mendips. Those whose delight is in sailing on inland water would promote the Norfolk Broads to the exclusion of all else. And so on. It must therefore be accepted that this purely arbitrary area of some three hundred square miles should be chosen for its beauty and variety, its 'feel', rather than for any one specific characteristic such as a rarely-climbed peak, a challenging and dangerous swallet-hole, or the freedom of open fresh-water and accommodating breeze.

Once this general principle has been agreed, then a very strong claimant and one that it would be very difficult to challenge with any degree of success, would be an area of just those dimensions. Much of it lies in the district of South Herefordshire, the south-western corner of the large English county of Hereford and Worcester; much in Welsh Gwent's eastern district of Monmouth—a hybrid land that is neither truly Welsh

The Border Lands

nor truly English but enjoys the best of both; while the western confine across the Black Mountains runs with the district of Brecknock, representing the southern third of Wales's county of Powys. Here is an area that offers what the poet, in a different context, has referred to as 'infinite riches in a little room'. It contains an expanse of high moorland hills that frequently top the 2000-foot mark. It contains a long stretch of one of our most beautiful rivers. It contains one of the most delectable valleys in all Britain. It contains one of the most perfectly sited medieval priories of all those that have survived the long centuries since their foundation. It contains a scattering of villages and hamlets, each one, you will find, lovelier than the last. It contains a cluster of thirteenth-century castles, each one memorable for some specific quality, whether of design or of setting. It contains. . . . But the time has come to pin-point this outstanding claimant to a throne that might be competed for by so many rival regions.

Its northern limit is established by a boldly curving reach of the Upper Wye, which here flows like a Gothic arch improbably composed of a sequence of infinitely varied loops and twists. The springing of this arch is, on the one hand, the little township of Hay-on-Wye, situated at the meeting-point of one English and two Welsh Districts (South Herefordshire, Brecknock and Radnor); and, on the other, Breinton, two or three miles to the west of Hereford. Its southern limit is a minor road running eastwards from Abergavenny in the heart of the Usk Valley to Rockfield, just short of Monmouth. Its western boundary therefore marches in part with that of England and Wales, while the eastern boundary of this arbitrarily-selected region runs from the wide and level valley of the Wye southwards to the lesser valley of the Monnow, on its leisurely way to the fortified bridge that is the western gateway to Monmouth itself.

Set out in these uncompromising terms, it may at first seem to have relatively little to commend it. It appears to be a sequence of small towns and river valleys, filling a rectangle pin-pointed almost as though latitude and longitude had been supplied. But glance at it on a map that gives contours in shades of brown and green, and the picture immediately takes on a three-dimensional quality.

Look at it here, glowing within the lightly-pencilled rectangle that defines our region, now lying outspread, inviting exploration. That boldly coloured mass in dark shades of brown that fills the left-hand portion, spreading westwards into Brecknock is named on your map 'Black Mountains'. And a little confusingly too, perhaps, for much farther to the west, beyond the Brecon Beacons (there's a name to stir the blood and fire curiosity!), there rises another range of high hills also named 'Black Mountain', though the word appears in the singular this time.

The north-western escarpment of the Black Mountains (in the plural) is a pattern of stubby fingers pointing downwards into the Wye Valley, each separated from its neighbour by a small *cwm*—the Welsh word, that would appear as 'combe' in the West Country and is a 'corrie' north of the Scottish Border. Through each of these hollows in the mountain or hill side there runs a minor stream: the Cilonw, it may be; or the Digedi; or the Dulos. The springs that give them birth are all on high ground: on Lord Hereford's Knob, for instance, at nearly 2300 feet; or on Hay Bluff, only a score or so feet less high. And it is from heights such as these, very soon reached from the Wye Valley to the north, that the great mass of the Black Mountains reach out south-eastwards, maintaining their near-uniform altitude for eight miles or more until they drop to the lower ground that separates them from Skirrid-fawr and Graig Serrerthin.

These high uplands are threaded by valleys that accentuate this south-easterly slant, or tilt. The River Monnow is born in the precincts of ruined Craswall Abbey, lost among the moors. It is reinforced by Olchon Brook, which has its origin on the highest ridge of the whole mass, at 2300 feet. This reinforcement gives it the strength and impetus to take a masterful sweep north-eastwards towards Pontrilas and then south-eastwards no less forthrightly to Skenfrith and Monmouth beyond. So loftily set are the birth-travails of the Olchon, in fact, that it could as easily have flowed westwards into Brecknock as south-eastwards into Herefordshire. There is a narrow road up the Monnow valley the whole way to the isolated hamlet of Craswall, whence it continues past the remains of the abbey to cross the border and descend to Hay-on-Wye.

Nor, in fact, are these your only choices. Barely a hand-span to the east there is a small road that climbs the steep valley of the Escley from Longtown to Michaelchurch Escley; beyond that point it narrows to track proportions and meanders on its way over the moors and past isolated farmsteads until it zigzags down the escarpment into the valley of the Wye a little to the east of Hay-on-Wye. There are tracks marked on your map which are smaller still, and certainly not practicable for motorists; but they offer splendid walking over terrain that is not too exacting, and they almost invariably rejoin some more definitely practicable road within two or three miles. There is one such, actually named Cefn Road, that runs parallel with the Monnow River in its highest reaches beyond Craswall.

These are, of course, the minor valleys, and the minor roads. Though negotiable—just—by car, they are essentially for the enterprising walker. Not one of them is over-exacting; not one of them is so long that it cannot be walked, out and back, within a comfortable three hours. But there remain two valleys, only one of which has been given a name, Golden Valley. The other is the valley down which the Afon Honddu runs. You will approach this best by taking the B 4350 southward in Hay-on-Wye, almost immediately hairpinning left to pass just south of the hamlet of Cusop, on the River Dulas below charmingly named Cusop Dingle. For a mile or two the narrow road climbs parallel to the border, but soon reaches a fork, the left arm of which is the lane from Craswall and the Monnow Valley. Your road, however, holds to the right, climbing into open country to reach Gospel Pass between Hay Bluff and Lord Hereford's Knob. Here, at over 1500 feet, you have reached the headwaters of Afon Honddu at the beginning of a magnificent, breathtakingly beautiful downward-sweeping valley.

Before you actually begin this descent you should stop and look back over the broad valley of the Wye, which has been turned south-westwards and now marks the border between Powys's districts of Brecknock and Radnor. The water-meadows are spacious, as they have been the whole way from Hereford. Through them serpentines the river, glinting in the sunlight, seemingly unable to make up its mind as to which side of the valley to favour. At Hay-on-Wye it runs along the south side of its valley; two miles farther on it has looped twice and touched the north side; a mile farther on again it once more shows its allegiance to the south side; but this is for a few hundred yards only, and then it is off again, making for the north side near Glasbury. A wayward stream indeed, this Upper Wye; it is small wonder that it fired the imagination of that fine writer and engraver, Robert Gibbings, and formed the subject of one of his trio of 'river' books. Wayward? You might fancifully excuse it, on the reasonable grounds that, accustomed to a valley career, it was apprehensive about the dominance of the heights on either side: the Black Mountains to the south and the hills of Clyro and Llanbedr to the immediate north.

From the crook of the road at the head of the tight little valley of the Afon Honddu you will see the valley of the Upper Wye at its best, for the sun at almost any time of the day will be shining more from behind you than in your eyes; last thing before sunset, in high summer, you will get an extra-special view of the valley because then the blue and gilt of the water will have been imbued with a deeper, warmer, tinge. To look down upon and across the Wye from the heights of Lord Hereford's Knob, or from Hay Bluff, is an experience not to be missed.

For almost the whole of its length, the valley you are about to enter is a close-set one. The main Black Mountains ridge parallels it closely on its left, rising a thousand feet in a good deal less than a mile, topped by the actual line of the border, which offers a magnificent ridge walk for an enthusiast with sufficient time on his hands. On the right-hand side, not paralleling it quite so closely but still for the most part less than a mile distant, runs the Fwddog Ridge. The average height of the two ridges is the same to within a few score feet at most, and this accentuates the impression you may have of being shut in between the two. Yet the foothills are sufficiently separate one from the other for there to be no risk of a sensation of true claustrophobia.

There is a magnetic quality about these two parallel ridges that almost compels one to divert from the narrow, hedge-bordered lane and, willy-nilly, attempt the adjacent heights. This compulsion is strongest when, as at Capel-y-Ffin for instance, a mountain stream flows down to join the Honddu, the slopes recede a little, and the inducement to explore becomes almost irresistible.

Here you have just passed out of Brecknock into that 'tongue' of hybrid Monmouth that shoots northwards as though minded to separate English South Herefordshire from the pure Welsh lands to the west. It is narrow at this point, not three miles wide from the Black Mountain Ridge across the valley to the steeply flowing mountain stream, the Grwyne Fawr, which forms Monmouth's western border all the way down into the valley of the Usk. This area of the Black Mountains which are actually in Monmouth still has rolling summits not far short of the 2000 foot mark, and it is between Rhiw Arw, to the east, and Bal-Mawr to the west that Llanthony Priory is situated. Its setting is reminiscent of that of Valle Crucis Abbey

St Non's Bay, looking eastwards, near St David's, Pembrokeshire

Coracle fishermen on the River Teifi

far to the north in Clwyd, for both these ancient ecclesiastical foundations are sited in valleys with views from their windows on to mountain slopes and heights. Like the Romans in their day, and for that matter the Iron Age men who built the hill-forts of Dorset and elsewhere in Britain, the monks of the Middle Ages had a genius for selecting an apt and rewarding site.

Cautiously following the valley road southwards from Capel-y-Ffin, for much of the way between hedge-topped banks, you could, were it not for a sign, quite easily pass by Llanthony, for it lies well back off the road at the end of a farm and guest house approach, the two having encroached upon some of the western portions of the priory.

If you are taking the exploration of noble medieval remains seriously then you should try to catch your first glimpse of Llanthony Priory by leaving the road a few hundred yards above it and making your way across an open field immediately to the north of its precincts. From this vantage-point you will obtain the most impressive view by far of what was certainly a most beautiful and noble building when it was completed in the first decades of the thirteenth century; it has remained so to a large degree in spite of the dilapidation that set in after the Dissolution of the Monasteries in the middle of the sixteenth century.

Llanthony Priory was actually established in the very first years of the twelfth century, a hundred years before the laying of the first of the stones that confront us today. Its founder was one William de Lacy, and the story reads like a fable, or a parable from the Bible. De Lacy was a knight who was well in the favour of King William Rufus. Apart from fighting, and attending on his monarch, his pleasure lay chiefly, as did that of so many of his fellow knights, in hunting. In the course of this pursuit he happened to enter the lower end of the Honddu Valley, and he stopped there for a while to shelter from inclement weather in a ruined chapel dedicated to St David, patron saint of Wales. It was while he sheltered there that, as with Saul twelve hundred years earlier, and possibly as much to his own surprise, he became 'converted'. There and then de Lacy vowed to renounce all his worldly goods, his place in the court, his duties as a knight attending on his king, and to devote the remainder of his days to religious contemplation.

His unexpected and sudden decision came to the notice of one Ernisius, who had been chaplain to Henry I's Queen Matilda, and the former chaplain there and then decided to throw in his lot with the former knight. The two men settled in Llanthony, and very soon their piety attracted a number of like-minded men. Between them they built a small church, on the site of the later Priory Church, and this was consecrated within five years of the date, in 1103, when the two men established their small community. Ten years later the settlement was designated an Augustinian priory—one of the first in Britain and actually the first to be so designated in Wales itself. Ernisius became its first prior, and within a very few years there were no fewer than forty canons in residence and the priory came under the direct patronage of Henry and Matilda, the first of a succession of monarchs who donated considerable sums from their exchequers in order that Llanthony Priory could be enlarged and beautified.

Towards the end of the century work was begun in earnest to replace the modest church built by the first members of the community, and its ancillary buildings such as dormitories. In little more than forty years of astonishing activity, it was completed: a presbytery, with chief altar, flanked by two chapels; a north and a south transept; a splendid tower built over the crossing; a nave consisting of three aisles divided from one another by rows of elaborate columns; and a north-west and a south-west tower, with a cloister laid out between the latter and the south transept and chapter-house.

Only a little of all this splendour remains to be seen today, of course, but from your vantage-point across the field to the north you can see the long and graceful north arcade of the nave, with a tower at either end, and there is sufficient hinted at behind these to tempt you to explore the remains more intimately. Within the site you can walk about the cloister and without undue difficulty locate such fundamental features of the whole congeries of buildings as the chapter-house and slype, which leads from it into the south transept, and the canons' choir beneath the crossing tower, the presbytery and the north transept and adjacent north chapel. Here and there you will find no more than the footings to indicate dimensions and proportions; elsewhere the walls rise to head height, even to as much as two storeys. The oldest surviving portions, those that date from the late twelfth century, are the main walls of the transepts and the presbytery; but succeeding builders married-in their work with that of their predecessors with such skill and understanding that there is a wholly satisfying uniformity of both design and execution.

Only the modern adaptations, where provision has been made for eating and drinking and sleeping, mar the general feel of the place; and this only to a very inconsiderable extent. Indeed, you would hardly realise, if you had not been told in advance, that a couple of centuries ago, the south tower was converted by one Colonel Wood into a shooting-box; or that the writer, Walter Savage Landor, actually lived there for some years in the early nineteenth century with the intention of marrying and establishing himself as 'a model country gentleman'. In this, it is said, he did not entirely succeed.

It would be difficult to find, anywhere in Britain, two valleys of comparable length, running parallel with one another and only some six or seven miles apart, more strongly contrasted than the valley of the Afon Honddu, which ends its run, below Llanthony, as the Vale of Ewyas, and Golden Valley, on the eastern flanks of the Black Mountains, in South

Llanthony Priory from the north-west

Herefordshire. Both are twelve or fourteen miles in length and both run
from north-west to south-east; both begin only a few miles south of the
Wye Valley and both have their lower ends in the valley that runs from
Abergavenny north-eastwards to Hereford. But these are only superficial
features that they possess in common; essentially, intrinsically, they are
valleys that belong to two different worlds. And this, of course, is one
persuasive reason for maintaining that this arbitrarily selected region of
mountain and valley.substantiates the claim originally made for it.

Two valleys, near neighbours, but belonging to two different worlds.
You could prove this for yourself in no more than an hour. Twelve miles
down the Honddu Valley from Hay-on-Wye to Llanvihangel; six miles up
the A 465 to Pontrilas; then twelve miles up Golden Valley on the B 4347
and the B 4348 to Bach (sometimes shown as The Bage) and unexpectedly
named Scotland Bank; thirty miles in all, and you have 'done' the two
valleys, one major and the other minor, and their link road! And in so
'doing' them, of course, you will have discovered one obvious fact: that
they are fundamentally as different as any two valleys, especially so close
together, could possibly be. Let us be fair and compare them in the same
north to south direction.

To enter Golden Valley from the north you must first climb up a very
modest gradient, by way of Middlewood to Newton. The hamlet lies

211

midway between the two hills that rise to a thousand feet a mile or so on either side of it. On the lower slopes of Merbach Hill you will find, if you care to go in search of it, the neolithic hummock that bears the name Newton Tump. Immediately beyond Newton, your road crosses the disused railway-line which helps to give you your bearings and at once merges with the B 4348, a bare half mile along which you come to the cluster of houses of The Bage or Bach, a very obviously Welsh name, though on the English side of the border.

Here, as so often, a choice awaits you. The B 4348 continues as far as Dorstone, a mile or two ahead; then, rather unexpectedly, it crosses to the other side of the river and the railway-track, to continue down the valley on that side for some miles (at Vowchurch becoming the B 4347) before re-crossing the river into Bacton to continue its southward run. But back at Bach, at the head of the valley, a branch road bears off to the left, to re-cross the railway-track and, for the first time, the head-waters of the river beneath the hill on which is sited Arthur's Stone. Since this lesser road, and the B 4348, rejoin one another at Dorstone, and since the lesser road affords you the opportunity to go and have a look at this exceptionally fine burial chamber, this is certainly the better choice of the two.

The lane by which you will approach Arthur's Stone is narrow, steep and even in places hazardous.. Hedges and lengths of wall make it impossible to see round many of its corners; but you have little need to worry, for this road is not popular with drivers and it is improbable that you will meet another vehicle, save perhaps on a bank holiday or during the height of the holiday season.

You will come upon Arthur's Stone suddenly, on the right-hand side of the lane, where fortunately there is a hedge clearance and you can momentarily relax. What confronts you is not, of course, Arthur's Stone at all, but the huge capstone and stone supports of a prehistoric tomb, a cromlech which an inscribed plaque informs you is a neolithic chambered cairn of around 5000 to 4000 B.C. So its date is countless centuries earlier than that of the legendary King Arthur. The site was superbly chosen. Standing on the turf from which the massive tumbled stones have been railed off, you look out westwards and southwards over a long reach of Golden Valley and the glorious range of the Black Mountains on the far side, forming a high, smooth, gently undulating skyline that is infinitely satisfying to the eye. There are nobler specimens of these neolithic tombs in many other parts of Britain, notably those of Trethevy Quoit and Lanyon Quoit in Cornwall; but Arthur's Stone has the distinction of being the sole specimen in the whole county of Hereford and Worcester.

By now, the river flowing at the foot of the rounded hill that carries the burial-chamber on its breast is large enough to have been given a name. It is the River Dore. The origin of place-names is usually debatable, but it is probable that the word here used is no more than an Anglicised variant of the Welsh word *dwr*, meaning water. South Herefordshire is so close to Wales that a great number of its place-names, particularly in its western areas, smack of Welsh rather than of English. Quite often two names stand side by side, topographically adjacent but otherwise distinct. Michael-church, and neighbouring Rhyd-ddu-bach, for example. Yet the Dore flows through Golden Valley, and it is evident that at some point—no one can say with any exactitude when this was—someone named the valley on the easy assumption, not that the origin is Welsh *dwr*, but that the river's name was a corruption of *d'Or*, literally 'golden'.

At Dorstone you again have a choice of roads. The better of the two, because it is the lesser of them, lies on the right bank of the Dore, running south-eastwards for three or four miles to Peterchurch, where it rejoins the B 4348 by re-crossing the river again to the opposite bank. Now the hills to the west have receded somewhat, and lessened in height generally; the valley is beginning to widen appreciably. At no point, of course, is it comparable in dramatic structure with that of the Afon Honddu; but it does not widen substantially until you come to a point half a mile or so to the south of Peterchurch, where Trenant Brook flows gently down off the hills to join the Dore. The miniature valley in which it runs is easy enough to accommodate a minor road that dips down into the main valley from Urishay Common, two miles or so uphill and a by no means exacting challenge. Parallel with it, a couple of miles down the valley, is a better road that runs downhill from Michaelchurch Escley to Turnastone and Vowchurch, twin hamlets whose small churches stand close together, one on either side of the river.

Inevitably with names such as Turnastone and Vowchurch, and so close one to the other, they are linked by a common story. Two sisters, so tradition maintains, were rivals in good deeds but unfortunately lacked true Christian humility. This is demonstrated (if the story is to be believed) in the fact that one sister said to the other: 'I *vow* my church shall be built before you *turn a stone* of yours.'

True or not, the two churches are charming specimens of thirteenth- or early fourteenth-century building, though both of them have been altered and added to since their foundation six or seven centuries ago. Turnastone's church offers a fine example of wagon-vaulting in the roof of its nave; and Vowchurch has a low-slung roof supported on oak posts, the inspiration of one John Abel, who was responsible also for the beautiful Jacobean communion-rails and screen installed in the second decade of the seventeenth century. Vowchurch is one of the many riches of Golden Valley that you come across so unexpectedly: memorials to the genius of men who lived and worked and died so many centuries ago in so remote and lovely an area.

Two or three miles beyond Turnastone and Vowchurch, where the road becomes the B 4347, you will come to Bacton, another of these Golden

Valley villages strung out along the gilded thread of the Dore, each one of which has something individual to offer. In this little church there is an effigy in alabaster of one Blanche ap Harry, whose name, among the first to surrender to English usage, was shortened to Parry. She was Gentlewoman-in-Chief of the Privy Chamber to Elizabeth I of England, and served her in one capacity or another until she died in 1589 at the age of eighty-two. Devoted to a queen whom she had served, in fact, since the queen was little more than a baby, her memorial-stone pays tribute to this. It is inscribed in the not unusual fashion of self-commemoration:

> . . . My time I pass'd away
> A maide in Court, and never no man's wyfe,
> Sworne to Quene Elizabeth's bedd-chamber allwaye,
> With Maiden Quene a Mayd did end my lyfe.

Her tomb is an impressive one for so small a church. Beneath the stone arch the cloaked figure of Queen Elizabeth, in full skirt, with ball and sceptre in hand and crown on head, gazes outwards into the church; on her right, facing her, looking at her mistress rather than on visitors to the place in search of her memorial, Blanche Parry kneels, hands clasped before her in gesture of service, her head not bowed but raised as though conscious of the respect due to her. By an odd freak of design, the head of this kneeling figure is on a level with that of her sovereign, who is standing. Is there some significance in this? Did the anonymous sculptor who created this memorable still-life-in-stone seek to establish Blanche's importance to her employer by this unobtrusive but impressive disproportion?

Now the road has crossed once more, and for the last time, both river and disused railway-line. A mile to the south and you come to Abbey Dore. You are right, of course, in supposing that the village is named from an abbey, though you will not find an abbey there today. But there was one. The Cistercian Order founded an abbey there over eight hundred years ago, in 1147. It throve, as did other abbeys in this and other parts of Britain, until the Dissolution of the Monasteries, when it suffered much the same fate as the rest of them. Its bells, incidentally, were salvaged and later installed in the church at Madley, a few miles to the north-east of Abbey Dore, where they may still be heard ringing on Sundays and Feast Days.

Nevertheless, you will in fact find a church at Abbey Dore and, though superlatives are at all times dangerous terms to handle, there are many connoisseurs who will unhesitatingly declare that this is one of the finest of the smaller churches, if not the finest of them all, in these border lands. It was built on the site of, and partly of the masonry from, the original Cistercian church, the focal feature of the abbey, under the sponsorship of Lord Scudamore and at the inspiration of that fine builder, architect and craftsman in stone and wood, John Abel. It was consecrated, and dedicated to the Holy Trinity in the year 1634.

Between them, Lord Scudamore and John Abel converted the remains of an ancient abbey church into the most memorable ecclesiastical feature of Golden Valley or indeed of the country for many miles around, though today it is known by the humbler name of Parish Church. Beautiful in itself, it lies in the heart of orchard country, the smiling open southern end of a valley whose beauty is made manifest in its first furlong or so beneath the slope that carries Arthur's Stone and increases in scope and variety with every delectable mile succeeding that first tentative furlong.

A couple of miles beyond Abbey Dore, by way of Ewyas Harold and Pontrilas, the river debouches into the Monnow, just where this larger river makes an almost violent south-eastwards turn from its hitherto north-easterly course that has brought it to Llangua and the Monmouth gap. The Monmouth border runs along it by way of Kentchurch and Grosmont to Skenfrith and Monmouth, twelve miles or so away: another valley, lying to begin with between the heights of Garway Hill and Graig Serrerthin, though soon it is to open out spaciously as it runs into lower-lying ground.

For many centuries this was always hotly disputed territory. To the west of the River Monnow lay Wales; to the east was England. The Normans coveted Welsh territory just as the Romans had done ten centuries earlier. But they were more assiduous in their efforts to acquire and retain territory than the Romans seem to have been in their day. Their technique was the standard one for medieval times: thrust strongly into any territory desired; establish bases there; fortify the bases and entrust them to powerful knights who would thereafter hold them against whatever odds might develop. The castles that survive reveal, by their condition, the ups and downs of fortune which swayed against and within their massive walls. In this region, the ancient Manor of Upper Gwent, on the west bank of the Monnow, three outstanding castles survive to this day, with history incised in their mouldering walls.

Of these, the first that you will come to as you enter the valley of the Monnow, just below Kentchurch and only a mile south of the main road, the A 465 from Abergavenny to Hereford, is on the B 4347, the continuation southwards of the Golden Valley road. Named Grosmont (and the name neatly combines an indication of its size and its site), it dominates the tiny hamlet of the same name, close to the water's edge just where the Monnow describes a violent, almost a hairpin-bend, to edge its way beneath the towering mass of Graig Serrerthin.

Grosmont Castle was one of a trio of castles all of which were built in the early years of the thirteenth century to replace the first strongholds established by the Normans when, towards the end of the eleventh century, they had penetrated thus far into Wild Wales and, temporarily at least, thrust the even wilder Welshmen that much farther westwards and away from conquered and occupied England. The other two castles are Skenfrith and Llantilio, the latter known also, and often indicated on the

Church at Abbey Dore

map as 'White Castle'. The three 'Trilaterals', as they are sometimes referred to, form an exact equilateral triangle, each being just five miles from its two neighbours.

Inevitably, of course, the passage of time, between seven and eight centuries, and long, bitter and sustained warfare between Welsh and Normans and their successors, has meant that the once magnificent castles have sadly deteriorated. But there is still sufficient of the masonry standing to give a clear and forceful impression not only of the strength of the original building but of the skilful utilisation of the site and its potentialities demonstrated by the military architects responsible. The bailey, or courtyard, at Grosmont is contained within a massive curtain-wall laid out in three equal lengths, with drum-towers at their intersections and an immense gate house at the south end. This consists of a vaulted passage no less than forty feet in length and topped by the remains of what was originally a two-storey building.

As you pass through the gateway you will find that the whole of the bailey is on a level substantially higher than that of the ground that surrounds the castle. The earth and rock used for this raising of the interior of the castle precincts no doubt came from the moat which surrounds it, taking the form of a perfect horseshoe with its tips united by one straight length. The moat is dry today, but was doubtless kept filled in the heyday of the castle by water extracted from the Monnow that runs close by on its eastern flank. You can still see the pit in which the counter-balance weights of the original drawbridge were lowered and raised. Needless to say, the main fortifications face westwards, challenging the men of Wales to do their worst.

Grosmont was designated a 'Royal Castle', and is known to have been visited from time to time by Henry III and his immediate successors. A century after it was built it had to face the most formidable challenge in all its long history, the sustained siege by Owen Glendower in 1405, which was only brought to an end by the personal intervention of Prince Henry and his relieving forces. If you are historically inclined you will find Grosmont an absorbing place; and you can of course read of it in far greater detail than would be appropriate here in the guide-books devoted to the subject and the period. But even if you are not particularly interested in history, you must still be deeply impressed by the feel of the castle precincts and its relationship with the setting in which it was so discerningly established.

Five miles farther along the valley, if you are still in search of Norman-built castles, you should turn left off the road you have been following and on to the B 4521. This minor road will take you directly, and in less than a mile, to the village of Skenfrith. It is on the east side of the village, close to another of these violent changes of direction that the Monnow so often makes, that you will come upon the second of these Trilaterals, Skenfrith

Castle. It is without question the most impressive of the trio, and certainly the largest in area.

You will be confronted by an irregularly shaped quadrangle whose greater axis is some eighty yards long and smaller axis about fifty. The diameter of Grosmont, by contrast, even with its encircling moat, was hardly more than sixty yards in all, and considerably less than that within its encircling walls. Skenfrith's walls are buttressed by five massive towers, one at each corner and, as you might expect, the extra one midway down the westward-facing wall, the one challenging the Welsh.

The dominating feature of the whole complex is, as usual, the keep. This great mass is circular, and stands roughly in the centre of the bailey, though somewhat to the south side; it stands on a *motte*, the customary mound of earth and stone artificially raised by Norman castle builders when such a feature was not already part of the selected site. Originally, of course, this raised mound of earth was simply strengthened by a heavy timber stockade and topped by a round or square fort of the same material. It could be built quickly, and would stand up to a considerable onslaught; but it inevitably had to be replaced by masonry as assault weaponry became more deadly. In any case, timber works were always hopelessly at the mercy of assault in which fire was used.

The Skenfrith *motte* is still some fifty feet in diameter at a height of fifteen feet above the general level of the quadrangular bailey of which it formed the central feature. On it stands what now remains of the keep, a three-storey building of immensely solid masonry with, as was so often the case, a basement hollowed partly out of the earth and rock on which the tower was built. One comparatively unusual feature of this keep is the remains of an external stairway, originally housed in a turret that carried it right up to the top storey; it is probable that the castle's commandant, or governor, had his private quarters here.

The castle at Skenfrith was built so close to the river that the water actually flowed beneath the eastern run of the curtain-wall. The other walls were flanked by an artificial moat some forty feet wide and buttressed with stonework. Over the centuries this has inevitably tended to become filled in, so you may not always find it easy to trace its line except by following it along the footings of the north, south and west wall lengths. If you look carefully, you may still be able to pick out the section of low wall near the south-east tower which was part of a system of sluices designed to trap water from the river close by and lead it into the moat to keep its level up to what was regarded as necessary when there were continued threats from the Welsh.

Curiously enough, the third of the trio does not stand close beside the river but some five miles to the west of it: farther, that is, into Wales. To locate it you must now retrace your route along the B 4521, past the junction with the road that led you southwards from Grosmont. Another five or six winding miles will bring you to the junction with another, and much smaller, road, just short of Llanvethcrine, which is signposted Llantilio Crossenny—another hamlet, incidentally, like those in Clwyd Vale, whose name is wholly disproportionate to its size. Less than a mile down this winding road you will come to Llantilio Castle, on your right, just where the road makes a dog's-leg turn. It is the least impressive of the Trilaterals, so it may seem odd that it should be the only one of them to have been awarded a nickname. The name 'White' derives from the fact that until comparatively recent times—recent, that is, by the time-scale of seven-centuries-old buildings—it still revealed extensive areas of white plaster-work which, if it had ever been included in the design of the other two castles, has certainly long since been lost and forgotten.

These are the only castles within the frame of our three-hundred-square-mile region, but there are of course others that lie only just outside it. Since the Welsh border country has always been a turbulent and potentially explosive area, it would be surprising if this were not so. King Offa of Mercia recognised this in the latter half of the eighth century, and so had his famous line of demarcation 'drawn' by turf wall and ditch from the Bristol Channel to the north coast of Wales, the unique 'Offa's Dyke'.

Ten miles or so outside the frame that has now been explored in some detail you will find, for example, Croft Castle. But this is certainly less obviously a castle, as ordinarily understood, than the Trilaterals in Monmouth; in fact, it is more of a fortified manor house, and is actually occupied by its owners. In the opposite direction, and well out of the area being explored, six miles and more to the south-east of Skenfrith, is Monmouth Castle. And farther away still, well into South Herefordshire and dominating a loop of the Wye near Symonds Yat, is Goodrich Castle, very well worth a visit before you finally turn away from this region.

The glutton for castles will find his time and effort well repaid at Goodrich. It lies just off the A 40, some four miles south of Ross-on-Wye. Unlike Grosmont and Skenfrith, it is magnificently sited on a spur of rock high above the right bank of the river; it was in fact built on this site in order to command an ancient and vital river crossing. The theory is strengthened by the fact that the village close to this river site is Walford—originally Wales-ford, or Welsh ford.

It might be as well to visit Goodrich Castle after, rather than before, visiting the Trilaterals, for it is a finer castle in every respect. There is more of it, to begin with; it is easier to grasp what its original design was; and the design itself is more impressive from every standpoint. Built in the twelfth and thirteenth centuries by Godrick Mappestone (whose first-name it bears, in corrupted form), it consists of a spacious bailey enclosed by massive walls, largely of red sandstone, which are themselves buttressed by three huge corner bastions and are pierced by a gateway protected by a barbican in a splendid state of preservation. The oldest part of the fabric, as so often, is the keep, an enormous rectangular edifice rising through three storeys and with one of the grimmest of medieval dungeons in its base. This is the only part of the whole castle that compares in stature and impressiveness with the gate-house barbican. You may well feel, if you have by now inspected the Trilaterals, and possibly Croft Castle in the north and Monmouth Castle to the south-east, that you have reached the apotheosis in such medieval remains when you pass through the ten-foot-thick semi-circular wall of the barbican to cross over the moat and enter the bailey by way of the gate house. Goodrich is a formidable experience; the memory of it will haunt you long after you have left the district in which it is without question the dominating feature.

It should not of course be supposed that the area deliberately selected to illustrate the resources of this Brecknock-South Herefordshire-Monmouth complex is alone worth exploration; such is far indeed from being the case. If you have enjoyed most the beauties of Golden Valley you may perhaps have followed the wider valley of the Wye that runs south-eastwards parallel with it just on the other side of the narrow range of hills, lower by far than the Black Mountains to the west. At Tyberton you may perhaps have taken a look at the fourteenth-century cross in the churchyard, with its engraving of Mary and the Child Jesus on one side and the Crucifixion on the other. From there you may have taken yet another of these winding and inviting roads southwards, one that crosses the A 465 to Hereford and leads you to another 'lost' hamlet, that of Kilpeck. Here you will find one of the most remarkable medieval doorways to be found anywhere, not merely in South Herefordshire but in the whole of Britain.

This valley village merits something more than a casual visit; but charming as it is in itself, its focal point is of course its church of Saints Mary & David. It was built as long ago as 1134, on a site given by William of Normandy to his henchman, William FitzNorman. The site, as the name of the village suggests, is more ancient by far than the Norman Conquest. Where 'kil', or one of its several variants, appears, the name has almost always come from an early British 'cell', or holy place. In this instance it was the cell of St Pedec, one of the earliest and perhaps least-known of the holy men who came from the far west to preach the Faith to the hitherto unenlightened. Though the main fabric of this lovely little church is Norman, there is evidence of earlier, Saxon, work to be seen in it, notably in the buttress on the north east side of the nave.

Such restoration as has proved imperative has been most skilfully and unobtrusively carried out. Indeed, there is surprisingly little of it, in view of the extreme antiquity of the church. It may in fact be said to stand in virtually the same condition in which it was when the last of the mason-sculptors laid down his mallet and chisel and went on his way to new work. There are features of the exterior which suggest to experts that the master mason, and possibly one or more of the men who worked under him, were members of the medieval Hereford School of Sculpture. Certainly some of them were humorists; you have only to glance upwards at the corbels surrounding the whole building beneath the eaves to recognise this truth. They are, almost every one of them, ornamented by grotesque heads and faces which seem to be laughing or sneering, mocking or disapproving, rarely appreciating what goes on beneath them. Gargoyles of course, are a feature common to most medieval churches and cathedrals; those of Notre Dame in Paris are world-famous. But these at Kilpeck, though admittedly on a lesser scale, are hardly less deserving of fame; for individually they are of quite astonishing force combined with fantasy.

The great glory of Kilpeck's church, however, is of course the South Portal. You will go far to find a single doorway that is richer, more elaborate, in its symbolic sculpturing, even in any European cathedral however famous, than this one. At first glance the detail confronting you is almost overwhelming; but it resolves itself, if you will only contemplate it patiently, and with an open mind, into the successive episodes of a 'story'.

The two door-jambs represent the Garden of Eden, the Temptation of Man, and his succumbing to the suggestion from Eve that he should partake of the fruit of the Tree of Knowledge both of Good and of Evil. On the capital at the head of the left-hand jamb there is a bold representation of a struggle between a lion and a dragon. Beneath this the Serpent, emblem of Evil, is sculptured with its tail uppermost and its head downward, symbolising the ultimate defeat of the Father of Evil, the Prince of Darkness. Intermingled with the figures on the door-jambs are some in costume that will surprise: figures wearing jerkins of mail, trousers, and headgear which is recognisably Phrygian in style. One of these somewhat unexpected figures represents the Church, as may be deduced from the fact that he holds a cross in one hand and a branch of palm in the other; State, as might be expected, brandishes a sword, but with his other hand he is, oddly enough, bestowing a blessing.

The capitals support a tympanum which incorporates the story of the Creation in astonishing detail. Birds, beasts and fishes are artistically intertwined with one another, inset in circles and scrolls that curve over the outer of the two concentric arches; beneath them, its ornate branches occupying the half-circle above the lintel, is a stylised Tree of Life. The whole conception is a rare and extraordinarily impressive example of medieval carving at its most liberal, imaginative—and professional. There is, too, artistry combined with craftsmanship of a rare order between the two door-jambs: the wrought-ironwork of the great hinges and door handles is comparable with that to be seen at Stillingfleet, in Yorkshire, also still *in situ*; and no tribute could be higher than that.

Far to the west of the frame in which these three-hundred square miles were contained, the mountains of Brecknock invite those for whom the

Kilpeck church – the south doorway

Black Mountains had an appeal stronger than that of the wide valleys and level pasture-lands of true South Herefordshire, with its dairy-farming acres and its hop-growing industry. Turn west, then, beyond Brecon itself, and pick up the A 470 to Merthyr Tydfil. Eight miles along that south-bound road, beneath the shadow of Cefn Crew, after passing the Brecon Beacons, which so nearly touch the 3000-foot mark, on your left, take the right-hand fork, the A 4059 to Aberdare. After some five miles you will see, slanting sharply back off your road on your right-hand side, a small road signposted to Ystradfellte, a village small even by south Brecknock standards. Here you will find the secluded valley, or minor gorge, of the Afon Mellte, a little river that tumbles headlong down between and over the rocks as though impatient to join the more leisurely waters in the Vale of Neath.

The best way to follow a river or stream, of course, is always along one or other of its banks. In the case of the Afon Mellte this is not too easy a thing to do, for it is such a tempestuous little stream; it is still busily carving its way, as it has done for aeons of time, through the close-set sides of a rocky gorge. Here and there, it is true, you can come quite close to it without actually wetting your feet; more often, if you are on the alert for the particular sound of music it makes, you can come upon it from the top of its gorge and look precariously down upon it as it sweeps and tumbles over step after step of rock.

It is at its most spectacular at the Clyn-Gwyn Falls, where it seems to spurt out of the rock itself, rather than flowing over it, and tumble downwards, step by dramatic step, leaving in its wake the occasional deep pool of water that, by contrast, gives the impression of being frozen into dark green immobility. Half a mile or so south of Ystradfellte it takes a leaf out of the book of the River Manifold on the Derbyshire-Staffordshire border and vanishes altogether in the gigantic Porth-yr-Ogof Cavern. But it is not lost for ever; it reappears again and continues briskly, if erratically, on its way to join the Neath.

Brecon folk will tell you that the Afon Mellte, though so small, is the most excitingly romantic river in the whole of Brecknock. Comparisons may be odious, so the partisan claim can be left without challenge. If you have the time, and the inclination, you might well try out some of the many other streams that tumble and sparkle among the mountains, and come to a decision of your own, without prejudice. In any case, mountainscape and valley: the choice here in the south-east corner of Wales and adjacent South Herefordshire is demonstrably wide.

SOUTH-WEST WALES

The first part of this chapter concluded with a tantalising glance westward from the Black Mountains; westward, that is, across the central and far country of Brecon Beacons National Park, uplands which are themselves southern tailpieces of those Cambrian Mountains that for all practical purposes line the whole north-south length of Wales. The problem here, in this high, open, brown and green land, is that roads are few and exploring thus becomes a matter of taking to your feet. Not that this necessarily matters. What does matter is that whether you are on foot, riding a pony or driving a car, exploration becomes a matter of scenery, and long distance scenery at that, rather than of specifics. All the same, as you journey westward from Kilpeck, or from whatever other place to which your exploration of the border country may have led you, there are some very worthwhile diversions away from the obvious A40 or A465, roads, both of them, in themselves of no more than passable scenic and other merit.

Brecon to Carmarthen

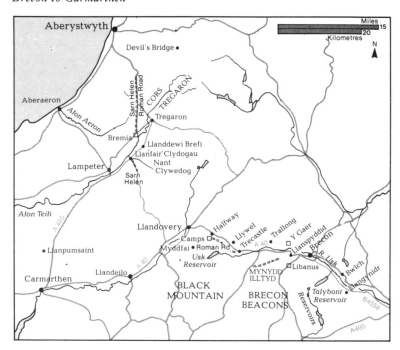

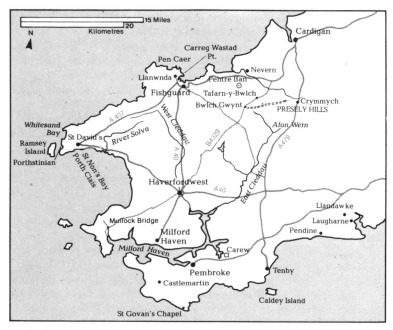

Pembroke

You might, for instance, aim for high-perched Bwlch halfway between Brecon and Abergavenny, thence dropping steeply to Llangynidr with its pleasing four-arch bridge across a lovely reach of the Usk. Here you can follow the B 4558 north, to break away at Talybont on to a forest road skirting a succession of reservoirs with names as musically Welsh as you could wish: Talybont, Pentwyn, Neuadd (two here) and Pontsticill, a string that surely disproves the adage that man can never improve on nature. This is no road to get you west even moderately fast, even less so if you are seduced by the Forestry Commission's enticing picnic sites and walks, but it is a road that will start you most pleasantly on your way. Neuadd reservoirs, by the way, are not actually on this road but up a short diversion northwards; one well worth making, not only on scenic grounds, for here you break out of the forest on to open moorland, but also because it leads you to a corner of travel history. That track lifting gently away to what is popularly and, as you will see, for obvious reasons known as The Gap was for centuries right up until the nineteenth the main horse and coach road from Brecon to Merthyr Tydfil and before that the Romans' way to their fort near Brecon, to them Cicutium but now simply Y Gaer, the Fort. And this fort is another place you would surely not regret seeking out on your drift westward. Surprisingly little visited, perhaps simply because it is on private land and permission should be sought at the nearby farm, you can, with any luck, stand alone within walls that once sheltered the Vettonian Spanish cavalry and the 2nd Legion.

By now, it may well be that the Brecon Beacons have enchanted you so much that you want to learn more; something which can be achieved by heading for the Mountain Centre, at 1000 feet on the upland common near Brecon, known as Mynydd Illtyd. Filling much of the western angle enclosed by the A 40 and A 470, it can be approached by car from either direction and you will find that not only is the Centre immensely and attractively instructive but also that the common itself with features spanning from prehistoric times to the twentieth century (a buried pipeline, a section of the oil link between Milford Haven and the Midlands) is well worth some pottering exploration. And you could well be almost alone here, for nine visitors out of ten choose the easier road from Libanus on the A 470 and, surprisingly, do not venture far beyond the Mountain Centre on the common's southern edge.

Obviously St Illtyd is the person who counts here, largely, it seems, on the strength of two stones and a small hollow long known as Bedd Illtyd, the Grave of Illtyd. But Illtyd was a distinguished scholar—a contemporary praises him as 'the most learned of all the Britons in knowledge of the scriptures'—and founder in about the year 500 of the famous teaching monastery of Llantwit Major, and for such a man this seems an unlikely spot in which to have ended his days, especially since there is reason to suppose he may have died in his native Brittany. However, no such doubts deterred the Victorians who built the nearby church and dedicated it to Illtyd in the belief that it was he who founded the first church on this site some thirteen centuries earlier. Yet, whether or not it was Illtyd, some holy man of Illtyd's time was certainly here, for this church stands within a circular boundary typical of a Celtic early Christian 'llan'—as good a reason as any for having a look at this place even if the church itself is locked, as it almost certainly will be. 'Llans', one might here explain, were enclosures of land granted by local lords to the much respected holy men, or missionaries, who thronged Wales during the Dark Ages; in Latin they were known as *Sancti*, a word which of course slid readily enough into Saint.

But there is more than just Illtyd up here on this inviting common. The hill-fort of Twyn-y-Gaer, for instance, where ancient cairns tell us that men were here long before the Iron Age builders of these ramparts and ditches; three standing stones, enigmatic as all such are but, since they more or less align, perhaps early route or boundary markers; the course of a Roman road, their Sarn Helen, a name which romantics trace to the lovely Helen. She was the Welsh lady of the Roman commander in the west, the Spaniard, Magnus Maximus, who accepted the title of Emperor from disaffected local soldiery and later, as Macsen Wledig, found his way

Mynydd Illtyd

into Welsh legend. (The less romantic argue that 'Helen' is suspiciously akin to the Welsh word 'heol', meaning a road.) On private land just off the western edge of the common, stands a castle motte still bearing fragments of a strong round tower which may have played its desperate part in Llewelyn the Last's doomed campaign to repulse Edward I.

To reach the south-west from Mynydd Illtyd the A 40 is the obvious if not the only choice, a wooded and undulating road along which the outside world tends to hurry, impatient for what awaits at the end, without the time or inclination or, to be charitable, perhaps without the knowledge to discover what lies to either side. Yet there are rewards enough for those content to settle for a relaxed pace and a criss-cross course.

Just after leaving Brecon you might, for instance, walk into the churchyard at Llanspyddid to seek out the gravestone said to be that of Brychan, that Dark Ages chieftain who has bequeathed his name to this whole lovely district. His pious daughter Tydfil was murdered, soon becoming a saint and also bequeathing her name to Merthyr Tydfil on the southern edge of the Brecon Beacons. Then there are the churches at Trallong and Llywel, both known for the Ogham stones which they shelter, one at Trallong and two at Llywel, although one of these latter is a replica of the original which is in London's British Museum.

It is worth a little attention, this intriguing Ogham script of short strokes either side of a horizontal or vertical line, for what you are looking at is the oldest known written form of Gaelic, the early writing used by the so-called Goidelic Celts, those people from the Danube basin who, perhaps four centuries before Christ, settled in Ireland (as opposed to their Brythonic, or British, kinsmen who either chose England and Wales or, more likely, were driven ashore here). There are many explanations as to why this essentially Irish script is found in Wales—Irish traders, Irish raiders and settlers (the Irish in fact ruled parts of the south-west for several centuries in the Dark Ages), Irish missionary priests. These particular stones date from around the fifth century A.D., the one at Llywel commemorating—and also in Latin—a certain Maccutrenus Salicidunus who, for all his resounding name, seems to be unknown in any other context. Look closer and you will find a small cross carved between the two words. It is said to post-date the Ogham and Latin by perhaps two centuries and must surely arouse speculation in anyone with some curiosity; perhaps some pious and superstitious descendant wanted to confer belated Christian respectability and salvation on a forebear he suspected of being a pagan. It may be that after seeing these stones you feel that you would also like to see the earliest known example of inscribed Brythonic, that is, of the early native Welsh. And this you can certainly do, although you will have to go a long way north and west, to Tywyn on Gwynedd's coast, where you will find what you want on St Cadfan's Stone in the church of the same name.

At Trecastle, just short of Llywel, it might make sense to stop and have a look at the map because there are two inviting possibilities to the south, one Roman and prehistoric, the other scenic and prehistoric. The Roman camps of Y Pigwn, at some 1400 feet and in lonely country, are, as the crow flies, only about a mile south of the A 40; the human approach, though, and most of the way on foot, is either from Trecastle in the east along the Roman road or, shorter, from the village of Halfway. Earthworks are about all you will find here—if your eye is attuned, one camp can be traced within a rather larger and slightly later one—but this is hardly surprising since the camps were thrown up at the very beginning of the Roman occupation, in perhaps A.D. 50 to 80, and were in any case only temporary. Look just to the east of the camps and you will find stone circles, evidence of man's activity here perhaps 2000 years before the Romans came along. Not a bad-weather objective, this, nor one for those bored by the Romans, but a fair-weather excuse for walking in some fine country. Usk Reservoir, nearly two miles long and banked by woods, is a less demanding diversion and one that can be made by car using the minor roads which work their way west from Trecastle. Here, if you look to the south of the south end of the dam, you will find a standing stone said to be the largest in the National Park and to weigh perhaps twenty tons.

From Usk Reservoir you can map-read yourself across the northern slopes of the Black Mountain—or Y Mynydd Ddu or Carmarthen Fan as it features on some maps—to reach Llandovery by way of the village of Myddfai. Should you, though, decide to continue along the A 40 you will find something very different indeed, even if it is yet another stone. A warning as relevant today as it was when erected, it stands beside the road about a mile and a half short of Llandovery and recalls the fate of a coachload of passengers spilt down the hillside when their drunken driver lost control of his team.

Christian churches within the confines of Roman forts, though rare, do turn up from time to time, and when they do must always command attention if only as examples of contrast, of how something essentially arrogant, pagan and warlike now shelters something humble, Christian and peaceful. The Saxons built a church within the mighty walls of Rome's Richborough. St Gybi did the same within the more modest fort at Holyhead. In both these cases there are still substantial Roman walls. But the venerable church of Llanfair-ar-y-Bryn, on its hillock immediately north of Llandovery, has only grassy earthworks. Yet there is a more evocative feel here than at other places, and, what is more, the pagan Romans have actually contributed to this church because you may pick out some traces of the distinctive Roman brick below the east window and in the north wall.

The boundary of Brecon Beacons National Park is drawn just east of Llandovery and Llandeilo beyond, but well before these places you will become aware that you have been dropping gently off the upland on your way to sea level at Carmarthen, southern gateway to Wales's south-west. The northern gateway is less easy to identify. Some would place it at Aberystwyth; others, imposing a far tighter definition, as far south as Cardigan. But it matters little, and for present purposes we will trace a line from Carmarthen through Lampeter and Tregaron—up the luxuriant and peaceful Teifi valley, that is, below the slopes that lift away to the east— and embrace all that fans out to the south-west and west of this datum.

Here is a land far removed from the high brown hills and snug, enclosed valleys you explored on the borders. Except for the Presely Hills—almost absurdly out of place but nonetheless welcome—this is a rolling, largely agricultural and wooded countryside, subdued rather than assertive and interlaced with a complicated network of little roads and lanes serving countless equally modest towns and villages, few of which, it has to be admitted, are of great character. To find character we must look to the many rivers, as quietly lovely in themselves as they are in their names. To the north coast flow Ystwyth, Aeron, Teifi and Nyfer; to the west, Solva and Cleddau; to the south, Taf, Cynin, Gwili and Twyi.

But it is the coastline which spotlights the essential difference between Wales's south-east and south-west. That along the south-east is shunned as urban and industrial, the land of cities such as Newport, Cardiff and Swansea, of the dying giants of steel, coal and shipping. That of the south-west is so beautiful that it has been designated a national park all the way round from Cardigan to Tenby and beyond.

Let us, then, look first at that baseline from Carmarthen and up the whole upper length of the valley of the Teifi. Next, at three chosen corners—the Presely Hills; Pen Caer above Fishguard, a lost clifftop which once experienced disturbing happenings; and that sainted peninsula around St David's. And, finally, at the southern quarter of the Pembroke peninsula across which we will linger at a number of places at which surprisingly few visitors seem to trouble to stop.

Carmarthen, so Merlin (or Myrddin, to give him his native name) prophesied, will fall down if or when the ancient oak in Priory Street falls down. So, since it is on your way out of town, you will of course want to satisfy yourself that the future is assured. What you will find is a sorry stump, well enough shored up with concrete and protected by an iron railing, good for a few more years perhaps but with no great promise of immortality. Why Merlin should have saddled Carmarthen with such a precarious future has never been explained. After all, this was his birthplace, scene of his royal mother's seduction by a spirit which took the form of a man, while Bryn Myrddin, just to the east, claims (as do of course a score of other places throughout Britain) to be where he rests.

For the next twenty miles or so, as far in fact as Lampeter, there is little enough to take your attention. Except, perhaps, after six miles, a sign to Llanpumsaint, the Church of the Five Saints. The saints—Ceitho, Celynen, Gwyn, Gwyno and Grynnaro—were brothers, sixth-century members of the leading Welsh family of Cunedda, and even given this semi-royal lineage one cannot but concede that this mass sanctification was no mean achievement. A signpost, this, to provoke a moment's thought, but not necessarily one to be followed, for although the drive is a pleasant one through meadows and woods the church at the other end will almost certainly be locked. However, should you manage to get in, you will find that the medieval altar bears no less than nine consecration crosses.

This Llanpumsaint should not be confused with the far better known Pumsaint almost twenty miles to the north-east on the A 482; better known because it is the site of famous Roman gold mines beside their important Sarn Helen which you may last have discovered as a trace across Mynydd Illtyd in the Brecon Beacons. Here, alongside the gold workings, now in the care of the National Trust, an ancient stone bears five indentations said to have been left by five saints—Ceitho and his brothers no doubt—who rested here and used the stone as a pillow.

On the outskirts of Lampeter you can escape from the main road and choose either of two quiet and pastoral minor ones ascending, but very gently, the right and left banks of the Teifi, a river on whose lower reaches that strange and timeless craft, the coracle—little changed from its Iron Age shape, some say—may occasionally be seen and which is also said to have been the last refuge in Britain of the beaver, though this was many centuries ago. It matters little which road you choose, though if you have an interest in hill-forts you should opt for the right bank since this one passes below no less than three (if the map word Castell has any meaning), all minor and all in fact more enticing in their names—Olwen, Allt-Goch, Goetre—than in themselves. But both roads soon reach the village of Llanfair Clydogau where the little Clywedog feeds the Teifi. Like Pumsaint eight miles to the south, the village is on the Roman Sarn Helen and is also the site of important mines, here silver rather than gold. Of these, though, no trace survives.

Sarn Helen soon crossed the river, but you will do better to keep to the B 4343 along the left bank which will quickly enough bring you to the fascinating church at Llanddewi Brefi, at which point you should be reminded that Dewi means David.

By church standards today's structure is not all that old—its tower is mainly of the twelfth century—nor is this church what it once was, since much of it, notably the two transepts, collapsed during the nineteenth century. What, rather, should claim your attention is the mound on which the church stands. Archaeologically and architecturally, this is certain evidence of a very early Christian foundation—whether or not you accept that this ground miraculously heaved up to provide St David with a platform when he came here to address a synod in 519. It must, indeed, have been a startlingly theatrical occasion since in addition to this convenient earthquake the Holy Spirit took the form of a dove and perched on David's shoulder, encouraging him to speak with a voice like a trumpet. Inside the church your interest is most likely to focus on the venerable stones at the foot of the tower, one, the tallest, known as St David's Staff, another bearing an Ogham inscription. But this latter has been sadly mutilated (it has been suggested that it commemorated a heretic of the persuasion David came here to condemn) and you will find better examples at Trallong and Llywel, mentioned earlier, or at St Dogmael's and Nevern on the coast south-west of Cardigan.

Be all this as it may, by a long way the most intriguing, indeed challenging, corner of this church is the north-west exterior of the nave, immediately above what was once the boiler house. Here, if you look up, you should be able to pick out two stones—or, rather, two pieces of the same stone—forming part of the fabric of the church and bearing, in one case almost upside down, fragmentary Latin inscription. Llanddewi Brefi indeed owes much to a scholar of 1698 who saw the stone, then presumably free-standing and intact, recognised that it dated back to long-lost centuries, and recorded the full inscription. It then read: 'hic jacet idnert filivs jacobi qui occisvus fvit propter predam sancti david'. Or, translated: 'Here lies Idnert son of Jacobus who was slain because of the plunder of the Sanctuary of David'.

Idnert is generally accepted to have been the murdered Bishop of Llanbadarn Fawr, parent village of Aberystwyth and seat of a bishopric until merged with St David's in the eighth century, but what is important here is not Idnert's identity but that this is the earliest known inscription referring to St David, one carved moreover within a century or so of when he was here. The tragedy is that during the eighteenth or nineteenth centuries the nave needed repair and the mason responsible—presumably illiterate, certainly no antiquarian, but professionally quick to spot a useful stone—broke it up and incorporated its pieces in the wall. Thus, today, only two separated fifths of the original can be seen, the remainder probably lying elsewhere in the wall with the inscription tantalisingly buried inwards.

There is in fact yet another stone here at Llanddewi Brefi, again only a fragment, but one identified as a part of the gravestone of a Roman soldier, doubtless a member of the garrison of the nearby fort of Bremia which provided patrols along this important section of Sarn Helen close to where it crossed the river. You can get to the fort, such as it is, by crossing the Teifi on to the A 485 and then bearing left to pass the junction with the B 4578 which, as is proper for a Roman road, comes in arrow-straight from the north. Almost immediately beyond this junction you take the second lane on your left, cross a tiny humped bridge over a disused railway and arrive at a farm where you can ask permission to visit the fort. Today, to the layman anyway, it is no more than seemingly haphazard banks and ditches together with a few sorry stones which represent the baths.

Your road northward—the A 485 if you have been to Bremia, otherwise still the B 4343—soon brings you to the small town of Tregaron, beyond which something very different awaits, for the landscape changes as suddenly as it does strangely. South below Tregaron the Teifi flowed through a pastoral, wooded and gentle valley; now it snakes sluggish, indecisive and lost to view across the centre of a peat bog—four miles long and up to a mile or so across—which owes its origin to a shallow lake formed here twenty thousand years ago at the close of the ice ages. Now a national nature reserve officially christened Cors Tregaron, the bog also enjoys the rather grander name of Cors Goch Glan Teifi (The Red Bog along the Banks of the Teifi), a name which surely must have been bestowed in autumn time, the season when the dying cotton sedges take on their deep red hue.

A place such as this is of course primarily of interest to naturalists, and even they require a permit to penetrate the inner reserve, but there is also much that the casual passer-by can both appreciate and learn. All you need do is park your car in a layby on the B 4343 two miles north of Tregaron and climb the few steps up on to the disused railway embankment which has in fact so far effectively hidden the bog from view. Now it is laid out before you; and, if you want to learn something about it, you have only to pay a small sum for an admirable Nature Conservancy Council booklet which you will find in an honesty box (the booklet tells you the story of the railway too) and set off as far as you feel inclined along the track which in a mile or so reaches an observation tower and bird-watchers' hide.

Our next chosen area, the Presely Hills, is contained within a fat pouch of the Pembrokeshire Coast National Park hanging southward between Cardigan and Fishguard. More precisely we are concerned with what lies within the boundaries of the coast on the north, the B 4313 along the west, the National Park boundary across the south from Greenway as far as the A 478, and this same A 478 providing the eastern confine. Across the centre, from south-west to north-east, diagonals the B 4329, generous with its views and a painless key to much of the obvious best of Presely.

But just what are these Presely Hills, or Mynydd Preseli, or any of a choice of other spellings? Physically, they could be said to be the last southern outriders of the Cambrian Mountains, that rather vague range running the length of Wales which, though named on most maps, is better known for its parts than for its whole. As such, Presely lifts, in places surprisingly abruptly, to 1760 feet above the surrounding pastoral landscape, an open, wide-shouldered brown moorland picked out with rocky outcrops not dissimilar from the tors of Dartmoor.

The slopes are easy and inviting, the views long, but there is more to these hills than just the exhilaration of open spaces, for Presely also offers much that is unexpected: as a sacred land of prehistory, as a setting for legend, and as an ancient trade route.

You have only to glance at a large-scale map to see that this whole area is exceptionally rich in those prehistoric monuments which can surely have had no other purpose than that of religious ritual. Standing stones, tumuli, cairns, stone circles, burial chambers, they are all here, indicating – proving one may indeed say – that these hills were, over perhaps millenia, a region revered far and wide as one of sacred and ritual mystery. And, if such be needed, there is even stronger evidence, for it was Presely that provided many of the megaliths for faraway Stonehenge and it seems highly improbable that people of perhaps three or more thousand years ago would have dragged and rafted all those stones weighing around four tons each over a distance of perhaps a hundred and forty miles solely on account of some geological suitability. The compulsion can only have been a religious one. But why these hills were sacred, and in honour or dread of what god or gods—these are questions unlikely ever to be answered.

As to legend, it was across Presely that Arthur and his companions, including two of his sons, hunted Twrch Trwyth, the monstrous boar which had once been a king until punished for his evil ways. Stand on Foel Cwmcerwyn, or Presely Top as this highest point is often marked, and you stand where Twrch Trwyth turned at bay, killing eight of Arthur's men, including his son Gwyrdre.

But if Presely had a religious significance it also had a commercial one. Around 1500 B.C. the people living on and around Salisbury Plain, the descendants of those who had sought the megaliths for Stonehenge, established a route which crossed Presely to reach Whitesand Bay beyond St David's, whence frail craft took them across to Ireland in search of the rich minerals of what we now know as Wicklow. Their path is still here today, generally known as the Bronze Age Track although other names point to later users. The Roman Way, for instance, though there is little evidence that they were here; the Pilgrims' Way, a far more convincing name because Presely lies athwart the approach to St David's, two pilgrimages to which equated with one to Rome; even the Flemings' Way, which may sound pretty puzzling until one recalls that in the early twelfth century Flemish colonies were planted in the Pembroke peninsula by Henry I. Perhaps Yr Hen Ffordd (The Old Road) is the best choice, simple, comprehensive and Welsh.

The track's principal section links Crymmych on the A 478 (it actually starts at Croesfihangel tumulus about a mile to the west) with Bwlch Gwynt, or Windy Pass, on the B 4329 a short way north of Greenway; six bracing moorland miles, plus some more if you make the diversions without which you would of course be missing much of the point of being here. A contrail may linger against the sky, a flash from a car's windscreen may catch your eye, the occasional forestry plantation may have locally changed the scene, you may pause beside traces of slate workings—but ignore such intrusions and your world will be little different from that of the prehistoric people who passed this way, their thoughts focused perhaps on setting up a ritual circle or lone stone; perhaps on laying a relative to rest in some communal burial chamber; perhaps, more mundanely, on the impending hazards of the crossing to Ireland and the profit likely to be made there. Of all these activities, except the last, you will find evidence. Foel Drygarn became an Iron Age hill-fort fifteen hundred or so long years after the blue dolerite for Stonehenge was sought here, as also at nearby Carnmenyn and Carnalw; cairns on Foel Drygarn, on Foel Cwmcerwyn and that of Carn Ferched all represent burial; Bedd Arthur, or Arthur's Grave, with its oval of stones, was a sacred site two thousand years before Arthur's time.

But, for one reason or another, this walk will not be for everybody, and it is a good feature about Presely that the hills, though not of course their detail, can be well seen by the motorist. The obvious road, the one mentioned earlier, is the B 4329, the key point along which is Bwlch Gwynt, the broad and open pass where the road is crossed by the Bronze

Age Track. Here you will certainly wish to stop—there is plenty of grassy, informal parking space—if only to enjoy the view. And, should you feel more active, you have a choice of rewarding directions; eastwards, perhaps, skirting Pantmaenog Forest until in about a mile you reach its corner below legendary Foel Cwmcerwyn, or westward, where the burial cairn crowning Foel Eryr may tempt you at least to start the not too demanding climb to 1535 feet.

However, despite its B classification, the B 4329 can be quite a popular road. You will get far closer to the true feel of Presely if you map-read your way along the adventurous minor road which hugs the southern slopes of the hills, its eastern half well within the National Park while its western marches with the border itself. Starting from Crymmych you drive first south-west and then west, within your first mile passing between the tumulus and burial chamber which mark the start of the Bronze Age Track. These are minor sites, though, features which set the tone of Presely but not much else, for the tumulus is an indifferent survival close to farm buildings while the burial chamber, hard to find in a bank to the left of the road, is little more than collapsed stones. Part through fields, part across moorland, part unfenced, this road gives you the best of two worlds; above you the promise of the brown hills, below, the wide green valley drained by Taf and Eastern Cleddau on their way to Dylan Thomas's Laugharne and the oil companies' Milford Haven.

About halfway between Crymmych and Greenway, at a lonely unfenced spot in open country where you cross the little Afon Wern at the boundary of the National Park, you should look up to your right where you will see two fine standing stones. They bear—locally, anyway, if not on your map—the almost regal name of Cerrig Meibion Arthur, the Stones of the Sons of Arthur. As you will doubtless have found in many places elsewhere—at Arthur's Stone, for instance, above Dorestone on Wales's eastern border—the name of Arthur is widely associated with prehistoric sites which were there literally thousands of years before that hero's time. The explanation lies in bardic legend and the hold which such legend, and especially that central figure, Arthur, held over Dark Ages and medieval people unable to grasp a time-span even as far back as the Romans, let alone beyond. Here, then, are two stones, archaeologically prehistoric but, if you prefer legend, monuments to those two sons of Arthur slain in their gallant but vain attempt to prevent the escape into Cornwall of the savage boar, Twrch Trwyth.

The sites around Presely are almost countless, if not always easy to reach, but there is one burial chamber you should not miss, a place which is archaeologically important, easily accessible, well signed and which lies in glorious country. It is called Pentre Ifan and to reach it you descend one mile north-east from Bwlch Gwynt to Tafarn-y-Bwlch, whence you follow minor roads northward for a couple or so miles. Dating from as long ago as 3000 B.C., yet with its fourteen-ton capstone still resting on its three supports, Pentre Ifan is remotely and appropriately sited on an open hillside, rocky moorland outcrops above, the tumbled summit of Carn Ingli with its Iron Age settlement filling the west, and below, a green countryside sloping towards the distant sea. There could be no more fitting conclusion to your exploration of Presely.

Westward from Pentre Ifan, the hills drop gently enough to Fishguard Bay, with the town of the same name on the grassy cliff above. An unpromising objective for exploration you might well protest, a place quickly enough identified for its ferry to Ireland but not readily striking any other chord. Yet Fishguard is associated with one of the most bizarre farces in British history—or in French history for that matter—and it is to try to capture something of the feel of this that you will have come here. You might start by asking yourself when was the last occasion on which Britain suffered foreign invasion. The Normans, some would doubtless say. Others might suggest the Jacobite ventures of the '15 and '45, or even that strange incident in 1719 when three hundred Spaniards, supporting the Old Pretender, landed in Scotland's Glen Shiel. But all would be wrong. The correct answer would be 'The French. Fishguard, 1797'.

The French plan—the destruction of ports such as Bristol and Liverpool and the fostering of revolution—was born of wishful-thinking and a lot grander in concept than in the measures taken for its execution. Command was given to a septuagenarian American adventurer, William Tate; his army amounted only to some 1400 men, most of them convicts offered the choice between gaol or military glory; apart from Republican zeal, the officers' only qualifications seem to have been inexperience and incompetence; and the invasion fleet comprised no more than four small ships. Finding himself off Fishguard, Tate ordered one of his ships into the harbour, from which, however, it quickly beat an undignified retreat, seemingly unaware that the battery that fired on it was equipped only with blanks. The invaders then withdrew to Carreg Wastad, on Pen Caer immediately to the west, at which highly unsuitable spot they landed, though not before eight men had been drowned when one of the boats capsized. After the landing the commander of the advance party, a young Irishman aged nineteen and with a more distinguished name (Barry St Ledger) than gift for disciplinary control, chose Trehowel as a suitable headquarters. Stocked ready for a wedding it certainly suited the soldiery who, as did other contingents elsewhere, proceeded to maraud, loot and drink themselves incapable.

Amid the general panic, only two locals attempted to stem the invasion, both being killed, and it was not until the energetic Lord Cawdor, a leading Pembroke landowner, organised resistance that the Welsh rallied. This show of strength was too much for the invaders—one story tells that they mistook a group of Welsh women, costumed in their tall hats and red cloaks, for military redcoats—and Tate, doubtless influenced by the fact that his rabble was threatening to shoot him if he didn't, sued for peace. To Lord Cawdor must go the credit for what is surely the quickest ever repulse of a foreign invasion. Tate landed at 5 p.m. on the 22nd of February and signed his surrender in Fishguard's Royal Oak Inn at 10 a.m. on the 24th.

The stage on which this Opéra Bouffe was played—the Pen Caer peninsula which forms the west side of Fishguard Bay—was then, and still is, lonely and sparsely inhabited country, steep above a rugged shore, dry and stony with narrow lanes below high banks and hedges. Not, as you will quickly judge when you get there, a land off which even an army such as Tate's could live for long, even less a place in which to ferment revolution.

You may plan to follow the fortunes of Tate, St Ledger, Cawdor and Jemima Nicholas (about whom more below) chronologically, but before you set off for Carreg Wastad it seems only fair to reveal that much can be achieved at the Royal Oak Inn, surely the only public house in Britain in which a whole campaign can be studied without stirring from the bar! For this inn was Cawdor's headquarters; it was here that two French officers came under a flag of truce bearing Tate's offer of surrender, and it was here that he signed that surrender. Today, at the bar, you can buy an admirable booklet-history of the invasion, and, while you enjoy your drink, you can see the table on which the surrender was signed and also souvenirs such as a French officer's water bottle, the bell rung to warn the town, and a French musket.

From the inn you can move on to adjacent St Mary's Church where you can get another glimpse of those stirring three days, in the form of the headstone of Jemima Nicholas 'The Welsh Heroine who boldly marched to meet the French invaders', personally capturing no less than fourteen Frenchmen. Aged forty-seven, a cobbler by profession and, it is reported, of brawny build and fearsome mien, she must indeed have been a daunting opponent. And the story must be true, for she was awarded a pension of £50 a year, a considerable sum for those days, enjoying it for thirty-five years until her death at the age of eighty-two.

On your way to Pen Caer you drop sharply to Goodwick with its marsh and sands, and here you might well pause to picture the scene as the excited locals of nearly two hundred years ago crowded these hills to watch the French march in to surrender their arms. Never since has Fishguard known such a day.

Up on Pen Caer, the greater part of which lies within the Pembrokeshire Coast National Park, the obvious objective for anybody prepared to walk a short distance must be Carreg Wastad, where a stone commemorates the landing. Stand here, perhaps make your way down to the water, picture this place in mid-February, and you will readily see how unsuitable a spot this was (not that Tate had much choice, given his inexplicable

Memory of
JEMIMA NICHOLAS
OF THIS TOWN,
"THE WELSH HEROINE"
WHO BOLDLY MARCHED TO MEET
THE FRENCH INVADERS
WHO LANDED ON OUR SHORES IN
FEBRUARY 1797.
SHE DIED IN MAIN STREET JULY 1832,
AGED 82 YEARS.
AT THE DATE OF THE INVASION SHE
WAS 47 YEARS OLD, AND
LIVED 35 YEARS AFTER THE EVENT.

ERECTED BY SUBSCRIPTION COLLECTED AT
THE CENTENARY BANQUET JULY 6.1897.

Jemima Nicholas memorial

determination to land somewhere along this rugged stretch of coast) and why it proved impossible to get any artillery ashore. On your way here you will pass the hamlet of Llanwnda whose trim little church, dedicated to an obscure saint called Gwyndaf, was attacked by the drunken Franco–Irish rabble and looted of its plate, a scene of violence hard to associate with this tranquil, lost corner. Giraldus, whose *Itinerarium Cambrense* of 1188 gives such a homely picture of the Wales of his day, was for a while rector here.

Having exhausted the oddities of the Fishguard invasion, you can move south-westwards to the peninsula of St David's, a shift of a mere seventeen miles in distance but, at any rate so far as the story of Wales is concerned, one of twelve centuries of time. To say that the sun does not shine here would be less than fair, and doubtless indignantly refuted by the locals. Yet more often than not the memory is of an austere place, of a terminal landscape which either cowers before a relentless wind or rests dank and chill within enveloping mist. And David himself is a figure in keeping with this peninsula which bears his name; a shadowy character about whom virtually nothing is known (what few records we have are suspect propaganda associated with later disputes over who should rightfully be bishop), yet a man who not only became Wales's patron saint but also achieved the rare distinction of both Celtic and Catholic canonisation.

St Non's Bay, half-a-mile due south of the village-city of St David's, could well be your first objective. It is not a promising road at first, a narrow turn out of the village centre past a hotel, but the houses soon give up, a cattle-grid is crossed, and there, below a parking place as pleasant as it is convenient, is the bay on the shores of which, if tradition is accepted, David was born in the opening years of the sixth century. His mother, we are told, was Non, who may have been a daughter of a chieftain called Brechan; his father Sandde, a member of that noble family of Cunedda which we have already come across in connection with the five saints of Llanpumsaint. Was Non a nun seduced or coerced by Sandde? Was she married to Sandde, becoming a nun on the latter's death? These are but two of the stories, and you can take your choice as you sit here above the gentle slope down to a modest green clifftop with, halfway, a chapel and a holy well. The well, at any rate as a natural source, must surely be at least contemporary with David's birth, a spring which could hardly fail to achieve sanctity as soon as this bay became accepted as the birth site. The chapel is also genuinely ancient and, in fact, in the care of the Historic Buildings and Monuments Commission; precisely how old, nobody knows, but pre-Norman for sure, while experts cite the primitive stonework around the south-west angle as typical of very early Christian construction indeed.

Should you want to continue to follow St David chronologically—along the path of tradition, that is, for there is nothing else—you should now make your way to Porth Clais, a creek hardby to the west, preferably on foot along the scenic clifftop, the way Non and her infant would have travelled. Here the future saint was baptised, at a spring beside the narrow, green-banked mouth of the Alun, an inlet later to become the harbour serving the monastery he founded and today the pretty home of small pleasure craft which cluster below the rough remains of a harbour wall that recalls the prosperous nineteenth-century days of coal and limestone.

Now, go north a short mile, then west another one, to reach Porthstinian, the second half of the word being a contraction of Justinian, the saint associated with Ramsey Island which breaks the view close offshore. A Breton nobleman, Justinian became a hermit on the island and also David's confessor and close friend, an association which led him into one particularly black adventure. Told by some sailors that his friend was sick and in need of his help, Justinian accepted their offer to row him across the mile-wide sound. Halfway across, however, he decided that these sailors were so ill-visaged that they must surely be devils, so he recited Psalm 79, whereupon (doubtless at the words 'Pour out thy wrath upon the heathen') the sailor-devils turned into carrion crows and flew away, a relieved Justinian presumably rowing himself the rest of the way. But it was to be a short-lived victory, for the thwarted devils later returned and took possession of Justinian's three servants (it seems that eremetical life was not without its comforts) who on their master's return attacked and beheaded him. Yet, even decapitated, Justinian remained resourceful, his arms retrieving his severed head and burying it at a spot which promptly became a place of miracles—though only for a brief period because David soon disinterred his friend's remains and moved them to a shrine in his new church.

It is sad, indeed, that, apart from the place's name, the only physical reminder here at Porthstinian of this doughty man should be a neglected, roofless chapel, a charmless relic of the sixteenth century which may or may not be successor to an earlier dedication to the saint. For the rest, Porthstinian is a picturesque corner where low green cliffs enclose an intimate bay in which the most dominant, if hardly aesthetic, feature is the lifeboat house perched high above its long slide down to the water. Beyond, Ramsey beckons, today a nature reserve known more for its flowers and seals and birds than for its sanctity and safely accessible without danger of devil-sailors.

Tradition associates David with many places—with Roman Caerleon, for instance, and Arthurian Glastonbury—but it seems that it was behind the sweep of Whitesand Bay, just north of Porthstinian and now a popular beach, that he founded the monastery out of which would grow the bishopric of St David's.

St David's represents both Wales's smallest city and its largest cathedral, the latter, together with its great ruined bishops' palace, coming close to filling narrow, steep-sided Glyn Rhosyn, the site, more genial than

Whitesand Bay near St David's

windswept Whitesand, to which David transferred his monastery in about the year 550. Stand on the hilltop beside the part-ruined gatehouse and look down, and you will be surveying what many consider to be the finest, largest and most satisfying medieval assemblage in all Britain; no trace, sadly, of whatever modest structure David may have built (today's cathedral is essentially a Norman achievement of the late twelfth century), but this site was of his choosing and, were he able to return, he surely would approve the undiminished sanctity of the cathedral.

Down there in the cathedral you will find much of both beauty and interest. But it is the see's founder who has been claiming your attention in this corner of Wales, and to complete his story you should make your way eastwards the length of nave, choir, presbytery and sanctuary into what is known as Bishop Vaughan's Chapel where, in the wall separating the chapel from the sanctuary, you will find a recess containing a coffer. Restoring the cathedral in the nineteenth century, Sir Gilbert Scott stumbled across this recess, then walled up, opened it and revealed that the mortar held human bones—bones which soon came to be accepted as those of David and Justinian, long the objective of veneration but assumed to have been hidden here during the iconoclasm of the Reformation. So here your pilgrimage ends, beside the coffer sheltering the saintly remains of the man whose life began less than a mile away at St Non's Bay and those of his murdered friend. Daunting characters they must have been, too, but also, tradition forces once to suspect, somewhat dull; Justinian, who refused to settle on Ramsey until two women said to be there had been removed, and David, dubbed 'Aquaticus' because water was all he would drink.

We planned earlier to round off our time in south-western Wales by exploring something of the southern quarter of what is loosely known as Pembroke; not so much the major features in which this district is so rich—features such as Pembroke's mighty ridge-perched castle in which the future Henry VII was born; or Manorbier Castle, birthplace and home of the scholarly Giraldus; or the tourist Mecca of Tenby—but rather some less obvious corners, less well-known but nonetheless not a whit less worthy of attention and each one astonishingly different from its predecessor.

St Govan's Chapel, for example, a place which both geographically and chronologically is as good a starting point as one could possibly select. You will already, for sure, have come across many a ruined chapel in Wales— there was one near Din Lligwy on Anglesey, and those down here in the south-west at St Non's and Porthstinian should be fresh in the mind—but it has to be admitted that, architecturally at least, many chapels can be disappointing. The local story is frequently as lost as is the original structure, and all that is left is a plain rootless and roofless rectangle, as likely as not a late medieval rebuilding on ancient foundations, sheltering perhaps some unidentifiable graveslabs of priest or knight. This Chapel of St Govan, though, is in every way—in atmosphere, story, structure and setting—a deeply satisfying exception.

You will, if you are lucky, find the chapel on the south shore of the Castlemartin peninsula, the north shore of which edges the long and historic anchorage of Milford Haven, once a channel of tranquil beauty but now to be avoided unless your interests embrace the oil industry which, however necessarily, has planted the land with refineries and pierced the natural course of the channel with the long Meccano-like jetties which provide the giant tankers with their terminals. The caveat 'if you are lucky' is necessary because the chapel lies close to a military Danger Area and access may be barred, but assuming, as is probable, that the way is clear, then you can drive to within a few yards of the cliff edge. On foot, you then literally go over the edge, to descend steps hewn within a narrow and precipitous cliff soon blocked by this surely unique chapel. Seemingly wedged into position, part construction and part cut into the cliff's rock, its steeply pitched roof and grey walls of local stone merge intimately and humbly into the surrounding scenic grandeur which with

St Govan's Chapel

its sheer drops, caves, clefts and lone limestone stacks ranks as perhaps the most spectacular stretch along the Pembrokeshire Coast Path.

But how old is this place? And who was Govan and what was he doing here? As to structural age, much if not all the stonework may be medieval replacement of some much earlier original, but there can be little doubt that the rock cell and well, the latter now dry but once able to grant your wishes and heal your afflictions, are very early Christian and, we may surely accept, contemporary with Govan. And, surprisingly perhaps, we do know who this worthy was, even if the events leading to his choice of this remote and perilous spot may strain our credulity. A sixth-century Irishman from Wexford, where he was abbot of Dairinis, he came in old age to Pembroke intending to live out his closing years as a contemplative hermit. Walking along these cliffs (and here legend takes over) he was attacked by ruffians, whereupon, in response to his prayer for help, the cliff opened, folded gently around him, and then opened again as soon as the terrified attackers had fled—leaving any good Celtic 'sanctus' with little option but to build his cell on this spot. He died in 586, and in a setting such as this one can readily accept that his remains lie below the stone altar. Indeed tradition is even more explicit, claiming that the fissure you will find in the cell is the precise one in which the saint was hidden.

Perhaps it is the sheer spiritual genuineness of this place that most appeals. Other chapels and holy wells occur along pilgrimage routes or within the many bays known to be safe havens during an age when, whether merchant or pilgrim, it was often more prudent to entrust oneself to the known perils of the sea rather than to man's lawlessness on land. Whether purpose-built or shrewdly developed out of some earlier foundation, such chapels and wells were pressed into serving the needs of a stream of pilgrims who required, or were easily enough persuaded that they required, both spiritual and medicinal encouragement. Doubtless there was holiness in plenty; but doubtless also there was superstition, and with it, gullibility and attendant commercialism. St Govan's Chapel has nothing of this. No pilgrim path passed this way, no sailor would willingly approach cliffs such as these. This chapel can only have been the refuge of some deeply pious recluse.

In miles it is not far from St Govan's Chapel to Carew Castle, a mere nine to the north-east, but the two places are centuries apart in time and an immeasurable span in spirit. There is nothing humble about Carew, built for war and three times remodelled for sumptuous living, and it is indeed for this duality of use as also for the castle's charming situation on a gentle green rise beside the tidal Carew creek that the place is of such interest. Drum towers, massive walls, and on the east flank, an outer curtain and a cunning narrow barbican recall the demands of battle, but within their defences the early Carews of the thirteenth and fourteenth centuries built a manor, of which little survives. Then in 1480 the castle was mortgaged to

View of Carew Castle from the north-east, across the Carew Creek

Sir Rhys ap Thomas, a man who engages our attention as much for his character as for his constructional work here. The latter is represented by the Great Hall with its porch and stairway, perhaps already completed by 1485 when Sir Rhys entertained Henry Tudor shortly after his landing near Dale at the northern entrance to Milford Haven. But had Sir Rhys really sworn to Richard III that if Henry attempted to pass through Pembroke it would only be over his body? And was he really so devious that he squared his conscience by lying under a bridge over which Henry would have to ride? Some authoritative books discount the story, but smoke means a fire of some kind and Mullock Bridge is still there—in modern form a shallow doubling among high reeds—and, as one crosses, it certainly adds entertainment to picture the powerful lord of Carew precariously clinging below. Be this as it may, Sir Rhys chose the winning side and a few years later Carew with its surrounding meadows was the setting for a glittering five-day-long tournament held to celebrate its master's investiture with the Order of the Garter.

In 1558 another colourful character came into possession; Sir John Perrot, rumoured to be a bastard of Henry VIII. Honoured as a bearer of the Canopy of State at the coronation of Elizabeth I and later a ruthless Lord Deputy in Ireland, he died in the Tower, to which he had been committed on charges trumped up by his enemies. Violent, brutal, delighting in physical strength, a raffish brawler. These are among the terms used to describe Perrot; terms, though, which are not easy to associate with the man who, although he died before the work was completed, effectively converted Carew into a palace and who conceived the graceful long windows and oriels that so soften and grace the castle's riverward face.

Without a detailed map you will not easily find Llandawke, a hamlet hiding along blind and narrow lanes in the heart of the little-visited country between the A 477 (the stretch from Red Roses to St Clears) and the A 4066 linking Pendine with Laugharne below the coastal escarpment. Yet no one with any feel for medieval and primitive churches should miss this place where the little thirteenth-century example, though sadly no longer in regular use, is as simple and evocative as any in Wales. It shelters an ancient stone, inscribed in Ogham and Latin some seven centuries before this church was built, and also the fourteenth-century effigy of a lady, perhaps Margaret, sister or daughter of Sir Guido de Brian, the local lord. The honorific of Saint which she sometimes enjoys seems to be a purely local canonisation, and if today the lady looks a little worn this is because she spent centuries out in the churchyard before being brought under cover.

Appropriately, we can leave south-west Wales remembering representatives of our own century, two of them also Welsh heroes, albeit in very opposing spheres. Today the name Pendine sounds an anything but glorious note, unless of course you are a holiday-maker in tune with caravans, cafés and souvenir shops. Yet in the 1920s and 1930s the five miles of firm beach known as Pendine Sands was synonymous with high courage and adventure, and if you can arrange to be out there on those long, wide sands when the crowds have retreated and the Ministry of Defence is inactive, then you may perhaps recapture something of the thrill of those days when Malcolm Campbell and the Welshman J.G. Parry Thomas between them five times assaulted the world's land speed record until Parry Thomas was killed here in 1927, in which same year his rival achieved nearly 175 m.p.h.; when, too, in 1933, Jim and Amy Mollison coaxed their frail and heavily-laden craft into the air in their attempt to reach New York non-stop, only to be defeated thirty-nine hours and forty-two minutes later when their fuel ran dry in the last sixty miles. To us, such achievements may seem paltry, but these visitors to Pendine were the pioneers who made possible the motoring and flying we now accept as commonplace.

At Laugharne, which you should pronounce 'larn', the hero is very different and very Welsh; Dylan Thomas, to whose simple grave and unpretentious home overlooking the broad and ever-changing tidal estuary admirers make their pilgrimage. But you do not have to be a Dylan Thomas enthusiast to enjoy this quiet, out-of-the-way waterside town, for there are some unusual things here—the tower of the town hall, for instance, which houses a strange little lock-up furnished with a wooden bench and built-in pillow; or, in St Martin's Church, the remains of a prehistoric man, a very early Celt one might say, a man who may have lived in one of those hut circles you have explored and been laid to rest under one of Wales's ubiquitous barrows.

IO

The Cotswolds

Perhaps no two people will agree exactly as to the boundary-lines of that delectable region of England loosely referred to as The Cotswolds. It derives its name from the range of uplands that average some six hundred feet above sea level, rising here and there to over a thousand feet, and are named on the map as the Cotswold Hills. But though these hills run from near Bath north-eastwards for some fifty miles to Chipping Campden, what most people mean by The Cotswolds consists of an area of about five hundred square miles sloping generally downwards to the east from the main escarpment near Cheltenham into the lower-lying region that bestrides the Gloucestershire-Oxfordshire border, to rise again in a sickle-like curve of higher ground to the north and east of Chipping Norton.

You could mark this out, roughly, as a quadrilateral having its two western corners near Evesham and Cirencester, respectively, and its two eastern corners just to the west of Banbury and Oxford. The border between the two main counties zigzags from north to south roughly half way across the area, the larger of the two portions being in Gloucestershire. Along the southern border of this area flows the Thames, eastwards from its disputed source at Thames Head, just south of Cirencester (Seven Springs, not far away, being the challenging rival source, though this has now been officially rebutted by the Thames Authority). In the northern part of the area Warwickshire makes a tentative but unimportant inroad for a mile or two.

It is thus a region of uplands interspersed with open valleys, of sequestered hamlets and rolling wolds, carved leisurely by the inexorable tools of time in the oolitic limestone belt that runs diagonally across England from the Dorset coast much of the way to Flamborough Head on the north-east coast. From the western escarpment of the Cotswold Hills you can look out over the estuary of the Severn, over the Forest of Dean, towards the hills of Powys; you can also look north-westwards across the Vale of Evesham to the Malvern Hills, which were ancient long before the sculptor had even started his work on the limestone on which you are standing. And you can look eastwards over one of the most beautiful and least spoiled (in spite of its popularity) regions in all Britain.

It is spanned by relatively few roads of any great load-carrying capacity. Close to its true centre lies Stow on the Wold. From this quiet township, it is true, eight roads radiate, spokewise, though none of them could be called a trunk road. One of them is the old Roman road, the Fosse Way, A 429. It runs northwards into the Midlands and southwards to Chippenham, in neighbouring Wiltshire. The A 436 runs south-westwards to merge with the Cheltenham-Bath road somewhere near Stroud. It runs eastwards, too, but only to become disheartened before reaching the Rollright Stones and Long Compton of the witch's prophecy.

The A 424 runs southwards for ten miles or so, but comes to an end at Burford. And no wonder, in a township of such abundant charms: who would want to proceed any farther into the southernmost Cotswolds— save perhaps to take in Eastleach Martin and Filkins and Broadwell?

The Cotswolds

There is one other main road, the A 44 linking Evesham with Chipping Norton: but this road by-passes Stow on the Wold on its north side, to take in Moreton in Marsh ('the' is customarily, but erroneously, inserted in this place-name), Bourton-on-the-Hill and Broadway. One other road of consequence does cross the Cotswolds. This is the A 40, which links Cheltenham with Oxford, forty miles away astride the Thames, under its alias, Isis; this road, happily, by-passes Stow-on-the-Wold to the south, though it comes all too close to lovely Burford.

These main roads afford easy access to and across the Cotswolds, dropping hints as to the rare treasures to be found but for the most part discreetly by-passing them so that they shall not be unduly disturbed. It is of course along the threads of the spider's webs that have been spun between each road and its fellow that the dew-pearls are to be found. But before actually leaving these roads, which for the most part tend to cling to the upper levels, the flowing ridge-lines, the higher contours, it is well worth making use of them, if only in their useful capacity as pointers to what awaits you once you have abandoned them.

There is something else, too, that justifies you in lingering deliberately along these busier roads. It is from this that you derive the most rewarding encounters with that basic and most characteristic feature of the Cotswolds: the drystone walls. For these walls not only bound the roads at sufficient distance to be appreciated as it were expansively; they can also be seen curving across the upper wolds, dividing field from field, forming enclosures, encircling stands of beech trees, linking copse with isolated copse in a diminishing perspective. They are, in themselves, stone ribs protruding through the flesh of these wolds, emphasising their contours, epitomising their strength, speaking eloquently of their essence, their origin.

The Cotswolds are of course not unique in the possession of hundreds of miles of this walling: a similar feature is characteristic of the whole of the Pennines, a hundred miles and more to the north. But in the Pennines the walls are composed of blocks and slabs of carboniferous limestone—a far cry indeed, both in hue and texture, from the very much later oolitic limestone of the Jurassic Age. No Yorkshireman, Lancastrian or other native of the Pennines, of course, will concede that the drystone walls of the Cotswolds can be compared with those of his region; nor perhaps can they: it is, after all, a matter of taste. But it would be a bold man indeed who sang the praises of his own particular walls too stridently in an alien camp! Carboniferous and oolitic: there is room for them both; but each has its appropriate setting, and between the two regions lie the broad acres of the Midlands, where you will search in vain for walls of either material.

Petrologists and geologists generally will divide and sub-divide the grades of stone that comprise what the ordinary person simply knows as 'Cotswold'. This 'ordinary person'—the loose term in any case is a dangerous one—is not really concerned. It suffices for him that this Cotswold stone, as he may have been told in advance and will certainly discover to his pure delight as soon as he crosses into this particular limestone belt, possesses a rare degree of beauty both in its texture and in the extraordinarily varied spectrum of its tones. It ranges from pale grey (softer by far than the characteristic weathered grey of the Pennine stone) by way of milk-white and cream, primrose and buttercup, to deepest ochre. And what is more: each of the myriad gradations of hue that this stone possesses can be magically varied by a shifting in the strength or direction of the sunlight that falls upon it from the spacious Cotswold heavens.

You can prove this for yourself, easily and simply. Whether on foot or by car, make a point of entering any village of your choice first from one end and then from the other. Because it is in all probability a village of one single street—curving, as in Upper Slaughter, or straight, as in Stanton— you will pass the same stone buildings first in one direction and then in the opposite. If you have a reasonable mental palette for colour you will immediately note either a greater or a lesser richness of tone in the stonework. If you are taking colour photographs you can record the facts at the time, and check your immediate impressions of the time by subsequently projecting the transparencies on your screen.

Your memory will less often be of the greyish Cotswold stone, delicately beautiful as this is, than of the richer, mellower stone that seems to glow beneath the sun, to radiate warmth that it has assimilated and stored for this very moment of your passing. Only an artist, perhaps, will have the vocabulary to define each successive gradation of stone that may be seen; but it is no exaggeration to state that Cotswold stone at its warmest, especially when seen in conditions of evening sunlight, has a near-incandescent quality; it is almost as though it had been cast in some fiery mould and was only now, after millions of years of life, beginning to cool.

Take a more deliberate look at these walls before you abandon the uplands for the valley and lower-slope hamlets. Though fundamentally all the same: breast-high, wedge-shaped in section, or with a slight 'batter', the courses following the undulations and sinuosities of the ground that bears them, they yet vary in detail. Some of them are composed of stones several inches thick; others of stones the thickness of Roman tile-bricks; others again almost as thin as the standard clay roofing-tiles familiar to us all. The thickness is governed by the characteristics of the quarry, almost always in the immediate neighbourhood, often close to the actual run of the wall, from which the stone was taken. The majority of these walls are old; unless there has been need for further extraction of stone, the quarries from which they derived have long since become turfed over by natural processes and are now little more than curved depressions, saucer- or cup-shaped according to the quantity of material that was taken from them;

sometimes the depression is so slight as to be visible only when the sun is low enough to fill the hollow with thin shadow.

These older walls, and happily some of these more recently built, are usually finished-off with 'cock-ups': roughish, substantial stones set on edge, shoulder to shoulder like heavy books on a shelf, no two of them identical yet in series contriving to present a pleasingly uniform impression. Seen against the sky, on a near horizon where a field curves over close at hand, they present a serrated edge, a *mons serratus* in miniature, you might say, extended lengthwise in either direction. The more recent lengths of wall—entirely new, for example, alongside newly widened roads or replacing older ones—are more usually finished-off with a cement capping smoothly rounded to lend stability and the hope of permanence to the uppermost course.

No true lover of the Cotswold scene accepts this variant with equanimity; he does so, if at all, with resignation, accepting the harsh twentieth-century fact that labour costs have soared astronomically and that to reproduce the cock-up-finished wall, even if craftsmen could be found capable of such skilled work, must add disproportionately to the overall cost of replacement. However, seen especially from a highish view-point, and preferably when the sun is low, the white snake-like course of such a cement-topped wall possesses an individuality that has the power to satisfy the not-too-exacting eye. The old-time Cotswold stone masons—and they were born with the tradition of generations of their ancestors in their bloodstream—accept this new-fangled style of drystone wall capping even less readily than we do.

Occasionally you may be fortunate enough to come upon a stretch of wall that is in process of being built. You will notice the curious wedge-shaped 'crutches' of timber framing that are set up at intervals, each linked to the next by a pair of taut and parallel lines, to ensure that the batter of the wall remains constant and conforms to the traditional proportions. A Cotswold drystone wall, like its starker fellow in the Pennines, must preserve these traditional lines, for they have evolved and proved 'right', and so been retained over generations that run into centuries.

Seen in section, these walls are a good deal more substantial than they may seem at first casual glance. Where the ground is uneven, additional devices have been incorporated to reinforce them, here as in the North Country. Basic among these is the use of the 'through', or 'through-stone', a relatively massive elongated stone laid athwart the run of the wall and protruding for six inches or more on either side. They are usually built-in about two-thirds of the way up the wall, set at intervals that are governed by the varying demands of the terrain. Seen against the sun, or with the sun at a low angle, they are capable of producing a pleasing pattern of knobbly shadow against the cream facade they embellish. They fulfil a secondary function, too: they offer a convenient foothold to anyone wishing to scale the wall, perhaps to follow a beaten path across an unsown field. Indeed, this may well be the origin of the characteristic Cotswold stone stile: a succession of these protruding through-stones running diagonally from left to right up one face of the wall and down the other, from ground level almost to cock-up.

Unhappily there are today long sections of this fine drystone walling, especially that flanking the minor roads, that have fallen into disrepair and have been in that state for so many years, even decades, that they have become engulfed in coarse weed. This straggle-weed is at once fine and tough; it clings as close and remorselessly as ivy. From a distance the effect is as though some giant cobweb has been spun all over the stonework; at close quarters you are confronted with a piece of fine Cotswold crafts-manship that has succumbed to a silent but inexorable foe. It has the power to bring a lump into the throat.

But there is another side to this particular coin. In village after village you will find that where the owner of a new house, or even an older one, has flanked his garden with a newly-built drystone wall he has left space between the parallel sides of the uppermost courses and in-filled this space with good earth. Now his wall is growing gay plants such as primulas, Californian poppies, wall-flowers and marigolds along its length. And of course the actual wall, like the garden rockeries composed of this same beautiful stone, is soon invaded by compact masses of aubrietia and other rock plants.

It is time, though, to leave the uplands, though you will certainly be impelled to return to them time and again, if only for that overall wide view under a wide sky that is so memorable a feature of the Cotswold scene. But it is in the little valleys, and clinging to the lower slopes of the wolds, that you repeatedly come upon the gems of sequestered villages and hamlets linked by their spider's web of wandering, tree-shaded roads, hardly more than country lanes which were originally just tracks beaten out by men and women and children passing between one small centre and another below the level at which the winds blew across open country, fierce and wild. Many of these follow the course of the Cotswold streams (rivers is all too grandiose a word for them)—Windrush and Evenlode (were ever two streams more euphoniously named?), Leach, Isbourne and Churn, Frome, Dikler and Coln, and even smaller, unnamed streams that form their modest tributaries and satellites.

You will come upon one such tracery of lanes, a filigree network of intercommunicating ways, set in the triangle formed by the main roads A 433, linking Cirencester with Burford; A 361, linking Burford with Lechlade; and A 417, linking Lechlade with Cirencester (the Roman Corinium), 'Sister' to the sophisticated and 'Siren' to the locals.

The main A 417 links Ampney Crucis, St Peter and St Mary strung along their Ampney Brook, while within the triangle names such as Coln

St Aldwyns and Eastleach Turville and Eastleach Martin remind you that
the Coln and Leach streams flow here. Only the somewhat unhappily
named Broughton Poggs lowers the standard of euphoniousness among
these sequestered little places; and even that is redeemed by the fact that it
is overlapped by a charming and close-set neighbour, little Filkins (it
sounds like a character out of Dickens), with its interesting Wool Weaving
Centre.

Just outside the main-road triangle that forms the frame for this
network of minor roads lie two more Coln hamlets: Coln Rogers and Coln
St Dennis. To reach these you have to cross to the other side of the A 433;
but this you will do at Bibury, still on the banks of the Coln. Here, though
the village is much better known than most, and thoroughly deserves to be,
you will certainly do well to linger, even though your main concern may be
with the little hamlets strung out along the lesser and rarely numbered
roads.

At Bibury, then, do not content yourself with the famous trout
hatcheries opposite the picturesque and much-frequented hotel; or even
with that lovely sequence of cottages called Arlington Row, now National
Trust property, that tilts down the slope towards the stream. Make for the
ancient church at the foot of the village, screened from you to begin with
by the noble beech trees that largely ring this village, held by many to be
the most beautiful in the Cotswolds. Superlatives are ever suspect, but no
less an authority than William Morris, artist and craftsman, made this
claim for Bibury, and it is a bold individual that will challenge such a man's
judgement in a matter of this kind.

The church of St Mary the Virgin, mainly thirteenth century though its
fabric incorporates masonry of a very much earlier date, recognisable by
the practised eye, is set among trees whose dark foliage beautifully draws
attention to the mellow stonework. To enter the churchyard you must pass
through a stone 'squeeze-belly'. This is incorporated in the wall at the
north-west corner of the churchyard, close to the village school and a
cottage or two whose windows look straight out over the shaven velvety
turf and embedded tombstones characteristic of this particular place. The
term squeeze-belly is self-explanatory: the two upright stones are so set
that you must pass sideways between them. They stand close-to at the
base, but curve outwards; thus sheep are prevented from passing between
them (and this has always been, and remains, sheep-farming country) yet
it is only a very portly individual who might find himself incommoded in
attempting the passage.

Before you enter the church, take a few steps across the level turf in the
direction of the chancel. Just beyond the beautiful Norman north
doorway, beyond the return of the outer wall which shows where aisle and
chancel meet within, you will see clear evidence of the Saxon origins of this
church. Set in the north-facing outer wall of the chancel there is a Saxon

Arlington Row, Bibury

gravestone bearing on its face a most unusual design. It consists of what is known as 'circle-and-pellet', a pattern that definitely indicates Scandinavian influence. The stone stands perhaps five feet in height. On its face there are seven of these interlocking circles, each containing four of the stone 'pellets', though of course two of these are shared by each of the interlocking circles. In fact, this undoubted Saxon gravestone was found elsewhere in the precincts of the church; but it has since been embedded here in the fabric of the wall, and to look at it one would think that it must have been there ever since the day it was carved and piously erected in honour of some dead chieftain.

Cotswold churches generally offer an unmatched feast for those whose interests lie that way; every one of them, however small, however isolated, has something to offer in addition to the sheer beauty of the stone of which it was built and the setting in which it was placed. Eastleach Turville and Eastleach Martin's churches are small in comparison even with the one at Bibury; but they are just about as ancient. In the one at Eastleach Martin you will see, if you care to examine it closely enough, that the roof of the nave is constructed much as a great tithe barn is, of giant elm boughs. The

255

timberwork looks ancient; in fact, it is not yet ninety years old. It came from elm trees felled within the boundaries of the parish and replaces the original timber roof constructed of Cotswold elm seven centuries ago. That the original roof lasted so long is proof not only of the quality of the timber used but of the degree of craftsmanship that went to its fashioning all those centuries ago. Gazing upwards at it, you may be inclined to feel that this new roof should enjoy a comparable life span.

Indeed, all the little churches in this gentle Coln Valley merit a leisurely visit. You may add to those of the three Coln-named hamlets the churches of Winson and Quenington. Nor should you dismiss these with the sweeping assertion that churches do not particularly interest you; for these small and beautifully designed buildings are the focal points of most of these hamlets. An exception, though, is Guiting Power farther north-east: the church serving this most charming hillside village above the Windrush stands curiously remote, seemingly aloof from it. The life of the villages and hamlets is embodied, enshrined, in these small churches; and the craftsmanship revealed in them is mainly that of local masons, whose hands manipulated with such understanding the stone that lies so close beneath the thin brown soil of the land, the stone that is the very skeleton of the country that bred them.

These masons fashioned millstones too, and you can see some impressive examples set vertically in a length of wall lining the minor road at Slaughter Farm just across the A 429 from Bourton-on-the-Water. If the sun is right, glancing athwart these stones, you can learn something of the art of the millwright and the niceties of fluting the hard stone surface with hammer and chisel. But, sunshine or not, the contrast between the level courses of Cotswold stone and the great circles of millstone inset among them is one that will linger in the memory, as the unexpected so often does.

A second tracery of minor lanes awaits you just to the north of the last one described. Its uppermost limit is Chipping Campden and it is enclosed roughly between the A 436 running eastwards of Cheltenham, as its southern border, the A 424 running north-westwards from Stow-on-the-Wold and just by-passing Campden, and the A 46 Cheltenham to Stratford on Avon road forming its western boundary. It is in this network of roads that you will find Stanton and Stanway, Cutsdean, Temple Guiting and Guiting Power, Snowshill ('Sno'zl' to Cotswold folk), Laverton and Buckland; and, south and east of these, near or on the Windrush, Naunton, Upper and Lower Swell, and Upper and Lower Slaughter.

Here, inevitably, frustration sets in. Asked to state a preference, to declare which of this unassuming galaxy should take pride of place above the others, the impossibility of so invidious a decision becomes immediately clear. Stanway can perhaps be ruled out. It is, after all, less an

Cottages at Chipping Camden, Cotswolds

The mill at Lower Slaughter, Cotswolds

Eastleach Martin – the River Leach and the Church

integrated village than a superb Cotswold manor house with an outstanding and strongly dominant seventeenth-century gateway, the work of Inigo Jones, and a magnificent Norman tithe-barn adjacent to it, originally a perquisite of Tewkesbury Abbey. The days of Stanway's importance as — believe it or not as you look about it today — a village whose inhabitants laboured in four local mills, corn mill, fulling-mill, paper mill and cider mill, are long since past, dead and forgotten.

Stanton, however, a mile or so to the north, might very well be the choice, especially if first seen with the sun towards the west and that single street rising gently but progressively steeply from the cricket-ground at its foot to the spectacularly-sited Mount Inn at its crest. It is a street lined with stone buildings of unsurpassed beauty of design, proportion and texture. Here the stone possesses an extraordinary richness of tone: gold is hardly a strong enough term; ochre is perhaps nearer to it, or perhaps apricot. On the other hand, Stanton falls down in respect of one feature that you may by now have come to regard as a *sine qua non* among Cotswold villages: the presence of water. This is an element found consistently elsewhere; at Lower Slaughter in particular; at Naunton, at Temple Guiting, at Bourton-on-the-Water, and at Lower Swell, to name but a few obvious examples. At lovely Stanton this is the one and only feature the lack of which must be placed on the debit side.

It is curious, but pleasing too, the way these villages go about in pairs, in trios, even in quartets, as in East Anglia, but without the patronage of a saint. There are the Slaughters and Swells, the Barringtons and Rissingtons, the Ampneys, two of which do have saintly patronage, a third a reference to the Cross of Christ; and if pedestrian Down Ampney is grouped with them they achieve the full quartet. Add to these Great and Little Tew, on the eastern fringe of the Cotswolds and denied full 'nationality' by the purist; Temple Guiting and Guiting Power, and Bourton-on-the-Water and Bourton-on-the-Hill—though these last are separated from one another by seven or eight long Cotswold miles.

The Guitings are an odd pair. Temple Guiting is set low down athwart the stripling Windrush, a few miles upstream from Naunton; Guiting Power is set on a slope of the wolds, a tilted village of mellow stone rising to a green overlooked by a few trim houses and bearing a modest war memorial that catches and holds the eye as you climb towards it.

You look in vain, at first, for that focal point of practically every English village you could name, the parish church. In Guiting Power it stands well clear of the rest of the village (though a newish estate has reached out towards it), somewhat to the south of it and so with a wide view from the churchyard in every direction but one. It is not among the most noteworthy of Cotswold churches, but there is detail for the finding. For example, carved out of the keystone over the South Porch there is a stone hour-glass. Was it placed at that vantage-point to remind the church-goer as he passed beneath that his span of life was inexorably running out? Or could it perhaps have been a gentle hint to the incumbent, carved by someone who was both craftsman and humorist (like the masons who worked on the church at Kilpeck), that he should not make his sermons over long?

A little farther down the valley the Windrush has widened as it approaches Naunton from the north and west. Like so many of these villages, this has just the one street, following the line of the valley from west to east. You may have caught a glimpse of Naunton from the B 4068, high above it, before you turned off at one or other of the two unobtrusive angled lanes that lead steeply down into it, one at each end. You will have noticed, then, its roofscape; as attractive a one as any you will find anywhere in the Cotswolds with the possible exception of Snowshill, seven or eight miles to the north. Here too you can perch on the edge of a road and obtain almost a bird's-eye view down over the roofs. It happens that the immediate neighbourhood of the village has always been noted for the quality of tiling stone, the thinner slabs just beneath the turf; tiles—or

Cotswold vernacular – barn with columbarium

slates, as they are sometimes mistakenly called—of Naunton stone cover
the roofs of these buildings, and those, too, of villages for many miles
around. They are much prized.

The great church tower at Naunton, comparable with some of the
'wool' churches of East Anglia, with which part of Britain, of course, the
Cotswolds share the long tradition of sheep rearing and the sale and
processing of wool, rises high above all but a few of the village roofs, the
few belonging to houses built on the steepish slope to the south of the
village. But it is dwarfed by the steeper slope of the wolds to the north of
the village, at whose feet the Windrush flows so unobtrusively. The
church of St Andrew is half screened by its staid assembly of yew trees,
between these two slopes.

Eastwards from Naunton some of these small, winding lanes will lead
you at length to Upper and Lower Slaughter. The name, particularly in so
idyllic a setting, strikes somewhat harshly on the ear, even before you
arrive in the villages: the suggestion of massacre, here, is unthinkable. Of
course. Happily, as so often, the name is a corrupt or debased form of a
much older word; in this instance it is a particularly unfortunate one.

There is a difference of opinion as to this among experts even now.
Some of them aver that the Saxon words *sloh* and *tre* represented (as seems
reasonable) the sloe tree—though the sloe can surely not be said to grow on
anything that could fairly be called a tree? More academic opinion rejects

this theory in favour of *sloh* being the origin of the word slough. So, they say, the place-of-the-slough is what the name means, using the *tre* element very loosely indeed and not too convincingly. It is a fact that, in spite of its name, Upper Slaughter, like its twin, Lower Slaughter, is located on well-watered ground. Before drainage was competently effected much of that ground through which a stream idles beneath the trees, providing good pasture for the cattle, may well have been swamp, and the name therefore aptly chosen.

Of the two Slaughters, undoubtedly Lower is the more immediately attractive. The River Eye flows right through it; a succession of small foot-bridges span the clear, shallow, embanked stream, each leading to the row of pleasant cottages on the opposite side and so to the village green at the farther end. It is a somewhat self-conscious village, though happily very much less so than, for example, Bourton-on-the-Water or, of course, "immaculate' Broadway just over the Worcestershire border.

In Lower Slaughter you gain the impression (as you do in Milton Abbas, in Dorset) that its dedicated inhabitants have been out since dawn clipping any unruly blade of grass or twig of bush within their purview, trimming the foliage of the trees, polishing the windows of their snug cottages, dusting the stonework, touching up with paint the white rails of the foot-bridge leading to their homes. Even the mill-wheel has been so contrived as to turn unobtrusively, noiselessly.

Upper Slaughter, a mile or so along the lane, is, to begin with at any rate, less prepossessing. For all that, its subtler charms steal over you insidiously. The Dikler, not the Windrush, flows through it, spanned by a clapper-bridge that looks a great deal older than in fact it is. If you have the choice of approach, it is more satisfying to come upon the village from below than from above, following the stream and passing the stepping-stones and small bridges before the road tilts upwards between high stone walls and you come, suddenly, into the very heart of the village: a triangular space dominated by a great chestnut tree on its lower side and a row of gabled cottages backed by the beautiful church of St Peter on the upper side.

That great Roman road, the Fosse Way, a hundred-and-seventy-odd miles long and, astonishingly, never more than six miles out of a dead-true line in the whole of its length north-eastwards from Axminster, passes through Stow-on-the-Wold a mile or so to the east of the Slaughters and the Swells—two villages that are only just less enchanting than the villages just described. Almost at once you find yourself in yet another of these delicate traceries of hidden lanes that link hamlet with hamlet. You are now in the wide and gentle valley of the Evenlode. Among these valley villages are Evenlode itself, and Daylesford and Oddington and Broad-well, with its shallow and tempting ford, its enormous tree-shaded, tree-encircled green and its stone cottages contrasting with the greater dignity

Lower Slaughter – the River Eye

of the manor house facing them. There is also Adlestrop, of which the First World War poet, Edward Thomas, wrote so nostalgically.

There is a reason for the greater profusion of fine trees hereabouts, and notably at Broadwell, than elsewhere generally in the Cotswolds. Here you are on the edge of the ancient Wychwood Forest, once a royal hunting preserve. The well-known six-centuries-old Shaven Crown Inn at Shipton-under-Wychwood was formerly the guest hospice for the medieval Bruern Abbey, and its name clearly commemorates the tonsure of the monks. Wychwood was in the very heart of this extensive royal forest.

After a great many years, however, the royal hunting lodge as it later became was handed over to the parish in the form of a charity, an essential proviso being that accommodation must be offered, free of all charge, to anyone who came knocking at its fine Tudor doorway in genuine need of assistance. It is an interesting fact that successive landlords have been bound, by the conditions of a Trust established to maintain this tradition, to conform to its terms. And Shipton is not the only survivor of the 'under Wychwood' nomenclature; we are reminded of the extent of this great forest, so little of which survives today except in isolated and scattered stands of noble trees, by other names too: Ascot-under-Wychwood, for instance, and Milton-under-Wychwood.

It is in this region, too, that the border between Gloucestershire and Oxfordshire wanders a little uncertainly north and south. The last-named villages, and many others of course, are all to be found on the Oxfordshire side of it. Another of them is Enstone, a little farther to the north and east; they are in reality two villages, not one: Enstone and Church Enstone. It is here that you will find one of the finest of Cotswold tithe-barns, a fourteenth-century perquisite of Winchcombe Abbey, on the far side of the wolds to the west. These great barns are always well worth a visit, if only to admire their cathedral-like qualities and the superb timber-work of their great roofs. The one at Great Coxwell, in Berkshire, ranks among the most famous, and there is of course the glorious example at Abbotsbury, in Dorset.

Just south of Enstone you will find on your map the two words, Hoar Stone. The spot marks just one more of the numerous Cotswold megalithic sites, of which Belas Knap, on the heights between Winchcombe and Cheltenham, is the most famous. The Hoar Stone is all that is left of a megalithic burial-chamber, reminiscent of Arthur's Stone above Golden Valley. But because it is so closely overhung by trees you could pass the cross-roads by which it stands a hundred times without spotting it. The tumbled stones, massive as they are, lack distinction, largely because of their unfortunate setting; they seem to crouch, secretively, as do the better-known stones that comprise Kit's Coty, near Maidstone, in Kent.

There are other villages hereabouts, each of which possesses some feature that makes it worth a visit. Charlbury, for instance, with its steep main street and medieval inn near its crest; Spelsbury, with an outstanding church; and Stonesfield, all set about (almost as its name implies) with the remains of quarries from which were taken the finest roofing-slates to be found anywhere in the Cotswolds, not even excepting those from Naunton. From this stone 'slates' were split that are comparable in quality, in texture and in endurance with the more massive 'Horsham Slabs' quarried and worked in Sussex.

It could be said, and with a reasonable degree of truth, that the eastern, or Oxfordshire, part of the Cotswolds is on the whole less memorable than the central and western parts. Such an observation, however, would lose a good deal of its conviction if Great Tew and neighbouring Little Tew were adduced by way of challenge. These are two villages to be found in a network of narrow roads and lanes equally distributed on either side of the A 34 main road from Oxford to Stratford on Avon, and they effectively balance the somewhat indeterminate claims of Charlbury, Spelsbury and Stonesfield.

In fact, it would be hard indeed to find two Cotswold villages with more beautiful stonework than that to be found in Great and Little Tew. About the only way in which the contention could be upheld that, generally speaking, the villages of the eastern Cotswolds are less memorable than those of the middle and western parts would be to point out that, lovely as these are, they stand almost alone in this respect, whereas in other parts of the Cotswolds there is almost an *embarras de choix*. Purists might contend that they are not in fact, and in the strictest interpretation of the term, Cotswold villages at all, being too far to the east. But they fully merit inclusion, for they are in the true Cotswold tradition of stone-built villages, and hardly more than five miles from Chipping Norton, a township which proudly, and with justification, claims to represent true Cotswold at its finest.

You will be struck immediately by the extraordinarily deep hue of the stone of the buildings, large and small, in Great and Little Tew. This particular grade of limestone must have been deeply impregnated with iron, among other minerals, to have attained this old-gold, this ochre, this near-russet tone. There is a richness about it of which you will have received an advance hint in the village of Adlestrop, a dozen winding miles to the west, which is richer in tone than any other that you will have found in Cotswold villages so far. Examining the warm, mellow stone of its church, you may have noticed the strong contrast with the hard, cold texture of the half-millstone which, unexpectedly, serves as threshold to the doorway. Incidentally, you will encounter this exaggerated richness of colouring in the stone as you journey farther north, crossing over the border into Northamptonshire, where the iron has very literally entered into the oolitic soul.

In Great Tew, the 'planned village', the stone is deeper in colour than that even of Adlestrop; in a moment of loose thinking you might almost be inclined to dub it 'gingerbread'; it is as though the stonework of the whole village is permanently illumined by a sun lying low in the west. Here you will find a steeply sloping village green, complete with stocks, part-sheltered by a massive stand of trees and dominated by the manor house up on the hill, out of sight of the village though so close to it, with the ancient church of St Michael standing in its grounds, many sizes too large, one would think, for so small a place as this.

It would be less than fair to speak of Great Tew without mentioning its near neighbour just along the lane. As its name suggests, it is the lesser village; nevertheless it has its own less obvious but very real charm. This is especially noticeable in the positioning of a fine conifer by the road side between the little church (one that is very much more in keeping with the size of the village than that of Great Tew) and the exceptionally beautiful manor house detached from the other buildings and half hidden behind its own screen of tall hedge and trees. Little Tew has been unkindly referred to as the 'shadow' of its better-known neighbour. Such an epithet is grossly unfair: the village is beautiful in its own right; and anyway—can stone so warm and glowing be fairly described in terms of shadow? Of course not.

But there is other stone in the Cotswolds, older by far than that which gives such aesthetic pleasure as one contemplates the walls and the facades and roofs of manor houses, cottages and tithe-barns. It is stone planted here, not by craftsmen of the Middle Ages and later centuries but by the Early Bronze Age Cotswold men of three to four thousand years ago. You have seen an example of such stones on the cross-roads just south of Enstone, the so-called Hoar Stone. But you will find the most spectacular example on both sides of a road so minor that it does not rate a number.

Three miles to the north of Chipping Norton, a mile or two short of the point where, at Long Compton, Warwickshire dips sharply southwards as though to drive a wedge between north Gloucestershire and north Oxfordshire, a road crosses the A 34 main road between Oxford and Stratford-on-Avon. A signpost points right-handedly to the hamlet of Great Rollright, which is notable solely for its church; in the opposite direction, that is to say westwards, this same small road starts out for Stow-on-the-Wold. You should certainly pursue this road for a mile at least, whatever may at this point be your main objective.

As you emerge from some trees, just as you breast the crown of a low hill, you come suddenly upon the megalithic Stone Circle known far and wide as 'The King's Men'. It lies on your left-hand side: an irregular, unditched circle consisting of some sixty or more stones of varying sizes on a diameter of about thirty yards. The site is worth more than a hurried inspection, for it is closely linked with two other prehistoric though smaller sites, one out of sight in a field sloping away from the Stone Circle itself, the other on a slight rise on the opposite side of the road a few yards farther on in the direction in which you are already facing. The first of these smaller sites, the one not immediately within your purview, is a collapsed dolmen, known as 'The Whispering Knights'; the second is a single Standing Stone of unusually evocative shape, known as 'The King Stone'.

Legend, of course, has inevitably built up about this trio of prehistoric sites, remote from main thoroughfares and possessed of a curiously powerful aura of mystery and secrecy. Popularly, it is held that a king was marching northwards over the Cotswolds with his band of knightly followers. He encountered a witch, at this point in his march. The witch halted him in his tracks, and both startled and pleased him by intoning:

> 'If Long Compton thou canst see,
> King of all England shalt thou be!'

Witches in those days, it seems, tended to speak in doggerel verse. In the mean-time, however, the crone had spread a mist across the valley that

Great Tew – stone gateway

intervened between this high ground and the village in question. She could now, therefore, complete her incantation to her own liking:

'Rise up, stick, and stand still, stone;
King of all England shalt thou be none!'

Her malevolent chant completed, the legend continues (and who is to dispute its truth, with so much evidence manifest all about him?), the king was forthwith literally petrified, and with him his circle of knightly followers grouped about him to listen, first, to the promise so clearly given to their monarch. Thus the luckless king became the King Stone. But the old beldame had not finished her evil work. Three of the supposedly loyal knights had previously detached themselves from the main body of their companions, and were already plotting to overthrow their liege lord. But they too were to be frustrated, for the witch's spell had fallen over them in passing. So, the three 'hoar stones', now known as the Whispering Knights, show what can happen to treacherous men. They are of course, as is the case with the Hoar Stones near Enstone, simply the main supporting stones of a dolmen, long since collapsed. But it happens that they are of such a size and shape, and so grouped, that they really bear an extraordinary likeness to three figures with hunched shoulders and heads close together, engaged in urgent conclave.

You may smile at the simple-mindedness of those who, long years ago, evolved these picturesque legends. But for all that, if it were your lot to come across the King's Men, the King Stone, and, above all, the Whispering Knights, after dusk had fallen and when there was no one else about, you might very well find yourself in sneaking sympathy with such superstition, and slightly shivering, as simpler folk than yourself have often been—ridiculous as this may seem in broad daylight beneath a blue Cotswold sky scattered with white galleons of cumulus cruising leisurely overhead.

Sussex and Kent

WEST AND EAST SUSSEX

Even a superficial glance at the map of south-east England suggests that the inhabitants of Greater London have been at some pains to ensure for themselves easy access to the sea. Certainly, to be anywhere between the metropolis and the coast on any fine week-end is to gain the impression that these inhabitants are a legion of lemmings bent on hurling themselves with the least possible delay over the cliffs and into the English Channel.

South-east, south and south-westwards a whole orchestra of roads span the fifty-odd miles, spreading out from the south London suburbs fanwise, like the tines of the familiar 'springbok' garden rake. Winchelsea and Rye, Hastings and Bexhill, Pevensey and Eastbourne, Seaford and Newhaven, Brighton and Hove, Shoreham-by-Sea and Worthing, Little-hampton and Bognor Regis: all these popular resorts are reached more or less directly by roads that spring southwards from a handful of distribution-points, bridges spanning the Thames such as Vauxhall, Westminster and Waterloo. It is small wonder that this county, whose two

West Sussex

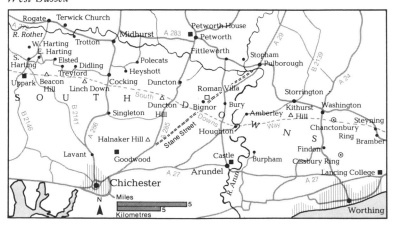

matched halves between them total more than seventy miles in length, if less than half that in depth, has long been known in song and story as 'Sussex-by-the-Sea'.

To develop the analogy of the garden rake, like the tines with their cross-brace these coast-seeking roads are crossed, some twelve or fifteen miles inland, by a major road, the A 272. This runs from west to east along the major axis of the county, from Petersfield, just over the Hampshire border, by way of Midhurst and Petworth, Haywards Heath and Uckfield, to Cross in Hand, where it becomes the A 265 and continues on its eastwards journey to Burwash and a point just short of Hawkhurst, in Kent, where it finally loses its identity; it is rather as though it has lost the momentum with which it set off, far away to the west in Winchester.

With such a multiplicity of roads criss-crossing the county, spacious as it is, lengthwise at any rate, the likelihood of finding out-of-the-way corners and off-the-beaten-tracks is small indeed in comparison with the prospects in, say, the Peak District of Derbyshire, Northumbria, or the Black Mountains of South Wales. Nevertheless, such corners do exist, even though so much of Sussex lies hemmed in between its own populous coastline and the commuter belt to the north.

To the great majority of holiday-makers Sussex is no more than an almost embarrassingly large selection of seaside resorts; to a lesser, though still substantial, number it is—The Downs. Both groups of partisans should be given their due; for the choices they have respectively made, though obvious, are nevertheless excellent ones. Especially, perhaps, the choice of the second group. But this, it must be admitted, is the judgment of someone who has a strong bias in that direction; for he has walked the full length of those downs, from Butser Hill to Birling Gap, time and again, and his 'Chalk Walk' was one of his earliest and most memorable experiments in learning to know a country through the soles of his boots. It followed shortly after the infinitely more challenging walk from Edale in Derbyshire to the Cheviots along the then unmarked route now known as the Pennine Way.

The downs referred to are of course the South Downs, the region that gave its name to the famed breed of sheep which once in their scores of thousands grazed the scant turf beneath which neolithic man probed for the black flint for his weapons and tools, the sheep which, many declare, provide the finest mutton in the world. These South Downs run for some fifty miles, from Old Winchester Hill in the west to Firle Beacon and the Long Man of Wilmington, a few miles short of Eastbourne. They have been carved into sections of varying length by small rivers such as the Arun and the Adur, the Ouse and the Cuckmere, which flow through valleys sloping gently down to the sea at Littlehampton, Shoreham and Newhaven. Between these intersecting valleys they rise to rolling summits that top the 700-foot and at times even the 800-foot mark. To walk from one end to the other of this chalk ridge, with the waters of the English Channel constantly in sight only a few miles to the south, is one of the most exhilarating experiences this 'soft' South Country has it in its gift to offer those who still take pleasure in long-distance walking.

This range of chalk is virtually all that remains in Sussex of the 3000-foot-high whaleback of chalk that in remote geological times, known as the Cretaceous Age, say a hundred and forty million years ago, not only covered the county and extended eastwards into Kent and westwards into Dorset but also arched over what is today the English Channel to link Britain physically with northern France. Thirty miles or so to the north, in the neighbouring county of Surrey, there is a matching remnant of this most ancient chalk, shown on the map as the North Downs, the other survivor of the original chalk dome that roofed southern England to a height comparable with that of Snowdon today. This stretch of downland runs eastwards from near Guildford, by-passes Redhill and Reigate to the north and then Sevenoaks and Maidstone in Kent, to slope down finally by way of Charing and peter out in the hinterland of Sandgate and Folkestone.

In overall length these North Downs are perhaps half as long again as the South Downs; in height they are often comparable. But in interest, in sheer beauty, in their power to imbue one with that rare sense of splendid isolation, they do not begin to compare. They are much too close to London, for one thing. The more sophisticated districts of London's southern dormitory sprawl across them. They may claim to possess such famed beauty-spots as Newlands Corner and Box Hill; but they do not possess the sense of space, of oneness with the heavens, that are an integral feature of the South Downs of Sussex.

Between the North Downs and the South Downs lies The Weald. It is a fairly common misconception that the word 'weald' is simply a variant of 'wold', and means highish rolling uplands, as in the case of the Yorkshire Wolds or, for that matter, the Cots Wolds. In fact this word is a variant of the Saxon word for forest, *wald*. It is in this fact that there lies the explanation of this area of Sussex, which extends also westwards into Hampshire, northwards into Surrey and eastwards into the Weald of Kent. It was in former times, quite simply, forest land.

For countless centuries trees, most notably oaks, grew here in such profusion, so densely, that the region was virtually impenetrable. Oak trees throve on the heavy clay and marl of the region that was laid bare when the south-flowing rivers had eroded the last of the chalk that lay between the North and the South Downs as we know them today. The Saxons who had by then moved into Britain dubbed the area *Andreadsweald* and referred to it as 'the forest where no man dwells'. They found, though, that it provided excellent feeding-grounds for their swine, who throve on the unlimited supply of acorns and oak-mast to be had there for the taking; so they cleared small areas of the weald, particularly in the east, in Kent, in which to establish themselves. The many villages and small townships of today that have the suffix 'den'—as in Biddenden, Bethersden, Frittenden and so on—are all relics of these scattered communities, the Saxon word meaning a settlement. There are records of chance visitors to the Weald in Saxon times intruding into these swineherds' settlements and falling victim not to the herdsmen but to the savagery of the wild boars roaming at will beneath the close-set oaks, grubbing among their roots.

You may reasonably wonder, therefore, where that forest is today that was once extensive enough to be known as *Andreadsweald*. The answer in fact is simple. Strange as it must seem to us who today think of iron foundries and steel works as being indigenous to Sheffield and Rotherham and the Black Country and South Wales, the first large-scale iron-working was carried on in the Weald of Sussex. The Romans started the industry in a tentative sort of way; but by the Middle Ages the Weald was, astonishingly, known as 'The Black Country', and in the middle of the sixteenth century there were more than a hundred furnaces, forges and 'bloomeries', as they were then called, in this hundred-mile stretch of south-east England between the North and the South Downs.

The first English cannon is reputed to have been cast in a foundry at Buxted, of all places, in the year 1543. On any large-scale map you will find echoes of this traditional Wealden industry in the very place-names: Iron Hill, Furnace Wood, Hammer Pond, Forge Farm, Furnace Lane are just a few obvious examples of these. Rudyard Kipling's home on the outskirts of the Sussex village of Burwash, *Bateman's*, was built in the seventeenth century by one of the great Sussex iron-masters, who had his furnaces and forge in the beautiful little Dudwell Valley, a stone's throw to the south of the house (now, happily, National Trust property), the setting, incidentally, for much of Kipling's little masterpiece, *Puck of Pook's Hill*. In Burwash church there is a memorial slab, appropriately enough not in slate or stone or even brass but in cast-iron. It bears the name of another Sussex iron-master, one who flourished in the district three centuries earlier.

The tradition of iron-working in the Weald lasted until comparatively recent times, when coal replaced wood as fuel for the insatiable furnaces. But by then the damage had been done. And irreparable damage it was, too; for the millions of fine oak trees that had populated, indeed constituted, the Weald had vanished up the chimneys of furnace and forge; today only a relatively small number of stands of those fine trees survive to remind us of their legions of vanished fellows.

To find the least spoiled areas of Sussex it is essential to keep close to the South Downs or actually on them; or at any rate to the 'tilted levels' immediately beneath the north-facing foot-hills of the downs, among the tiny villages nestling beneath them and the 'many-coloured fields spotted with farms' that so engagingly fill in the spaces between them. There are, of course, other rewarding areas, particularly in West Sussex, farther from the South Downs; but always, unless your goal is the seaside resorts and the ribbon-development between them that is so steadily destroying the former beauty of the coastline, this must be looked for to the north of the downs; not too far to the north, though, or you will find yourself on that main highway running west-eastwards through the heart of the Weald, the A 272.

Almost on the border between West Sussex and Hampshire, midway between the A 272 and the western flank of the South Downs, lies a trio of small villages, the Hartings, East, West and South; little more than a mile separates any one of them from its neighbours. The Hartings form as good an introduction as you could hope to find to this stretch of the Weald that is bordered on its southern side by the swelling rampart of the Downs. Of the trio, probably the most interesting is the last named. It is comfortably the largest of them, which is no doubt why, conscious of its seniority in this respect, it has the habit of dropping the 'South' from its name. Not that reference to differences in size really counts for much, here: these foot-of-the-Downs villages are as modest in their size as they are unobtrusive in their siting; and this of course is all to the good.

There is a record of incumbents of the Parish Church of St Mary and St Gabriel, in this village, that goes back to the twelfth century; but the greater part of the fabric as you see it today dates from the thirteenth and fourteenth centuries, and much of this had to be substantially restored after a disastrous fire in the latter part of the sixteenth century. It dominates the road and the village itself from an elevated position approached by a slope from a small triangle of neutral ground.

On the edge of this, close beside the gateway, there stands a pair of stocks, complete with whipping-post. A small detail on this tells, or at least implies, a simple but pathetic story. Look at the three pairs of iron wrist-cuffs, and you will notice that one of them is smaller, and lower, than the others. This suggests that it was not only the adult sturdy rogue and vagabond of those days who was publicly whipped before being placed in the adjacent stocks, but also quite small children. Looking up from the stocks, you will notice the fine Sussex 'broach' spire, so conspicuous a feature of churches throughout this county and on into Kent. And a noteworthy feature inside the church is the beautiful timber roof of the chancel, the work of Elizabethan craftsmen following the fire in 1576: it is a complex pattern of trusses and king-posts highly satisfying to the questing eye.

The church overlooks four cross-roads. One of these comes in from Hampshire; another makes northwards for Rogate and Liss, where it leaves the county; a third runs due south until it touches the fringe of the great deer park, in the heart of which is the mansion simply known as Uppark; the fourth bears eastwards, approaching very close indeed to the foot of Harting Downs and signposted for Elsted. This is a tiny hamlet, with a church that is entirely in keeping, one that is not only smaller by far than that at South Harting but also far older. Though its exact date has not been established, it is known to have been standing here a long while before the Norman Conquest. There is Saxon herring-bone work in the west end of the fabric, said by connoisseurs to be the finest in the county and among the finest to be found anywhere in Britain. In pre-Conquest times the building consisted simply of a nave some thirty feet long by about half that width. The Normans pierced the east wall and built on to it a small chancel, which was enlarged in the thirteenth century—before the main fabric of St Mary and St Gabriel's in near-by South Harting was even begun. It is something more than pure imagination that makes you feel that you are treading not only on holy ground but on a most ancient site, as you pass beneath the tall trees that embower it, either through the little gateway or by clambering over an awkward stone stile in the wall facing the farm buildings.

The north face of the Downs, hereabouts, is a sequence of alternating steep slopes and narrow valley mouths—though the term valley is perhaps too grandiose for such relatively small indentations between shoulder and shoulder of the great chalk mass. The road which you are now following eastwards, narrow and twisting, every now and then takes a violent dog's-leg turn to left or right, as though nervous of approaching too closely to foot-hills that rise to almost eight hundred feet at Beacon Hill and top that figure soon afterwards at Linch Down. It is along this stretch that the contour lines crowd so closely together that it is almost impossible to separate them without the use of a magnifying-glass.

Just beyond Treyford, and beneath the shadow cast by Treyford Hill, there is a lane on your right, hardly more than a farm track, that peters out within a few hundred yards, opposite a yew tree. Behind the yew stands the minuscule church of St Andrew, yet another of these edge-of-the-Downs church-lets that date from the thirteenth century. The diminutive '-let' is certainly justified in this instance, for it is doubtful whether a congregation of more than thirty-six in all could be accommodated on those black oak benches, installed in the early fifteenth century and still satisfyingly medieval with their individual candle-holders.

Matching those somewhat crude benches is the small pulpit, the handiwork of a Jacobean incumbent who dabbled in joinery in his plentiful spare time. He constructed his pulpit from an oak chest, and ornamented it with an amateur's hand that was manifestly not too well accustomed to a wood-carver's tools, however handy he might be with hammer and saw. You will see a very roughly carved head, just below the lectern: it was placed there to conceal as best it might what is quite

Looking towards Chanctonbury Ring from Cissbury Ring, Sussex

Glyndebourne, Sussex, famed for its opera: the lawn and flower borders on the garden front of the house

Barfreston Church, Kent — detail of the tympanum over the south door

Medieval bridge over the River Rother at Trotton

obviously a keyhole designed to accommodate the massive wrought-iron key to the chest. The small reading-stand, hardly in fact a lectern, is another example of an amateur's handiwork; yet it is surprisingly effective in its simplicity, as you will readily find out by examining its ingenious device for adjustment of height.

The lane that ends beneath the branches of the yew tree provides as good an approach to the ridge of the Downs as you could hope to find at this western end. A track leads due south from it, beyond the gate, dipping slightly for the first hundred yards or so and then climbing purposefully upwards on to Linch Down, at 818 feet. Here the South Downs are a mile and more wide, the slope seawards being so gentle that it is almost imperceptible. Nowhere along their whole length, in fact, are they wider, except perhaps at Duncton Hill, seven miles to the east.

The track clings to the top of the escarpment, immediately above the steeply-falling slope. Standing on it, you look northwards over the roofs of the hamlet of Didling, which is well beyond its tiny church, to the equally

273

small hamlet of Trotton, where the A 272 is carried over the stripling Rother on a beautiful little medieval bridge that ought long before now to have been by-passed in case the ever-growing weight of the traffic it is obliged to carry brings about its collapse.

Incidentally, Trotton also has its interesting little church of St George. It is interesting primarily for its fine brasses, including one believed to be the oldest in England to commemorate a lady, and for its fourteenth-century wall-paintings discovered no more than sixty or seventy years ago on the west wall. They bear the unmistakable imprint of their time. Christ sits in judgment; Moses holds the Tables of the Law; on one side you may see the traditional Good Man practising the Seven Good Deeds of Mercy, including the clothing of the naked and the feeding of the hungry; on the left side there is the naked figure of the traditional Evil Man encircled by the Seven Deadly Sins, too familiar to require enumeration. The figures that symbolise these sins appear to be issuing from the gaping jaws of the dragon-like monsters easily recognisable by the simple folk for whom these solemn admonishments were so often presented in pictorial form.

A mile or so along the road westwards you will see, in a field and partly surrounded by a fine square-cut hedge, Terwick's church of St Peter. It is always known, and for obvious reasons, as the Church-in-the-Field. Like Didling's church beneath the yew tree, it lies remote from the few scattered houses whose occupants it serves. No one has ever established why the church should have been built, some time about the middle of the twelfth century, in the middle of a field. The only clue to the mystery is to be found in what is known as a Northumbrian Preaching Cross, the remains of which now stand immediately opposite the west door. Its presence suggests that this field may have been a very ancient burial-ground, dating back to Saxon times, and suggesting itself to the Norman builders of the little church itself.

But it is time to return to the downland ridge from which this fair display of low-lying ground extends northwards, westwards and eastwards across the wide valley of the upper Rother. From here you can look towards the western flank of the North Downs, twenty miles away, your view interrupted only by the isolated hill known as Woolbeding Common, now National Trust property, and the uplands on which Hindhead stands, just over the Surrey border. There is now a track beneath your feet; indeed, a choice of tracks. For here the Downs form a spacious plateau, near-level to the west, south and east. The turf is smooth, unbroken. Here and there are trees: small stands only, for the most part, of chalk-loving beech. It is farther to the east that they become more clearly shaped and defined, and have been endowed with names, such as Chanctonbury Ring, and thus become named landmarks on one of the most breath-takingly beautiful skylines in all Britain.

Beacon Hill, at 795 feet, Treyford Hill and the Devil's Jumps, Didling

Hill and Linch Down, with Linchball Wood immediately behind it, and Cocking Down, with its tumuli, are all within a radius of not more than three and a half miles from you. At Cocking Down again you have a choice. You can take the track that slopes purposefully down towards the village of Cocking, through which a north-south road, the A 286, passes between Haslemere and Chichester, to cleave the line of the South Downs at right angles to the track you have been following. Or you can remain on your downland track, dip downwards on to the intrusive road near Hacking Copse and climb up and away from it to regain the heights between Herringdean Wood and Singleton Forest—both of these names being somewhat grandiosely chosen for the relatively small tree communities they represent.

Now follows a glorious stretch of the Downs. Once again (and for that matter as usual) the best walking track is the one that clings fairly closely to the northward-facing slopes. It leads you to the tumuli at Cross Dykes, close against Heyshott Down; and beyond that, less than two miles of exhilarating yet easy walking, to Graffham Down and yet more tumuli. If you are not particularly interested in churches generally, or even in these tiny, unusual churches that nestle at the foot of the Downs, each seemingly smaller than the last, then you may like to remain on this splendid track that leads you eastwards along the escarpment. But if by now you have been captivated by these little 'lost' churches, as they are sometimes called, then before you go any farther along the track you should visit one more, to be found barely three miles to the north on the outskirts of Selham.

Hereabouts, the minor road from South Harting gives the impression of having lost all hope of clinging to these foot-hills. At Cocking it branched northwards, briefly merging with the A 286, but apparently soon thought better of its decision and turned eastwards again, farther by a mile or two from the Downs than it had been up to that point, to wander through the rusticity of Heyshott Green and menacingly named Polecats before entering Selham from the south-west; and it is on the outskirts of the village, before you come in sight of the first of its few houses, that you will see the little church of St James the Apostle, standing back from the road on your right.

Unprepossessing as to its setting, it is nevertheless a church that amply repays a visit, small and insignificant as it appears at first sight. The corners of its walls offer a good example of the traditional building-method of the Saxons in the 'long-and-short work' characteristic of that exceptionally early period in the matching of the quoins. This, together with the herring-bone work in the north side of the chancel, establishes the earliest portions of this church as Saxon. The doorway, on the north side for once, is exceptionally narrow, so narrow indeed that a coffin could only just be manoeuvred through it.

Exteriorly this church is not among the most attractive of those lying beneath the South Downs; but its interior is quite outstanding. A strikingly beautiful arch separates the tiny nave from the even tinier chancel. It is elaborately carved, and much of the carving reveals Scandinavian influence. There is for instance a grotesque and fantastic monster facing outwards from the arch into the nave, supposedly to deter evil-minded men from penetrating the sanctuary of the chancel itself. This ornamentation apart, the church is notably simple and in its way, unexpectedly perhaps, one of the most impressive of all these small churches; only the one at Elsted, with its Saxon herring-bone work, seems in any respect comparable with it.

You can return to the ridge walk that you temporarily discontinued to go in search of Selham by way of a small road that will lead you to Woolavington Down. Thence your track will take you eastwards to Duncton Down, where it takes a sharpish turn southwards for a mile or two before swinging south-eastwards over Bignor Hill, with its tumuli and prehistoric hill-fort dominating a stretch of the track somewhat oddly named The Denture. It is here that your downland trek brings you nearest to the site of the Roman Villa in the flat plain below Bignor Hill. And this, for anyone seeking out the treasures to be found immediately to the north of these Downs, is a site that must surely not be missed.

If you possess a map on a reasonably large scale you will have no difficulty in spotting a dead-straight dotted line running north-eastwards from Chichester towards London and marked, at intervals along its length, Stane Street. It is of course the relic of an original Roman road, one of many of which traces remain in open country or have been utilised, as their Fosse Way was utilised, and a section of Ermine Street to the north of Lincoln, to take two examples only, as the basis for a more modern road. Stane Street is embodied in the A 285 as far as Halnakar Hill, with its fine windmill on top of it, a landmark for miles in every direction save one. At that point the modern road departs from it, to the left, while the Roman road continues north-eastwards to the top of Bignor Hill and soon afterwards, at Pulborough, becomes incorporated in the A 29, which in due course becomes the A 24 and so crosses the Surrey border to the south of Dorking. But no sooner has it dropped down the north slope of Bignor Hill than it skirts a site marked on the map just east of the village of Bignor, 'Roman Villa'.

It is not, of course, a villa as ordinarily understood today; far from it. It is in fact a site laid out perhaps eighteen centuries ago by a Roman of some importance—quite possibly the governor of that particular province during the occupation—and developed by a succession of Romano-Britons of consequence during the years that immediately followed the departure of the Romans in the fourth century A.D. It is a site of which it could be said, in the modern condensed form of the advertising house agents, that it was equipped with 'all mod. con.'

Mosaic of Medusa from the Roman Villa, Bignor

Discovered quite by chance, as has been the case with so many Roman and other remains in various parts of the country, by a farmer ploughing one of his fields, it has been skilfully and intelligently, patiently and imaginatively excavated over a number of years since the first fragments of a tessellated pavement were laid bare in 1811. The result is one of the most remarkably complete and revealing of all the Roman sites hitherto excavated; it is, indeed, comparable with that of Chedworth, in Gloucestershire.

There is a near-rectangular courtyard a hundred feet in length and more than half that in breadth; a corridor ran round all four sides of this, and a succession of chambers large and small opened off three of the sides. The fourth, or east, side opened into the Outer Court, larger by far than the courtyard itself and containing a number of outbuildings such as servants' quarters, labourers' quarters, stabling and cattle sheds and a granary. In the south-east corner of the main block of buildings were the *hypocausts*, prime-movers in the central-heating system which, eighteen hundred years ago, was the prototype of today's beneath-the-floor heating. There were also the *calidarium*, or 'hot room', the *tepidarium*, or 'warm room', and the *frigidarium*, whose Latin name speaks eloquently enough for itself: these were of course the graduated bath-rooms of the standard Roman 'Turkish bath'. Romans of the leisured classes, both at home and in the far-flung colonies they were in process of civilising, knew the general principles of this type of bathing long before modern civilisations did; 'all mod. con.' is no misnomer here at Bignor.

Some of the finest tessellated pavements and wall-mosaics anywhere in the vast Roman empire were laid bare at this site. They are particularly noteworthy in the north wing of the Villa, in a large chamber thirty feet long by twenty feet in width and heated by its own hypocaust beneath the floor. Here the mosaic is that of 'Venus and the Gladiators': Venus is accompanied by Cupid, and there are a dozen gladiators in four separate groups, some of them engaged in armed combat, others preparing for combat or lying recovering from their wounds. In an adjacent but much smaller room there is a pavement, or floor, most elaborately designed in a series of geometrical figures of squares, diamonds, oblongs and quatrefoils that incorporate stereotyped flowers and foliage of various exotic types wholly out of keeping with the relatively cold English scene.

Such elaborate ornamentation, so many amenities of varying kinds, indicate that Bignor was established and developed during a period of peaceful occupation by the Romans and an even longer period following their departure when the well-to-do Briton, who had learned something of the finer arts of life from the Romans into whose place he succeeded, was in residence, maintaining an established tradition that was wholly admirable. The site was almost certainly in continuous occupation for at least three hundred years, and covers in all something like four and a half acres. On really large-scale maps, of the type that record the names of actual fields, the one in which the Villa was laid out is shown as 'Bury Field'. The name, of course, has nothing to do with burial; it is one of the many contractions of the old word 'burgh', meaning a fortified, or at any rate firmly occupied, place.

The existence of this name today shows that the old tradition, dating back some fourteen hundred years, has survived the Dark Ages and all the changes of fortune that the Sussex Weald has known throughout that long period. It is pleasant to be able to record that the site, and the remains of the Roman buildings on it, still belong to the family that farmed here when the great-great-great-grandfather of the present owner first broke through the turf with his ploughshare and brought to light the treasures that had been so long hidden beneath the turf.

In the trim village of Bignor, near the church, you will find a building that deserves more than a passing glance, even though it is many centuries less old than those that the Romans erected, for this is in fact one of the most perfectly preserved non-ecclesiastical ancient buildings (other than castles) in the country. Built as long ago as 1485, it is today a private house, privately occupied, but for long years it was Bignor's village store.

The framework of the house, like those of so many houses in East and West Sussex and neighbouring Hampshire and Kent on either side, is of

'The old shop', Bignor

massive oak timbers. It was built, of course, when forests of oak filled the region and a man could take his pick of the finest timber the building trade has ever known. But the timber framing is in-filled with brick, laid either herringbone-wise or horizontally. The lower panels contain the horizontal courses, and are nearly square; the upper ones, above the diamond-paned windows, are taller than they are wide and contain seven successive courses of bricks tilted left or right. Elsewhere the timber framing has been in-filled with flint set in cement. The facade of this five-centuries-old house, as deserving, surely, of the epithet 'ancient', though it makes no claim to this, as the famous Ancient House in Ipswich with its pargetting panels recording the then-known four continents, is unusual. The two outer portions, above the ground floor, overhang, supported on massive oak joists; the middle portion is similarly framed but does not overhang. Instead, it is set back a couple of feet, continuing upwards the line of the ground floor. Two curved beams frame it, at the same time bracing the heavy, steeply-slanting roof above, the eaves of which cast a shadow half way down the wall when the sun stands high at noon.

But now, it may well be, the Downs call again. Before you turn back to them, though, take a look at the fourteenth-century bridge that spans the Arun between Stopham (after which it takes its name) and Pulborough, three or four miles to the north of Bignor and still short by a mile or so of that busy west-to-east road, the A 272, that can never be too far away from the South Downs to satisfy a true downland lover. It is a bridge so beautiful in its proportions, quite apart from its setting, that it makes the Trotton bridge, a product of the same century and perhaps from the hand and eye of the same builders, seem almost commonplace. Beneath its seven beautifully graduated arches the darkly glinting water flows; above it lean the great boughs of the overhanging trees; it is a place of silence and peace, comparable perhaps with that which has lain over Bignor's Roman Villa for a dozen centuries and more, though that place was a thousand years old at least when the masons first arrived with their tools to quarry stone for the bridge that was to replace the time-honoured ferry.

East of Bignor the road returns to a line close under the north face of the Downs. You may care to stay on it for a while, rather than climb back on to the Downs themselves, for the vast expanse of Arundel Park and the Earl Marshal's ancient castle intervene for a mile or two. In this case you will pass through the village of Houghton, having descended the long winding hill that deposits you outside the George & Dragon Inn. Brick and local flint throughout, but the upper storey is reinforced by timber framing; and the whole structure is braced by three massive brick buttresses, as though at some time it had been feared that the heavy tiled roof would cause the loose-knit walls to bulge outwards and collapse. The inn claims a royal connection. 'Charles II, on his ride to the coast after the battle of Worcester,' a plaque informs you, 'stopped to take ale at this Inn, October 14th, 1651.' You may feel inclined to follow suit before returning to the downland ridge that has, with interruptions, led you as far as this.

Nevertheless, Houghton is only one of a trio of villages in the vicinity that well repay a visit. The other two are Bury and Amberley, close together and only a mile or so to the north of the George & Dragon. If it must be one or the other, let your choice be Amberley, for this is surely one of the most perfect of all Sussex villages.

You may go to Amberley primarily to look at the remains of its fourteenth-century castle, today no more than a shell; or you may go there to look at the even older Norman church of St Michael, one of the most beautiful in all Sussex, the outstanding feature of which is perhaps the moulding of the chancel arch. But what is likely to leave the strongest impression of all, and one that will linger with you longer than that made by castle or church, is the sheer 'feel' of Amberley as a whole. It is easier by far to describe the masonry of the castle, or the individual lengths of zigzag moulding on that chancel arch, than to convey the atmosphere of this village that lies so far off the beaten track yet so close to both road and rail.

Here is serenity epitomised. The houses, large and small (and there are not many of the former), the cottages, the few shops, the old smithy, the former bakehouse: every building of whatever degree is perfectly matched and in tune with its neighbour. Here is mellow stone; here are subtly proportioned dormer windows; here is thatch so deep and thick and shapely that you would think it had grown there naturally, not been laid by thatchers with beetle, comb and shears. Some of the cottages have gardens laid out at head height that run to the top of the six- or eight-foot walls, themselves topped with channels of gay flowers to gladden the heart of the passer-by as well as those who look out over them from their upper windows.

The one road that runs through Amberley seems to double back on itself, to return whence it came; if it is indeed a through road, why then, it leads to nowhere with something of a secret smile. There is, it must be said, a slight suspicion of complacency here in Amberley; yet it can hardly be termed an offensive, even a righteous complacency. It is not in the least surprising that its occupants—the word seems more appropriate than 'inhabitants'—should more than once have been awarded the prize for the Best-Kept Sussex Village.

And so, at last, back to the South Downs once more. You can rejoin your original route by a gentle climb along a track that branches southwards off the B 2139 road to Storrington. It lead you on to Amberley Mount, and then eastwards, past the Celtic Fields (yet another reminder, like the tumuli and hill-forts, of the antiquity of the district) to Rackham Hill at something over six hundred feet above the level of the sea that is still screened for you by the sheer mass of the Downs themselves. Then, leisurely, to Kithurst Hill, nearly a hundred feet higher, where the north slopes are once again steep; steeper by far than those you have seen for the past twelve miles and more.

Just beyond Kithurst Hill, on Chantry Hill, there is a veritable network of alternative tracks. One of them continues straight onwards, but only to fork left and right about half a mile ahead; another follows the curving crest of the Downs left-handedly, round a horseshoe-shaped combe, and widens into a lane that slopes downwards for Storrington, in the valley below. Two others branch off right-handedly, dropping a hundred and fifty feet as they do so, their objectives a mile and a half and two miles distant respectively being ancient Flint Mines. They are of course shown on the map in Gothic type, as being recognised historic sites.

The nearer and better known of the two is named Harrow Hill. Here you will find relics of neolithic man that will remind you of Grimes Graves, on the Norfolk-Suffolk border near Brandon. Here at Harrow Hill four thousand years and more ago he delved into the downland chalk with antler-pick to extract the nuggets of black flint from which he would laboriously shape his tools and weapons; nuggets as precious to him as

Cottages in Amberley

nuggets of gold were to the prospectors of '98. You can still see, as you could in those other flint mines, the marks of his antler-picks and the smears of smoke from his crude oil lamps on the chalk that he worked some forty centuries ago.

At frequent intervals as you were making your way eastwards along the Downs you will have caught far glimpses of Chanctonbury Ring, silhouetted on the distant skyline. This mass of close-set beech trees on the crest of the Downs marking the prehistoric hill-fort is visible from miles away to the north, the north-west and the north-east; it is indeed one of the best-known landmarks in the whole of the south of England. Now it is no more than three miles ahead, on the far side of another of these main roads that make their way southwards through the intermittent gaps in the Downs, this time the A 24 from Dorking to the coast at Worthing. You have no option: you must inevitably cross this road, dropping fairly steeply off the downland track, to climb about as steeply up the opposite slope between Frieslands and Elbourne House, if you are to set foot within the Ring itself. When you do so, you will obtain perhaps the finest view from a downland crest to be found anywhere along the whole length of the South Downs.

On the other hand, you may be on the road that runs along the foot of the Downs from Storrington to Washington and on to Steyning. In this case you will be looking upwards at the Ring, and it will be surprising indeed if the mere sight of that great assembly of beeches does not fire you with the determination to climb until you can stand among them. You will find there a huge elliptical ring of trees wholly enclosing an Iron Age camp at a height of almost eight hundred feet above sea level. The 'camp', so-called, is of course prehistoric; the beech trees, on the other hand, were planted round it a mere two centuries ago.

The ground lies low to the immediate north of Chanctonbury Ring. The A 24 main road to Horsham and London thrusts across it, almost at your feet, close to the valley of the Adur. Seven miles north of where you stand it crosses straight over the A 272. Look in that direction, and then a mile or two to the left of the junction of the two roads. If the light is good, and the trees in the valley are not too rich in foliage, you should just be able to descry, even without the aid of glasses, the great white octagonal weather-boarded 'smock' mill at Shipley. It stands boldly on that level plain, giving the impression, as did the tower mill at Billingford on the Norfolk-Suffolk border, of being a lighthouse in a great turf sea.

You can of course come close to the mill. It is one of the relatively few objects that make the A 272 worth while, apart from its being a handy and fast road from east to west. You branch off this main road a couple of miles to the west of its junction with the A 24, on to a minor road, the B 2224, which serpentines about for a mile or so before depositing you in the very shadow of the windmill. This is 'Hilaire Belloc's Mill'. Here that great writer and ardent lover and interpreter of the Sussex scene lived from the beginning of this century until his death, at the age of eighty-three, in 1953. He did not live in the actual windmill—though people today do occasionally take over abandoned windmills and, at enormous expense, turn them into relatively comfortable dwellings. There is one such at Aldeburgh in Suffolk, another at Burnham Overy in Norfolk, and yet another at High Salvington, behind Worthing, in Sussex. But he lived and wrote in the house close alongside, so close indeed to the windmill that when its great sails turned they cast long sweeping shadows over it. It was here that he wrote that superb book about Sussex, the most riotous effusion to come from his vigorous pen, a book that breathes the very essence of Sussex, *The Four Men*. He is, perhaps, but little read today; he died, tragically, in his beloved home at Shipley, within view of Chanctonbury Ring; those who do not know his work are the poorer for this.

Eastwards of Chanctonbury Ring the South Downs diminish into the wide Adur Valley and at the same time come closer to the coast than they have been so far or will be again until they make their final gesture on the outskirts of Eastbourne. To look at what industry is doing in this region is

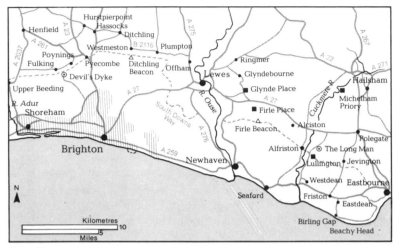

East Sussex

to make one wonder whether even this great mass of chalk land can hope to survive man's depredations. This valley is the widest of those that carry the rivers southwards to the sea. The low-lying ground immediately to the north of villages such as Steyning and Bramber and Upper Beeding is beset by immense quarries and their attendant works; the former small and engaging roads are being widened into dual carriageways, with flyovers and junctions and goodness-knows-what-else either on the drawing-boards of the surveyors and engineers responsible for this desecration of this corner of Sussex or in actual process of construction. Inevitably, of course; for this is the direct route to the coast, midway between Worthing and Brighton.

You cannot avoid crossing this gap between the main length of the South Downs and their dwindling eastwards extremity. As several times already, two courses now lie open to you. From Chanctonbury Ring, if you are on foot, you can continue on your way almost due east, following a track that drops gently downwards by way of Wiston and so into the village of Steyning, with Bramber and Upper Beeding beyond, either side of the Adur; from just north of Upper Beeding a minor road runs close beneath the north shoulder of the Downs eastwards to Fulking, Poynings and Pyecombe. Alternatively, you can here climb back onto the Downs themselves and continue walking on fine smooth turf high above this road with a view southwards to the sea but unhappily including the vast sprawl of this major south coast town, Brighton itself.

As an alternative to this route, however, you can leave Chanctonbury Ring by a track that at first runs almost due south and will take you to another of the great prehistoric hill-forts, Cissbury Ring. From here the view southwards and eastwards is as impressive as the view northwards from Chanctonbury Ring. You can see as far as Beachy Head in one direction and the Isle of Wight in the other. This hill-fort is not only remarkable in itself but also includes a number of flint mines similar to those on Harrow Hill, if not quite so extensive. From Cissbury, though, you must in any case descend, whatever direction you decide upon. A track will take you eastwards, down steepish contours to begin with, until you come quite close to Lancing College. Few visitors will deny that the dominant feature here is Lancing College Chapel, which has been appropriately called a 'Gothic Masterpiece'.

It is hardly surprising that this gigantic building has come to be known generally as the 'Cathedral of the Downs' (reminding one of the church at Tideswell, in Derbyshire, which acquired the title 'Cathedral of the Peak'). Certainly it is more cathedral than church, let alone chapel—its official title, as is usual in the case of schools and colleges. The first stones of this great edifice were laid just over a century ago. The architect is on record as having aimed at achieving the same spectacular scale as that to be found in the nave of York Minster or Westminster Abbey. The tradition of the great Gothic cathedrals was to be observed in such details as, for example, the use of stone quarried and carved, so far as was practicable, locally and by local masons. In fundamentally chalk country, this of course led to problems. Nor were such problems new. Many of the great cathedrals of Europe stand in regions where suitable stone is not abundant, and stone from the famous quarries at Caen had often to be transported over great distances.

This 'Cathedral of the Downs' is of course dear to all alumni of the famous college for whose benefit it was erected a century or more ago by Nathaniel Woodward as a mother church for all the other schools of his foundation. The public can usually go inside after asking at the porter's lodge near the West Entrance. The interior is well worth seeing. It is admired by many who have no connection with the college for the ambitious quality of its conception. But yet there may be some who feel that on account of its very splendour it is perhaps less in keeping with the Downs and the Weald beneath them than are the many modest little churches such as those of Elsted and Didling, Trotton and Terwick and Selham. We leave Lancing College and its cathedral-like chapel with wonder in our hearts; we remember those others with an emotion more akin to affection.

Since this alternative route takes you so close to the sprawling and still growing conurbation of Shoreham-by-Sea, Hove and Brighton (already virtually fused into one), it is obvious that the other is the better choice: to leave the Downs just short of Steyning, cross the wide valley by way of Bramber and Upper Beeding, and on the other side of the valley aim for the Downs again on Truleigh Hill, or keep close beneath their north face on the charming little lane that winds close alongside them to Fulking and the other small villages that lie just beyond this.

Inevitably, thanks to their situation in this broad valley of the Adur, Steyning, Bramber and Upper Beeding are all in danger of being destroyed. The heart of each village, even though modern-style shops and stores may be opening, retains much of beauty. There are Georgian houses, which are of course always distinctive; there are houses of an earlier date, finely half-timbered; there is an outstanding Norman church in Steyning, dedicated to St Andrew and built by the Order of Benedictines on a site on which a much earlier church had been built, in the eighth century, by St Cuthman. He is one of the few saints with whom a legend that is basically comic has been associated. The story goes that St Cuthman reached Steyning during the hay harvest of some indeterminate year twelve centuries ago. The odd feature of his visit is that he arrived wheeling his aged mother in a barrow. This story may or may not be true, but the large-scale maps of this part of Sussex do indicate a 'Cuthman's Field' on the outskirts of Steyning.

Bramber, a mile to the east and right on the river's edge—the Adur was a navigable river up to comparatively recent times and Bramber, now so quiet a village, was for that reason a township of some importance centuries ago—is noteworthy today chiefly for its castle, which stands high among trees near the top of the hill by which you approach it from the direction of Steyning. There is not a great deal left of this castle, built by the Normans not long after the Conquest and for long relied upon to command the navigable Adur and warn off any who dared to sail up its wide waters with hostile intentions. Like so many of our castles, it was sadly damaged during the Civil War and today, even though it is National Trust property, there is not sufficient of it standing to enable anyone, save an expert in these matters, to form an adequate notion of what it originally looked like. Though it is impressively sited, it is easy enough to miss it altogether from the road, behind a bank of trees, if you do not know exactly where to look out for it.

The smallest of this trio, Upper Beeding, lies just on the other side of the river. The A 2037 sweeps through it, and there really seems very little chance that the village can much longer survive the pressure of traffic that passes beneath the frontages of its shops and small houses. It is unlikely, too, that it will be by-passed, for there is a useful bridge just here across the Adur and it might well be regarded as uneconomical to build another in order to spare the village further damage.

Beyond Upper Beeding the A 2037 takes an abrupt turn northwards, making for Henfield, four miles distant. If you know, and therefore love, the poetry (and prose, too) of the late Walter de la Mare you may like to have a look at the village, for he lived here for many years before his death. It is a village in which you will find, among other things, some good examples of true Sussex thatch, notably at Lavender Cottage, overlooking the spacious green. And here too you will find, if you walk part way up a lane that leads to the church, that odd feature of Henfield known to everyone as The Cat House.

It is a half-timbered cottage heavily (and admirably) thatched. You will notice that all round it, just beneath the overhanging eaves, there is what could be called a frieze of cats: one black cat apiece in each of the oak-framed, white-washed panels, and every one of them in silhouette. There is, of course, a story behind this odd feature.

The cottage used to be occupied by a somewhat eccentric old lady whose sole companion was a well-loved canary. The vicar of the parish church, a bachelor, had for his sole companion a well-loved cat. The cat used to accompany him everywhere, so that on his way up the lane to the church on Sundays and other occasions when his presence was required there, he and his cat passed close to the cottage, almost beneath its eaves. And, inevitably, one day disaster struck: the canary had momentarily escaped from its cage, and the cat, happening to be passing at the time, seized both the opportunity and the canary.

As a reprisal, the old lady, distraught at the loss of her pet, had an effigy of the vicar's cat made and hung on a pole outside the door of her cottage, so that the vicar would be reminded every time he passed of the heinous crime committed by his cat. Eventually the old lady died, and the feud between parish priest and parishioner died with her. The cottage passed into other hands. But because village traditions are slow to die—indeed are often, and rightly , deliberately kept alive—the memory of the delinquent cat was preserved in this novel form. And the canary, too, achieved immortality: look carefully, and you will see that every cat-in-silhouette holds in its mouth a diminutive canary in its death-agony!

This northwards turn of the A 2037 is forced upon it by a massive shoulder of the South Downs immediately to the east of the river. But a mile or less along that road a minor and most inviting lane branches off to the right, signposted to Edburton and Fulking. The best way, of course, to get the true feel of this next section of the Downs is by walking along the top of them; but a good alternative is to be found in this unspoiled lane that runs so close alongside them at their feet; closer, in fact, even than the best portions of the corresponding lane that you may have followed eastwards from the trio of Hartings to Didling, Duncton and Bignor.

A mile along this lane, on your left, is Truleigh Farm. It takes its name from the summit beneath which it shelters, Truleigh Hill, at seven hundred feet. Here the contour lines once more crowd closely together and the hard track that leads steeply away from opposite the farm gate climbs

Looking towards Seven Sisters cliffs from Seaford Head

these contours, to bring you out on a beaten turf track running southwards to the prehistoric hill-fort resoundingly named Thundersbarrow, and then eastwards to Castle Ring high on Edburton Hill. This is indeed a noble stretch of the South Downs, rich in the remains of tumuli, Celtic fields and other relics of the prehistoric inhabitants of these chalk uplands. Six hundred feet and more below you, to the north, is the wide expanse of open country, the 'tilted levels' of which Sheila Kaye-Smith, the Sussex-born novelist, wrote, and the 'many-coloured fields spotted with farms'. And here and there, of course, are small villages; Fulking, for instance.

Unlike so many of these villages, however small, Fulking does not possess a church; not even one like Didling's, situated well outside the cluster of houses that make up that village; not even one like the Church-in-the-Field at Terwick. But it does possess a most charming, and charmingly sited, inn, the Shepherd & Dog. Yellow-washed, and secure behind a high flint wall, it stands at the foot of a short, steepish hill that climbs from a sharp turn at its foot in a crook of the Downs.

Beyond Fulking the narrow lane wanders on, still close beneath the Downs, to Poynings, whose church is large enough for two villages, which

288

is perhaps just as well since neighbouring Fulking has no church of its own. Between the two villages, on the crest of the Downs, there is the curious feature known as the Devil's Dyke. It is the site, if tradition is to be believed, of a set-to between Old Nick and St Dunstan who, perhaps to his own surprise and certainly to that of Old Nick, succeeded in preventing him from achieving his purpose, which was nothing more nor less than to carve a channel through the Downs just here that would allow the sea to flow inland and flood the Weald with salt water.

And still, mile upon mile of these glorious Downs lie ahead of you. In Pyecombe, close to former iron-working country, the finest of all Sussex shepherds' crooks were made; and it is not only the descendants of the Pyecombe craftsmen who make this claim, for Sussex shepherds almost without exception pay tribute to them. High above Pyecombe, yet not so high as would be the case in other parts, for the village stands higher than many others, is Newtimber Hill to the south-west, matched by Wolstonbury Hill with its prehistoric hill-fort to the north. Then a narrow lane, branching off just to the east of Clayton Tunnel (with the extraordinary castellated tunnel entrance that is fit to rank among the eighteenth-century 'Follies' even though it was constructed a hundred years later) takes you once again along the very foot of the Downs, through Westmeston and Plumpton, on the B 2116, and eventually by way of Offham village down into Lewes, where for a mile or so you must in any case leave the South Downs, whether you are driving or walking on them.

They start again immediately to the east of the county town of East Sussex, beyond the broad valley of the Ouse. But by now you will of course have left behind you, and somewhat to the north, the villages of Ditchling and Hassocks. They will almost certainly be already known to you by name, for they have been associated with crafts and craftsmen not only in olden times but comparatively recently, when Eric Gill's community of craftsmen lived and worked here. Now, unhappily, the villages have become somewhat self-conscious, and the true, unspoiled village atmosphere, such as may still be savoured in so many of the smaller, less-renowned, villages of the region, has gone for ever.

A solitary chunk—there is really no other word for it—of the South Downs rises to the east of Lewes, beyond the Ouse, topped by the remains of a Long Barrow, a tumulus or two and the relics of another small area of Celtic fields. On the east slopes is Glyndebourne, beloved of Mozart enthusiasts the world over. Then, beyond a stretch of water known as Glynde Reach, to the south of Firle Park and its mansion, the Downs swell once more to something like their earlier grandeur and you can follow them right through to their eastern terminus just to the south of the Long Man of Wilmington, with but one brief interruption when you must descend to the Cuckmere Valley at Alfriston. Only some twelve miles of the Downs remain to be explored as they curve gradually southwards, following the line of the coast but closing in on it all the time till they merge with it above Birling Gap.

The Long Barrow on Firle Beacon is seven hundred feet and more above the sea, now just four miles from you to the south. There is no longer a minor road, or even a lane, to follow close beneath the north shoulder of the Downs; instead, a main road, the A 27, running eastwards from Lewes and leading to Eastbourne, Bexhill, Hastings and the Channel resorts of Kent as well as Sussex. More than ever, if you wish truly to savour the Downs for the last few miles, you should contrive to be on the high tracks that were trodden by the inhabitants of these parts long centuries before any roads were built in the low-lying, afforested and often swampy areas to the north. But if this is not practicable, you can still come close to the Downs by following this main road and branching off it right-handedly at intervals along the narrow and winding roads that eventually tilt upwards among the foot-hills.

One such minor road, no more than a brief section of lane, in fact, will take you to the hamlet of Alciston; from here you can quite easily climb on to Bostal Hill at something over six hundred feet. Another, and wider road, will take you to Alfriston, one of East Sussex's show villages; here you will find, among much else of interest, the beautiful half-timbered inn, The Star, comparable in quality with the finest medieval inns not merely in Sussex but in the country as a whole, and one of the oldest, too. It was built some time in the middle of the fifteenth century by the Abbot of neighbouring Battle Abbey as a hostel for mendicant friars. Being the property of an abbey it could provide sanctuary to anyone who sought it beneath the hostel roof; but it was intended primarily for the mendicant friars and for pilgrims on their way to and from the shrine of St Richard, at Chichester in West Sussex.

The great roof, of Horsham slabs, is supported on a framework of massive oak timbers – Sussex oak, of course. Between these, three beautifully proportioned oriel windows project outwards beyond the overhanging upper storey. There is a sequence of carvings in the oak beams and elsewhere: St Michael fighting the Basilisk (not, as is commonly supposed, St George fighting the Dragon); two heraldic beasts, two snakes with intertwining tails, a quaint little terrier, a bishop wearing his mitre. All these are the work of medieval craftsmen, and the oak in which they did their carving is so iron-hard that it has survived some five hundred years and still looks as though it could survive another comparable span of time.

Do not miss, by the way, the odd-looking monster jutting out from the corner at pavement level, at the end of the alternating courses of brick and flint of which, like so many buildings in Alfriston, this ancient house was constructed. A monster it certainly is: a lion's head, heavily crowned, is joined to a trunk of a body by a short, thick neck. It was not placed there by the men who built this ecclesiastical hostel five centuries ago, but it is certainly old. In fact, it is a figurehead taken from a vessel ship-wrecked off this coast three hundred years ago.

And do not turn away from the inn with the idea that Alfriston has nothing else to show save tea-shops and souvenir-shops (of which some might say that there are too many). There is a fine medieval church here, disproportionately large for the size of the village, so large in fact that it was known as the 'Cathedral of the Downs' long years before Lancing College Chapel was even dreamed of in the mid-nineteenth century. It was at one time attached to the Augustinian Priory of Michelham, five or six miles to the north. Alfriston also has what is believed to be the sole surviving example of a Clergy House. Indeed, it is true to say of this small village in the Cuckmere Valley between two shoulders of the Downs that here are 'infinite riches in a little room'. This, of course, is a phrase that can be applied to a great many villages the length and breadth of the country as a whole, but there is no good reason why, cliché as it may be, this tribute should not be paid where it is so well deserved.

Just across the Cuckmere is the tiny village of Lullington, all flint nicely intermixed with brick: two or three houses, a little village hall and, well signed up the hill towards Wilmington, the alleged smallest church in England. Hidden among trees at the end of a footpath, it is built on a slanting piece of roughish turf scattered with a few gravestones and also some half-buried lengths of what appear to be 'footings', foundation-stones.

The internal dimensions of this church can hardly be more than fifteen feet from wall to wall in either direction; close-crowded, elbow to elbow, it might at a pinch seat a congregation of eighteen—only half the congregation that was the estimated capacity of the minute church of St Andrew, near Didling, in West Sussex. It has an altar, a lectern and a font; and that is about all. Those partisans who claim that it is the smallest church in England, smaller even than the one at Culbone, in Somerset, conveniently forget that in fact Lullington's church, as you see it today, is merely the sole remaining portion of an originally much larger church, the chancel, in fact. You can judge this for yourself by tracing out the lines of those foundations that extend westwards from the present small entrance to the church. Nevertheless what has remained gives the impression of being whole and complete, if on a miniature scale. It is capped by a white weather-boarded belfry, small in proportion, and this in turn is topped by a miniature broach spire. No one, however, seems to know why the church should have been made so difficult of access from the village in the valley at its feet. Perhaps its situation on the slope of a steepish hill is the simple explanation of why it has now ceased to exist save as one small portion of a once relatively capacious House of God.

And now you are close indeed to the final buttress of the South Downs.

The contours decline gradually, spreading outwards rather than upwards, as the chalk mass approaches its demise. Beyond Alfriston and Lullington is the beautiful small hamlet of Wilmington, less self-conscious than some other Sussex villages, less exploited than neighbouring Alfriston, mindful still, perhaps, of the Benedictine Priory at the top of the hill which, after the Dissolution, became a private dwelling. Now in the care of the Sussex Archaeological Society, the priory shelters an agricultural museum.

From a stone seat near the entrance to the priory-that-was, a seat dedicated to the memory of the writer Jeffery Farnol, you can obtain a magnificent view of the so-called Long Man of Wilmington, set in a north-eastwards-facing hollow of Windover Hill. This is an extraordinary turf-cut figure, reminiscent a little of the Giant of Cerne on the chalk hill immediately above the Dorset village of that name (and above a priory, too, as it happens). A bulky, somewhat shapeless figure, he stands (or lies) on the concave face of the Downs, holding a staff in each hand at arm's length. Whoever carved the figure, and more particularly the two staves, must have had a good eye; for in spite of the concave curve out of which he was cut the two staves are rule-straight for the whole two hundred feet of their length, which in fact slightly exceeds the height of the figure himself.

Who carved him there, and when, no one can say with any degree of certainty. There are those who say that he was carved as a *jeu d'esprit* by the monks at the priory. They point out, in support of their theory, that unlike the Giant of Cerne an important feature of the male anatomy is wholly lacking here. In any case, though, would any prior ever be so broad-minded as to let his fraternity of holy men loose on this slope of the Downs to carve anything other than, say, a Cross, or some other religious symbol? Surely not. So it can be taken for granted that any date that could be ascribed to the original carving in the turf of the Wilmington Long Man is earlier by many centuries than the Benedictines whose priory faced him across the hollow at the foot of Windover Hill.

Another theory is that he represents the Scandinavian god, Baldur. The theory is supported by the fact that the figure is carved in such a position as (very nearly) to face the rising sun. He would thus be holding in his two hands the posts that support the legendary 'Gateway of the Morning'. It is a pleasantly romantic theory; but the words 'very nearly' tend to invalidate it. The Egyptians, and possibly the early inhabitants of Britain, had the knowledge and skill to foretell and establish the movements of the sun at varying times of the year, whether in the land of the pyramids or on the open wastes of Salisbury Plain on which the latter sited Stonehenge. But by no stretch of imagination can the two staves held by the Long Man of Wilmington be identified with the Portals of the Morning.

A more promising theory as to the origin of the Long Man is that his two staves represent those that have always been used by surveyors laying-out roads in many parts of the country. But this, too, has an element of fantasy

The Long Man of Wilmington

in it. The tracks along these Downs, and the corresponding ones along the Berkshire Downs, notably the Berkshire Ridgeway, date back so many hundreds of years, even into prehistoric time, that it is hard to believe that they were established by men with such relatively sophisticated equipment as sighting-poles and measuring-tapes. And in any case there would be no need for these on the Downs; for a man, and the cattle he herded, automatically and instinctively followed the tracks beaten out for him by those who had earlier travelled that way; and those routes were always the natural ones that sought the driest and therefore most consistently practicable terrain through and over which he had need to travel. At any rate, Wilmington's famous Long Man was not even discovered until some time in the middle of the eighteenth century; there are no references to his existence earlier than that. He may well have rested there, staves at the ready, for a thousand, may be two or even three thousand years, before being laid bare; thus it is improbable that his secret will ever be learned.

You are now within sight of the eastern terminus of the South Downs. Their level rises to 638 feet at the prehistoric camp on Combe Hill. A track leads thence south-eastwards into the outskirts of Eastbourne; another leads south-westwards into the hamlet of Jevington. For once it is safe to recommend a visit to a place lying on the south side of the downland rampart, which has (rightly or wrongly) been so studiously avoided ever since the Hartings were left behind. Jevington is another of these charmingly secluded downland villages: flint and brick, of course, with a beautiful, and beautifully sited, church, dedicated to St Andrew.

The road on which quiet Jevington lies will lead you southwards by way of Friston, whence the A 259 will take you either to Eastdean, once a beautiful village but now unhappily virtually incorporated in the outskirts of Eastbourne; or to Westdean, by way of the oddly named village of Exceat. Westdean happily lies just off the road and is as good a village as any in these parts at which to complete your tally of those that East Sussex has to offer. There is a serenity about these few houses of brick and flint nestling beneath the hanging woods that so nearly surround them that epitomises all that you may have felt about these many villages interspersed among the novelist Sheila Kaye-Smith's 'many-coloured fields spotted with farms', and yet not succeeded in expressing.

But since for the most part the South Downs themselves, and the Weald to the north of them, have been the subject of this leisurely exploration, perhaps it might best be completed by continuing onwards as far as Birling Gap, which lies between the elevated earthworks and tumuli, curiously named Belle Tout—though they are most emphatically British rather than, as the name suggests, French; these are to the east; and the Seven Sisters (now happily in part National Trust property) to the west.

It was to Birling Gap, along the track following the escarpment of the South Downs, that the first fruits of the Cornish tin mines were conveyed, by pack-animals, centuries ago, for shipment to the Continent. It was into the secret maw of Birling Gap that, for many centuries and indeed right through almost (if not quite) to our own day, contraband was delivered from the Continent, for dispersal throughout Sussex and north-westwards to London and beyond. Here came the 'brandy for the parson, baccy for the clerk' of Kipling's verse.

To obtain your final view of the South Downs, however (if this is practicable), you should board a small boat at any convenient point of embarkation and make your way a mile or two out to sea. Then, turn about and feast your eyes on the undulating cliff-line that forms a thin green peak above the chalk-white faces of the Seven Sisters. This is, as it were, a cross-section of the Downs that have now curved towards the sea, to be cut off short, as with a sharp knife. It is a visual reminder of the oft-stated fact that Sussex (and part of Kent to the east and Hampshire and Dorset to the west) once lay beneath a solid mass of chalk, originally the bed of a primeval ocean that was in time to be thrown up to form an elongated dome three thousand and more feet high. That dome, of which the South

Downs are now virtually the only relic left from that unimaginably remote period when south-eastern England and north-western France were an entity: a 'belle tout', to adopt a local name that almost represents not fancy but fact.

KENT

If Sussex does not readily offer itself for exploration, even less so does Kent. True, this county's coastal resorts are fewer and, some would hold, less distinguished; but they still demand quick road links with London, and all the more so since two of these resorts, Folkestone and Dover, together with Sheerness on Sheppey where the Medway meets the Thames, are important cross-channel ports fed by motorways and trunk roads, the former at any rate something virtually unknown in Sussex. And the South Downs, which provided the varied axis of your route all the way from the Hartings to Eastbourne, seem to lose heart in Kent and become mere characterless outriders of their western selves, unrecognisable as anything more than a modest escarpment until reinforced by the North Downs creeping uncertainly down from London's confines to end abruptly as the white cliffs of Dover.

The backbone of these North Downs separates two motorway or trunk road systems across the northern and eastern parts of the county. These are the M2, roughly paralleling the Thames estuary and serving Gravesend, Rochester, the cathedral city of Canterbury and the port of Dover; and, only a few miles to the west and south, the M25 and M20 which join Sevenoaks, Maidstone, Ashford and Folkestone.

For the rest, Kent, the 'Garden of England', is a county of orchards, of hop fields, of market gardens and of several of England's most famed stately homes, these including Sissinghurst, Mecca of garden enthusiasts; Leeds Castle, not without reason claiming to be 'the loveliest castle in England'; Knole, Penshurst, Hever (where Henry VIII first met Anne Boleyn) and Winston Churchill's Chartwell. Thus the crowds that spill out of London into Kent form two streams; those who tour the county for its own sake, and those who see it as mere transit territory to be hurtled through on the way to the Continent. The latter keep to the motorways and trunk roads and should not worry the rambler; the others—at any rate in fine weather and at holiday times – can clog roads that under other circumstances are refreshingly unpretentious.

Kent, one may then say, is a sophisticated, widely known and very accessible county. Yet there are two corners to which only the last of these adjectives applies. The first, immediately east of the border with Sussex, is Romney Marsh. The second, on the map a clumsy claw separating

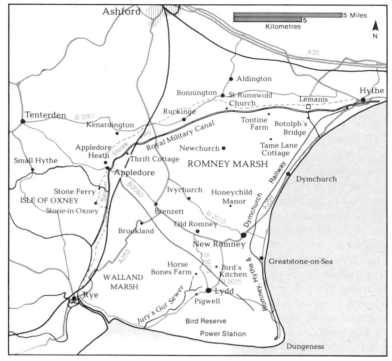

Romney Marsh

Thames from Medway, is officially and rather pompously the northern sector of the District of Rochester upon Medway, but unofficially the peninsula of Hoo, or just plain Hoo.

In fact to speak of Romney Marsh—if we mean, as we do here, the whole stretch between Sussex's Rye and Kent's Hythe—is to be imprecise, for the area comprises two individual wetlands; that of Walland to the south-west and that of Romney to the north-east, the two separated by the A259, a road that traces the ancient Rhee Wall which in the sixteenth century made possible the reclamation of, first, Romney and then Walland. Officially, then, two names, but visually a single flat expanse which over millenia has vacillated between sea and land or something halfway. Hence such oddities as Small Hythe—Hythe meaning a landing place—now all of six or seven miles from navigable water but once a bustling wool port on a broad tidal waterway which today survives only in indignity as the insignificant Reading Sewer (the one-time Harbour Master's house enjoys greater dignity as the home, now a museum, of the actress Ellen Terry); or the Isle of Oxney, today simply sleepy, pastoral land, though a purist, allowing Reading Sewer rather more than its modern due, could insist that this is still an island; or Stone Ferry, where a road crosses what is now no more than a glorified ditch beside which the modern long-distance footpath, the Saxon Shore Way, emphasises that in Roman times salt water lapped here.

These names can be readily explained. But down on the marsh there are many others, to be gleaned and savoured from a detailed map or simply encountered while meandering around, which can hardly fail to spur speculation. Pigwell and Horse Bones, for instance; Birds Kitchen, Jury's Gut, Tame Lane, Tontine Farm, Honeychild and Thrift. But if such names are teasing—suggesting, perhaps, domestic and farming successes and disasters and joys and virtues – those identifying the small houses along the characterless shore carry a clearer message, maybe of the nostalgia or unrealised dreams of their retired owners. The Helm and The Chart are here, alongside Sea Symphony, Blue Haze, Tossing Waves and, by contrast, Even Keel.

Hardly a shore, this, on which to linger. But you may have no choice, for the children will surely clamour for a ride on the toy Romney, Hythe and Dymchurch Railway which has plied the thirteen miles from Hythe to Dungeness for over fifty-five years and claims not only to be the world's longest miniature railway but also the only one used officially for the transport of children to and from school. Nor can Dungeness simply be dismissed, for here is a gem if ever there was one for the connoisseur of the appalling. Desolate and as often as not windswept even in sunshine, this blunt, shingle promontory is a litter of haphazard bungalows and shacks, their roofs in many cases secured by sandbags; of gravel pits, dismantled railway, pylons, defeated vegetation and basic-looking boats stranded like unhappy mammals on shingle ridges. Vague, unfenced, temporary-looking roads lead seemingly nowhere or peter out around the mass of the nuclear power station which dwarfs everything, including the adjacent lighthouses. Yet aesthetics are not everything and there are those who cannot keep away from this place. Bird lovers make for the sanctuaries around the pits; ship spotters, armed with binoculars and dreaming of far places, stand absorbed out on the shingle tip; pebble collectors enjoy access to limitless trove.

Nor, it must be conceded, will the marsh appeal to everyone. In almost every sense except distance far removed from familiar cosy and conventional Kent, Walland and Romney are essentially for two types of person. For those at one with flat wetland, wide skies and the constant presence of water and its flora and fauna; and for those who cannot resist churches. Whether gaunt skeletons recalling a more pious or perhaps a more thickly populated era, or whether still in use as one of the ten making up the modern parish, churches are hard to avoid here.

Romney, Hythe and Dymchurch railway—the 'Typhoon' leaving Hythe

Smuggling, too, is of the essence in this place. Not the sordid, modern drug pushers of Heathrow, Gatwick and the Channel ports, but those—to our eyes anyway—more picturesque eighteenth- and nineteenth-century characters who beached on the secret Dungeness shingle, then made their way inland. At first it was all pretty open: 'Five and twenty ponies, Trotting through the dark, Brandy for the parson, 'Baccy for the clerk', to quote Kipling. The 'gentlemen' felt, reasonably enough, that they were supplying a public need. Why else did the parson so often turn a blind eye to the fact that his church served as a safe distribution point? But it was too good to last, of course, and whatever element of romance there may have been vanished after Waterloo when the authorities, free now of the worries of the French wars, clamped down and, for both smugglers and excise officers, smuggling became, as you will learn when you reach Brookland, a very vicious scene.

Since you are in country so long moulded by sea and tide and storm, you could do worse than start your meander—and that is what it will have to be—at New Romney, where you may be surprised to find that should you wish to visit the fine Norman church you will have to step down into it. Seven hundred years ago this was not so, but in 1287 a devastating storm deposited so much shingle that seven centuries later the ground level has still not subsided to what it once was. What the storm did to the church could have been at worst an inconvenience. What it did to this whole district was disastrous, for the shingle so blocked the Rother's mouth here that New Romney lost its harbour, and with it its life, while the river had to find a new course to a new mouth at Rye. Thus as you drive along the two or so miles to Old Romney, you are following the ancient course of the river to a place which until that day in 1287 was a bustling trading and shipbuilding port but which today is a sleepy hamlet below rook-filled trees. Have a look inside the largely thirteenth-century church. You will find a vaulted ceiling, a medieval stone altar cut with consecration crosses, box pews and, perhaps most intriguing of all, in the little belfry a primitive ladder-stair opposite a window arch cunningly offset to light it.

Should you be tempted by curiosities you can now briefly divert northwards to Ivychurch where you will be rewarded by a church porch that once served as village school and also by a slightly comic but highly practical portable shelter known as a 'hudd' and used in the eighteenth century by parsons determined to keep themselves dry while officiating at the graveside. No ivy here, by the way; the name derives from the Saxon *ey* and means The Church on the Island, a timely reminder that had you chosen to visit here a few centuries ago you would have had to find a boat.

Whether you divert to Ivychurch or not, your next objective will surely be Brookland. The church here is known to have been one of those which doubled as a smugglers' cache and was probably the objective of a large armed gang who one February night in 1821 landed their contraband on Camber Sands to the south-east of Rye. Detected, they were harried across the marsh until near Brookland there was something like a pitched battle in the course of which the Blockaders' leader was killed as were also four smugglers, while the wounded numbered eighteen, sixteen of them smugglers. Of this bloody affray, only the story remains, but the church at its centre, probably the most interesting on the marshes, now welcomes more law-abiding visitors who come to admire the complicated, detached, timber belfry and, inside, the alarming angles of the nave arches, the collection of tithe weights and measures, and, above all, the famous Norman font, superbly decorated with the signs of the zodiac and the occupations of the months.

Brookland's church is well set within its village. Brenzett's, rather over a mile to the north-east, lies clear and despite the adjacent main road hides idyllic behind trees below which sheep graze the rough churchyard and in summer lie sprawled warm on the flat graveslabs. It is dedicated to Eanswith, a little-known saint who in fact enjoys two claims to fame: as granddaughter of that Ethelbert who welcomed St Augustine ashore at Ebbsfleet (we shall find ourselves there later), and as the founder at Folkestone of what was almost certainly England's first convent. Sadly, the evil eye must have lighted on the place, for after being sacked by

Vikings, it was rebuilt as a monastery, only to suffer the indignity of sliding into the sea as the cliffs eroded. However, Eanswith's relics were rescued and should you wish to continue your acquaintance with this talented lady—stretching wooden beams, curing blindness, and causing water to flow uphill were among her accomplishments—you have only to visit the Church of Saints Mary and Eanswith at Folkestone. But to revert to Brenzett. As so often happens with churches, it is some small half-hidden feature that most touches the memory; here it is a bricked-up priest's door with, on one jamb, a medieval scratch-dial used to indicate the times of services.

For devotees, the marshlands to the north-east will continue to beckon: to Newchurch, perhaps, where the church's tower has taken a startling lurch and the churchyard looks as if it had suffered an earthquake; or to Eastbridge, beyond, whose church long ago gave up, resigned to crumbling into gaunt ruin and the cartographical anonymity of 'Church (rems of)'; or even to brave the vulgarities of Dymchurch for the sake of its Martello towers. But it may well be that you are hankering for a change, if only a temporary one, and thus succumb to the promise of the gentle escarpment that cradles the marsh, offering many an attractive corner as well as long views towards Dungeness and its coasts. But first you will have to cross what is grandly marked on the map 'Royal Military Canal'—a dignity sharply cut down to size by the qualification 'disused' in brackets. This canal, which starts near the centre of Hythe and for some twenty-three miles hugs the foot of the escarpment until its waters merge with those of the Rother near Rye, was dug in 1804–6 as part of a defensive system which, together with those Martello towers along the coast, was to deter the French. And, one may well say, it succeeded. In any event the French never came. Maybe, though, they had already learnt their lesson from that debacle near Fishguard seven years earlier, the farcical course of which you can trace should you be in western Wales and so minded. Today the canal is for angling, boating and strolling, a tranquil man-made successor to the tidal river and sea inlets that once ebbed and flowed here.

Along this escarpment—and scenically it is a total contrast to the wetland only a few yards away beyond the canal—you will find Roman, Viking and medieval associations, although in the church at Stone-in-Oxney there is something infinitely older, namely the bones of an iguanodon, a beast which died near here perhaps seventy million years ago, thereafter resting hidden until revealed by quarrying in 1935. Alongside there is a battered and ancient stone, of local geology, bearing an incised bull; dug up in the chancel during the eighteenth century, it is claimed to be a Roman or Romano-British pagan altar, perhaps in active use on or near this site until its rites, whatever they may have been, were ousted by those of Christianity. Sadly, the chances are that you will find that both these curiosities are behind a locked door. However, there is a

St Clement's Church, Old Romney, on Romney Marsh

wide grille through which you can look, and any particularly interested and determined visitor will surely be able to negotiate closer access.

The churches at both Appledore and Kenardington stand amid traces of Viking encampments. Appledore is a neat but elongated small town with a wide street, green verges and some sixteenth-century houses, trim and conventionally Kentish despite its being a mere stone's throw above the marsh. By contrast, Kenardington is a hamlet, a place in which you can still find evidence of the harsh presence of the Viking invaders though this long ago ceded place to Christianity and what must be one of the humblest of churches, primitive within and without, a gem with tiled paving, rough walls, candle lighting and the simplest of furnishing.

At Ruckinge—a scatter of no particular character three or more miles farther east—you once again run into villains for this was the home of the notorious Ransley gang. Although hanged in 1800, two Ransley brothers nevertheless rest in the churchyard, though in a weird grave marked by a crude plank resting on iron supports, while local ambivalence has conferred respectability by naming a nearby residential area Ransley

Green. A tiny church appropriately dedicated to a tiny saint is what you will find next, at Bonnington, another three or so miles to the east; or, more precisely, well outside its village and just above the canal. The saint is Rumswold. Born in 662 (but not here), he at once announced 'Christianus sum' and discoursed on the Faith with both eloquence and erudition; on his second day he delivered a sermon on the Trinity, and on his third he foretold his own end and thereupon expired. After this it seems bathos to mention, if only for the benefit of alumni of Durham, that William van Mildert, founder of their university in 1832, was Assistant Curate here in 1789. A far better-known cleric, the great Erasmus, was in 1511 granted the living of adjacent Aldington, one of many favours he managed to attract during his short years in England and one he speedily traded in for a pension of £20 a year. But then Aldington was no ordinary living, for here once stood a country palace of the archbishops of Canterbury, a place of grace and elegance crumbled today into earthwork hummocks beyond the church. But take a look at this church, at its exterior north wall where you will find a blocked doorway; strangely tall and narrow, this, it seems, was the archbishops' personal entrance.

Your tour along the escarpment began with a pagan altar and it seems appropriate that it should end with the place from which this altar may have come, Rome's fortified port of Lemanis. The site, a sizeable one spilling down the lower contours, is best appreciated if seen as a whole from a distance and this of course means returning to the marsh and then following the road eastward past Lower Wall and Tontine Farm towards Botolph's Bridge. But well before you reach this last you should be scanning the slopes to your north where you should have no difficulty in picking out the considerable remains of a place which must have seemed welcome indeed to many a Roman, standing where you now stand but on the deck of a ship (as likely as not a proud unit of that resoundingly named fleet, the *Classis Britannica*) feeling its way home through the treacherous tidal shallows of the river Limen. Doubtless this port was first established as an ancillary of the main base at Rutupiae (Richborough) soon after the Romans' arrival in Britain in A.D. 43, and it would have been a mature fortress in its own right by the third century when Marcus Aurelius Carausius was appointed admiral with orders to put a stop to the ever more successful Saxon raids. For a man like Carausius virtual ownership of a fleet was an opportunity not to be missed and in 286 he declared himself autonomous ruler of Britain, a position he enjoyed for seven years until murdered by one of his own officers. Rome then re-occupied Britain and disbanded the now disgraced *Classis Britannica*. But the Saxon threat gathered inexorably, fortresses had to be built or strengthened along the length of the endangered coast (revealingly, it was called the *Litus Saxonicum*, the Saxon Shore), and though its stones may well first have

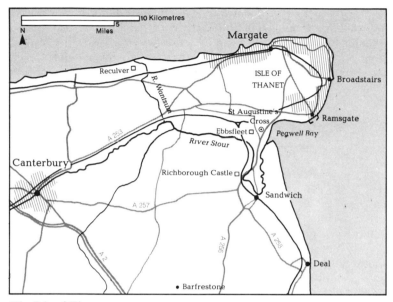

The Isle of Thanet

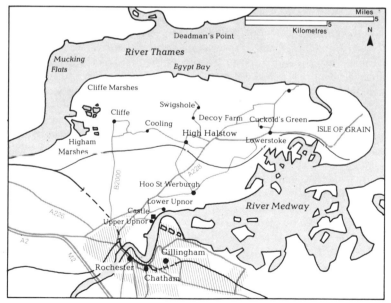

The Hoo Peninsula

been used in A.D. 43, the Lemanis you are looking at now represents this panic building of the early fourth century.

Should you feel like pursuing this Roman and Saxon theme more intimately—and it is of course at the roots of these islands' story—then you could do worse than drive the few miles through Folkestone and Dover to Pegwell Bay, immediately south of Ramsgate. Or, better, plot your course along the minor roads well behind the coast, pausing halfway at Barfrestone to admire the Norman stonework that has earned modest fame for the church here. Nor is this carving all, for you will also find two curiosities. One is a blocked entrance on the north, known as the Devil's door and in more credulous days opened at baptisms so that the Devil could escape after being summoned out of the infant by the priest; the other is the church bell which you will be surprised to find hanging in a yew tree.

It would be misleading to claim scenic interest for this corner of Kent. You will probably pass coal mines on your way here, and when you arrive you will find multi-national industry, a huge power-station and an unpromising coast, discouragingly annotated on the map as 'Mud and Sand'. Yet this small patch—Pegwell Bay and its hinterland—is historic ground which has seen much of both the beginnings and of the renewals of Britain's history. It will not appeal to everybody, of course, but it will surely lure anyone with a feel for origins and the ability to ignore a drab, modern environment while peopling it with scenes from the past; and it may also attract some of those who find themselves in Folkestone or Dover faced with an empty hour or two before the ferry sails.

Julius Caesar was the first to land here; the first recorded, that is, for surely many of the prehistoric immigrant waves must over millenia have passed this way. Caesar came twice, in 55 and 54 B.C., beaching we are told near what is now Deal, though the beach he knew must have been well inland of today's. On the first occasion he achieved little; on the second, not much more, for although he crossed the Thames and imposed tribute on the local chief, Cassivelaunus, he was soon forced to withdraw empty-handed.

But if these Romans left no trace, those of just under a century later have left plenty in the shape of the great walls of Richborough Castle. Like Caesar, though, these Romans did not see the landscape we see today. In A.D. 43 when Aulus Plautius landed with his 40 000 men, what is still marked on the map as the Isle of Thanet really was an island, cut off by a tidal channel running from Reculver on the Thames estuary to Ebbsfleet, just south-west of modern Ramsgate. With a bit of footwork you can still trace this through marshes and levels threaded by the little rivers Stour and Wantsum. But what Aulus Plautius found was a large, safe anchorage, and it was here that he landed, establishing and fortifying the port of

Rutupiae (Richborough), destined to serve as Rome's main base throughout some four hundred years of conquest and occupation.

To say that Aulus Plautius left his physical mark may not be strictly true. Some masonry doubtless survives of the Rutupiae which he built, but essentially the walls you see here are, like those of Lemanis above Romney Marsh, those designed to repel the Saxon menace at the turn of the third and fourth centuries. Nevertheless there is one impressive survival from only a few years after Plautius's time, for you will find within this great square the foundations of a grandiose memorial erected to celebrate the final subjugation of Britain shortly before the close of the first century.

The forts of the Saxon Shore—Regulbium (Reculver), Rutupiae, Dubris (Dover), Lemanis, Anderida (Pevensey) and others – could do no more than delay the Saxon flood and, since it is always helpful to anchor to a date, that of 449 seems the obvious one. This was the year in which Hengest and Horsa landed at Ebbsfleet, today a map entry in Gothic print within a marshy little-heeded triangle enclosed by the shore of Pegwell Bay, the B 2048 on the west, a railway and minor road across the north, and crossed by the A 256. These brothers, who, strictly, seem to have been Jutes, probably from Jutland, were not invaders but invited in by the British King Vortigern because he needed help against the Picts and Scots. But however dire Vortigern's need, the invitation was a rash one, for soon these and other Saxons began to oust the native British, Vortigern himself fleeing to Wales to become woven into legend. Thus as you drive around this tiny triangle of Ebbsfleet, it is sobering to reflect that it was as a direct result of what took place here in 449 that the Celtic British withdrew westward to become Cornishmen and Welshmen, while England became Anglo-Saxon. Not surprisingly, perhaps, Hengest and Horsa left no physical evidence of their arrival, but their direct descendants have done so, for in 1949 to celebrate the 1500th anniversary of their forebears' voyage, some Danes sailed across in a longship which now rather incongruously decorates the shore of Pegwell Bay.

One hundred and fifty years after Hengest and Horsa, in 596, St Augustine stepped ashore here, to be welcomed by Ethelbert of Kent and his already Christian wife Bertha and preach his first sermon to the English before going on to found the see of Canterbury and start the spread of the Roman Church throughout Britain. As with Hengest and Horsa, Augustine's landing spot has also been marked in modern times, in the saint's case by a large cross erected in 1884. Its claim, however, that he imported Christianity goes too far, for Queen Bertha was already Christian and if you go to Lullingstone Roman Villa in north-western Kent you will find that Christians lived and worshipped here perhaps two centuries earlier. Nevertheless the cross does purport to stand where Augustine first stood, and you will find it on the northern edge of the Ebbsfleet triangle where the railway crosses a minor road. It is not an uplifting place, between golf links, railway and road, but nonetheless it can hardly fail to provoke thought.

If the Isle of Thanet represents Kent at the outer end of the Thames estuary, Hoo represents the inner end. And where Thanet, despite its resorts, has something of a coastal frontier feel, Hoo, empty and lost though it is, perversely never lets you forget that you are on one of London's murkier fringes. A snub, fat promontory resting on the A 228 but bounded on its other three sides by Thames and Medway, Hoo is unusual in several ways. Although rural and remote, it exists within a horizon of oil tanks, flares and the stately progress of ships, large and small. Yet the eastern end, the Isle of Grain, is not only a world apart but a contradiction in itself being neither an island nor a source of grain. Ignore the horizon, perhaps, though it does convey an excitement of its own, certainly ignore the Isle of Grain, and Hoo becomes a place which invites exploration on a number of counts: because it is a promontory and thus a temptation; because so few people come here; because narrow roads and lanes can tempt you to lost places with strange names; because, at least for admirers of Charles Dickens, this was the land of *Great Expectations*.

You might start at Upper Upnor on the Medway's left bank just clear of Rochester, where the village's main street is as satisfyingly quaint as you could wish. Descend this and you will find what is called a castle but is in fact an Elizabethan gun platform built for the defence of Chatham dockyard, a role which it discharged ingloriously since on the only occasion on which it was challenged, when the Dutch sailed up the Medway in 1667, it was almost wholly ineffective. You can't, by the way, take your car down here; but there is convenient parking in the woods above and the walk is no more than a short stroll. At nearby Lower Upnor, though, you can park near the water; if you are indolent, simply to watch the modest shipping; if you are energetic, to climb Beacon Hill and enjoy the view.

From the Upnors it is just about due north to High Halstow, a village on Hoo's central ridge from which you can look down across the flats and sands to the Thames whose northern shore, an unreal toy world at four miles distance, is lined by oil refineries, jetties and places suffering from such names as Mucking Flats and Deadman's Point. Tiring of distance, the eye focuses more readily on the marshes below, cultivated and grazed in summer but largely surrendered to waterfowl in winter, a desolate land in which the names are even more challenging than those beyond the river; Egypt Bay, for instance, Swigshole, Decoy Farm and Cuckold's Green with its arch hint of past infidelities.

At Cooling—a name which has nothing to do with temperature but which has conferred something approaching immortality on a Saxon landowner called Cul—you meet Charles Dickens, or, rather, Pip of *Great Expectations*, for this little place, little more than a mile west of High Halstow, claims to be Pip's village. Certainly the churchyard contains the 'little stone lozenges' to which Pip refers. Not just five, but thirteen; a saddening reminder of the hazards of eighteenth-century infancy, for no less than ten shelter the pathetic remains of as many Comport children, not one of whom survived beyond seventeen months, while the other three cover little Bakers, aged one, three and five months. Cooling Castle, with its great gateway, moat and seemingly haphazard walls all gloriously set amid trees and flowers, provides a refreshing contrast to that melancholy churchyard. Yet even here a cruel death is cited as the main historical feature, for one of Cooling's owners, back in 1414, was the Lollard Sir John Oldcastle, who was rash enough to rebel against Henry V, as a result being 'hanged and burned, gallows and all'.

One mile farther west and you are in Cliffe. Perched on one end of Hoo's central ridge and with a main street lined with weatherboard-fronted cottages and small houses, this is a place of rare character and one which can hardly fail to conjure up an atmosphere of sail, smuggling and press-gangs; the sort of place, in fact, you would be happy to accept as just the right conclusion to your exploration of Hoo, if not indeed of Kent. However, should you feel further need of exploration and atmosphere, or for that matter simply be interested in water birds, then you have only to descend on foot northwards or westwards, on to the estuary flats, where lagoons, marshes, saltings and disused quarries back a desolate shore whose reeking shallows once knew the notorious prison hulks.

12

Hampshire and Wiltshire

Hampshire is a sadly under-rated county. Though it is beloved by anglers, for the Itchen, Test and, to a lesser extent, the Meon rank among the finest of our trout streams; by all traditional cricketers, since their game was 'born' there, on Broadhalfpenny Down at Hambledon; by those who have lost their hearts to the New Forest and its wild ponies—for most people it is just a county that one hurries through in order to reach the West Country or Southampton and the Isle of Wight.

Furthermore, Hampshire's road system tends to encourage swift passage through the county. The busy A 3 trunk road from London to Portsmouth clips off a portion of it in the south-east corner. The A 34, carrying a vast surge of traffic from Manchester, where it begins its long run southwards through the Potteries and the Black Country and Birmingham and its satellite towns, to Winchester, almost exactly bisects the county from north to south. The A 31 slants purposefully across the centre, making for the West Country. The A 272 thrusts in from West Sussex, to bisect east-westwards, and does not relinquish its grip until it reaches Stockbridge, almost on the western border with Wiltshire. And, finally, the A 30 with its companion M 3 cuts across the north. Thus it is small wonder that Hampshire, at least so far as the road map generally is concerned, gives the impression of being a 'transit' county, and nothing more. And this, of course, is all the more reason for challenging what the road maps suggest and going to find out for oneself just how far they represent the truth.

Take, then, the A 31. It crosses the Surrey-Hampshire border midway between Farnham and Bentley, a small and not particularly attractive village that sprawls along this main road. The trees that are a welcome feature of this district are the last survivors of the great forest known in medieval times as Alice Holt (a 'holt' being one of the old names for forest land), itself a westwards spur of the Forest of Anderida, the ancient *Andreadsweald*, that stretched throughout what is now the Weald of Kent and Sussex. This was rough country in its day: thick forest land in which the very few roads, such as this one through Bentley, were virtually swallowed up by undergrowth and overgrowth and a tradition of

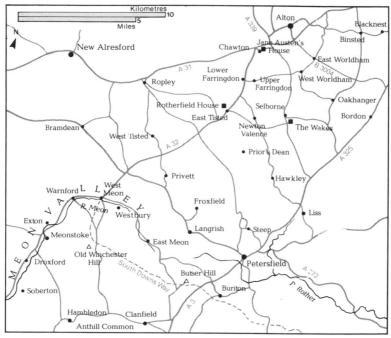

The Meon Valley

lawlessness obtained that made passage for merchants and couriers bound to and fro between London and Winchester hazardous in the extreme.

Bentley village deliberately reminds us of this. Glance to your right as you pass through it and you will see, sheltering beneath a lych gate type structure, a giant 'book', open wide. The left-hand page carries a historical chart in Gothic type portraying and dating the chief events in which, from Saxon days onwards, this area has been closely involved. It is the first hint you will have been given, only three miles or so over the border into Hampshire, of the richness and variety that this county has to offer you, once you depart from the beaten track.

A few miles beyond Bentley you should turn off to the left, taking what is little more than a lane, the first of a sequence of such minor roads, most of them criss-crossing one another or turning at abrupt right angles. They are not generously signposted; but this hardly matters, for no one lane is more or less interesting than another, and you are bound to come in time— and time should not be a factor of any significance in this curious pocket of Hampshire—to each of these out-of-the-world hamlets interspersed with well-maintained farmsteads and trim old-world cottages.

'Giant Book', Bentley

You will come quite suddenly upon, for instance, West Worldham. It possesses a minuscule church, the church of St Nicholas. With its tiled roof and singularly un-church-like windows, it looks more like an extension of the farm buildings immediately alongside than a real church, however small.

Nevertheless it really is a church. It was founded in the twelfth century as a Chapel of Ease for Hamble Priory, though only its very modest South Porch survives of the original fabric. It was restored at irregular intervals by Winchester College, owners of much of the land hereabouts, for the tiny community it has served down the centuries has never been affluent enough to keep the church in constant repair. Just one year before the end of World War Two it came perilously near to obliteration. A plaque inside records that lighting was installed as a thank-offering because the bomb that was dropped on this community of twelve households on the night of 15th May, 1944, failed to explode and so destroy the whole hamlet. Twelve households: that is all. You have to look about you with some persistence to locate more than two or three of them; this is indeed as 'lost' a fragment of a county as you are likely to find anywhere at all within forty-odd miles of London.

East Worldham lies a little way along the next lane; and tiny Wyck a mile or two beyond that; and Binstead and Blacknest; and in the other direction Oakhanger—another hint of the forest land once so ubiquitous on the Surrey-Hampshire border. But do not go too far eastwards, following these enticing little lanes, for you will then find yourself in the region of Bordon Camp and be reminded of the very features that you were so glad to escape as you fled south-westwards from Aldershot.

You may prefer to turn westwards for a while, if only to find relief from a sense of involvement that these close-set lanes tend to induce. The B 3006 will lead you out on to the A 32, just below Alton and almost in the heart of Chawton, with its Jane Austen associations. No lover of her novels can stay long away from this village and the comely house in which she wrote *Mansfield Park, Emma*, and *Persuasion* in the last eight years before her death in 1817. Her other well-known novels, *Pride and Prejudice, Sense and Sensibility* and *Northanger Abbey*, she had written in another Hampshire village, Steventon, not many miles away to the north-west of Chawton.

From Chawton there is a choice of two main roads. The A 31, which you left just on this side of Bentley, would take you over the uplands and down to New Alresford ('Awlsford' is the pronunciation of this oddly-spelled name) and so on to Winchester; the A 32 will take you southwards over a more generous spread of uplands and so into the delectable Meon Valley, by way of such villages as Farringdon. There are in fact, and unexpectedly in view of its modest extent, two halves to this village, Upper Farringdon and Lower Farringdon; the former, to the east, is by far the more attractive.

Here there is little more than one low-slung street, flanked on one side by a row of beautiful cottages, one of them being a fine example, rare today, of a cruck-built cottage. Unlike the cruck cottage at Lacock, or the larger house in Pewsey, both in neighbouring Wiltshire, the cruck here is no longer actually to be seen; it is possible that as a result of a fire which nearly destroyed the cottage a few years ago it has had to be built over in order to add the necessary reinforcement. In this same row there is 'Gilbert's Cottage', a reminder that the famous clerical naturalist, Gilbert White, of neighbouring Selborne, acted as curate to the little church of All Saints which stands on the opposite side of this road in its beautifully tree-shaded churchyard. White fulfilled this curacy for more than twenty years, riding over from his own village of Selborne, three miles to the east, along the winding lane that gives the impression of not having changed essentially during the two hundred years that have elapsed since his day.

In his book, *Antiquities*, White refers to the ancient custom of hanging from the nave beams of both his own church at Selborne and the sister church at Upper Farringdon garlands and pieces of white paper fashioned to resemble gloves and frills. They were hung there, he wrote, 'in honour of young women of the parish reputed to have died virgins. I recollect to have seen the Clerk's wife cutting in white paper the resemblance of gloves and ribbons to be twisted in knots and roses, to decorate these memorials of chastity'. But there are none of these to be seen today, either at Farringdon or at Selborne.

This is well wooded country. Among its most attractive features are the so-called 'hanging woods', the tree-clad slopes, often surprisingly steep, such as those that are to be seen in the few miles that separate Farringdon from Selborne. These were well known to White, who, with his Clerk, used to ride back and forth that way between church and church on Sundays and other Holy Days.

But of course the best-known of all the villages in this corner of Hampshire is Selborne itself, the home of the naturalist for so many years, the setting for his church, amid the fields and lanes and tree-clad slopes that he knew so well and described and interpreted with such love and intelligence. The lanes are most of them narrow, the hedges tall, riding along high banks so that you might at times think you were a hundred and fifty miles to the west, in Devonshire. The houses and cottages are of flint, with freestone, or brick quoins that are richly-toned enough to set off the coldness of the flint and stone. There is also homely thatch. And where tiles have been used in its stead the tradition of thatch seems to have been deliberately carried out in the other medium: the tiled roofs slant and curve, undulating over small dormer windows and between gables just as well-laid thatch would do.

This part of Hampshire would seem to be noteworthy, so far as its churchyards are concerned, for the enormous yew trees, of almost unbelievable age, to be found in them. One of the most remarkable of these you will pass as you approach the South Porch of the Church of St Mary, Selborne. Its bole is a full thirty feet in girth at head height, and its enormous lower boughs, as massive as the bole of any lesser tree, have had to be supported on an array of sturdy posts set in the ground all about it. You may not feel that the church itself has a very great deal to commend it, apart from its intimate association with the naturalist. Gilbert White was born in Selborne, at the house known as *The Wakes*, which is now a memorial to him. It stands within a stone's-throw of the church which he served as curate for half a century, though he never became its vicar, being content to remain as curate and divide his time between his own parish and that of Farringdon. His grave is to be found in his own churchyard, where he was buried at the then ripe old age of seventy-three, Selborne's greatest son.

But inside his church there is one feature that should make and leave a lasting impression on anyone who has even the slightest interest in natural history, especially ornithology. It is a window placed in the south wall of

'The Wakes', Gilbert White's House, Selborne

the church as recently as 1920, in memory of the naturalist. You will see in it a replica of the famous yew tree in the churchyard, said by experts to be at least a thousand years old and quite possibly twelve hundred and more; its true age will not of course be established until the day when it is felled and its rings can be counted—a day which every true Selbornian, whether parishioner or follower of Gilbert White, hopes will be long delayed.

You will see in it also a representation of St Francis preaching to the birds. Beneath the window there is a list of the actual birds portrayed; the tally is a remarkable one: no fewer than eighty-two. Among them, immediately recognisable to any bird-lover, are Brambling and Corn Bunting, Sedge Warbler and Wax Wing, Wheat Ear and Redstart, Whinchat and Pied Wagtail, Woodchat, Shrike and Wryneck, Ring Ouzel and Hoopoe; and there are some seventy more besides. It is a virtuoso performance by the stained-glass window artist commissioned by the donors of the window to create this most appropriate and beautiful memorial.

There is a similar window, on a less pretentious scale, dated 1906, in the twelfth-century church of St Mary at Newton Valence, a few miles along the lane south-west of Selborne. Here St Francis is again preaching to his feathered congregations, though there are fewer of these than in the larger window at Selborne. But at the saint's feet, in an extraordinarily realistic posture, is a white stoat which, small as it is, steals the thunder even from the central figure himself. Outside the church door is another of these famous yew trees, not quite comparable with the giant that dominates the churchyard at Selborne, but remarkable enough.

These churches diminish in size, but possibly increase in interest, as you wander along these secluded lanes from one small village to the next. The isolated church in the diminutive hamlet of Prior's Dean, near Hawkley, a few miles farther south still, again has its yew tree, and is in fact more immediately attractive than any of the others so far visited. Above its roof soars a miniature steeple of shingled timber framing. Go inside, and you will find something quite rare: the steeple is supported on four enormous baulks of timber, virtually tree-trunks roughly shaped with the adze, and said to date from Saxon times or very soon thereafter. They stand clear of the stone fabric, which appears (though this is improbable) to have been built round the four great pillars of oak which are more impressive than the stonework itself. In the chancel, the great supporting beams were deliberately exposed when, comparatively recently, some highly intelligent restoration was carried out here, and they at once act as foils to the stone and balance the more considerable timbers at the farther end of the church.

This use of massive timbers to support a belfry or steeple is comparatively rare. You will find another example of the practice, on a more ambitious scale, in another Hampshire village, Bishops Sutton, a few miles to the west. Its twelfth-century church of St Nicholas has similar beams, though of even greater size, supporting a very much more substantial bell-tower and steeple. But in fact there is one tiny detail at Prior's Dean that you may possibly remember before all else, after you have closed the church door behind you. Instead of the massive wrought-iron ring, often so harsh in the hand, with which in most churches the latch is lifted and released with a muffled clang, Prior's Dean church door is fastened by an oak latch that slides smoothly into and out of its socket, quite noiselessly yet with fitting finality.

Its strong contrast with this cluster of small churches, all of them so obviously in dedicated use today, though their congregations can never be other than small, is the church in the charmingly named village of Privett. It stands on highish ground, on the outskirts of the small group of houses, and is out of all proportion to the setting which it almost menacingly dominates. Flint abounds here, and the few cottages and one or two houses comprising the village are all built of this locally quarried material, intermixed with the mellow red and russet brick that goes so well with the cold, glassy stone. Nevertheless, well before you come to the church it is probable that you will have begun somehow to feel uneasy; there is a sense of desolation here, or at any rate of something seriously amiss. A notice informs any interested visitor that the church, though still consecrated, is maintained by the redundant churches fund; it has, moreover, been stripped of its interior fittings, and these have been distributed as seemed best among the churches of the neighbourhood fortunate enough still to be able to attract their own congregations. One leaves this pleasant upland village with a sense of depression in the mind and spirit; something vital, one feels, something that was once the focal point of village life, has been given the kiss, not of life but of death.

These Hampshire villages, with their small churches, their air of seclusion, approached by winding, hedge-bordered lanes, screened from main roads by fine stands of trees, are all on, or on the lower slopes of, the uplands that flow southwards, undulating gently as they lose height, but remaining somewhere about the 500-foot contour. The uplands rise a few miles south of Basingstoke, top the 700-foot mark a little to the west of Chawton, and then gradually lose height as they approach Petersfield. Just to the south of this pleasant old market town there is Butser Hill, only a little short of nine hundred feet in height, the westernmost spur of the glorious South Downs.

It is just to the south of these declining uplands, and before they rise again to the three fine summits of Butser Hill, Salt Hill and Old Winchester Hill, that the beautiful River Meon is born. From its source a few miles west of Buriton—which many lovers of Hampshire declare is the most beautiful village in all the county—it flows west-by-north for a few miles, giving its name first to the village of East Meon and, two or three miles farther along its wide-open valley, to the village of West Meon. Then it turns almost due south, to reach the Solent twenty miles away just to the west of Gosport. Dedicated anglers may insist that the Itchen and the Test are the finest of all Hampshire's trout streams; may be so, and may be it is true that the Meon does not quite qualify for inclusion in the supreme category. But for the lover of modest streams set in open, gentle, unpretentious valleys, small as it is the Meon can hold its own with the others, and with something to spare.

This small river has gathered about itself a veritable galaxy of unpretentiously beautiful villages and hamlets, every one of them a little jewel of delight. East and West Meon are the first of them, with little Westbury sandwiched in between them. Then come Warnford and Exton, Corhampton and Meonstoke, Droxford and Soberton; and hardly more than four valley miles separate the first-named from the last. You will not find it easy to name another valley, anywhere in Britain, in which so many hamlets, and hamlets of such individual charm, are to be found so close together: gay beads strung along the thread of so alluring a stream. Nor is the tally completed at Soberton; there are others farther down stream,

The exterior and interior of Jane Austen's house, Chawton

such as Wickham and Titchfield. But by then you are coming all too close to urban areas, and within the ambience of Fareham and Gosport. Better, surely to follow the Meon only as far as the last of this covey of valley hamlets, Soberton, and then branch off eastwards for a mile or two, if you are so minded, to pay tribute to Hambledon and Broadhalfpenny Down, where cricket first saw the light.

East Meon has one obvious advantage over its fellow three miles along the valley to the west: it lies on a minor road, so the busy traffic on the A 32 by-passes it with room to spare. The valley, too, has not really opened out yet, as it will do farther to the west and south; it is still, almost if not quite, a 'tight' valley; the stream, here not much more than a streamlet, has only just left the chalk uplands that gave it birth, and the higher ground to north and south squeeze both stream and the minor road from Petersfield which now parallels it quite close together.

As you descend the gentle hill into the village you become immediately aware of this fact, for the great cruciform church of All Saints which is its noblest feature seems almost to hang over it on the steep slope of the northern side, and so far as the stream itself is concerned it has temporarily vanished from sight. You will have to turn away from the church, and go down into the village which it overlooks, before you come upon the little Meon, temporarily channelled among the cottages and clustered small shops. But do not do this before you have given yourself time to look closely at the church itself. It is partly of the twelfth century; at least, its fine central tower and a few of its main arches date from that period. A hint as to its great age lies in the massive construction of its walls, some of which are no less than four feet in thickness. It is a church with a long and honourable tradition, and closely associated with Winchester itself.

Leaving the churchyard, you will pass through an unusual feature, consisting of what is in effect a double lych gate. From that viewpoint, to the left immediately across the sunken road, you will see the noble Court House, a medieval building which was used by the successive bishops of Winchester for their occasional deliberations. Like the church that looms so impressively above it, a glorious monument in flint and freestone, the Court House has walls four feet thick. Its actual date may be later, but it was built by the same type of native craftsmen and, as with all their work, built to last out the centuries.

Westwards from East Meon the valley opens out a little more, the stream growing in stature until, very soon, it can be dignified—just—by the term river. Its valley widens subtly, the water-meadows spreading right and left from its reed-screened banks. Here and there a little footbridge gives access from one bank to the other, braced perhaps against the roots of a pollarded willow. But immediately beyond these lush meadows the slopes to right and left begin again, for this road and accompanying stream are as it were still having to elbow their way out between the impending chalk masses to north and south, the uplands that we so recently left, and the chain of individual heights running westwards of the A 3 trunk road from London to Portsmouth.

In West Meon the upper valley road meets the busy A 32, which carries more traffic than you may have seen for some time past while you have been threading the lanes that link the Worldhams and Selborne, Farringdon and Privett and Froxfield and their close neighbours like Prior's Dean and Hawkley. You may feel tempted to stop as soon as you see the magnificent specimen of a Hampshire thatched house which stands at this junction. But this is a busy corner and you would be wiser to cross to the other side of the A 32; it is not only quieter, but the house can also be better enjoyed from here.

Close by, a narrow road climbs away from the village towards the church, and though it is possible that you do not feel any particular interest in churches as such, and may even have felt yourself recommended to look at too many of them already, you should not omit to go to this one, if only for the glorious view southwards down the Meon Valley (your next objective) which you can obtain from the high terrace on which it was built. And there are other reasons for a visit, besides this one.

Simply as a church, dedicated to St John the Evangelist, this does not compare with any of those recently mentioned, whether in Hampshire or in the neighbouring county of West Sussex. It is little more than a hundred years old, having replaced, as recently as 1843, the older and smaller church whose remains are some fifty yards down the hill at the foot of the present churchyard. But its exterior—quite apart from the pillar-box-red gold-studded door in the South Porch, which may strike the visitor more as an eyesore than as an impressive contrast to the stonework of the fabric, is notable for the excellence of its flush-work. This consists, of course, in dressed flints; but the interesting thing about this particular example of the craft is the extreme smallness and the absolute uniformity of the flints. They are all of them just two inches from top to bottom and specifically either two inches or two and a half inches from side to side. They are thus very much smaller than the fine Suffolk examples of this traditional craft to be seen in such churches as the one at Kersey.

More interesting still is the story behind the flint knapping. It was all carried out, not by professional flint knappers such as those at Brandon, but by the womenfolk of this small Hampshire community. Just above the church, at the top of the hill and shaded by trees, there is a small enclave named Knaps Hard. Today it is a small residential estate of modern houses; but it was here that, a century and more ago, the village women lived who so methodically and accurately shaped the rough flint into these perfect rectangles. So accurately where they shaped, and so skilfully laid edge to edge in panels inside the freestone, that it would be impossible to insert even a knife blade between any one flint rectangle and the next.

Some idea of the total number of these knapped flints produced by the women of West Meon can be obtained by a small measurement and quick calculation based on this. A representative panel of flints contained within the freestone 'frames' of the church's south wall will be found to be ten feet in length and six feet in height. This means exactly thirty-six courses averaging sixty flints in each—a total of 2160 individual knapped flints. And this is just one panel, between a pair of stone buttresses, beneath a window, of many more extending to right and left and above and below it. The total number of flints shaped by hand to these precise and unvarying dimensions must be astronomical.

One wonders what these village women were paid for their immense and taxing labour. Possibly the rates were rather better than those that obtained for labour generally in the mid-nineteenth century. For the then rector, who in fact was responsible for replacing the original church by this very new one, happened to be an extremely wealthy man of independent means, an Archdeacon of Stow, in Lincolnshire, and at the same time a Canon of Westminster Abbey. Records show that he purchased the land on which this church was built and in addition paid some £11 000 out of his own pocket—a very substantial sum in the 1840s; the small balance seems to have been raised by contributions subscribed by his parishioners. It is to be hoped that the Venerable Henry Vincent Bayley, prime mover of the enterprise, made no attempt to persuade the women of the village that it was their Christian duty to knap these hundreds of thousands of flints solely to the Greater Glory of God.

As you descend from the church, another look across at that fine thatched house which we noted on first entering West Meon may remind you that there is of course much other good thatch in Hampshire. You come upon admirable examples of it at every turn. Wherwell, far to the west near Stockbridge, in the Test Valley, is perhaps the Hampshire village in which superb specimens of it are most abundant; but you will find good thatch in practically every village or hamlet you pass through, and also on the scattered and often surprisingly isolated cottages and farmsteads between village and village. There is a charming specimen set all by itself at a coming-together of minor lanes only a mile or so from Privett. Here the upper thatch, beneath the ridge-pole, is beautifully scalloped as well as being patterned with a subtle tracery of spars and withies, and the tiny dormer windows on either side of the small central porch, also thatched, have each of them an 'eyebrow' of snug thatch, so that they seem to be cautiously winking from the safety of their individual shelters.

If a poll were to be taken as to which, *inter pares*, of the villages in the Meon Valley could claim to be the most perfect, a very strong case indeed could be made for Exton, a mile or two farther down the valley than Warnford, which is probably the least engaging of this little galaxy of

Meon villages and hamlets. It has one advantage that is not common to the others, though Soberton shares this to a certain extent, and Meonstoke too. This is that it lies in the valley but not on the road that threads this valley alongside the now disused railway-line. You turn off on a lane that is no more than a few hundred yards long, with the village in sight but, luckily for its handful of inhabitants, out of ear-shot of the road; almost before you realise it, you have come within its ambience.

Flint walls, intermixed with red and russet brickwork; trees; well-clipped yew hedges backing and sometimes topping the walls. One or two of these walls run a sinuous line from the edge of the village, near the green that separates it from the main road, leading the eye into the heart of the village and beyond. Presumably such walls enclose small private estates. The notion is strengthened by the glimpses one has of fine stands of trees rising splendidly behind them, through which sunlight glints on spacious windows. There is a quite extraordinary sense of timelessness in Exton; a sense of leisure, of a tempo one associates with an older, more expansive, less tempestuous age than this. There are glimpses of trim velvet lawns, interspersed with shapely and well-populated flower-beds, lovingly tended. Many of the cottages have wells in their gardens. They may no longer be in use, for mains water, like electricity, has come to the village; but they are well preserved, sometimes gaily painted and with bright chains and barrels depending from them.

The church of St Peter & St Paul is part-thirteenth century, part-fourteenth and later. It could hardly offer a stronger contrast to that unhappy relic of a church at Privett, not so many miles to the north, which for lack of use has been de-consecrated, its interior fittings removed and distributed. Here, it seems most probable, a regular and affluent congregation meets regularly; and it obviously takes pride in seeing to it that the meeting-place is maintained as it should be. One has the impression that these homely and well-preserved cottages, some of them at any rate, today house retired or leisured folk of independent means who cherish their amenities materially as well as emotionally. They can hardly be blamed for this, even if their moving-in has entailed the departure of some cottage owner who had lived there and his father and grandfather and great-grandfather before him: Exton, after all, has everything to offer that a lover of peace and quiet and beauty unimpaired could demand for his years of retirement.

You have hardly returned to the main road, just below Exton, before you run into Corhampton. Like West Meon and Warnford, it lies astride the road and therefore, inevitably, loses some of the character it might have retained had it not been so unfortunately placed. You may feel tempted to continue straight on through the village, without lingering long enough to find out what riches, if any, it possesses. And this would be a mistake indeed, for then you would miss entirely its greatest treasure, its undoubted Saxon church, standing on what may well be a prehistoric man-made mound, the base of which is washed by the Meon. The nave and parts of the chancel are thought to belong to the first quarter of the eleventh century, the chief evidence being the typical Saxon 'long-and-short' work of the quoins, as also, to the east of the south porch, the Saxon sundial, marked, as was contemporary custom, with eight divisions representing the tides. Inside the church you will find murals which may be Saxon though it seems more likely they were painted about a century later, a perfect Saxon chancel arch, and, on the north side of the chancel, an ancient altar stone bearing six consecration crosses.

Outside the South Porch, the only entrance to the church, stands yet another of the splendid yew trees that are such frequent incumbents of these churchyards. Reputed to be at least a thousand years old—planted, perhaps, in the same year as the first stones of the church were laboriously brought to the site and laid in place—it is not far short of thirty feet in girth at shoulder height, and therefore comparable with the giant at Selborne. Alongside sits a crude stone coffin, dug up nearby in 1917; dating from Roman times, it is open now and neatly serves as a flower bed while the body it contained was reinterred at Meonstoke.

Just below Corhampton and still on the main road, lies Droxford. Its church of St Mary & All Saints lies well off the road, screened by a noble stand of chestnuts and set about with fine turf and an unusually well tended churchyard. It is by no means as old as the Saxon church at Corhampton, the earliest portions of the fabric dating only from the twelfth century; but it is known that it replaces a Saxon church that was probably contemporary with the other one just up the road.

It is unfortunate that so much of this lovely Meon Valley must be threaded by way of a fairly busy main road. But at Droxford you may (though you are not officially permitted to do so) continue your journey southwards along the track of the disused railway-line, which runs close to and indeed almost through the churchyard itself. Shoppers from neighbouring Soberton in search of commodities that can only be bought in Droxford, or farther afield, have a habit of walking along this track between one village and the next, and there is rarely anyone in authority to say them nay. The line presumably linked Alton in the north, beyond the valley, with Wickham, well to the south, where it joined the east-west running line between Southampton and the towns that line the long West and East Sussex coast.

In fact, however, you can follow the Meon southwards from Corhampton without keeping strictly to the main road, and this offers a very pleasant and rewarding alternative, as minor roads so consistently do. At Corhampton there is this minor road, which runs almost parallel with the main road but half a mile or so to the east of it and so closely beset by hedges and trees that it is entirely screened from it and you would hardly know that the main road existed at all were it not for the occasional glint of a car in a gap between the trees.

This road branches off the main road and leads you at once, across the river and into the village of Meonstoke. And there you have a good Saxon name: Meon plus *stoke*; that is, the settlement-by-the-Meon. It was probably little more than a very small community of simple agriculturalists who found running water and fertile land there for the taking twelve or thirteen centuries ago. And today you will find that the place is not all that much larger. For the minor road leads across a low and level bridge to an inn, a house or two, a cottage or two, climbing up a gentle slope eastwards and away from the main road. Look back from here and you will see wide water-meadows through which the stream wriggles like an eel between its rush-filled banks.

A little surprisingly perhaps, from those very water-meadows, separated from them only by a stretch of green sward lovingly mown and ornamented with an elaborate pattern of well-filled flower-beds, there rises the mass of Meonstoke's thirteenth-century church of St Andrew. It does not look its age, and you may have to convince yourself that it does date from that century by glancing down the long list of its incumbents. The first of these, you find, was inducted in the year 1262.

The English village tradition, of course, is to have its church almost at its centre, perhaps overlooking a green. Here, however, as at Droxford and as at Guiting Power in the Cotswolds, the tradition is broken. This church is set apart from the village, a place on its own. You can approach it only by a narrow lane that twists behind the inn at the foot of the hill and first passes the vicarage. But if your immediate impression is that the church has deliberately made itself unwelcoming by that difficult approach, the notion is challenged by the welcome implicit in the outspread apron of lawn and flower-beds that suggest a well-kept private estate rather than the precincts of a church. The flower-beds ride up close to the lych gate through which you pass to enter the churchyard; and the pastoral element is reiterated in the trees that crowd close up behind the church, supplying a variegated backcloth to the ridge of the nave and chancel roofs and the squat but shapely tower and open belfry that tops it. A stone's-throw from the west end of the church is an old thatched cottage that might have stepped straight out of a canvas by Constable. The stream flows by, virtually beneath its doorstep. Here, presumably, the churchwarden or gardener-gravedigger lives, as other servants of the church of Meonstoke have lived for generations before him.

It is a relief to approach a village such as this by a road that is not a main road; the habit was formed among the hamlets on the uplands in which Farringdon and Selborne and their neighbours are so happily set. It was broken at Corhampton, and again at Droxford; now it is picked up again. A winding lane, overhung by trees, set between hedges, rising and falling, twisting and turning, will bring you all in good time—and it is a mistake ever to allow oneself to hurry in country such as this—to the last of this cluster of Meon Valley villages, Soberton.

It is a village whose virtues seem to be as yet unsung. This is surprising, for it is as attractive as any you are likely to come across; it is well looked after, and possesses a village green overlooked by church and rectory, with the local Great House (now flats) not far away: so, it is thoroughly in keeping with the best village traditions. And like so many of these self-effacing Hampshire villages, it possesses an outstandingly interesting church, that of St Peter, approached up a short, straight lane beside the green that ends right beside the churchyard. From it a fine view southwards down the widening Meon Valley can be obtained.

As with so many of these churches, parts are much older than the rest. As at Droxford, for example, the twelfth-century portions, such as the north aisle, stand on foundations laid very much earlier than that, and most certainly prior to the Norman Conquest. Most of what confronts you today, however, dates from between four hundred and fifty and five hundred years ago—long enough, surely, to satisfy all but the most exacting connoisseurs of these medieval and earlier ecclesiastical foundations.

Probably the most interesting feature of this church of St Peter, Soberton, is the very handsome tower, which dates only from the earliest years of the sixteenth century. It differs from the style of tower to which one has become accustomed while wandering about this part of the country, for there is a considerable area of chequer-work in freestone intermixed with panels of the more familiar flint. Compare it in your mind, for instance, with that at West Meon, and you will immediately recognise the difference in emphasis between the two types of stone used in the fabric. Particularly interesting, though you must crane your neck upwards at an uncomfortable angle to study the unusual feature in detail, is the use of diaper-pattern lattice-work, in stone, to fill and ornament the windows in the uppermost part of the tower. This feature is certainly unusual, hereabouts at any rate; but it is very satisfying to the eye when it has once been recognised and understood.

There is, however, another and very much more unusual feature associated with this tower. It is one which demands yet keener scrutiny, and preferably in the late afternoon when the sun has rounded the south-west angle. On the west face, high up, there is a carving in stone of a pair of heads, about life-size, though considerably diminished by the height at which they were set by the sculptor. Between the two heads there is what appears to be either a bucket or a roughly shaped bag; there is also a massive key. The local explanation, one of those traditions that survive in spite of the sophisticated sceptic of today, is that the original tower fell into disrepair and, by the end of the fifteenth century, had to be replaced. It was in fact almost entirely rebuilt in the early years of the following century. But this was no parallel to the West Meon church, built by a wealthy incumbent; the money for its rebuilding was, if this tradition is to be accepted, subscribed by the dairymaids and indoor and outdoor servants of the farmers and gentry living in the district served by the church.

Can this really be true? Were servants' wages four and a half centuries ago generous enough for dairymaids and butlers, cow-herds and footmen (if these existed in 1520 and earlier) and their like to be able to afford the sort of money that would pay for a handsome church tower like this—or indeed for any church tower? Even allowing for the low degree of wages payable to masons in those days, and for the fact that there would have been a fair supply of usable stone lying ready to hand on account of the decay and collapse of the original tower, a very considerable sum of money would have been required. So, the story of the generous and public-spirited farm-hands and indoor servants is almost certainly apocryphal. Nevertheless, something must account for the existence of a pair of heads facing one another across a key—the symbol, surely, of the châtelaine or the chief servant of a household—and what certainly looks uncommonly like a milkmaid's bucket.

Now move round to the south. Here, standing solid on turf beneath the flint and freestone of the church wall, is an enormous stone trough. Take a closer look at this. Is it, in fact, a trough? You will not be long before coming to a quite different conclusion. Eight feet in length, two feet at the near end and half as wide again at the farther end, and a couple of feet in height, this 'trough' is supported on two or three rough blocks of stone that have been half crushed into the ground by the weight they have to support. And this is hardly surprising; for it is said to weigh between two and a half and three tons, its sides and ends being full six inches thick and its base considerably more than that. In fact, this is no trough at all; it is an extremely ancient coffin, hewn in one piece out of a solid block of stone.

It was discovered about a hundred years ago by a farmer who was deep-ploughing a field that had lain fallow as long as he had owned the farm. As is so often the case—in the Roman Villa at Bignor, to mention just one obvious example—the ploughshare unearthed something more solid than earth and loose stones. The farmer had the wit to seek advice. An archaeologist known to someone at the Great House near by urged caution in further digging. The result was that, little by little, from the chalky soil beneath the Hampshire turf there eventually emerged this remarkable specimen of a stone coffin said by the experts to date back at least to the second century A.D. That made it almost certainly Roman in origin. There is no certainty of truth in the local tradition that the skeleton of a tall man, wearing the toga and other trappings fitting to his patrician rank, was found inside the coffin, though this is a tradition that the villagers will not willingly allow to die. After all, they may say in support of their belief,

Thatched cottages, Wherwell

there was that skeleton in the coffin which now rests in Corhampton's churchyard only a few miles farther up the valley; so why not here at Soberton, too? Well, you feel tempted to assent, may be there was such a skeleton, trappings and all, and it has since been mysteriously spirited away!

With or without the skeleton, the huge stone coffin was laboriously conveyed the half mile or so across the field where it had been so unexpectedly unearthed, and deposited for safe-keeping in the south transept of the church; and there it remained a while. But now it has been relegated to a less honoured site, a long stone's-throw from the part of the field where, in 1880 or thereabouts, it was revealed by the ploughshare. It now stands on the broken fragments, each of which weighs a hundredweight or more, of the lid that originally lay over it. It is in fact a good thing that the lid has been removed, though it is a pity that it has been so badly shattered; for it enables one to see, if one looks closely, a beautiful and strangely moving feature which in all probability the great majority of visitors to this church fail to notice at all. In the middle of the upper edge of the wider end of the coffin is the fossilised imprint of a scallop shell.

Quite apart from its intrinsic beauty and its sheer unexpectedness, this is a tacit reminder that once this good land, parts of Hampshire, West and East Sussex, Kent to the east and Dorset to the west, formed a sea bed on to which creatures in their untold billions were deposited over aeons of time. The sea bed, of course, that was later up-thrust to form the great chalk rampart still to be seen at and behind England's southern coastline and the northern coastline of France; and later still, as we have seen, sufficiently eroded away and denuded for the waters of the Atlantic to flow eastwards and merge with the North Sea, severing Britain from the Continent once and for all.

So, this, the last of the handful of small churches to be found in the lovely Meon Valley, has perhaps the strangest of all tales to tell. And with this look at what Soberton and its church have to offer, we leave this corner of Hampshire, having sampled, it is true, but a tithe of its reserves. Now it is time to work our way north-westwards to its border with Berkshire, to the north, and with Wiltshire, to the west, in search of who knows what unexpected and memorable impressions there may be lying in wait for the curious and appreciative eye.

Look at any map of Hampshire in which the contours are coloured or shaded and you will see at a glance that the southern portion of the county, a triangle with its three points at Winchester, Portsmouth and Bourne-mouth (this last in fact in Dorset), lies nearest to sea level. There are two main areas of uplands: those in the east, above the Meon Valley, and those in the far north-west angle of the county where it meets Berkshire, on its northern border, and Wiltshire to the west. Though these last-mentioned cover a lesser area than the others, they are in general higher. They range well above the 500-foot contour, reaching six, seven and eight hundred feet and, at Pilot Hill, literally on the Berkshire border, no less than 938 feet. Just over the border, only a mile or so away, is Inkpen Beacon, with the grisly relic of Combe Gibbet as its most pronounced feature apart from the megalithic Long Barrow close by.

Hereabouts the three counties interlock in such a tangled fashion that only a large-scale map will enable you to know for sure in which of them you are actually standing. In fact, with a little skill, and equipped with such a map, you could contrive to stand with a foot each in two of them and your walking-stick in the third. It will depend on the manner in which you have distributed these three points as to whether you are looking out over the uplands of Hampshire or what has been described by a true Wiltshireman as 'an ocean of rolling grass with a distinct and yet unaccented separateness, informed by a spirit of isolation'. It is a descriptive comment which you may not perhaps fully appreciate, or even believe, until you have gone there and seen and felt it for yourself.

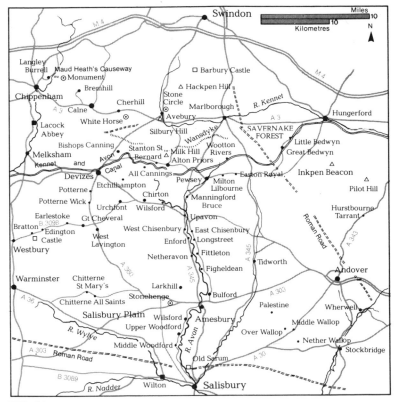

Wiltshire

It is indeed a far cry from those sunny little villages in the ever broadening valley of the Meon to the splendid isolation of Pilot Hill and its close neighbour across the border, Inkpen Beacon. Not in distance, of course: by way of Winchester and Whitchurch and Hurstbourne Tarrant it is hardly more than fifty miles all told. No, not in distance—but in spirit. For here, on this triple frontier, you are in, for want of a better word, ancient country. (An echo here, but with a difference, of Breckland, on the Norfolk-Suffolk border.) The great rolling mass of the Berkshire Downs to the north bears on its whaleback one of the oldest 'roads' in the world, the Berkshire Ridge Way, that ran, and still runs, from the Thames Gap between Goring and Streatley to Old Sarum, in Wiltshire. It passes on its route the great Long and Round Barrows of prehistoric man, the first inhabitants of this island. One of the best known of them, of course, is Wayland's Smithy. And there is Segsbury Camp, and Uffington Castle, and the White Horse on Dragon Hill, and the Blowing Stone at Kingston

Lisle (allegedly used by King Alfred to summon his men to battle), and the West Kennet megalithic Stone Avenue, and Barbury, and Hackpen Hill, and the Avebury Stone Circle, and the 'Grey Wethers'—the innumerable sarsen stones scattered with generous hand by who knows whom and so long ago that Time was still a boy. Certainly the Berkshire Ridge Way is prolific in prehistoric record.

But it is a counsel of perfection to adjure people to walk the Ridge Way from Streatley to Old Sarum and then to walk the South Downs eastwards from Winchester on to Butser Hill and so by way of Chanctonbury Ring to Birling Gap. For this, after all, is not basically a walking book. Though the only true and lasting way to come to know a stretch of country is through the soles of one's boots, for most people time is at a premium and it is only the happy few who can find, or make, sufficient time to embark on such ventures. That Ridge Way walk, and the return by way of the corresponding chalk ridges in Hampshire and Sussex, remain, after a quarter of a century, among the most vivid and memorable of a long series of such leisurely explorations, at home and abroad; it was recorded in loving detail many years ago in a book long since out of print, the present writer's *The Road Before Me*.

Still, there is this stretch of countryside, half in Hampshire, half just over the border in Wiltshire, adequately supplied with roads major and minor to tempt wheels as well as footsteps, and generously rewarding whatever may be your taste. Let its north-west limit be the Wiltshire township of Calne; its north boundary, for present purposes, a line drawn thence by way of Avebury and Marlborough along the A 4 Bath Road; its east boundary a line drawn southwards a little beyond the summits of Inkpen, Combe Gibbet and Pilot Hill down to a point just short of Winchester; and let its southern boundary be a line that just clears that city and Salisbury, twenty-odd miles to the west. Once again, an arbitrarily selected area; but then, as they say, one must draw the line somewhere, and the area enclosed within these four lines, like that in the south-east corner of Wales and overlapping into Herefordshire, has much to commend it.

This northernmost portion of the area is highish ground. At this point the A 4 Bath Road crosses it above the 500-foot mark near Silbury Hill, the largest man-made mound not only in this country but in all Europe. Just south of this there rises a very much higher, but this time natural, eminence, Milk Hill, which almost reaches the 1000-foot mark. From this summit you can look northwards across the valley of the Kennet to Hackpen Hill and Barbury Castle, a prehistoric hill-fort on Marlborough Downs, only seven miles away as the crow flies and very nearly the same height above sea level as that on which you are standing.

Turn about, though, and you look immediately southwards to the lovely Vale of Pewsey, almost at your feet. The ground rises, though not to quite the same contours, on the south side of the Vale, and then the vast,

Looking northwards from Milton Hill Farm, near Milton Lilbourne, Vale of Pewsey

seemingly limitless expanse of Salisbury Plain lies spread out before you, epitome of that 'ocean of rolling grass with a distinct and yet unaccented separateness' of which that good native of Wiltshire so expressively wrote.

You should linger in the Vale, among the sequestered hamlets whose names are a delicate music on the ear: Pewsey and Easton Royal, Wootton Rivers and Milton Lilbourne, Stanton St Bernard and Alton Priors, Woodborough and Manningford Bruce, All Cannings and Wedhampton, Potterne and Potterne Wick. ('What,' you cry, echoing Macbeth, 'will the line stretch out to the crack of doom?' Yes: there are more than these, and every individual one of them well worth more than a swift turn of the head as you pass on to the next. Urchfont and Chirton, for instance; and again Etchilhampton; and, just outside this close-knit area, lovely Erlestoke, with its near neighbours Great and Little Cheverell, nestling at the foot of Little Down.)

A hint is perhaps appropriate as to what is to be found among them, again selecting very much at random. Pewsey, of course, is something more than a village; it is in fact a small country township. It boasts—as other and larger places rightly do—a statue of King Alfred the Great. It does not boast, though some may feel that it should do, of possessing one of the finest examples of a half-timbered house with a cruck-ended gable to be found anywhere in the country. Not many of these medieval cruck-built houses survive to this day. There is of course the one at Lacock, in the same county, and at Upper Farringdon in neighbouring Hampshire.

Manningford Bruce is a tiny place by contrast even with Pewsey, and is own cousin to neighbouring Manningford Abbots and Manningford Bohune. It has a beautifully sited early Norman church, all set about with tall trees so that its diminutive stature is yet further diminished by their presence. It is built of flint and freestone and topped by a toy belfry rising from its steeply-pitched little roof. Stanton St Bernard is larger, though not all that much so. Some of its buildings, notably the seventeenth-century manor house, have incorporated those blue-grey sarsen stones found on the uplands to north and south of the Vale of Pewsey and for centuries a source of supply of reasonably good building material lying ready to hand.

The word 'sarsen' is often spelt with a capital initial letter. This tends to give substance to the popular belief that these random blocks of hard sandstone, so prevalent in this region, were originally brought here by the 'Saracens'. To the simple folk among whom the belief was born, Saracens were as remote and incomprehensible as Martians, and their ways reputedly wondrous strange. Because of their uniform greyness, their unevenly rounded lines, and perhaps above all because they tend to be found isolated on otherwise empty stretches of this grey-green turf thin-stretched over the native chalk of these downs, they are also often referred to as 'wethers'. Nor is this surprising: even in good light, and certainly in poorish light, these blocks of stone bear a curious resemblance to old and dormant grazing sheep.

There is a notable cluster of these, actually shown on the larger-scale maps as the Grey Wethers, near Fyfield, some four miles west of Marlborough and just off the main A 4 Bath Road. There is another such group, similarly named, and likewise owned by the National Trust, at Lockeridge Dene, a mile or so to the south of the first group. To find these—and, indeed, to take the pleasantest route into the Vale of Pewsey, you should turn off the main Bath Road some two to three miles west of Marlborough, a minor road that will introduce you to major delights within a very few minutes. It leaves the main road at a sign pointing to the Who'd Have Thought It Inn.

This road runs south-westwards, skirting the eastern slopes of Milk Hill, the highest summit in Wiltshire at 964 feet, and close to the Alton Barnes White Horse. Though the actual area is relatively small, you will find yourself in a strangely empty region to begin with, and an ancient one too, for beyond the sarsens of Lockeridge Dene the road crosses the long earthwork of sixth- or seventh-century Wansdyke before linking with a spur of the Berkshire Ridge Way and curving between a neolithic camp to the east and the long barrow known as Adam's Grave on the west. And, as you travel this road, you may well also feel that it affords some of the finest views of the downs and hill summits to be found anywhere in all Wiltshire.

The sarsens of this empty region have something of the haunting quality that is possessed by so many of the Stone Circles and Standing Stones, which themselves so often consist of sarsens; like other prehistoric relics they tend to accumulate about themselves legends that many people are quite content to accept as history, not myth. Two hundred years ago there were vastly more of these scattered stones than you will find today, for so many of them have been broken up and embedded in farms and other houses, insulted by being made to serve as foundations for mean buildings of many kinds. Among the most impressive survivors are those that have been incorporated in the so-called 'Druid' monument on Salisbury Plain, Stonehenge. Not all its stones, however, are sarsens; there are also the great 'blue' boulders that were brought to the site at infinite cost in labour and ingenuity from the far-off Prescelly Mountains in South Wales. There has, unhappily, been vandalism even among these spectacular stones during the long centuries that have rolled over them, and especially in recent years characterised by this ever-growing wave of sheer wanton destructiveness. But now, happily, this most ancient of Ancient Monuments is in the expert and dedicated care of the Historic Buildings and Monuments Commission and so is virtually safe for as many more thousand years as have already passed over it.

All Cannings at the western and open end of the Vale, would seem to have gathered to itself the other Cannings villages of the district; but it has obviously overlooked Bishops Cannings, a mile or two to the west. Perhaps this is because of the splendour of the great church of St Mary which, as so often, seems out of all proportion to the size of the community living in the few thatched houses and cottages spread around its feet. All Cannings has its own church, of course: another that is disproportionately large and at the same time perhaps not in quite the same class as St Mary's, though parts of it are claimed to be Norman; all too much of it, however, shows signs of comparatively recent and not entirely successful, some will say, restoration.

Another of these Vale of Pewsey churches that seems to have been designed by someone who anticipated larger congregations than perhaps ever assembled in its pews is that of St Mary, at Potterne. It dates from the same period as Salisbury Cathedral itself, the early to middle thirteenth century, though it has little else in common with that supremely lovely edifice, with its tapering four-hundred-and-four-foot spire, tallest and loveliest in all Britain.

If your taste is for the humbler type of church altogether, then you should explore the twin Vale of Pewsey villages, Alton Priors and Alton Barnes. Like the curious little early Norman Church-in-the-Field near Terwick, in West Sussex, that of Alton Priors stands in a field, not closely set about with houses and cottages, as is so often the case in these unspoilt villages. And not far away is the equally small and modest church of St Mary at neighbouring Alton Barnes, beside a little lane used by the occupants of the few small cottages that make up this isolated hamlet. It is very old. The 'long-and-short' work of the quoins denotes, as it did at Corhampton and elsewhere, true Saxon workmanship.

Quite apart from the villages, the hamlets, the individual scattered buildings to be found hereabouts, the Vale of Pewsey is lovely in its own right. It is a gracious as well as spacious item of landscape, watered by the Kennet & Avon Canal that runs by way of Great and Little Bedwyn and the interesting pumping-station at Crofton, almost on the border between Wiltshire and Berkshire. Here at Crofton are lovingly preserved the great beam engines used for pumping water into the canal and installed here a hundred and seventy years ago. You may see them in the engine-house that lies just beneath the level of the road alongside but still well above the level of the canal whose quiet waters reflect the fine brickwork of the building and its pipe-line.

Great and Little Bedwyn are villages still unspoilt even though they are cut by a main railway line and lie so perilously close to the Bath Road, the A 4, near Hungerford. Of the two, Little Bedwyn, as you might guess from its name, is the more attractive. Here you will find a profusion of mellow Georgian brickwork in the manor house; flint and freestone in its lovely little church of St Michael, with its shapely and finely proportioned spire; an abundance of trees, including some fine yews that set off the stone and brickwork that are so effectively mingled in the village; and, of course, the placid canal below lush meadows.

From the uplands that circumscribe it to north and south you can look down into the Vale of Pewsey, and every prospect pleases. True, a railway line threads it, inevitably following pretty much the line of the Kennet & Avon Canal, but somehow the trains seem to be absorbed by their surroundings. Quite often they are unheard; but you discern a silent, snake-like progress along the water-meadows, interrupted here and there by trees, vanishing just long enough to make you watch closely in case the train does not reappear. Finally it leaves the Vale of Pewsey altogether, making for Westbury and Frome and points south-west beyond. Wait long enough, and you will see a train creep into the Vale, unassumingly, as though conscious that it will be regarded as an intruder in so sequestered a spot as this if it does not behave itself in seemly fashion. Not often can one be grateful for the fact that the steam locomotive has now been universally replaced by characterless successors; but here, perhaps, one may be truly grateful. No billow of smoke lies over the Vale of Pewsey when the train passes through it; the wide fields on either side of the track, sloping up towards the trees on a low horizon, are unsullied by soot or ash.

And happily, too, no main or even secondary road runs through the Vale, except to the east of Pewsey itself. To the west, among the scattered hamlets already named and perhaps perfunctorily described, and their neighbours only named, a series of indeterminate lanes wander and criss-cross one another, leisurely leading you hither and yon; you could not ask anything better of them than that they should do just this.

Westbury was mentioned. It lies just beyond the western border of this area, but you will go there if only to see the famous White Horse on its westward-facing slope. This is an eighteenth-century turf-cut figure, less ancient, therefore, by far than the Giant of Cerne or the Long Man of Wilmington; and less ancient by far, too, than the Uffington White Horse on the north face of the Berkshire Downs, though there may have been an earlier figure cut on this very site. You can see this White Horse very well indeed from the railway-line; less well, though, from the B 3098 road that runs along the foot of these downs by way of lovely Erlestoke, Tinhead, Edington and Bratton. It is well worth the climb from this road up any one of a number of tracks cut in the chalk to reach the prehistoric hill-fort above Bratton and then to continue along the chalk ridge south-westwards right over the top of the turf-cut figure itself. This is spacious, expansive walking; there is always a strong breeze, growing now and then into a challenging wind. But you know as you walk that within a mile or two or three you will come to another track cut in the chalk which you can then follow downhill all the way to rejoin the road you temporarily abandoned at Edington or Bratton.

One thing only will perhaps irk you. The nearer you come to the White Horse the less easy it is to grasp its impressive proportions, let alone obtain an adequate photograph of it. Even if it has been recently 'scoured' (and the author of *Tom Brown's Schooldays* also wrote a fine account of the scouring of the White Horse of Uffington) there still remains the almost insuperable problem of a satisfactory viewpoint. Immediately above or below it, you are too close; view it from the train, and its proportions fall suitably into relationship with one another—but then you are not only in motion but also too far away even for a camera with a normal telephoto lens. The answer, clearly, is a helicopter, chartered to do exactly what you enjoin upon its pilot; and this of course will be to hover high enough above the road at the foot of the downs on which the White Horse sprawls, and far enough away from it for you to see it undistorted and in its entirety.

This White Horse is only one of quite a number that have been carved on these chalk downs at one time and another. There is one on the slope above the village of Alton Barnes, cut in the chalk flesh of Walker's Hill little more than a century and a half ago. There is another, deservedly better known, that overlooks Cherhill, a village that lies almost astride the

Bath Road, a few miles to the east of Calne. There is not a great deal to commend the village, inevitably marred by its proximity to a very busy highway; but you can obtain a magnificent view of the Cherhill White Horse from any number of vantage-points there, and not least from the churchyard of St James.

You will do much better, though, to leave the village behind you and climb a chalk track that slopes pretty steeply up the downs on the south side of the Bath Road, the A 4. The horse, cut in the turf in about 1780, and therefore earlier by several decades than its neighbours at Westbury and Alton Barnes, is sprawled out somewhat uncomfortably on a concave slope above a sort of combe; the concavity increases beneath the horse's belly, and towards this its long, ungainly and spindly legs, inadequately integrated, Sir Alfred Munnings would have been quick to point out, with the body, extend vaguely downwards. A crown of typically downland trees rests on the skyline immediately above its head. The animal is of course far more recognisably a horse than is the so-called White Horse of Uffington, which is more like a dragon than a horse. This point is forcefully made by the name Dragon Hill on which the figure spreads its disjointed and extraordinary length of 374 feet from nostrils to tail-tip; some attempt, however, has been made to establish its identity as a true horse by naming the combe just beneath it 'The Manger'.

It may seem inconsistent to leave this corner of Wiltshire without specific reference to the Avebury Stone Circle; even more so virtually to ignore Stonehenge, fifteen miles or so to the south. But to deal adequately with these famous prehistoric sites would involve chapter upon chapter, each crammed with description and discussion of conflicting theories about them and the attempted elucidation of points that have puzzled professional experts ever since they began to take Ancient Monuments as seriously as they deserve. This book is no place for academic studies; there are monographs and volumes galore of this kind, and by the most competent authorities; by men who, exploring this portion of Wiltshire, so close to the Hampshire border, and corresponding portions of Brittany, such as Carnac, find themselves becoming more and more obsessed by the mysteries implicit in these prehistoric remains. Anyone more than casually interested in what is to be seen here can soon build up several shelves of such works; and they are being added to all the time.

Before leaving these uplands altogether in order to follow some minor roads southwards down such valleys as that of the Avon (not the Stratford Avon, of course: the word is a Celtic one for river or stream, as in the ubiquitous Welsh *afon*), there is an oddity to be looked for and located a few miles outside the area immediately under consideration, between Calne, at its north-west corner, and the larger Wiltshire town of Chippenham—an old market, or 'bartering' town, as the first part, from the Saxon *ceap*, reveals (Chipping Norton and Chipping Campden and

London's old Cheapside all echo the word). Here, five centuries ago, lived Maud Heath, farmer's wife. She achieved immortality in a most unusual fashion, and her simple story is all too little known.

Just west of Calne a road leading off north and signed Bremhill soon reaches a modest summit named Wick Hill, where you will find a solitary farmhouse somewhat unexpectedly named Monument Farm. The reason for the name becomes evident as you look through the farm gate across a field to the left of the house, that slopes slightly upwards from the road. For, standing in the middle of it is a forty-foot-high eight-sided stone column on top of which there sits a solid looking countrywoman with the twisted handle of a stone basket slung over the crook of her left arm. She is looking due west, over a steep escarpment, towards the market town of Chippenham, four or five miles away across the Avon Valley. And for a very good reason: it was to this small market town that, during the greater part of her life, first as a farmer's daughter and later as a farmer's wife, she went to sell her eggs and poultry.

You may find nothing unusual in that. But in fact, there was. For the wide and shallow Bristol Avon valley used to flood, and remain flooded, for long periods in late autumn, winter and spring, yet the journey to market and back, ten miles in all, had still to be made. Maud Heath did not like getting her feet wet; and she was public-spirited enough not to wish her neighbours to suffer the same discomfort. So she carefully saved the money she made from her eggs and poultry at Chippenham market and in due course had sufficient to set in hand the building of a raised causeway to span the full width of the water meadows on either side of the river.

Her generous gesture is commemorated in various ways. On the plinth of the obelisk at Monument Farm, that, strangely enough, was erected only a century and a half ago, more than three hundred years after her death, appear the words:

> Thou who dost pause on this aerial height
> Where Maud Heath's pathway winds in shade or light,
> Christian Wayfarer, in a world of strife,
> Be still, and ponder on the Way of Life.

Beside the road, at the top of the steep hill, facing the gateway into the field that contains the obelisk, there is a stone pillar inscribed with the words:

> From this Wick Hill begins the Praise
> Of Maud Heath's Gift to these Highways

From this stone you now descend Wick Hill in search of this much trumpeted pathway. You will be surprised to find that it far exceeds your expectations. At the foot of the hill the lane levels out and the water-meadows spread like a green carpet on either hand. At first there is no sign of the Avon, for except during periods of heavy rainfall it lies well below its rush-filled banks. Its line is indicated by a bridge that carries the lane over it, towards the attractive village of Langley Burrell; but a few yards before you reach the actual bridge you come upon Maud Heath's five-hundred-year-old 'causey', or causeway, and a remarkable construction it proves to be.

Its builders knew their job. The causeway runs, parallel with the lane, on the left-hand side, for some two hundred yards: a path carried over a series of arches, each with a span of some seven feet and stoutly constructed of brick and stonework. The grading has been so skilfully done that the rise from the level of the lane at each end to the highest point, about six feet in all, in the middle of the bridge is hardly perceptible to the unpractised eye.

At the east end of the bridge is a square column on three of whose faces there are small, delicately inscribed sundials. Beneath each of them there is an inscription, conceived in the vein always deemed appropriate in association with sundials. They read, with a nicely judged blend of resignation and of homely admonition:

> Life Steals away this Hour, Oh Man, is lent Thee
> Patiently work the Work of Him Who sent Thee;
>
> Haste, Traveller! The Sun is sinking now;
> He shall return again — but never Thou!
>
and   Oh Early Passenger, look up, be Wise,
> And think how, night and day, Time onward flies!

This small sundial-bearing obelisk is older by far than the larger obelisk in the field behind Monument Farm, at the top of Wick Hill. But lest any 'passenger', or passer-by, should fail to appreciate its significance it carries yet another inscription:

> To the Memory of the worthy MAUD HEATH, of Langley Burrell, WIDOW. Who in the Year of Grace 1474, for the Good of Travellers, did in Charity Bestow, in land and houses, about 8 Pounds a year, FOR EVER, to be laid out on the highways and CAUSEY leading from Wick Hill to Chippenham Clift. This PILLER was set up by the FEOFFEES, in 1698. INJURE ME NOT.

Versions of the charity here commemorated vary. From the appearance of Maud Heath as shown on the obelisk at Monument Farm she was a buxom farmer's wife, her egg-and-poultry basket (most skilfully rendered in stone) her badge of office. But in 1474 the sum of £8 was a very considerable one. Since she is referred to by the Feoffees (trustees of a bequeathed estate) as a widow of Langley Burrell it is possible that in fact she was not able to have the causeway built in time to keep her own feet

The bird window in the Church of St Mary, Selborne

The rare marsh gentian; this one was found on Slepe Heath, east of Wareham, Dorset

View of Wiltshire countryside

dry, but, widowed, found the money to build the causeway as a landmark
in the valley by which she is to be remembered 'for ever'. And so she is
remembered, and generously remembered, in this lush little corner of
Wiltshire watered by the Avon as it flows southwards in the direction of
Bradford on Avon and Bath and Bristol, and so to Avonmouth in the
Severn Estuary.

Yet another Avon, the Hampshire Avon, flows out of the Vale of Pewsey
almost due south down the eastern edge of Salisbury Plain by way of
Manningford Bruce and on by way of a necklet of villages strung out
between Pewsey and Amesbury. Here, for example, is Upavon, at the
junction of the A 345 and the A 342, in a cutting between two low spurs of
chalk downs carved by a remote forbear of the stream you see there today.
You may like to linger in the village enough to admire the fine flush work of
the thirteenth-century church, whose walls are bright with the contrast
between the alternating bands of freestone and obsidian-like black flint.

Below Upavon you have a choice of roads. The larger one, the A 345,
parallels the river on its west side, beyond which stretch the rolling slopes
of Wilsford and Charlton Downs, the northern outliers of Salisbury Plain

itself. The minor road, which is much to be preferred by anyone except a person unwise enough to be in a hurry, runs southwards on the opposite bank. Between them, the roads feed the small villages of West Chisenbury and East Chisenbury, where there is a Jacobean house that was once a priory and where, as so often among these hamlets built along river banks, there is a most satisfying relationship between thatched cottage and its garden and the water that flows past beneath them.

Farther down stream are Enfold and inappropriately named Longstreet, Netheravon and Fittleton and Figheldean; but by now you will have caught sight of such names as Bulford and Larkhill Camps and, all too close, Tidworth Barracks; you will therefore know at once and without question that the army has been here before you.

Do not, however, choose the main road south from Amesbury, the A 345, which has entered it from the north. It will only bring you, in eight swift, uneventful miles, to Salisbury. Instead, branch off a little to the right, on to one or other of two unnumbered minor roads which, like those that you have already followed southwards from Upavon, run along the banks of the Avon. There is little if anything to choose between them, and in any case they criss-cross one another midway along their length between Amesbury and Salisbury. But in their brief seven or eight miles they meander through some of the most delectable country to be found anywhere so close to the vast grey-green desert that is 'The Plain'.

You will come almost at once to West Amesbury, a trim little village strung out along the lane and notable for the obvious pride that its inhabitants take in the appearance of their houses and cottages. Here you will see, possibly for the first time, a feature characteristic of Wiltshire and parts of Berkshire in particular: the thatched wall. You may have seen this type of wall in the beautiful little village of Blewbury, in Berkshire, the setting, incidentally, for Kenneth Grahame's *The Wind in the Willows*, where the small, twisting lanes are most of them flanked by high walls topped with thatch. Alas, Blewbury now finds itself uncomfortably close to the vast and sinister Government Research Station of Harwell, only a couple of miles or so to the north-west: had this been in existence in Kenneth Grahame's day he would certainly have looked elsewhere for the setting for Rattie and Mole and Mr Toad's activities.

There are not many parts of the country where this tradition of thatched walls has been established and maintained, as it has been in these two adjoining counties. There is, as always, a good reason for this thatch capping. A region builds in the raw materials readiest to hand; or at any rate it did so before the days when basic heavy materials could be easily transported by road and rail. Here in Wiltshire, as in Berkshire, chalk was abundant, and flint too. These old walls—many of them date back to the eighteenth century and even earlier—were largely made by setting up heavy 'shuttering' in parallel runs and in-filling the space between with puddled chalk and water This resulted in a sort of whitish-grey mud, containing loose fragments of flint and other stone, deliberately included to supply 'bulk' but not essential to the principle of construction. The local name for the mixture was, and remains to this day, 'pug'. When the boards were removed, if the right consistency had been achieved the 'pug' wall stood firm.

It would of course have been laid on stone—all too frequently broken fragments of the sarsens from the nearest source of supply on the downs or Salisbury Plain. But it was necessarily highly vulnerable to wet weather; and this explains that cheap and reliable form of capping to the walls: the thatch already in almost universal use among the smaller buildings of the region. It is true that this had to be replaced at intervals and without delay if the rains had begun and there were noticeable gaps through which it could intrude; otherwise the wall would virtually dissolve. But wall-thatching is quickly done and does not demand the same skill and finesse that is so evident in the thatching of roofs. There is a saying in Wiltshire that is familiar to all who live in districts where this form of building is traditional, to the effect that a wall must be given 'a good hat and a good pair of boots'; the metaphor is self-explanatory.

There are many good examples of these thatched walls in these charming small villages strung out along the length of the Avon, now happily running well to the west of the busy main road so that they are likely to remain unspoilt for the foreseeable future. The trio of hamlets, Upper, Middle and Lower Woodford, for instance, all have such walls. They have, too, many buildings in freestone and dressed flint that lend them distinction. Of the three, perhaps Middle Woodford, with its flint-work and its air of compactness, is the most attractive; though Lower Woodford, with its very pleasing little inn and a wealth of chequered freestone and flint, runs it very close. None of the Woodfords, however, can compare with the trim beauty of West Amesbury, a little farther up this stream-side lane.

Quite apart from the sheer attractiveness of these hamlets the roads, especially the one that runs along the west bank of the river, are lovely in themselves. Embowered with close-set trees, with a thatched and half-timbered cottage at every other turn, or a brick-and-flint-and-cob out-building of some sort, or a glimpse through a gap in the trees of some more notable building, a Georgian mansion of modestly appropriate size, for example, they lead you on from one object of beauty to the next. And dipping down towards the river from time to time there will be a leafy lane, almost totally overhung with fine trees, leading perhaps to some 'lost' church-let such as the diminutive Church of St Michael on the outskirts of Wilsford, a mile or two south of West Amesbury, almost obliterated by the noble stand of beeches that flank the narrow lane on either side and continue on into the churchyard itself.

It is lanes such as these that bring us back in spirit to those explored in the north-east corner of Hampshire long before crossing the border into Wiltshire: those on the uplands between Alton and Selborne, for instance; and those in and about the Meon Valley, from Meonstoke to Soberton and on to Hambledon and Broadhalfpenny Down. Some parts of these two adjoining counties share this homely feature between them. It is of course true that nowhere in Hampshire can you find anything quite on the scale of that 'ocean of rolling grass' that is perhaps the essence of Wiltshire and, in particular, 'The Plain'. But there is a hint of this as you look out from the summit of Pilot Hill which, so close to the Berkshire Downs, gives promise of distance. There is not the sense of antiquity in Hampshire that is so dominant in much of Wiltshire, as it is too in Berkshire when you are treading the ancient Ridge Way with its prehistoric hill-forts and camp sites; but on the other hand there is, in Hampshire, a rare impression of intimacy, of half-hidden delights only waiting to be fully unveiled by someone in search of experiences less exhilarating, perhaps, but in the long run certainly no less memorable.

13

The West Country

DORSET

The midway point along England's six-hundred-mile southern coastline is marked by the Isle of Wight; ten miles or so to the west of this, beyond Hampshire's New Forest area, is the border between that county and Dorset, the first of the four counties that comprise the West Country. It is by a good deal the smallest of the four. It is little more than half the size of Somerset, which overlies it to the north, and little more than one-third the size of its western neighbour, Devonshire. Perhaps for that very reason, or perhaps because it possesses only seventy miles out of the seven hundred-odd miles of English Channel and Atlantic coastline that form the total periphery of this peninsula, it is less well known, less disturbed by traffic, than the other three. Much of Dorset sleeps on, as it has slept ever since prehistoric man moved in and settled, perhaps five thousand years ago. But by no means all. For here too, alas, as on Salisbury Plain and parts of Hampshire and Surrey, Norfolk and Suffolk, Yorkshire and the Cheviots, the Army has set its inescapable imprint.

Much of the county is chalk uplands, peppered with ancient hill-forts, like the chalk downs of Sussex, the Berkshire Downs and neighbouring areas of Wiltshire. Its highest point, Pilsdon Pen, comes very close to the 1000-foot mark, and eastwards from this summit there are contour lines running at six, seven and eight hundred feet. Bulbarrow Hill comes to within ten feet or so of the height of Pilsdon Pen; from almost any one of the many ancient hill-fort sites you can obtain (as their builders intended should be the case, though for the benefit of their look-outs) magnificent open views in all directions across the lesser uplands to other hill-fort sites. It is no exaggeration to say that Dorset's heritage in this respect is as rich and as rewarding to archaeologists and antiquarians as that of any other county in the land, with the possible exception of Wiltshire. Dorset may not have Stonehenge, Avebury and Silbury Hill; but it has the incomparable Maiden Castle, the most impressive as well as the largest by far of all our hill-fort sites. And it has others of distinction, too: those of Eggardon, Rawlsbury Camp, Hambledon Hill, Badbury Rings, Maumbury Rings (in fact a Roman amphitheatre, not a prehistoric fort), and Hod Hill Camp, to mention no more than a handful of these.

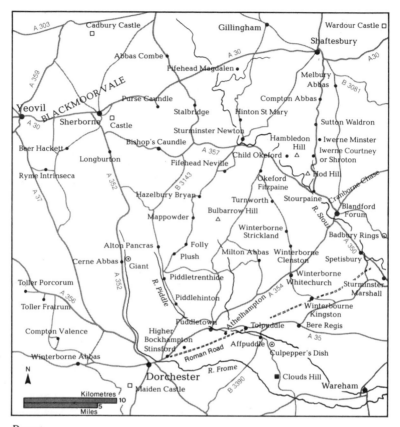

Dorset

Look at a relief map of the county. You will see at once that the chalk
uplands of western Wiltshire, to the south of Salisbury Plain, the uplands
that carry Cranborne Chase south-westwards along Wiltshire's border
with Hampshire, slant diagonally down into Dorset. They are momentarily interrupted by the River Stour (one of many in the country), which
over the aeons has carved for itself a channel through the chalk. It now
runs south–eastwards by way of Blandford Forum and Sturminster (Stour
Minster) Marshall and, having joined forces with the Hampshire Avon,
finds its exit in the English Channel near Bournemouth. But these chalk
uplands rouse themselves after this interruption, to reach even more
impressive heights and to shoulder their way across the heart of the county
as far as the valley of the Axe, the border with Devonshire, where once
again they are momentarily checked in their westwards-flowing course.

North and south of this fine and invigorating terrain are Dorset's open valleys, notably Blackmoor Vale, which flows out of Somerset to the west of Shaftesbury, to end on the northern slopes of the chalk. In its widest reaches lie such truly Dorset villages as beautifully named Fifehead Neville and Fifehead Magdalen, Sturminster Newton, Hinton St Mary, Bishop's Caundle, Purse Caundle and Child Okeford. It is questionable whether any other county in all Britain possesses so many enchantingly-named villages and hamlets as are to be found in Dorset. They ring in the ear, whether for their sheer music or for some elusive quality that arouses speculation or lifts the eyebrow of curiosity. Hazelbury Bryan is one such; Toller Fratrum and Toller Porcorum, and near neighbours Piddle-trenthide, Folly, Mappowder and Plush are others. Compton Valence has a romantic as well as a distinguished sound to it; Beer Hackett and Long Burton, with their inevitable connotation of the raised glass, are near neighbours; Ryme Intrinseca evokes speculation without solution. Not, perhaps, until you reach Cornwall, with its Indian Queens and Zelah and Peranzabuloe, will you be at once so attracted and at the same time so puzzled by the minor names scattered about a map.

A rewarding cross-section of this county, threshold, you might say, to the true West Country, and an admirable one at that, could contain part of Blackmoor Vale, a fine stretch of the chalk uplands, and just a hint of the low-lying terrain watered by the River Frome to the east of Dorchester itself. Three hundred square miles, with Shaftesbury (Shaston on the older milestones and in the mouths of the older residents) in the top right-hand corner and Dorchester (the Romans' Durnovaria), the county town, in the bottom left-hand corner. In such an area you will find all that is best, most truly representative, of the county; all, that is, save its very attractive but now sadly over-populated coastline, and the nobility of the Purbeck marble on which Corfe Castle rears its gaunt and shattered skeleton to the empty sky.

Two roads run due south from Shaftesbury to Blandford Forum, twelve miles away. The larger of the two is the A 350, which has left the A 4, the Bath Road, far to the north near Chippenham and is to end its run on the edge of Poole Harbour. For a main road it is unusually pleasant; but then, this is Dorset, and even its more important roads seem somehow to come under the spell of this lovely county. Almost parallel with it, a mile to the east and on a higher level, for it runs along the foot-hills of the chalk ridge carrying the western extremity of Cranborne Chase, another road links the two towns twelve miles apart. It is very much a minor road, and in fact has only one village along its length, that of Melbury Abbas, a couple of miles south of Shaftesbury. If you are seeking absolute solitude, then this is your road. Moreover, it offers a series of minor roads branching off eastwards into the heart of Cranborne Chase, on ground that rises steadily and from which you can look southwards over the lower reaches of the

Stour Valley, to the uplands south of Wimborne Minster, and to the unique Isle of Purbeck beyond, soaring above Poole Bay. You can also look back westwards, over your shoulder, to the lower reaches of lovely Blackmoor Vale and to the uplands that rise beyond it, curving horseshoe-wise about the town of Sherborne. This is richness for the taking indeed.

If you have entered Dorset from the north-east, that is from Wiltshire, Melbury Abbas may well be the first of the county's hundreds of secluded villages that it will be your good fortune to explore. The stone here—almost every building in Dorset is either of Portland stone or of the warmer-hued stone from quarries to the north and west of Portland, golden, even ochre in tone—is just a shade warmer than that which predominates in Wiltshire and Hampshire. The farther west you go, of course, the richer in tone it tends to become. You will see the native oolitic limestone at its best in the outcrops in the cliffs of Burton Bradstock, and in quarried and hewn form of course in Dorchester, in Sherborne, in Cerne Abbas, and in a host of smaller places all over the county as you come closer to the true limestone belt that runs north-eastwards across England from this very point. The terminal 'Abbas' will remind you that originally this small village, Melbury, had ecclesiastical associations. The word appears countless times: Cerne Abbas, Milton Abbas, Compton Abbas (only a mile or so from Melbury), Winterbourne Abbas and Abbas Combe are but a few examples of these.

You will find more of these charming Dorset villages on the larger of the two roads, the A 350; and you may take this road without apprehension, for it does not carry an undue amount of traffic, hereabouts at any rate, and it does lead you through a succession of characteristic villages. Leaving Melbury Abbas to the east, in a hollow sunk between Melbury Hill and Melbury Down, it leads you soon to Compton Abbas, in the hollow below Fontmell Down, beyond which, in a crook of the road, lies Fontmell Magna. The suffix, as so often, is misleading: this is no 'great' town; like the other hamlets strung out along this road, and along its continuation south-eastwards beyond Blandford down the valley of the Stour, such as Spettisbury, it is little more than a small village of stone-built and for the most part beautifully thatched houses of modest pretensions and more numerous humbler cottages. The churches, such as that of St Andrew, in Fontmell, have fragments that date back to the fifteenth century and earlier; sometimes they claim to possess such treasures as twelfth-century fonts or other very early relics; but the quick eye will detect all too often the hand of the restorer, often of Victorian date, which has dealt not too successfully with a decaying fabric in need of sympathetic and imaginative treatment.

Farther down the valley you will come to Sutton Waldron—a name that does not seem to fit the Dorset vein quite so well as most; but soon afterwards you come to the unmistakable Dorset-style name, Iwerne

Corfe Castle from the west

Minster, lying snugly within a crook below Iwerne Hill. Its church of St Mary reveals fairly modern restoration work, and an actual addition, the South Chapel, which is not yet a hundred years old. Nevertheless the church has more than a trace of the twelfth century in its main fabric, and it also claims to have one of the few really old spires to be found among the smaller churches in the county.

Beyond Iwerne Minster you come to Stourpaine—evidence, apart from anything else, that you have now entered the Stour Valley, into which the trickle of the Fontmell has just unobtrusively flowed. The close-set hills of the chalk uplands to east and west almost immediately relinquish their grip on the road and the valley opens out to accommodate the old market town of Blandford Forum. The name immediately suggests a Roman origin. In fact, unlike Dorchester, it is not of Roman provenance at all, in spite of its suffix, *forum*. The story goes that a medieval ecclesiast, conscious of the strong monastic tradition implicit in the Abbas, Minster and similar suffices, replaced the good old 'chipping', or market, tag by the loftier sounding word; so, Blandford Forum, instead of Chipping Blandford, it is to this day.

From Blandford you should now turn your face westwards rather than southwards, unless you wish to reach Dorchester with the least possible delay along the A 354. You will soon find a choice of very minor, seeming indeterminate, roads that weave about the chalk uplands to form a nodal point high on Woolland Hill, very close indeed to the 900-foot contour and close to Bulbarrow Hill and the prehistoric hill-fort, Rawlsbury Camp. At least six 'spokes' invite exploration from this nodal point, equally spaced round the points of the compass. All of them dip off this summit, one or two of them gradually and in the main to the south-east, south, and south-west, the others more steeply since they make for the lower end of Blackmoor Vale. In a district as deliberately circumscribed as this you have plenty of time to explore each one of them in turn.

There is a fine ridge run, north-eastwards along Woolland Hill towards Okeford Fitzpaine, a hamlet that nestles immediately beneath Okeford Hill, the eastward extension of Woolland Hill. It is a place that gives a strong impression of compactness, of reluctance to extend outwards as so many villages tend to do; but it can only be a matter of time before it is forced to succumb to the temptation, as its fellows have done. Okeford Fitzpaine is less uniformly stone built than villages farther to the west, and you will find here a good deal of flint, and even brick, as well as the freestone. There is also an admixture of half-timbering, a style of building that is not so prevalent in Dorset as it is in some other counties.

From Okeford Fitzpaine a minor road will lead you over Okeford Hill, a steepish climb, southwards to the hamlet of Turnworth, which is little more than a string of cottages and the church of St Mary, much of which dates from the thirteenth century and which has one strong claim to uniqueness in that it is the only church in Dorset that was restored under the supervision of that great interpreter of the county, Thomas Hardy. This, of course, was during the period when he was working as an architect and before he began writing his incomparable Wessex novels.

This is, of course, all 'Hardy Country'. The poet-novelist was born in Higher Bockhampton, not four miles out of Dorchester; he lived at Max Gate, not far from Dorchester, the 'Casterbridge' of his novels; and when he died, though his ashes were buried in Westminster Abbey his heart was buried in Stinsford, two miles from his birthplace, in the county he loved and made so positively his own.

One does not look for sophistication in Dorset, save perhaps among the upper crust of Dorchester and the owners of Stately Homes such as Athelhampton (a gem of a place) and Creech Grange and Forde Abbey, that miracle in golden stone from the famous Ham quarries and ornamented by Inigo Jones himself, and a few other such outstanding places open to the public at certain seasons of the year. The element is not indigenous to Dorset; nor would the true lover of the county wish that it were otherwise. Its treasures are for the most part half-hidden; you must

Melbury Bubb village from Bubb Down Hill

go and look for them; with a little persistence you are unlikely to look for them in vain; and it is quite certain that, having located them, you will never be disappointed in what you have found.

Travelling westwards along these uplands from their summit plateau near Bulbarrow, you may come upon a signpost that will surprise you: was ever such a gallimaufry of improbable place-names to be seen on one small finger-post as Mappowder, Folly and Plush? Yet these are three Dorset villages, the first separated by not more than a mile and a half from the last, and the second, fittingly, between them. Mappowder lies on low ground, just south of melodiously named Hazelbury Bryan. Its name is almost certainly a corruption of Domesday's 'maple-dre'. One of the cluster of cottages standing close to the church that is dedicated to St Peter and St Paul was the home of the Dorset novelist and short story writer T. F. Powys, one of a trio of strange but gifted brothers of whom John Cowper (of *A Glastonbury Romance*) and Llewellyn were probably the better known. Their powerful writing is largely forgotten today; to read their books is to find oneself deeply involved, willy-nilly, in the Dorset and neighbouring Somerset scene.

The next place along this narrow, tree-hung, hedge-bounded lane is Folly. It is smaller altogether than Mappowder; so small indeed that it rarely scrapes into the guide-books, and even on a relatively large-scale map it is printed in type so small that you might think it had privately asked the cartographer not to draw attention to it. It stands very close to the 600-foot contour, but is squeezed hard between two much higher shoulders of hill, on each of which there are the remains of a prehistoric camp. Then the road begins unobtrusively to drop, and in a mile or so you are entering the hamlet of Plush, which appears on the map in equally minuscule type. You puzzle a little over the name. The association of 'powder' and 'plush' perhaps comes unbidden into your mind: 'powder-rooms', 'plush' upholstery, luxury and good taste in olden times? you muse. But of course not. The first name has already been explained away; and this name, the last of the trio, is neither more nor less than a faint corruption of an older word, *plesh*, indicating a shallow piece of water. There is, still, a shallow reach of water, close to the handful of cottages that make up this improbably-named hamlet.

The church of St John the Baptist lies somewhat outside the village itself and is not really worth more than a rapid, even superficial, glance; in any case it is almost hidden by a stand of mixed yews and cedars on a slope above the tight valley into which the houses are compressed. At the foot of the hill you will find the village inn, the Brace of Pheasants. You can see at a glance that this was originally a pair of low-roofed cottages, with a smithy (now of course no longer operating) at the far end. The three buildings have been skilfully and imaginatively welded into one unit: a long, stone-built, whitewashed and thatched building that carries over its entrance a bracket supporting a most unusual sign.

It is in fact a glass case in which a cock and a hen pheasant, expertly stuffed, perch in a most lifelike fashion, one facing outwards to catch your attention and the other inwards to indicate what is expected of you. They are so realistically posed that, glancing upwards at them even before you have had your glass, you would be prepared to swear that they are alive. And Plush has another unexpected surprise in store for you; here in this diminutive Dorset village there is a quite flourishing industry: nothing less than the growing for export of orchids!

Just below Plush you will come to the junction of the lane you have been following with a somewhat larger but still very minor road, the B 3143. This clings to the edge of a stream named the Piddle. It has given its name to a succession of villages: Piddletrenthide, standing right at this road junction, is the first you will come to. It has a remarkably fine church in which there is some twelfth-century work, notably in the doorway, though the greater part of the fabric dates from three centuries and more later. In this fabric there is an interesting blend of the cold grey and the warmer yellow limestone of the county, each throwing the other into relief and each, incidentally, thrown into relief by the presence of bands of the even colder grey-black glassy flint.

This name, Piddle, looked less off-putting in Domesday, when it was spelt 'Pidele', which unwittingly gave it the overtone and connotation of the word 'fidele'. Down the centuries it has been alternatively written as 'Puddle', and you will find that, small as the river is, a whole galaxy of villages has been named after it, utilising one spelling or the other. You may add Piddlehinton to the already named Piddletrenthide. But the form preferred by most authorities, and certainly in the nineteenth century when one was more inhibited than one is today, and even piano-legs were sometimes kept decorously encased, was the alternative 'Puddle'. In this small valley you will encounter Puddletown and Affpuddle, Bryants Puddle and Turners Puddle, Little Puddle Hill and Tolpuddle (of the 'Martyrs' episode), and so on. A hint that neither name entirely satisfied the authorities at one time is shown by the fact that against the name Piddle, attached to the stream of that name, is the addition 'or Trent'. It was presumably as a wide gesture to susceptibilities that both names were incorporated in that village set where one small stream merges with another just large enough to have a name of its own, Piddletrenthide.

From Puddletown, where you join the main A 354 road from Dorchester to Blandford, it is only a mile or two to the very beautiful Stately Home of Athelhampton, hidden from immediate view by a massive array of trees bordering the road. A mile or two beyond that you will come to Tolpuddle, with its memorial to George Loveless and his five companions, who formed a union to challenge the then pitiful agricultural wage of 8s 6d a week. The year was 1833. Their sentence was a savage one: transportation to Australia for a term of not less than seven years, though in fact this was later slightly reduced as a result of the storm of protest the sentence evoked. The memorial to the six men may or may not, in the light of what trades unionists get up to today, seem either appropriate or adequate. Just a hundred years after the scandalous trial and transportation of the men, the T.U.C. caused to be erected a row of memorial cottages to house pensioners who had spent their entire lifetimes in an industry which, even today, is felt by some to be grossly underpaid.

The larger-scale maps of this area show that from Tolpuddle, running dead-straight north-eastwards across the valley and the lowest foot-hills of the chalk uplands you have just left behind you, is the relic of a Roman road constructed some eighteen centuries ago to link their Durnovaria (our Dorchester) with their base at Old Sarum, on the Wiltshire Downs between modern Salisbury and Amesbury. Today it demands a keen eye and perhaps more than a little imagination to detect just where that old road ran. It ran, in fact, by way of Bere Down, a mile or so north of Bere Regis, on the main road, to Winterborne Kingston and for miles beyond that. You could attempt to pick it out, if you are inclined that way and are equipped with an adequate map; but you will probably do better to branch southwards off the main road, making for the trio of Puddles—those of Turners, Bryants and Aff.

The last-named lies among wide water-meadows, only a hundred feet or so above sea level. After the exhilaration of the uplands the setting is perhaps somewhat uninspiring, reminiscent a little of parts of Lincolnshire or Bedfordshire. The one notable feature of Affpuddle is its church of St Laurence, the earliest portions of which date back to the early thirteenth century, though there may well have been a church of some sort on this site as early as the year 987, when one Alfrith, or Affrith, donated 'a parcel of land' to the Abbey of Cerne ten miles away to the north-west. The church is finely set among tall, well trimmed yews and other trees. Again there is that interesting contrast of the relatively cold grey stone intermixed with the darker flint and topped by the richer-hued, near-golden stone from entirely different quarries.

Inside the church there is an unexpected feature: on the wall of the North Chancel there is a memorial to one Edward Lawrence which includes the Lawrence coat-of-arms. As shown here, it is not difficult to believe the tradition strongly held in Affpuddle that his coat-of-arms was the original inspiration for the flag of the United States; George Washington's mother was in fact a Miss Lawrence before her marriage, and her arms are thus quartered with the stars and stripes of 'Old Glory'.

Close to Affpuddle, though in fact closer to the other two Puddles, is an odd topographical feature shown on the map by the improbable sounding reference 'Culpepper's Dish'. You will find it within a few hundred yards of the southern edge of Bryants Puddle, where the ground begins to slope upwards on to Affpuddle Heath, a very modest height perhaps a hundred feet at most above the level of the valley as a whole. It is a hollow in the ground about a hundred yards across and not more than about forty feet deep, partly filled with small trees and scrub. If you had come across this in the carboniferous limestone region of, say, Yorkshire you would have taken it to be an exaggeratedly large and rather unusually proportioned specimen of a swallet-hole. But this is emphatically not carboniferous limestone country (though this type of limestone occurs some forty miles to the north-west, in the Mendips). It is of course chalk country, with an admixture of gravel. Though the locals incline to talk of caves occupied here by prehistoric man, the romantic theory is challenged by geologists, who state with conviction that the great hollow so nicely named Culpepper's Dish is in fact simply the result of a subsidence in the chalk that underlies the gravel found in much of this valley, and probably caused by the movement of underground water that gradually diluted and so removed the chalk.

Go much farther to the south and east and you will come all too close to military installations: tank-testing grounds, artillery ranges. You are

The Stately Home of Athelhampton

within hail of the great expanse of heathland that Hardy immortalised in the opening pages of perhaps his finest novel, certainly one of his four truly great novels, *The Return of the Native*. But alas, today this is no place for the casual visitor; it is better to read of it in those immortal paragraphs at the beginning of that book, and return to it when you come to the scene of the throwing of the dice by the light of the glow-worms between the two men, Christian Cantle and Damon Wildeve. The book was written half a century before the army took possession of Egdon Heath.

Retrace your steps, then, north-westwards up the valley of the Piddle to Piddletrenthide and on up to Alton Pancras a mile or two beyond, from which place a minor road called Rake Hill will take you cross-country, steeply climbing some four hundred feet in not much more than a mile, to Cerne Abbas. Or you may, if you prefer, approach this lovely old priory village either direct from Piddletrenthide, or by main road from the south, leaving Dorchester by the A 352. By either route it is no great distance from Affpuddle: perhaps fifteen miles by the longer route of the two. It is in Cerne Abbas that you will find some of the loveliest stonework in all Dorset—and that is saying a good deal; only the best of the Cotswolds can really be mentioned in the same breath. There was a Benedictine abbey here in the Middle Ages; today all that remains of it, though breath-

351

takingly beautiful, is part of the original main gateway, the three-storey porch of the Abbot's Hall, and a building which may have been the Guest House for pilgrims and abbots and other ecclesiasts visiting the abbey from far afield.

But 'religion' of a much older day is hinted at here. On the upper slopes of a great chalk mound known appropriately as Giant Hill, immediately to the north of the village, a giant male figure—indubitably male, you will find—sprawls its 180-foot length and brandishes its enormous shillelagh to the sky. It is comparable in size, though in little else, with the Long Man of Wilmington in East Sussex. Experts disagree as to the exact date of this elaborately turf-cut figure, and even as to its provenance; but a majority verdict is that it is Romano-British in origin, a representation of some powerful god, probably Hercules.

But there are those who would like to believe (and they may of course be right) that the figure dates back to a vastly earlier age, an age of fertility rites in Britain that were basically similar to those found the world over. Certainly the predominant feature here is not the irregularly shaped club brandished in the outstretched right hand, high above the foreshortened head, but the challengingly erect male member, perhaps twenty feet long and armed with a formidable pair of testicles. There are of course those who have felt, and may still feel, that the grass should be allowed to grow over the chalk lines that delineate the stark anatomy with such power. At one time such people had their way, and when, more recently, some more enlightened people set to work to clear away the overgrowing turf there was an outcry from the puritan element. But the others won their case. In this permissive age it is unlikely that anyone would ever again think of impropriety in the grotesque figure sprawled on the hill-top, trumpeting its potency.

Strangely (or perhaps not so strangely) there are even today young couples who, hand in hand, will make the steep ascent of the slippery turf to take their joint stance on the relevant part of the anatomy and wish, in silence and in faith, that their union shall be a fruitful one. Certainly, as one stands there, without any specific motive for doing so other than mere curiosity or the mere resultant sense of achievement, one becomes increasingly conscious that the uplands of Dorset in particular are 'ancient' country; one senses, almost in spite of oneself, that prehistoric man and his immediate descendants and their mysterious way of life lie buried not so very deeply beneath the thin turf that is stretched so tightly over the county's chalk and stone.

View of the Quantock Hills, Somerset

Dartmoor, Devon, looking southwards towards Cator Common, near Postbridge

Vixen Tor, Dartmoor

The Bedruthan Steps, near Newquay, Cornwall

SOMERSET

From the Bristol Channel almost to the English—the gap is a mere seven miles—Somerset's western border marches with that of Devonshire, and indeed it is not always easy to be quite certain as to which side of that border you are on. On the coast, where you can look across the Bristol Channel towards South Wales, twelve miles or so away, the Somerset-Devon border stands at a point about three miles east of the summit of Countisbury Hill; it is known as County Gate. But immediately to the south of this point the border line makes a series of abrupt dog's-leg turns into Exmoor Forest, part of the Exmoor National Park shared between the two adjacent counties. Thereafter it slopes more or less consistently south-east by way of Winsford Hill, Bampton (which it skirts to the east), and on to the Blackdown Hills before skirting Chard and merging with the Dorset-Devon border near Pilsdon Pen. The Dorset-Devon border reaches the English Channel at Lyme Regis.

For the great majority of holiday-makers, and certainly for those entering this south-west peninsula from the Midlands and points north, this, rather than Dorset, represents the true springboard for the West Country. Once the lovely range known as the Quantock Hills lies behind you, you are truly in the West Country; this westwards spur of the county that curves upwards with the coastline to Bristol and Bath points a broad finger into the peninsula that is (alas for those who today seek quiet and seclusion) by far the most popular holiday area in all Britain.

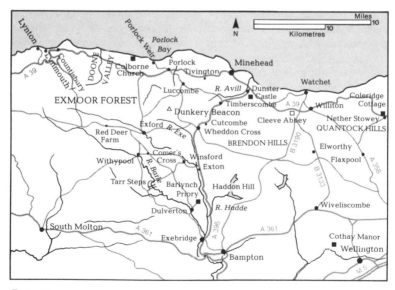

Exmoor

The busy A 39 skirts its north coast and will take you down into the heart of Cornwall, where it merges with the A 30 to take you to Land's End. The even busier A 38 and accompanying M 5 stride purposefully across the northern limit of the Blackdown Hills at Taunton, making for Exeter, Plymouth and Bodmin, where A 38 too merges with the A 30 and the Land's End route. But between these two trunk roads, tucked away close to the Somerset-Devon border at its northernmost extremity, there is an escape-route which offers some degree of quiet and seclusion; and this can be savoured, as it should be, amid scenery that lingers long in the memory when it has at last been left behind. The northern limit of this region is of course the coastline of the Bristol Channel, delineated by majestic cliffs that tower a thousand feet and more above the water.

They are not, of course, sheer cliffs; in this sense they are not comparable with, for example, the astonishing cliffs of Moher, in Eire, or with some of the Atlantic coastal cliffs in the Orkney or Shetland Isles. But they have the eventual height, even if they are 'stepped' and interrupted here and there by shelving combes. To reach their summit you must climb westwards out of Porlock, or eastwards out of Lynmouth, up hills that even with today's efficient car engines can offer a very real challenge. In both cases, of course, you start from a point very near indeed to sea level.

The ascent from Porlock is notorious. Porlock Hill has been a trap for motorists who have hitherto believed that they had nothing to learn about the negotiation of hairpin-bends on gradients close to one-in-four while keeping their engines running fast enough to take them over what seem interminable miles of steady, unrelenting climb. Not for nothing are there barrels of water by the roadside for the emergency replenishment of exhausted radiators and cooling-systems. This hill (and for that matter its opposite number climbing eastwards out of Lynmouth) challenges from the outset. The initial hairpin-bend is virtually in the village itself, so that there is no opportunity to take a brisk run at the hill to obtain a good start. The hill climbs to some fourteen hundred feet. So, of course, does the toll-road, that zigzags up the cliff face to the north of the main road. Some motorists, especially those faced with the ascent for the first time, feel that it is a worthwhile alternative; others maintain that though the gradient in general is less severe this benefit is counteracted by the greater number of hairpin-bends. Certainly these present a very real hazard when up-going and down-coming vehicles come face to face. So, you takes your choice and, in one case, pays your money for the privilege.

But before leaving Porlock there are two churches you may well wish to see. One is at Tivington, just south of the A 39 some three miles to the east; diminutive and abutting a cottage, it goes back to the fifteenth century and with its thatch is as charming as it is architecturally rare. A visit to the other church, that of Culbone, involves a beautiful walk of about one and a half miles from a toll and car park in Ashley Combe near Porlock Weir.

Perhaps the smallest medieval church in England, it squats on a slight slope, with the cliff sides rising steeply to west and east of it, softened by trees that creep right down to the perimeter of the diminutive churchyard. All is entirely in keeping, as though originally designed to be erected in Lilliput. The church may be thirty-five feet long, and is certainly not more than twelve feet in width. It contains one family box-pew that could seat perhaps half a dozen members at a pinch, and it would be a pinch; it contains in addition two-some pews that would accommodate a dozen more, at most. Are they, one is inclined to wonder, ever filled?

You would hardly expect a church so small to have features of recognised architectural beauty, and you would be right in this. But the church certainly possesses some features of interest, over and above the sheer charm of its Lilliputian dimensions. Its tiny chancel, for instance, is lit on the north, or seaward, side by a small, square window which is unusually interesting because, as can easily be established by looking closely at it, from the outside rather than from within, the whole window, its square frame, its mullion and its transom, has been carved out of one solid block of sandstone. The main fabric of this remarkable little church dates from the twelfth century, and this is manifest in the proportions and in the mode of building of the little South Porch. But it has of course been restored over the centuries since the first stones were laid, and additions, notably the small, slate-covered and oddly truncated steeple, have also been made.

The little churchyard reveals that parishioners, in the last century at least, have been buried here. Between the great tree-clad slopes of this isolated and truly 'lost' combe there are gravestones many of which bear the surname Red. An odd name, perhaps; but an evocative one. A frequent variant of it is—Ridd. And was not one of the characters in *Lorna Doone* the famous Jan Ridd? The setting for this novel is only three or four miles to the south-west of Culbone Church, across the moor.

There is a small postscript to this. The poet Coleridge lived for a time at Nether Stowey. One of the most remarkable poems he ever wrote is *Kubla Khan*. The poem was never completed. For, as he tells us, he was awakened from the trance, in which the immortal lines had their birth, by 'a person from Porlock' who called upon him unexpectedly when he was a temporary guest at a farmhouse at the head of this very combe at whose foot lies the little 'lost' church of Culbone. In his poem there appear the magic lines:

> But O, that deep romantic chasm which slanted
> Down the green hill athwart a cedarn cover!
> A savage place! As holy and enchanted
> As e'er beneath a waning moon was haunted
> By woman wailing for her demon-lover!

There is no evidence that, when he was staying at this farmhouse, he ever scrambled down the steep path through the trees (no cedars among them, anyway, but that can be regarded as legitimate poetic licence) to Culbone Church; but equally there is no evidence that he did not. And the poem was written during the period that he spent down here in the West Country.

With Porlock left far below, the wide and almost unbroken expanse of Exmoor calls you. Dunkery Beacon, at 1707 feet, dominates the landscape, but this Exmoor maintains a general level in excess of a thousand feet, and even the valleys that interlace it, such as Badgworthy Water, Doone Water and Haccombe Water, along the last of which the Devonshire border runs for a while, are to be found on relatively high uplands. The River Exe, for instance, rises, at Exe Head, at a height of nearly fifteen hundred feet, to flow south-eastwards for twenty serpentining miles through Somerset before entering the county with which it is always associated, at Exebridge, and then continuing on its way down an ever-widening valley to Tiverton and Exeter and its broad estuary below Topsham, thirty and more miles away.

There is one bold road that spans this part of Somerset, southwards from Dunster to Bampton and on again to Tiverton: the A 396. From Dunster, in the north, it climbs alongside the River Avill by way of Timberscombe and Cutcombe to Wheddon Cross, where it swings a little to the left and enters the Quarme Valley, which it follows as far as Exton, where Quarme meets Exe. From there it continues southwards, but now in the upper Exe Valley, as beautiful a valley main road as any you are likely to find anywhere along the Somerset-Devon border, or for that matter very much farther afield. A tight valley, with plateaux on either side on the 1000-foot contour shouldering a road and accompanying river still running at more than half that height, and indeed shouldering them very closely for much of the way. These are not road miles over which anyone should be tempted to hurry.

But both to the east and to the west of this solitary main road there is a scattering of minor roads. At Wheddon Cross, for example, as the name of the place signifies, a road crosses this main road, running east and west. From the east it has run along the inspiriting ridge of the Brendon Hills, at about twelve hundred feet and parallel with a small railway-line long since abandoned. From this, looking north by west, you can obtain a magnificent view of Dunkery Hill and its Beacon, five miles distant across the intervening valley, itself lying on relatively high ground, for Wheddon Cross is close to the 1000-foot contour.

The road continues westwards, skirting the foot-hills of Dunkery, by way of Luckwell Bridge and Larcombe. (How frequently in these parts 'combe' is found as the suffix of a place-name. And no wonder, for this is the county of combes, matching in character the *cwms* of Wales.) It arrives

Culbone Church

at Exford, and here of course there was once a ford across the river of that name; now there is an adequate bridge. But here you will leave the Exe, which turns northwards for a while, and continue along the road parallel with the engagingly named Pennycombe Water, the charm of whose name is balanced by the less attractive name of Muddicombe on the other side of the road. Soon you come to a solitary house shown on the larger scale maps as Red Deer Farm: you are close to Exmoor Forest, and the name will remind you, perhaps to your shame, that we still, some of us, hunt the red deer of this dramatic countryside.

Glance to left and right from time to time and you will notice unobtrusive little signposts, small oaken posts bearing a horizontal wooden bar at the tip of which is a small triangular pointer in yellow, green or red as the case may be. A clearly printed inscription indicates that the footpath or track leads to such-and-such a place, at such-and-such a distance. These are of course moorland paths and tracks, and as such should be followed realistically. Only natives of the region can afford to take the risk of following their own paths, short-cuts which, to the inexperienced, can prove to be very long cuts indeed—if not something worse. These small signposts, clear but unobtrusive, are a wholly excellent amenity designed to assist the bona fide walker. They have something in common with the symbols to be found on trees and stones along the innumerable *wanderwegen* of Switzerland, Germany and Austria, which cover so many hundreds of miles of first-class mountain and valley walking in those enlightened countries.

From Exford, working your way southwards, you can pick up a minor road that will lead you into the valley of the Pennycombe, which you can follow down into Withypool, the focal point of a network of minor roads branching out in many directions. One of these would take you due east to Comer's Cross at nearly twelve hundred feet, and thence along the lower slopes of Bye Common (which separates this little valley from that of the Exe to the north) as far as Winsford. This last is as perfect a West Somerset village as you can hope to find. Admittedly it tends to be on the tourist track, for here lies perfection in so many forms; but you might be fortunate enough to come upon it on a day when others had by-passed it.

A place of thatched cob-walled cottages set within a wooded loop of the Exe and threaded by the diminutive Winn, the village enjoys a green, a ford and no less than eight packhorse bridges. Cross one of these and stand—or, if you prefer, sit, for there are inviting benches—on the green. On one side the tall tower of the church lifts against the hillside; on the other, the thatched village inn, the Royal Oak, is as truly village-English as anyone could wish. So much so, in fact, that a few years back the organisers of the British Exhibition held in New York selected this inn as the 'model' for the Britannia Inn erected over there to represent this particular and traditional aspect of the British way of life.

A sign in the village points to Tarr Steps, three miles away by minor roads and lanes. And these are lovely miles indeed, first up over open Winsford Hill to a crossroads where the Caratacus Stone of perhaps the sixth century honours some descendant of that early British hero, and then down into the wooded valley of the River Barle, crossed here by what are now known as Tarr Steps, in fact one of the most notable of the West Country clapper-bridges. Possibly the longest in the country, the bridge bestrides the river at a point where the valley has temporarily widened beneath the trees so that water-meadows extend on either side. Maps indicate that there is a ford here; and indeed there would have to be, for no cart or wagon could cross by this bridge and even a laden horse or other pack-animal would have to mind its tread. Because the ground, particularly on the near, or east, side of the bridge is so low lying it is crossed by a long stone causeway that merges with the actual mammoth slabs that constitute the bridge itself. So, except in periods of unusually wet weather, when the moorland streams are in spate, you can pass from one side to the other relatively dry-shod.

These clapper and clam bridges (in the former type there is a succession of slabs, whereas in the latter, and more primitive, type one sole immense slab forms the actual bridge) never have parapets. They were designed to withstand the pressure of rivers whose waters were swollen; this they could never have done if they had been furnished with parapets, for these, or at least the ones on the upstream side of the bridge, would have set up resistance to the flow. As a result of this, first the water above the bridge would have built up and flooded the low-lying ground on either side; and eventually the sheer weight of the accumulated water would have carried away the parapets and with them the footway itself, however massive the slabs of which it was composed.

The great stone slabs that form Tarr Steps are worn smooth by the continuous passage down the centuries of men's feet and pack-horse-train hooves. How many centuries? No one can give a positive answer to that query. There are guide-books of repute that state categorically that clapper-bridges such as this one were built in prehistoric times. This, however, is most improbable, for prehistoric man was unlikely to bother over-much about getting his feet wet, and he would not be sending laden animals from one part of his territory to another. Almost certainly, then, Tarr Steps, and other bridges of the kind, are medieval—possibly very early medieval—in date; there is no real point in attempting to establish the date any more closely than that.

There are many other examples of this interesting type of bridge, up and down the country; Somerset's close neighbour, Devonshire, is for example, particularly rich in such treasures, one of the most notable being on Dartmoor, at Postbridge between Moretonhampstead and Princetown. Here three enormous granite slabs, each twelve or fifteen feet long and four feet or so wide and proportionately thick, mounted on great buttresses of the same local stone, span the East Dart. But, impressive though it is, to many people Postbridge's clapper does not compare with Tarr Steps. And it is certainly less ancient, for the experts say that it cannot be earlier than the thirteenth century. Nor is the bridge at Postbridge the only one in Devonshire's district of steep hills and fast-running streams like the East and the West Dart which cannot be crossed by ford save during the rare periods of exceptional drought and must therefore be spanned by bridges high enough to stand clear even of deep water. There is another such bridge not far away at Wallabrook, impressive enough even though it was conceived on a less gigantic scale. Yet another is to be found near Fernworthy, at Teign Head, while probably the best known of all is the one at Dartmeet where East and West Dart have their confluence.

It may be true to say that there are more of these medieval clapper- and clam-type bridges still to be found in the West Country than anywhere else in Britain; but there are others. Among these, one of the most famous is at Wycoller, on the border between Lancashire and the West Riding of

Winsford village – packhorse bridge

Yorkshire. That the points chosen for the installation of such bridges were fundamentally sound is proved by the fact that bridges built considerably later, notably of the pack-horse type, are still to be found close alongside the earlier bridges. There are even sites where ford, stepping-stones, clapper and the semi-circular pack-horse type all exist close alongside one another. So, the history of developing aids to transport is exemplified in juxtaposition: not exactly the 'sermons in stones' or even the 'books in running brooks' of the banished duke in the Forest of Arden, but at least non-military history in boulder, slab and quarried stone.

The Devon border 'comes cranking in' close to the point where Tarr Steps cross the River Barle. That border has flowed down off the heights, though it is still close to the 1000-foot contour, following the narrow valley of a moorland stream named Litton Water which, just below Hawkridge, becomes Danes Brook. Danes Brook merges with the Barle some three miles below Tarr Steps, and here once again the border between the two counties falls steeply away southwards for a while before branching east again to cross the valley of the Exe just below Dulverton. You can hardly go wrong here. The Exe Valley and its enclosed road, the A 396, run almost due south, though never straight for more than a few hundred yards at a time, following the likeliest contours of the hills that shoulder inwards upon it to west and east. You have left behind you Winsford Hill and the valley of the Barle; they are balanced on the other side of the main valley by the long, flowing range known as Haddon Hill and the valley of the River Haddeo which flows at its feet from its distant source somewhere on the southern slopes of the Brendon Hills. A gentle valley, tree-filled and lush—though not so lush and verdant as the valleys you will thread in South Devon and farther west in Cornwall: Luxulyan Valley, for example, a delight to come.

Only a mile or two to the south of Dulverton you cross the border into Devonshire. The valley road has now dropped below the 400-foot mark and you have the choice of following it in its generous curve along the left bank of the Exe or, more directly, taking the moorland road by way of Combe Head at over seven hundred feet before dropping gently down into Bampton, in its low-lying valley of the River Batherm.

Bampton is the small town which, almost from time immemorial, has been famous for its October Exmoor Pony Fair. If you happen to be there in that month you will find it a very different place from its normal sleepy self, snug on the Somerset-Devon border. But whether you are there in October or in some other month, you should make a point of having a look at its church of St Michael & All Angels. Here, quite apart from its more important features, you will find, set low in the west wall of the tower, a quaintly worded plaque. It commemorates the unlikely and pitiful death of the parish clerk's son, over two centuries ago. It should be recited aloud rather than silently read, for obvious reasons:

> Bless my I.I.I.I.I.I.
> Here he lies
> In a sad Pickle,
> Killed by Icicle
> In the Year 1776

No one seems to remember just how the boy died, or at what exact age. Presumably an icicle from the eaves of the church roof, or perhaps his parents' cottage, fell during a thaw and, dropping like the sword of Damocles, pierced his thin skull. Just round the corner of the tower wall you will find the village stocks, placed, as so often, close to the church. Sometimes, as at St Feock in Cornwall, the stocks are to be found actually in the church porch, for safe-keeping—and perhaps with the subconscious thought that one day they may come again into their own.

Uplands and valleys, combes and woodlands, ridges like those of the Brendon Hills and Winsford and Haddon; cob and thatch; windy heights and seemingly endless level acres scattered with trees, rich in good farm land spreading round snug and trim farms where the soil is good: this is

Annual sheep fair, Brendon Hills

western Somerset. Not such notable wealth in respect of prehistoric remains as in neighbouring Wiltshire, beyond the county's distant eastern frontier, or even in neighbouring Dorset, beyond its south-eastern border. But elsewhere in Somerset, of course, there are the glories and mysteries of Glastonbury and Glastonbury Thorn and Cadbury Rings and Meare Village and memories of King Arthur and his Round Table, which will crop up yet again much further to the west, where the rocks of Tintagel Castle mark the seaward horizon. Nevertheless, there is wealth enough and to spare even in so small and circumscribed an area as this, which extends south-eastwards from the great cliffs overlooking the Bristol Channel but little more than twenty miles to the north, and over a breadth from west to east of not more than fifteen miles or so. This is proof, yet again, if you still require it, that you do not need to cover great distances in order to savour the resources of this country to the full.

DEVONSHIRE

Devonshire is a large county, something like one-tenth of which, some three hundred square miles in all, is represented by Dartmoor, a lozenge-shaped plateau of granite extending some twenty-odd miles from north to south between Okehampton and Ivybridge, and for some eighteen miles from east to west between Bovey Tracey and Tavistock. For all those to whom the coastline, with its understandably popular seaside resorts, is not all-important, Dartmoor, quite simply, *is* Devon. No excuse, therefore, is necessary for selecting an area of Dartmoor that is enormously rich in what it has to offer, rather than Devon's long and lovely English Channel and Atlantic coastline and immediate hinterland.

Dartmoor is circumscribed to the north by the broad sweep of the A 30, the main road from Exeter by way of Okehampton to Land's End; to the west by the A 386 which forks off the A 30 just below Okehampton, making for Tavistock and Plymouth beyond; and to the south and east by the A 38 main road from Plymouth by way of Ashburton back to Exeter. Only two roads of any consequence dare to cross the moor, and even then only on its lower half. These are the B 3357 Tavistock to Ashburton road and the B 3212 between Moretonhampstead and Yelverton. They intersect at Two Bridges, close to Princetown, in the dead centre of the lower portion of the moor. Only in the triangle formed between them to the east of Two Bridges will you find any truly negotiable roads, and even these, enticing as they may be, must be followed with circumspection. They will very swiftly deflate the carelessly casual driver who has not yet come to terms with the demands of lanes cut through granite country.

It is inevitable that, save for the hardy walker, the experienced veteran, who can risk treading the boglands and leaping the granite outcrops and scaling the less accessible tors, such as Yes Tor, at well over 2000 feet in the far north of Dartmoor (and no one embarks on such an enterprise without compass and whistle and a modicum of 'iron rations' for real emergency), Dartmoor must so far as possible be explored by road.

This is almost certainly best done from the east, where the introduction to the grandeur of Dartmoor is at once least baffling and most variegated. You could enter this triangle-of-plenty either from the south, from Ashburton, or from the north, by way of Moretonhampstead; there is little if anything to choose between the two, for the scribble of minor roads, dodging the most challenging summits, picking their way along the most promising valleys—the word is almost too grandiose save for that of the River Bovey, that rises just below Moretonhampstead and finds its way south-eastwards eventually to Bovey Tracey, beyond which it merges with the Teign—this scribble of minor roads nicely fills the area, zigzagging mainly between north and south, with spurs to east and west.

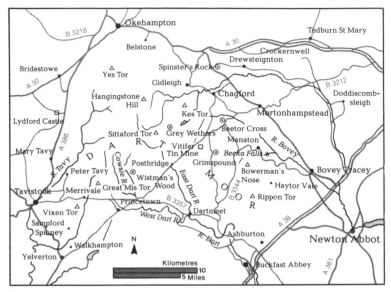

Dartmoor

But there is a third approach, one so unpretentious that without a large-scale map you might overlook it altogether. It winds westwards from Bovey Tracey, following very roughly the line of little Becka Brook and just to the south of this stream. Becka Brook itself, without question one of the minor gems among the waters that flow through Dartmoor's few valleys, rises far to the south on the western slopes of Saddle Tor; surprisingly, it flows northwards for some three or four miles to the hauntingly lovely Becka Fall (popularly the Becky Falls) where it tumbles down the loose granite boulders beneath close-set overhanging trees and then turns east to flow leisurely into the upper valley of the Bovey and, alas, lose the identity, the individuality, that it has possessed for those half-dozen or so true moorland miles.

A narrow road (B 3344) skirting Trendlebere Down will lead you to Becka Fall. There, though you will hardly be conscious of this until you have made your way out of and beyond the sheltering trees, you will find yourself at the foot of steeply rising ground in every direction save one, that by which in fact you approached Becka. Black Hill and Haytor Down, on the 1300-foot contour, rise to the south of you; Hound Tor and inappropriately-named Honeybag Tor rise to the south-west of you; Hayne Down rises to the west of you; and Manaton Tor and Hunter's Tor rise to the north of you. There seems no escape, save by way of these formidable summits.

But in fact there are three escapes. A minor road running south skirts close beneath the eastern slopes of Black Hill and Haytor Down to reach Haytor Vale; the B 3344 will take you northwards through Manaton (just beyond which a gated lane leading south soon passes below the granite stack known as Bowerman's Nose—about which more later) and thence into the lovely wooded valley of the upper Bovey between Manaton and Hunter's Tors; while a third choice, a lane initially, curves south and west between the Hound Tors (so called because their scattered crags have been seen as a gathering of wild dogs) to reach a crossroads from which the small northerly gated road is the other end of the one already mentioned as passing Bowerman's Nose.

The Dartmoor 'tors', or towers, are the surviving remains of a granite plateau, almost certainly of volcanic origin; now greatly reduced in height, they are believed once to have risen at least eighteen thousand feet above sea level. The figure may well be in excess of the true one, which of course can now never be accurately assessed. Nor does this matter over much, for what remains is sufficiently imposing. It consists of an enormous granite plateau rising generally to well over two thousand feet, the giant brother of neighbouring Bodmin Moor to the west, Cornwall's lesser granite mass that is, in fact, hardly less impressive even though so much smaller. The outcrops of this highly resistant granite towering to the heavens are its dominant features. Only three or four of them are known to the generality of holiday-makers: Yes Tor, which is the doyen of them all, Hay Tor, Great Mis Tor and Hound Tor, for example. But there are scores of others: topographers of the region list no fewer than one hundred and seventy, of which at least thirty bear accepted names, such as Raven and Belstone, Rippon, Sharp, Longaford and Kes.

No two of them, of course, bear the slightest resemblance to one another, save in their sheer mass. They range from gigantic, sprawling congeries of stones, like those that constitute Hay Tor, to what are virtually single distorted shafts that are only visible when they can be seen against the skyline. Many of them are distinctive enough in shape to have won for themselves nicknames. This is most frequently the case where they are relatively small. Bowerman's Nose is an example of one of these: as distinctive in shape as, for instance, the so-called Dancing Bear in far-away Brimham Rocks near Pateley Bridge in Yorkshire, though that rock is gritstone, not granite.

Others again have officially recognised names, often names that do not strike the casual, or even the persistent, visitor as being in the slightest degree apt. Vixen Tor is one such. But so suggestive are most of the tors, particularly the smaller ones, that the variants on their possible nicknames become legion. Granite, of course, ranks among our hardest, most resistant, stones; the fact that these outcrops have weathered in such an extraordinary fashion is evidence of their almost inconceivable antiquity.

Wind and weather, frozen rain and blistering sun (in an older epoch, of course) have worked their will on this highly resistant rock over uncountable aeons, and what we see today is the result of this massive erosive onslaught that has been in operation continuously since the very dawn of time. The effect of erosion is more easily accepted on sandstone, and even on the relatively tough gritstone of the Yorkshire moors; that granite can be shaped as it has been on Dartmoor is as good an indication of the sheer dimensions of geological time as any that could be conceived.

But we are now at that strange stack called Bowerman's Nose, a natural feature remarkable not only as such but also for being so fortunately placed for the camera enthusiast, since it silhouettes so starkly against the open sky. A slope through bracken scattered over rough turf interrupted by loose, treacherous boulders and equally treacherous patches of unexpected marshy ground leads you gently upwards for a couple of hundred yards; with every successive step this assembly of granite blocks takes on a more and more convincing identity.

The term 'assembly of blocks' is wholly appropriate. For the Bowerman's Nose, like so many of these rock masses, like the Devil's Chimney, too, on the western escarpment of the Cotswolds, gives the strongest possible impression of having been deliberately constructed, erected, from suitable graduated blocks of stone, and by human hands rather than by the agency of wind and weather down the ages. The plinth on which they stand is dead level, though cracked across from top to bottom; it is, of course, simply a continuation upwards of the virgin granite of the moor at this point. Poised on this is the largest single block of the whole composition, split, as you will soon see, both vertically and near-horizontally. It supports two wedge-shaped blocks that between them correct the slope of its upper surface. These blocks in their turn support the next largest single block, the one that constitutes the Bowerman's head; and this is capped by a final stone that ends, westwards, with what you may take either for the peak of a cap or for the figure's actual nose, according to the angle from which you contemplate it.

The Bowerman is no beauty. If, as local tradition has it, this rock-pile (it only just scrapes into the category of true tor) was named after a man who once lived among the dog-like crags on the slopes of Hound Tor, then this fellow Bowerman must have been ugly indeed! There is something simian about the Bowerman; or if not simian then Neanderthal. Something primitive, at any rate; and therefore entirely in keeping with the moor of which it is here so conspicuous a feature. It may not be the highest rock-pile on the moor; indeed, it is not much over twenty feet in all. It may not even be the most interesting of the scattered rock-piles. But in part thanks to its superb setting it possesses an indubitable quality of distinction. Stand against it, and you can look out over lower-lying country in most directions. It dominates a landscape even as spectacular as this area of Dartmoor—which must be some indication of its splendour.

The more one explores these rock masses, large or small, the harder it is to accept the fact that they are all of them granite masses eroded and abraded by Nature and not sculpted by the hand and tools of man. It is true that the impression of sculpting is not quite as strong, here on Hayne Down, as on some other sites, for the granite has very evidently been split and cracked both vertically and horizontally rather than been deliberately shaped like this by chisel and hammer. But there are other rock masses in which the chiselling seems less haphazard, more deliberate; where you would almost swear you could discern the passage of chisel-edge over the stone, where the curves are subtler, the lines bolder, more calculated, less crude. But then you may remind yourself that Nature moves in mysterious ways, its wonders to perform; and that to Nature time is no object, she has no deadline to meet, her watch is set to eternity. Nowhere is this conception more emphatically brought home to one than on the windswept heights of Dartmoor.

Now, below you lies Manaton, a moorland fringe village and a good base from which to explore the wooded valley squeezed between Manaton and Hunter's Tors and the beauty-spot known as Lustleigh Cleave. This is homely country indeed, compared with the desolate wastes of true Dartmoor; it is moor fringe-land, so to speak, with Moretonhampstead only a mile or two to the north and all the contours hereabouts content to remain in three figures rather than in four, like so much of the rest of the moor to the south, south-west and west. Lovers of Galsworthy's novels and plays may like to be reminded that here for some time he made his home; he could hardly have chosen better.

If you are using a large-scale map (and it is really profitless to explore the moor without one) you will have noticed the entry, probably in Gothic lettering, a mile or two to the west of the Bowerman's Nose: Grimspound. The two words, Hut Circles, may be attached to the name. This is just one, though among the largest and finest of the prehistoric communal dwellings which, perhaps fifteen centuries B.C., were occupied by Bronze Age herdsmen and their families; they occupied them for generations, probably for centuries, without a break in continuity.

You can reach this prehistoric site by taking the road from Manaton north-westwards, the B 3344, over the moors to Beetor Cross, where it meets the main B 3212 road linking Moretonhampstead with Yelverton almost at right angles. Turn left at this point, follow the road for a mile and a half, and then branch off to the left where a signpost indicates Widecombe along a narrow road with passing-places at intervals along its length. The ground slopes downwards on your right, and gently upwards on your left towards the three summits on Hamildon Down at over 1700 feet. Grimspound lies on the lower part of the slope, not far from the road, but visible only if the light is fairly good, for most of the great stones of which it was constructed three thousand-and-five-hundred years ago have now either fallen on their sides or been sucked down into the bog.

In this context 'pound' is an old word: there are of course sheep-pounds and cattle-pounds all over the country, many of them dating back almost, if not quite, to medieval times. Grimspound is a true 'pound' in the accepted sense; but it is not only infinitely older but vastly larger in extent. To be more precise, it is in fact a collection of individual pounds, or relatively small enclosures, varying in size from two or three yards in diameter (most of them were constructed either round or oval) to very considerably more. In all, there were originally more than a score of them, closely grouped, sometimes inter-communicating, and ringed by a periphery wall that, according to a survey made many years ago when it was in a much better state of preservation, was between a quarter and half a mile in circumference. You might say that these are visual echoes of the *clochans* on the Fahan Peninsula, Co. Kerry, or the prehistoric dwellings of Skara Brae, in Orkney.

Here at Grimspound Bronze Age men grazed their sheep, and perhaps a few small cattle, of a type that could subsist on the relatively poor herbage of the moor; they may also have grown a little barley, though it would have been very short in the straw and of poor quality compared with the barley grown today. But they were resourceful enough to make good provision for themselves, weather-wise. Though experts tell us that Dartmoor weather was less fearsome three thousand and more years ago than it can be today, it still demanded that anyone bent on living within its grim confines must take what precautions he could. The individual pounds, or huts, perhaps shared between families and their scant livestock, were constructed of upright granite blocks six or seven feet long and set firmly in the ground, so that their effective height, inside, would not be more than about five feet. This, however, would be adequate for the Bronze Age occupant. A pole, or a slender granite column, would be set up in the centre, and a cone-shaped roof of rough thatch, heather, bracken or turf would be held up by this, with a gap in it to release smoke from a fire lit on the stone hearth.

Grimspound was only one of these settlements on Dartmoor, and not by any means the largest. Broadun Ring, in the valley of the East Dart, for instance, covered some fourteen acres—perhaps three times the acreage of the other. Another of these settlements, with the romantic name of Riders Rings, far to the south near Buckfastleigh, was also much larger than Grimspound, probably half as large again, though it seems to have had only about the same number of individual dwellings. It may be that these primitive communities (unlike communities in our own day and age) had arrived at what was the optimum number of individuals in any one community, together with the necessary livestock that should be permitted to live in close association with one another.

Dartmoor generally is richer in prehistoric remains than all but a very few other districts. In addition to hut circles, or pounds, such as those

Coastal view of north Devon, looking down on Lynton

mentioned, there are a great number of Standing Stones, or menhirs; there
is the magnificent cromlech, or dolmen near Drewsteignton, for instance,
most inappropriately known as the Spinster's Rock. It is comparable with
the glorious specimens in Cornwall such as Trethevy Quoit and Lanyon
Quoit. Like Wiltshire, Dartmoor can show some remarkable specimens of
Grey Wethers. They are of course of different stone, for the moor is wholly
and unashamedly granitic; but they are set out in stone circles such as the
one actually marked on the map as Grey Wethers to the east of Sittaford
Tor, and the Scorhill Circle overlooking the valley of the Wallabrook. In
fact, no fewer than ninety such stone circles, ranging from a hundred feet
or so in diameter to less than twelve, have been counted and recorded on
the moor: evidence of course of intense 'religious' life concentrated in a
relatively small area, a life that must have demanded an inborn sense of
purpose and conviction to have been so widely distributed in a region so
deficient in anything that might be termed amenity. In the light of all this,
and much more besides, it is not difficult to accept the archaeologist's
comment that 'the granite upland of Dartmoor should be accepted as a
single monument of antiquity on which, when the light is favourable, one
can almost restore the prehistoric landscape'.

369

From Grimspound you can look across the line of the road to the uplands to the west which no road crosses, however small. A trickle of water, shown on the large-scale map as Vitifer Leat, meanders north-westwards from the abandoned tin mine of the same name and its close neighbour, romantically-named Golden Dagger Mine, which is separated from the first-named by a brief Stone Avenue (from Grimspound it can be made out on the skyline) dating of course from prehistoric times. This, a small one only, is but one of sixty and more such stone alignments that have been traced and pin-pointed on Dartmoor. They vary greatly in length, from a row near Merrivale that is less than fifty yards long to that on Stall Moor which runs over high ground for two and a half miles to a burial-mound on Green Hill. There is much speculation as to the significance of these Stone Avenues, the majority of which tend to run along the east-west axis of the moor, though a few run from north to south. They are almost invariably associated with a barrow or burial-site, and one theory, which it is pleasant to accept, is that the length of the avenue and the number of stones marking its sides correspond to the importance of the chieftain for whom the barrow was raised.

Vitifer Leat makes north-westwards for several miles into the heart of the moor, carving its way between the heights of White Ridge (another gross mis-nomer!) and Assacombe Hill. It passes to the left of another of these very modest Stone Avenues and then curves forthrightly beneath the slopes of White Hill in the direction of Sittaford Tor, which rises to a height of nearly eighteen hundred feet. On its eastern slope are groups of ancient Standing Stones, some hut circles, the Hemstone Rocks, and the great Stone Circle known as Grey Wethers. This is remote territory indeed, accessible only in fair weather and, unless you are a native of the district, accompanied by someone who knows the terrain intimately and can challenge the conditions it imposes on the would-be visitor. Here, perhaps unexpectedly, you would come upon a trickle of dark water, lost in the peat among the granite boulders; it is, in fact, the source of the River Teign. From here the stream flows first northwards past Chagford, eventually to turn south-eastwards down a broadening, extremely lush valley and pass through Newton Abbot to merge with the sea in its own spacious estuary, all memories of the moorland which saw its uneasy birth now left far behind.

You will be wise not to attempt to pursue Vitifer Leat to that prehistoric site, however great your enthusiasm for such matters may be: the brief moorland trek would not be without very considerable hazard. Better to continue on your way down the B 3212 for another mile or two or three as far as Postbridge, where you will find on your left the clapper-bridge, sometimes referred to as a 'Cyclopean' bridge because of the sheer massiveness of the slabs of stone of which it is constructed. It spans a small stream, the East Dart, in fact, though it has not yet matured; and it was a bridge long before the road was constructed that now runs south-westwards so close to it. It carried one of a multiplicity of ancient trackways across the moor, trackways which converged just at this point. (For more about this and other similar bridges, turn back to Somerset's Tarr Steps.)

Few of the old trackways, of course, are so to speak decipherable today, for they have since disuse tended to become swallowed up in the peat-bogs which they were originally intended to skirt but to which they so often eventually fell victim. One of them, however, is still just discernible, running westwards from the bridge and following for a brief while the right bank of the stream before swerving away from it with, it would appear, a point between Lower and Higher White Tor, at 1700 feet, as its objective. It must have been viable not only in medieval times but in prehistoric times too, for where it peters out today there is a cluster of hut circles and a small Stone Avenue, lost in the rank turf. Just beyond is the stripling West Dart, flowing southwards to merge with the River Blackbrook and River Cowsic close to Two Bridges among yet another group of hut circles. Three or four miles farther to the east it merges with its twin, the East Dart, at picturesque and, inevitably, sadly-exploited Dartmeet.

The road drops, not too steeply, to Two Bridges, the crossing-point of the only two roads that may truly be said to have been laid athwart the moor. But even as you cross the bridge in front of the hotel you are still well above the 1100-foot contour. These altitudes, of course, are relative. Because the 2000-foot Yes Tor, and the nearly comparable heights of Hangingstone Hill and Wild Tor and Watern Tor are out of sight ten moorland miles to the north of you, you do not easily accept the fact that the contours on which you are travelling are modest by comparison. The level, in spite of the presence of running water, seems exalted. And there are more impressive heights all about you: Hessary Tor, at nearly 1500 feet, to the south; North Hessary Tor, to the west and more than a hundred feet higher; and to the north, Beardown Tor, a hundred feet higher still. You may be highly placed, but you are seated at a table of giants.

Just beyond Two Bridges the road forks. The B 3212 branches south-westwards for Yelverton, passing on its way the grim convict prison of Princetown—known to all who have served sentences there simply as 'The Moor'. A morbid fascination lures visitors to Dartmoor into this granite township, where the very smell of prison seems to predominate, for all the efforts of the authorities to avoid just this impression. Years ago you would have seen men at work marked with the traditional 'broad arrow' of the convict; not so today, however.

Here in Princetown the native granite of the region has well and truly come into its own, and may be seen to have done so. 'Abandon Hope All Ye

Who Enter Here' might well be inscribed over almost every doorway, for surely no prison has a grimmer, more forbidding setting than this? Dartmoor, unlike Alcatraz (now abandoned as a convict prison), may not have sharks swimming about it to snap up the rare escapee; but it presents other challenges hardly less terrible. The number of men who have escaped, and remained free of, the granite walls of this prison is small indeed. Yet promoters of penal reform are loud in their demands that The Moor shall eventually be done away with altogether. Certainly no one will be better pleased when this prison ceases to exist than the prison officers whose lot it is to work within these walls and live continuously within sight of them.

Beyond Princetown, at about 1400 feet above sea level, the road crosses a beck at a point marked Devil's Bridge and continues on and over Walkhampton Common—though only the hardy and seemingly indestructible Dartmoor pony would ever accept the implicit invitation to walk on this 'common'. Black Tor, Harter Tor and Cramber Tor, with the remains of hut circles and a brief Stone Avenue, will be found to the left, or east side, of the road; to the right is Leeden Tor, not far short of 1400 feet, with the remains of yet more hut circles. The Bronze Age men who quarried the granite and constructed these circles were free men, not convicts, and lived here for choice, not of necessity. This is as strong evidence as any that the meteorologists can adduce for the fact that in that age Dartmoor was a more hospitable region than it is today.

And now, beyond Sharpitor and Peak Hill, the road dips more pronouncedly, and almost before you know it you are running off the moor to Yelverton. A final reminder of the heights that, a while back, crowded so closely about you is caught by a glimpse of Burrator and Sheep's Tor, to the east; but these two are well beneath the 1000-foot mark and so, by now, hardly worth your notice! Here you can very nearly smell the sea; here at Yelverton you are on the edge of the valley of the Meavy, overflow from Burrator Reservoir, that runs into the widening Bickleigh Vale to join the Plym just to the east of the town to which the river gives its name. Only a couple of miles to the west is the even more attractive valley of the Tavy, a river that first saw light in the dead heart of the northern area of the moor, flowed off this to the south-west, formed its own valley and came to mark the western boundary of the moor as it ran idly between Mary Tavy and Peter Tavy to Tavistock, and thence channelled for itself a course as circuitous as that of the Wye, to form the estuary between Plymouth and Devonport, fifteen meandering miles and more to the south.

There is still, however, the westward extension of the A 384 to explore, at least as far as Tavistock. Ideally this road should be followed from that town into the heart of the moor rather than the other way about. It should preferably be done when the sun is in the south or south-west, so that it is not in your eyes and is in fact shining away from you on to the rising slopes that lead to the great tors to the north of Two Bridges. In any case it is not much more than eight miles from Tavistock to the junction of the two roads, so that if you have already done it once in the reverse direction it is easy enough to turn about and cover those eight miles once more from west to east. An easy enough run, and certainly a most rewarding one.

The road will climb, of course, for Tavistock (a wholly delightful little market town of granite construction) is situated some two thousand feet below the major summits of Dartmoor to the east. But for the first two or three miles it hardly seems to do so. This gently sloping road offers a leisurely, even deceptively simple, introduction to what lies ahead. But then, at about the third milestone, it seems to have a change of heart. Now the gradient steepens noticeably, and what has hitherto been a straight road resolves itself into a series of loops that will bring it, in a short distance, on to a very different contour; within a mile you have been lifted to nearly eleven hundred feet. Take the opportunity to pause here. Two or three minor becks pass beneath the road, having gathered their waters from the southern slopes of a trio of heights, Great, Middle and Little Staple Tors, just to the north of the road. They rise some four hundred feet above the level on which you are standing as you look about you, and so perhaps seem rather bigger than in fact they are; but you now know, of course, having seen so many of their giant brethren elsewhere on the moor, that they are no more than lowly cousins of those others.

Just to the east of them, beneath their flanks, there runs a beck with the grandiose name, Grimstone Sortride Leat. It has its origin well to the north, beyond the noble summit of Great Mis Tor, which rises to 1761 feet and is the nearest giant actually in view. There are hut circles, stone circles and stone rows all the way up the right bank of this moorland beck: evidence once again of the attraction that these granite uplands held for prehistoric man. At least he was not as exposed here as he was farther to the east; the heights were less pronounced, and there must have been an adequate supply of water for himself and his womenfolk and children and all-important livestock.

Look southwards, too, from this vantage-point. The ground falls away, terraced in spacious steps that would take you down to low-lying ground intersected by streams where a trio of hamlets all bearing the first name, Sampford—an indication that they all stood close to small river fords—are distinguished as Sampfords Peverell, Courtenay and Spiney, the names of the owners of the land in feudal times. A fourth name, Sampford Barton, suggests that this was the main farmyard, or 'barley-tun', serving the area. Beyond the Sampfords lies Yelverton, a centre of sheep-farming and the basis from which annual sheep-dog trials are held. Beyond this, of course, lies Bickleigh Vale, and the first intrusive summons of the sea.

Now turn eastwards again, but without hurrying. Ahead of you, on the farther side of Grimstone Sortride Leat, the road runs nearly level for a mile or so before dipping to Merrivale Bridge, with its disfiguring quarry and its inn on one side overlooking the remains of hut circles on the other, close beside the road, and of a stone row just beyond. Well before the road begins to dip there is one of the most remarkable and, incidentally, most accessible of all Dartmoor's major tors; it is only a few hundred yards to the right, or south side, of the road. To pass it without taking the trouble to visit and inspect it at close quarters would be a shame indeed. This, in fact, is Vixen Tor.

Vixen Tor is a contradiction in terms in more senses than one. Instead of being a granite peak on a steepish upward slope, as are most of the tors, large and small alike, it actually lies below the level of the road; thus, once you leave the road and take to the shaggy, boulder-strewn and sometimes marshy turf, you proceed down hill rather than up. It does not seem to make sense. But in spite of this, Vixen Tor, measured from its turf base where the virgin rock first emerges and the underlying granite plinth on which it stands, is actually the highest rock-pile to be found anywhere on the moor: on its steepest side it is very nearly a hundred feet from toe to top.

Southward from the road the ground dips gently. It is rough turf, typically moorland turf, scattered with odd lumps of granite and interspersed with brief patches of soft, spongy ground even in dry weather. Tussocks of bent enable even the least handy walker to proceed from one dry patch to another, and ten minutes will see you to the vicinity of the tor, which you are of course approaching from the north-west if you have come from Tavistock; it is equally accessible from the opposite direction.

From a distance even more than from close at hand you will quickly note the inappropriateness of the name it bears. This is no vixen; rather, it presents the aspect of a sphinx—at least when viewed from the west side. Or, if not a sphinx, it could, just, have been the inspiration of Landseer's lions at the base of the Nelson Column in Trafalgar Square. Most certainly this is no vixen: there is no sharp nose or cocked ear, from whichever direction you view it; bluntness, and a certain inscrutability, is all.

The scale of the rocks forming Vixen (or Sphinx) Tor is enormous. Beside these rocks the stack known as Bowerman's Nose dwindles almost into insignificance (though the unmatched splendour of its siting cannot be so dismissed: it is incomparably finer than that of Vixen Tor). Here of course is the same evidence of cleavage and erosion; and naturally, for the same forces have been at work over the aeons. The cleavage-planes run mainly near-horizontal and, mass for mass, there are perhaps fewer of the vertical clefts than were in evidence on Hayne Down. The sculptor took on a far greater commission, here, than he did when he started work on Bowerman's Nose. If the result here is not as self-explanatory as it is on Hayne Down this may simply be due to the disposition of his basic raw

West Dart, Dartmoor

material, the granite outcropping from its vast igneous bed beneath the thick and shaggy covering of spongy turf.

Once within the periphery wall you can walk round the tor and view it at your leisure from every conceivable angle. On one side the ground falls away slightly, and so the rock mass seems to tower more dominantly; on another side the ground rises gently, as though encouraging you to set foot upon the plinth from which the great sphinx-like head rises so powerfully and with such dignity. But from whatever angle you view this tor, it offers you a new, and often surprising, even startling, impression of beast-like rather than purely static, immobile presence. Seen in half-light (though to approach Vixen Tor across that spongy turf in such conditions could be a risky business), or in mist, or even by day beneath a heavily overcast sky, it could give the impression that it is, for all its mass, potentially alive and on the move.

It is undoubtedly seen at its best when the midday sun shines down upon it. Photographically speaking, this may seem odd, for everyone knows that objects are normally best photographed when the sun is not too high in the heavens. But there is a reason for this apparent exception. Most of the cleavage-planes on Vixen Tor are horizontal; the mass is therefore seen by the camera lens at its most three-dimensional when there is shadow in these planes of cleavage. With the light from immediately above and the consequent shadow beneath, the anatomical lines of this sphinx (or what you will) derive emphasis and strength which they do not possess in such degree when the light is poor either in concentration or in lateral direction.

From this tor there is a magnificent view north–north–eastwards, across the road and up the lower slopes of Little Mis Tor to the noble summit of its giant neighbour just behind, Great Mis Tor, at 1761 feet, two miles distant in a direct line. This is true Dartmoor country; not at its grimmest, however, but at its most inviting. Indeed, it is vistas such as this which produce the proverbial 'itchy feet'; but the itch is, as has already been emphasised, something to resist save where there is evidence that no real danger or hazard exists. As to this, advice can always be sought from anyone living locally—the inn-keeper, the roadman, the cattleman who may be encountered by chance even in the most empty-looking districts. And such advice, it will be found, errs always on the side of caution, of discretion; it is a very foolish visitor who ignores it, for he will certainly do so at his peril. The impact of Dartmoor is second only to that of the Lake District; those who are fortunate enough to come to know both of these magnificent regions of Britain will, if they are honest with themselves, probably admit that of the two, the sheer impact of Dartmoor remains the greater.

CORNWALL

Cornwall comes somewhere about half way up the scale in English counties, so far as size is concerned; but with more than three hundred miles of coastline—half as much again as that of Devonshire, twice as much as that of Lancashire or Kent, more by fifty miles indeed than the whole of East Anglia, the country's eastward extension—she ranks as a giant.

Yet the term seems somehow inappropriate—unless one adds some such modifying epithet as 'lazy', or 'sleeping'. For though her cliffs are certainly the most magnificently spectacular in all England, and worthily comparable with the finest in Scotland or on the Atlantic coastline of the Republic of Ireland, and though she possesses 'a little Dartmoor' in the shape of the stern granite uplands of Bodmin Moor, one yet instinctively thinks of her as a sun-bathed and generally soporific westwards extension of the land, walled by granite to resist the onslaught of the Atlantic Ocean, offering seclusion, warmth and comfort, beauty for the taking, and a strangely persuasive peace which baffles understanding to the extent that one comes to accept it readily and without conscious question.

Liskeard to Falmouth

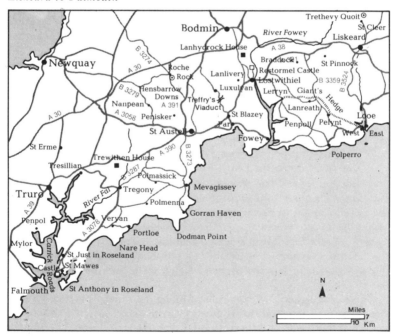

Compared with the rest of the country, compared even with neighbouring Devonshire, Cornwall is as 'foreign' as, for instance, Connemara is 'foreign' in comparison with the rest of the Republic. It is little more than a century since Brunel built his magnificent Saltash Bridge across the Tamar and thus admitted a railway-line at last into the county. Until then, the only direct access to Cornwall had been by way of the medieval bridge at Gunnislake, also spanning the Tamar. This bridge spans the river still at that point; but now, of course, there is a new and fine road bridge over the Tamar alongside Brunel's masterpiece of 1859. Car-borne visitors as well as rail-borne can now penetrate with ease into what a true Cornishman has called, and not without a hint of quiet contentment, this 'bony extremity a long way from the English heart of things'.

Note the 'English'. He writes, of course, as a Celt; certainly his forbears, like those of all true Cornishmen, were Celts. In many respects Cornwall has substantially more in common with Brittany, where the French variant, *Cornouailles*, appears, than with other parts of Britain. If you are inclined to doubt this, glance at the names of Cornish saints, as commemorated in place-names, in lowly churches, in ancient parish crosses and other relics of the past. They are to be found also, often almost letter for letter, on the other side of the English Channel. Saint Ives and St Yves, for example. And lesser-known names of saints such as Mabyn and Feock, Piran and Wenn, Breock and Petroc. Study the *Calvaires* of Brittany next time you find yourself near Morlaix or Lannion or Tréguier or a hundred other spots less well known, and a breath of Cornwall-across-the-water will fan your cheek.

St Petroc, incidentally, is an interesting case where a variant makes his name at first hearing unidentifiable. He is found, among many other sites, at Little Petherick in north Cornwall, a couple of miles south of Padstow and the estuary of the River Camel. The original name of this remote hamlet was St Petroc Minor of Nansfounteyn. The name commemorated the saint who in the sixth century came by coracle from Ireland with the laudable objective of converting the people of the south-west to the Christian faith. Petroc had with him (the coracle must have been sadly overloaded) three companions: two men named Medan and Croidan and a boy named Dagan. Of the four missionaries, Dagan, in spite of a name all too close in sound to that of an established pagan god, was to become a bishop. But long before that, indeed immediately on landing from the estuary which offered them at least a material welcome from the rigours of the Atlantic crossing from Ireland, they formed a small brotherhood of monks, drawing in converts to their religion as the months and years went by.

Theirs was a grimly ascetic order. Among their many practices of self-abasement was to stand up to their necks in water, ice-cold among the granite of Cornwall, and there recite their psalters and pray by the hour that those who were still heathen might swiftly become converted to Christianity. If example is worth anything, their prayers should have met with instant response.

Little Petherick, as St Petroc's base in due course became, is one of the more charming of the hamlets in the immediate hinterland of this Atlantic coastline. A stone bridge crosses the stream at the foot of the steep and narrow hill that descends past the church. The road is laid upon an old pack-horse track that formerly linked the ports of Wadebridge and Padstow with Bodmin, fifteen miles distant across the swelling uplands of the moor. It is probably no exaggeration to say that today, in this second half of the twentieth century, the road carries less traffic than it did in medieval and subsequent times. Beside the road, on the left hand side as you descend it, almost entirely overshadowed by trees, is the church dedicated to St Petroc. This dedication took place in the fourteenth century, but the church itself is older by a century and more; its record of incumbents dates back to the year 1264. It may be read, not off a sheet of printed paper, or even illuminated parchment, but incised on a fine slab of slate from the gigantic quarry at Delabole twenty or so miles up the coast.

It is a curious fact, but one that can easily be checked by looking carefully at a map of this south-west peninsula of sufficient scale, that to all intents and purposes Cornwall is not just the westernmost county of England but, virtually, an island. Not obviously an island, as are the Isles of Scilly (all too often loosely referred to as 'the Scilly Isles', to their occupants' justifiable indignation), but very nearly so. How can this be? The explanation is quite simple.

Trace the line of the Tamar, the county boundary with Devonshire, northwards from Brunel's Saltash Bridge. It ties itself in knots between Calstock and Gunnislake; northwards of Gunnislake its course as far as Dunterton is hardly less tortuous, its ox-bows being comparable with those of the Wye near Symonds Yat; north of Dunterton it zigzags its way between Launceston and Lifton, less tortuously now that the terrain is more level; northwards again it passes in a more or less straight line midway between Bude, on the coast, and Holsworthy in Devon; and finally it peters out as no more than a spring on the 700-foot contour of the uplands close to Welcombe, just behind Morwenstow, three or four miles at most from the sea. So, if a man were to amuse himself by digging a trench along those last three or four miles, Cornwall would become, literally, an island, linked to its neighbour, Devonshire, only by a succession of bridges of varying importance from the source of the Tamar to its estuary spanned by Brunel's bridge. There is an odd parallel to this. If the sources of the Rhine and the Rhône, high on the Grimsel and Furka Passes, were only a little closer, you could say that the continent of Europe was cleft asunder by two waterways debouching respectively into the North Sea and the Mediterranean.

There is another, and more popularly recognised, indication that Cornwall is 'different' from the rest of the country: its place-names. Every schoolchild has heard the refrain: 'By Tre-, Pol, and Pen- Ye shall know Cornishmen'. The prefixes are, of course, Celtic in origin; you meet them, and their close variants, in Brittany. It is rare to find place-names elsewhere in Britain that have these prefixes; where they do occur, spasmodically, and notably of course in Wales, it is because of the Celtic tradition. Most Cornish place-names are immediately identifiable; most, that is, not all. It is a little startling to find the name 'Brighton' within hail of a cluster of true Cornish names such as Trewhela and Penhale, Polwhele and Treneague. But for every one such bold alien there will be found a hundred, may be a thousand, indigenous names.

As with Devonshire, it is of course the coastline that chiefly attracts. It must be admitted that generally speaking (and in so far as generalities are ever acceptable) the interior of Cornwall is not in quite the same category as the interior of its neighbour. Its villages are that much starker, its granite more prevalent, its cob walls, so characteristic and picturesque a feature of Devonshire, so much farther to seek. Granite is more generally the primary raw material; its chief alternative is slate, and this, for all its beautiful coloration in the area of Delabole, is almost as cold and harsh in its impact on the questing eye.

For the present purpose, however, Cornwall's magnificent coastline will be almost entirely disregarded as too well known (and too abundantly exploited and commercialised, more's the pity); the great granite plateau of Bodmin Moor, too, will be largely ignored. This, surely, is only fair: for it was the granite moor that dominated our attention in Devonshire and, with all due respect to every loyal Cornishman who may happen across these words, Bodmin Moor is not quite in the same class as Dartmoor.

Nevertheless, Cornwall, independently of her coastline and granite heights, has riches in plenty of her own. Indeed, one of the most rewarding of her hunting-grounds lies between coastline and moor, with the moor just impinging on its north-eastern extremity. It is an area, in round figures, some thirty-five miles in length by a dozen or so in breadth, say four hundred-and-odd square miles in all. And this is in south Cornwall, specifically; there is a comparable stretch on the opposite side of the peninsula which is hardly less rewarding.

The A 390 from Tavistock will lead you into Cornwall over the medieval bridge across the Tamar at Gunnislake. This is as good an introduction to the county as any, though of course it is much less dramatic and spectacular than the route of the A 30 from Launceston over Bodmin Moor by way of Bolventor and the Jamaica Inn of Daphne du Maurier's famous novel. Why is it so good? Quite simply because at almost every turn there is something worth lingering to enjoy, some odd feature worth going out of your way to locate and examine, some beauty-spot as yet unspoiled by an overdose of popularity, something essentially Cornish in spirit to savour—perhaps, if you are lucky, actually for the first time in your life. Such places may involve time and a little trouble and effort to search out, the careful use of a map, perhaps, or diligent inquiry from some native of the district. The Well-chapel at Dupath, for instance.

Cornwall is peculiarly rich in these otherwise unusual, and unusually charming, relics of medieval times and ingrained piety; and here too the feature is matched by Cornwall-over-the-water, *Cornouailles*, Brittany. A precious spring is trapped, controlled, housed, and gratefully dedicated to the local patron saint or to some other worthy who 'belongs' here. It is not always remembered that Christianity came to Cornwall long before it reached, say, the Meon Valley and other far-flung parts of Britain. There were Celtic Holy Men in Cornwall, bringers of The Faith from Ireland, fifteen centuries ago. Holy Wells, and Well-chapels such as the one at Dupath were among the memorials to these men, who became saints after their death and often were regarded as such even during their lives.

So, three or four miles after you have climbed from the bridge at Gunnislake you begin to approach Callington. Just short of this little town a minor road branches off to the left to merge with the A 388 main road to St Mellion (named after yet another of these little-known saints) and Saltash. Less than half a mile along this narrow road a lane dips steeply downwards to the left, and comes to a group of farm buildings. Dupath Well-chapel is to be found here: older by some centuries than the farmhouse and its outbuildings, this beautiful chapel-in-miniature certainly dates from the early sixteenth century and in all probability from the century before that. Its sides consist of four courses of immense granite blocks; each corner carries a tapered granite finial; the west end of the steeply-pitched moorstone slab roof carries a miniature stone belfry, ornately designed, and composed in such a way that, standing on the rising ground before it, you can look eastwards across the valley to the hills beyond. An oak door, with fine scrolled hinges of local wrought-ironwork gives access to the interior of the chapel.

Inside, it is perhaps eight feet square or a little more in one direction. A trickle of bright water flows in beneath the sill of the door, along a shallow channel, and out beneath the wall at the other end from a little trough. It is crystal clear. And that is virtually all that there is to be seen: a well, or rather a spring, temporarily stayed in its course and then graciously released. It is reminiscent of the Holy Wells of Derbyshire, at Tissington and elsewhere.

Inevitably of course there is an accretion of legend here at Dupath. Though it is regarded as a Holy Well, and is in fact probably the best preserved of all those in Cornwall, it almost certainly stands on what was, before the coming of the Holy Men of Ireland, a pagan site. It almost certainly witnessed the practice of ancient fertility rites. But some time in the Middle Ages, if not earlier than that, the Church was at pains to sanctify the site, as was its practice throughout the length and breadth of Christendom. It became a minor baptistry. It became a focal point for the gathering of men and women from the scattered farmsteads of the region in medieval and later times. In this it would have been comparable with the wayside shrines to be found in such isolated areas as the Val Maggia and Val Bavona in the Ticino Province of Switzerland, at which the itinerant priests still gather their scattered mountain congregations. One local tradition, however, differs from the rest. This holds that the chapel was built as a gesture of penance by a local Cornishman who had slain in individual combat a neighbour who was a rival for the hand of the girl he wished to marry, and that he lived out his last years, alone with his conscience, within its comfortless granite walls.

Beyond Callington the road rises and falls over a succession of uplands and the intervening valleys of the Lynher, which makes for Newton Ferrers and its own estuary to the west of Saltash; the Tiddy, which flows down to Tideford, where it was once crossed on foot, and so into the Lynher Estuary; and the Seaton, which flows past Menheniot (a very ancient Cornish name), famous for five hundred years for the stone excavated from its quarries, a compact little 'lost' village-in-a-valley with a fine church dedicated to yet another of these unfamiliar saints, St Anietus.

Follow any one of these valleys south-eastwards from the road to Liskeard and you will not feel that your time has been wasted. At the end of them you will meet, perhaps for the first time, that characteristic feature of the south Cornish coastline, the wide and deep estuary that curves and twists and thrusts its way far inland, its banks heavily wooded, its herbage lush, its air warm and fragrant—almost spiced. Westwards from Saltash these are plentiful. There is the estuary of the Lynher, of the East Looe, of the Fowey (with Penpoll and Lerryn Creeks perhaps the most beautiful of them all); and beyond these, that of the Percuil, above St Anthony in Roseland, and Carrick Roads, leading to Mylor Creek, Restronguet Creek, King Harry's Reach, and the secluded estuaries of the rivers Truro, Tressilian and Fal. A catalogue, it is true; but what a galaxy of evocative names!

Westwards of Liskeard, a fine old Cornish town and former seat of King Cerruyt, the road lifts out of the valley of the upper East Looe River and runs for a mile or two before splitting. Now the choice is hard indeed, for it lies between entering the upper reaches of the lush and lovely valley of the upper Fowey, by the right-hand road, or climbing on to the uplands at nearly seven hundred feet before dropping south-westwards into the small town with, surely, the most hauntingly musical name in all Cornwall—Lostwithiel. The first, which is the main A 38 road to Bodmin, Cornwall's County Town, is the lovelier of the two, though the other, the A 390, also has much to commend it. But hereabouts we are in the main concerned with Cornwall's valleys rather than her uplands; and since it is still possible to approach Lostwithiel from the Bodmin road by taking a small branch road south immediately beyond Bodmin Road station, let that be the deciding factor. Not least because it will enable you to continue to follow the Fowey Valley long after the main road to Bodmin has turned northwards from it.

The road is better than it was in the early days, now that the famous seventeenth-century Lanhydrock House has been thrown open to the public and access has had to be made easier in order to accommodate motor-coaches instead of horses and private carriages. The Great House lies to the right of the road in the valley, and if you are in search of Britain's Stately Homes this may well be the first in Cornwall that you will visit, though you may possibly have called in at the Tudor Cothele House near Calstock immediately after passing out of Devonshire and before you went in search of the Dupath Well-chapel. Both are beautiful, and memorable, though so disparate in period and style.

Lostwithiel is just five miles upstream from the mouth of the Fowey and possesses the superb fifteenth-century Greyston Bridge, the first to be built over this river. Its five arches, with their shapely cut-waters, replace a ford that would often have been impassable when the river was swollen by tributaries running into it off the southern slopes of Bodmin Moor. The small town dates back to the twelfth century. Fortunately it has been to a large extent by-passed, and so you can wander about its small streets and among its granite buildings almost undisturbed—a rare experience these days. It is hard to believe that this little town, today so quiet, was the old capital of Cornwall; but until the time of Elizabeth I the Fowey was navigable for comparatively large vessels as far upstream as this, and in medieval times the town was actually the focal point for the then flourishing Cornish tin industry. Tin was an immensely valuable commodity, then as now, and vessels could sail up the Fowey, take on their cargoes of the precious ore and then sail back into and across the English Channel to where the markets were rapidly increasing in number and the demand in urgency.

It is better, though, to think of Lostwithiel as the township it is today, a quiet, withdrawn place, its former industrious life a memory only of yesterday. If you wish to be yet further reminded of olden times you should follow the minor road up the right, or west, bank of the river for just over a mile and you will then come to one of England's oldest, and admittedly smallest, castles. Its name, you may feel, matches in mellifluousness that of the little town it has overlooked for seven hundred years: Restormel.

Ideally, Restormel is best seen from the air, though this is unlikely to be a practicable proposition for the average visitor. The reason is that the castle presents so perfect an example of a shell-keep on a Norman *motte*, its circular layout given additional emphasis by the perfectly circular ditch that surrounds its base. The curtain-wall is some four hundred feet in circumference, eight feet in thickness and rises to more than twenty feet. It is older, of course, by far than even the oldest portions of Lostwithiel itself, having been built less than forty years after the Norman Conquest.

If you look for it, you can still find the quarry from which, over eight and a half centuries ago, the Pentewan stone was taken for its construction. Restormel has been fortunate. Compared with the great majority of Norman and post-Norman castles in the country it seems to have escaped involvement in real warfare; so, there is more to be seen on this site than is often the case even with castles that were originally conceived on an infinitely more ambitious scale. It symbolises, perhaps, this element that is so characteristic of some parts of Cornwall which will be found again at Luxulyan, for instance, some miles to the west: its withdrawnness, its innate reluctance to become involved with 'the outside world'.

A little network of lanes and minor roads fills the area between the West and the East Looe rivers, to the east, and the valley of the Fowey as it meanders southwards from Lostwithiel. Here there is nothing magnificent, nothing that forcibly strikes the eye; but there is much, all the same, to delight and soothe. Between Fowey and Lerryn and Trebant Water and the twin rivers above the town of Looe there are modest uplands and diminutive vales, with a multiplicity of hidden farmsteads at the ends of deep-cut, narrow, hunch-shouldered lanes; and of course a village or two, a hamlet or two, such as Pelynt, Lanreath, Braddock and St Pinnock. The last of these, as you may well guess, is named after yet another of these saints who are so little known outside Cornwall and Brittany: St Pynnocus. Alas, his church is not as old as you would hope from the antiquity of the name it bears; and alas again, it has been not too successfully restored.

More striking by far—and this is unexpected, for though the railway has come to Cornwall one tends not to think of this county in railway terms—is the giant viaduct close to the village. It spans the upper reach of the West Looe at the astonishing height of a hundred and fifty feet above the water, running deep in its lush valley. The engineers who built this railway, a hundred and thirty-five or so years ago, were faced with the problem of spanning valley after valley, the majority of them running directly southwards athwart the route surveyed. There are more than thirty of these viaducts in the fifty or so miles between the Devonshire border and Truro. In fact, here on the outskirts of St Pinnock, two viaducts were built. The first, completed in the same year as Brunel's Saltash Bridge, was replaced twenty years later by another and finer one close alongside. You can stand beneath one of them and look across the steeply sloping valley side at the great piers designed and built by Brunel to carry the original track, and since replaced.

The village of Braddock lies a few miles to the west of St Pinnock, and also near the head of a valley, this time that of the Lerryn. It is more secluded even than its neighbour, and it may come as a surprise to find on the large-scale map, not half a mile from the village and certainly within its parish boundary, the legend: Site of Battle, 1643. It was here that the forces of Charles I, led by a man who bore one of the most distinguished of West Country names, Sir Beville Grenville, defeated the forces of Cromwell and drove them eastwards out of Cornwall altogether.

On the opposite side of the parish, far from the battlefield of more than three centuries ago, there is a whole cluster of the viaducts built by the railwaymen of the mid-nineteenth century to span valleys large and small, half a dozen of them having been replaced, as the St Pinnock one was, within twenty years or so of building when the railway was re-aligned. You may not be over-much interested in railway architecture, as such; but these relics of the work and ambitions of the intrepid men who followed the instructions of the great Brunel have a quality that evokes an emotion deeper than mere admiration for difficulties overcome and conquests achieved.

The third of this little group of villages, Lanreath, takes some finding. Though it is quite clearly marked on the map, it has contrived somehow to detach itself from the route which seems to be indicated. Nevertheless it well repays the effort of discovery. It has a seventeenth-century manor house; it has one of the most memorable of this country's inns, the Punch Bowl, with a painted wrought-iron sign attributed to Augustus John and bedrooms equipped with half-testers; and it has a church, dedicated to St Manaccus and St Dunstan, the earliest portions of which are certainly Norman though much of it dates back only to the fifteenth century.

But Lanreath is set amid relics that are older by many centuries than either manor house, inn, or church. To north and south of the village, on Bury Down and Tregarrick, there are the remains of prehistoric hill-forts and camps, almost certainly occupied well into the early centuries of the Christian era. And, more unusual than hill-fort or camp, a curious parallel ditch and turf wall combined runs from near the head of Trebant Water, at Kingote, eastwards and then southwards round the northern perimeter of the village. This curious landmark bears the even more curious name, Giants' Hedge. Giant and Devil are of course inevitable 'names' given to any feature improperly understood: Giants' Graves and Devils' Dykes proliferate throughout the country. But the word Hedge, in such a context, is rare if not unique.

It is time now to cross the Fowey and penetrate westwards deeper into Cornwall. Luxulyan, and its incomparably lovely valley, shall be the objective. To get there means first climbing on to higher ground. Not actually high ground, of course, or certainly not high ground in comparison with that which lies to the east, beyond the border with Devonshire. The contours range only about the 500- and 600-foot mark, though beyond Luxulyan, on the moors above St Austell, you will climb close to the 1000-foot mark on Hensbarrow Down. Some of the place-names in this upland region are unexpected or unusual: to the west of Hensbarrow Downs, for instance, at almost one thousand feet, you will come across 'America'; to the south are Wheal Bunney and Yondertown. But Treverbyn, Treskillin and Penisker are near by, too, to remind you that you are truly in Cornwall.

From Lostwithiel you climb out of the valley of one of the Fowey's tributaries, branch right-handedly off the St Blazey road and take a very minor road that is signposted Lanlivery. This hamlet is little more than a mile away, but is so isolated that it seems remote even from the rest of the district. You will see first the 100-foot tower of its granite-built-church, one of the finest in a county proud of its church towers. The church itself is less old than that of Lanreath and others, but it is remarkable for its size, for the impression of antiquity that it imparts, and perhaps above all for the size of the local granite blocks of which it was built.

It would seem that the fifteenth-century masons who quarried and built here must have been giants; the raw materials in which they worked would have defeated any but the strongest of their breed. Many of the blocks they incorporated in the fabric of this church, notably in the south side of the tower, are up to eight feet in length and must have been of prodigious weight. And for that matter, their counterparts are to be seen on every hand: field boundary walls and the walls of minor buildings dotted about along the road side and elsewhere contain blocks and slabs hardly less Cyclopean. Indeed, this may be truly called 'Cyclopean' architecture, of the kind to be met with on the road that wanders up the Atlantic coastline north of Sennen, for example. To match these enormous granite blocks built into the church at Lanlivery you will find, in the churchyard, opposite the church's main entrance, a huge stone coffin, shaped so that there is a separate curved hollow for the occupant's head; the fact that it has no lid adds to the impression of solidity and sheer weight that it conveys. Local tradition has it that it was the last resting-place of a Cornish princeling who died long ago at Restormel Castle.

Luxulyan is set on uplands that slope more or less steeply down into the valley. Again, the church is the dominant feature: a granite church dedicated to Saints Cyriac and Julitta that dates from the fifteenth century. You may notice that it is rather more crudely built than some others you have seen. The craftsmanship suggests local work, the handiwork possibly of granite workers of the immediate neighbourhood. For the granite quarries of Luxulyan have been famous ever since man first exploited the stone. Here again the term Cyclopean instantly comes into the mind. The entrance to the church, at the south-west corner, a mere gateway, is marked by an enormous slab of granite at least nine feet long, laid there five centuries ago as a coffin-rest. There is no lych gate to shelter those who accompanied the coffin, but an ancient Cornish cross gives sanctity to the site immediately alongside. Crosses such as this—and few other things in Cornwall convey such a haunting aura of a simple antiquity—will increasingly be found the farther west you go.

Most of the cottages in the village, except perhaps a few on the western outskirts which are of quite recent date, are built of granite from the local quarries. This particular stone has a quality that is not to be found in all Cornish granite, and it is therefore in great demand by architects seeking the very best quality for buildings of their designing. The tomb of the Duke of Wellington, in St Paul's Cathedral, for instance, was constructed in this granite from Luxulyan, which possesses an unusual sparkle and a curious pinkish tone that contrasts strikingly with the other. On a humbler note, because of its exceptional resistance to wear and tear a great many of London's kerbstones are hewn from this same Luxulyan granite.

At the upper end of the village, nearly a mile from the church in a field behind the high banked hedge that borders the road, there is an enormous rounded block of granite known to all in the district, and much farther afield too, as the Devil's Stone. It is reminiscent of the famous granite Cloven Stone of Easky, on the Atlantic coast of Eire, save that, happily, it remains entire. Legends of course have accumulated about this stone, as they have about the one near Easky, quite apart from the fact that it has been ascribed, like so many others, to His Satanic Majesty. Children will tell you that if you walk three times round the block as the hour approaches midnight you will hear the Devil's chains rattle; if you are courageous enough to continue until you have walked round the block seven times (the magic number, of course!) in all, you will meet the Devil in person. It is not a form of nocturnal entertainment that is ordinarily indulged in by the people of Luxulyan.

The stream flowing past the foot of the hill on which the village of Luxulyan stands, which curiously enough does not seem to have been given a name on the maps of this area, rises high on Helman Tor, four miles to the north. This fact explains why it is a milk-white stream; for to the north of the village, and for many miles to the north-west, lies that strange region of the china clay pits. The china clay which is excavated here in such enormous quantities, and has been for so many generations, is a disintegrated form of granite. Knowing the extreme hardness of granite, it is difficult for anyone save a geologist or petrologist to accept such a statement; nevertheless, it is true. The whole of this landscape, especially that portion extending between Roche, to the north, and St Austell, to the south, has a sort of nightmare quality; it is as though a stretch of lunar landscape had been uprooted and brought back complete, to be deposited here in Cornwall.

However, in the valley that runs steeply down from Luxulyan to St Blazey and on to Par, formerly an important point of despatch for

Cornish-mined tin but since the mid-nineteenth century concerned chiefly with the china clay trade, you are remote from this nightmare region. The sole reminder of it is the milky stream that tumbles and gurgles over rounded granite boulders, themselves long since 'painted' a creamy-white by the water passing over them, between high banks overhung by stunted trees in-filled with dense scrub. The narrow road meanders alongside it, close to its left bank; it is so tortuous that it is risky to take one's eyes off the road in order to savour the beauty of the valley. However, fortunately there are a number of lay-bys, often just small quarries from which stone for the road has been excavated, the quarry face having been left to accumulate its growth of fern and plant, always wet with the hidden springs that jet unseen among the dark clefts and are only discernible because of the richness that they impart to the natural decoration of the stone. It is well worth leaving the car in one of these natural recesses and following the stream in each direction for a mile or two—it is barely three miles from Luxulyan down to the main road that leads on to St Blazey, in any case.

There is a further good reason for taking to one's feet. High above the valley there is the magnificent aqueduct which was built by Joseph Treffry in 1839—twenty years before Brunel and his men started work on the railway viaducts already visited. In fact, it was a viaduct as well as being an aqueduct, for Treffrey's objective in building it was a twofold one. He needed to carry water across this unusually deep valley to a mine on the other side; and he needed a set of narrow-gauge rails for the horse-drawn wagons to convey the ore to the crushing and processing mills.

It is a magnificent structure, even by modern standards. A succession of gigantic granite piers thrust skywards from the heart of the valley, where road and stream come close together; and on either side, up the near-precipitous slopes of the valley, a succession of beautifully graduated piers of lessening height are 'stepped' out of the native rock, seeming almost to grow there, like columnar trees of stone. The combined water channel and narrow-gauge line are carried a hundred feet overhead; looking upwards from the close confines of the valley at this point, one gains the same impression of slightness, almost of ethereality, that is conveyed by Telford's Pontcysyllte Aqueduct striding over the River Dee on the outskirts of Llangollen.

Treffry must have been a very remarkable man; indeed, little short of a genius. He was doing, long before Brunel himself, what that great civil engineer was to do on a major scale with his viaducts and railway-line between Plymouth and Truro. One way to pay tribute to his genius is to attempt the steep and exacting climb up the track that winds sinuously up the valley side to where the viaduct merges with the natural rock. From the top of the valley slope there is a glorious view northwards to the very edge of the china clay country; to the south, a grand vista out over St Blazey's roofs to Par and the open water of St Austell Bay beyond.

Perhaps it may be felt that the terms 'nightmare', or even 'lunar', are unduly strong to describe the china clay region of Cornwall that fills the uplands, and the lower-lying ground too, west of St Blazey, north of St Austell, which was the centre of distribution for the Cornish tin until, in the mid-nineteenth century, this other commodity became its chief concern. You could certainly not find a stronger contrast with the lush secluded valleys between the Fowey and West Looe rivers, or that to the south of Luxulyan beneath Treffry's Aqueduct, than you will find when you turn your face towards Hensbarrow Downs, which actually top the 1000-foot mark. Gigantic cones of this china clay thrust upwards from the ground, ranging in size from 'young' ones, still only on the threshold of life, to the true giants that have already reached maturity. Startlingly white when seen against the remainder of the landscape, and even more so when seen against a blue sky, they challenge curiosity and fire the imagination. Compared with these man-made glistening white pyramids even the enormous salt hills among the salt-pans on the Spanish coast north of Torrevieja seem to have been conceived in a lower key. They too are seen at their most magical, most memorable by night, and beneath a full moon.

Now turn your back on St Austell and make your way north along any one of a remarkable choice of minor roads, almost any one of which will take you in the direction of Roche—a self-explanatory name to anyone with a smattering of French. The more spectacular of the approach roads is that which runs along a ridge on the west side of Hensbarrow Downs. You may get on to it by taking the A 3058 road westward out of St Austell for about three miles and then turning north, on the B 3279, for a couple of miles or so. Near the village of Nanpean you will have to branch off right-handedly on to a smaller road that passes through Curyan north-eastwards. This road, or an even higher-pitched road running almost parallel with it to the right, will bring you in a very few miles to Roche itself, which lies on the B 3274.

Long before you come to the village of Roche, however, your eye will have been caught and held by an excrescence of rock fundamentally different from all the china clay pyramids of the region to which you have been becoming accustomed in spite of their strangeness. This rock mass is clearly natural, not man-made; yet there is something about it that, even from a distance, suggests that man has been associated with it in some way or other. And your supposition will be proved correct—though not, perhaps, quite in the way anticipated.

Roche Rock, as it is called, is a gaunt outcrop of granite that juts out of the bracken-clad tumble of loose boulders about its feet as though in some frantic effort to free itself from some giant's grasp beneath the turf. It is of

Roche Rock

no great height; but because the terrain all about it is, for Cornwall, comparatively level, it gives the impression of dominating an otherwise somewhat featureless landscape almost as the china clay pyramids do in their own peculiar individualistic fashion. Roche Rock, indeed, is not unlike some of the Dartmoor tors in the variety of its cleavage-planes, its rounded edges, and above all its impression of antiquity. If you come upon it from the north face, which is to say from the direction of the village, you will see little other than the virgin granite of this pile, though you may even at that have a half-felt impression that man has at some time been at work upon the material of the pile. As you come past it on the road that runs southwards out of Roche and close beneath its east face, however, not a hundred yards away, you at once see that your suspicion is justified.

For, topping the granite mass is, quite manifestly, a small building of shaped granite blocks. It is roofless, certainly, but it has a window facing south over more tumbled boulders, and a smaller window immediately beneath this one; and there is an unmistakable buttress reinforcing one corner of the structure. The whole gives the impression almost of growing out of, rather than having been superimposed upon, this granite mass; and it most certainly invites closer inspection.

It is, in fact, a diminutive chapel, dedicated as long ago as the year 1409 to St Michael. After clambering over and among the scattered boulders strewn about the foot of the rock in an attempt to follow the narrow and twisting path that threads them, for much of the way totally obliterated by rampaging bracken, you find an iron-runged ladder built into the natural rock and rigid as the granite in which it is pegged. Climb this, and you come at length into the upper part of this tiny chapel; the sense of height experienced is considerably greater than you may have anticipated. You can, if you have a sure foot and a good head for heights, step out of the chapel, over a broken portion of its massive wall, on to the topmost crag of rock. From this vantage-point you will obtain one of the most remarkable and memorable views across Cornwall to be obtained anywhere save on one or other of the summits of Bodmin Moor. From this vantage-point, too, the huge china clay pyramids become temporarily dwarfed; they will, however, regain their fantastic proportions when you descend to ground level once more and begin circulating among them.

What is this strange chapel of Roche Rock? Why is it here? There are the inevitable legends; but for once the Devil's name is not to be found among them. The tradition has more plausibility than most; it may even be authentic. Centuries before the china clay was discovered here, and even longer before it began to be exploited on a commercial basis, this huge expanse of granite landscape was already notable for this one giant 'molar'—the word is as apt as any that might come to mind. So, it was of course the obvious site for a chapel to be built to the glory of God, a focal point for a Faith so recently brought to this land. The chapel was built. And incorporated within it, as a sort of basement hewn out of the solid granite, was a cell for the use of the priest. The cell came in time to be known as the Hermit's Cell; and for a very good reason. Long after the chapel was built and consecrated, a man, possibly the last of a family of local landowners, the Tregarricks, fell victim to leprosy. He was public-spirited enough to incarcerate himself voluntarily here, to rot away until death mercifully released him from his agonising disease; in this way he could reasonably hope that he would not communicate leprosy to his fellow-men. His daughter Gundred, later to be canonised, dedicated her life to serving him. She brought him food and water every day until his death. Then, knowing that she might herself have become contaminated through her devoted service, she took possession of the cell and there lived out the remainder of her days in self-imposed incarceration. Tradition does not say whether in fact she fell victim to leprosy or not; but in any case her gesture was a noble one.

Westwards from Hensbarrow Downs the ground falls away in a pronounced fashion to the valley of the River Fal and, beyond that, to the valley of the Tressilian, whose waters rise only a few miles to the west of the source of the Fal, on the uplands between Penhale and Goss Moor.

'Pen-' and 'Tre-' are well represented in this area, with such euphonious
Cornish names as Tregony and Trelasker, Penvose and Penpell, Tre-
waters and Pengalley; but you must go farther south and east to find the
third of the triumvirate represented, in places such as Polmassick,
Polmenna, and Polsue.

South and south-east of the cathedral city of Truro the estuaries of the
Fal, the Truro and the Tressilian, with their ancillary creeks, form the
most extraordinary network of starfish-like arms reaching into the lush
hinterland with their thickly wooded banks. The roads hereabouts, most
of them little more than narrow lanes running between high-banked
hedges have the disconcerting habit of ending abruptly at the water's edge,
where there may or may not be a ferry to take you to the other side; or, if
there is one, it does not happen to run again that day. No matter: this is no
countryside for hurrying through; better to accept the tempo imposed
upon you and luxuriate (as nature herself is doing) to the full.

Between St Blazey and Falmouth a succession of deep horseshoe bays
indent the coastline: Mevagissey, Veryan, Gerran's Bay being the named
ones, though each has its own minor indentations, such as Gorran Haven,
Porthluney Cove and Porthbean Bay, for example. If it is the coast, the
alternating rock and sandy beach, the high cliff bisected with narrow creek
or inlet, and all 'undiscovered' country compared with the busy and
exploited main seaside resorts, then—this is your country. But not less
rewarding are the odd spots in the hinterland, intersected by these
meandering lanes, almost devoid of villages or hamlets, though sprinkled
with farms hidden snugly at the ends of improbable looking tracks
between high-banked hedges or walls. Among these, behind Nare Head,
which separates Veryan Bay from Gerran's Bay, lies the village of Veryan
itself. It is set on a steep hill that runs north and south and is crossed by a
minor road that vanishes eastwards to lovely Portloe and westwards to join
the A 3078 to St Mawes and Falmouth. Try Veryan for size, as it were:
what you will encounter there will both surprise and please you.

It is a trim and shapely village, with rather more thatch than is
commonly seen in Cornwall. Round its irregular perimeter, and that of
Veryan Green just to the north, there will be found a succession of odd,
small buildings which are known as Veryan's Round Houses. They are not
all in fact literally round, though some of them are; but those that are
hexagonal instead have corners so gently fashioned that they give the
appearance of being round. Most of these little houses are thatched. Some
of them have diminutive thatched porches exactly matching their roofs.
They give the impression of being 'one-up-and-one-down', though this
may not be literally true. There is certainly a Walt Disney look about each
of them. And this impression is strengthened by the fact that the majority
of them have small, often unusually-shaped, windows picked out with
pebbles and shells, their entire frames sometimes being composed of this

Veryan's Round Houses

unlikely material. No two of these small houses are identical; but they all possess much in common, and would seem to have been built about the same time, designed perhaps by the same man; and the fact that each of them has a cross on top of the cone-like thatched roof suggests (quite correctly, as it happens) that they were all built with the same objective in mind.

   Like all peoples of Celtic origin, Cornishmen have always been noted for the intensity of the superstition they share among themselves. It is not always easy to draw a clear-cut line distinguishing between superstition and religion, and this is certainly the case here. The presence of these Veryan Round Houses has a recognised explanation. They were so designed in order to confuse the Devil. Knowing that at all times he was on the look-out for souls to call his own, the problem was to frustrate him and check his malign activities. Hence the crosses erected on the thatched roofs. But this was not the only expedient. By constructing a number of these Round Houses on the perimeter of the village there was a reasonable hope that he would become so confused that in the end, being unable to find his way between them without coming so close to them as to be affected by the power of the crosses, he would eventually give up his evil intentions towards the good people of Veryan, and seek his prey elsewhere. Where that other choice might be was, of course, of little importance to the villagers: in those days communication between one village and another was difficult and therefore rare; and the people of Veryan would argue that the inhabitants of other villages could surely take similar steps to look after themselves. Religion is catered for, here in Veryan, as well as superstition: its church is interesting, and not least for the fact that it is dedicated to one of the least-known of these Cornish-based saints, St Symphorian.

Westwards of Veryan a promontory between the curve of Gerran's Bay and Carrick Roads thrusts southwards to Zone Point. St Mawes, with its fine castle, built to the orders of Henry VIII in 1543 to face Pendennis Castle on the west bank of the Roads and likewise built to his orders, is the only place of any size in this region; and there is little enough of it anyway. Smaller by far are two of Cornwall's most melodiously named sites, St Anthony in Roseland and St Just in Roseland, the former across the Percuil River from St Mawes, the latter a mile or so north on an inlet off the Roads. The name Roseland is deceptive. It does not mean, as is so generally supposed, 'Land of Roses', but derives from the Celtic *rhos*, meaning peninsula. Nevertheless the two names linger hauntingly in the memory and one may be excused for ignoring etymology for once and thinking instead in terms of pure beauty such as the word 'rose' is sure to evoke.

And beautiful indeed this lost corner of the peninsula is. Of all Cornish churches, that of St Just in Roseland, at any rate as regards its setting, must rank as one of the most beautiful and memorable. A steep lane drops down to a fine granite lych gate that gives access to verdant, almost subtropical grounds at the foot of which the church stands at the water's edge.

The church was dedicated to one of those Celtic missionaries who came to Britain in the fifth and sixth centuries; in this case it was St Just, to whom churches and memorial stones and places too are dedicated in many parts of western Cornwall. It was built on the site of the original chapel, or cell occupied by a holy man, which dates from about the year A.D. 550. Records, possibly not absolutely accurate, suggest that this foundation was served by a succession of Celtic missionaries for several centuries until, about a hundred years before the Norman Conquest, it was taken from the Celtic Church by the Bishops of Cornwall and Exeter. This church of St Just, as you see it today, is by comparison with the original chapel almost modern, for it was built only as long ago as the year 1261. The chancel survives from this period of building, though other portions are later, or have been restored over a protracted period. It is not, perhaps, the most beautiful church that Cornwall has to offer; but the sheer beauty of its setting is incomparable.

Church of St Just in Roseland

The lych gate, built of granite and slate, Cornwall's two basic commodities, is beautifully proportioned, unusually massive yet surprisingly graceful, especially in view of the sheer weight of stone embodied in it. Below, beside the water, there is another stone lych gate, modest compared to this upper one but, some would say, less formal and more evocative.

It is inevitable that, the farther west into Cornwall your road leads you, the more congested the country becomes. In the very 'toe' of the county, with Penzance at the arch of the 'instep', a radius no more than eight miles long gives you a half-circle from St Ives in the north by way of Gurnard's Head, Pendeen lighthouse, Cape Cornwall and Land's End, and so round to Gwennap Head to Porthcurno (and the Minack Theatre), Lamorna Cove and Mousehole ('Muz'l' to those who really know the place); and this is a circuit of hardly more than thirty miles in all; the area that it encloses is a good deal less than a hundred square miles.

Consider it for a moment, with a view to quartering it conveniently. The main road, the A 30, drives straight across this area south-westwards to Sennen and Land's End itself. A somewhat lesser road, the A 3071,

395

branches off this just to the west of Penzance and runs almost due west to St Just. (This, of course, is not St Just in Roseland but the saint's name commemorated *tout simple*.) The few remaining roads are all 'B' roads, or else unnumbered roads that have yet to earn official recognition. The B 3306 runs round the north coast from Land's End to St Ives; the B 3315 runs round the south coast, somewhat farther inland, from Land's End to Penzance; the B 3311, B 3312 and B 3283 criss-cross the relatively empty spaces to be found between the two coast roads and the trunk road, and those spaces are further intersected by the handful of unnumbered roads already referred to. There are many parts of Britain in which those authorities responsible for the signposting and other marking of the roads could learn much from the intelligent work that has been done in this very small area of granite upland declining in all directions to the less elevated coastal strip.

In this area, the largest type on the map, apart from that of Penzance and St Ives, will be found in St Just, whose full, though rarely used, name is St Just in Penwith; it is the most westerly township in Cornwall, and therefore in all England. It is no beauty, though its granite buildings large and small have the uncompromising and challenging dignity that is so often found in this county that builds predominantly in this indestructible raw material. St Just was once renowned as a centre for the coming-together of the Cornishmen who wrestled annually for the coveted prize of

Land's End

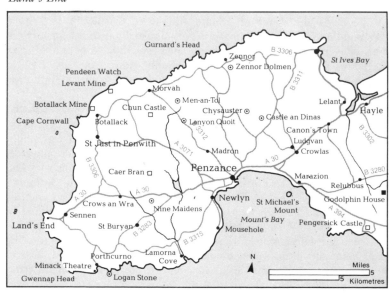

the gold-laced tricorne. It knew real prosperity in the heyday of tin streaming. The abandoned tin mines that helped to bring it this prosperity until a century and a half ago still dominate the scene inland from the road that runs northwards up this gaunt coastline. Few individual objects in all Cornwall make a stronger, more memorable, impact on the eye than the great chimney-stacks and adjoining engine-houses of these old mines. Seen against an empty sky, and especially against a westering sun, or seen in full daylight against the white galleons of clouds sweeping across the Penwith peninsula, they have a stark nobility about them which makes a deep, and leaves an abiding, impression.

It is in this region that the strangest of all the Cornish tin mines is to be located—the famous Botallack Mine. Botallack is famous not simply because in its heyday it was producing a notable supply of first-rate tin ore and also copper ore and, perhaps surprisingly to the layman, arsenic, but because, unlike the many tin mines scattered about on the uplands, this one had its workings *under* the sea, beyond the great cliffs that range to the north and south of Botallack Head. Today you can take your car beyond the village to within a few yards of the cliff's edge and look down at the gaunt remains of the engine-house perched on a granite outcrop from the base of the cliffs only just above the level of high water.

The miners who worked in the narrow and low-ceilinged corridors of Botallack, hewing their way ever farther and farther out beneath the sea in pursuit of the most profitable seams, could, it is said, hear the rumble of loosened granite boulders and pebbles being trundled to and fro by the restless waves all too close above their heads. When a seam had to be followed upwards, instead of on the level or downwards, the miners came perilously close to the sea bed, and watched their straining pit-props with anxious eye. Few, save perhaps those who made their money from the profits in selling the tin and copper, can have been truly grieved when Botallack Mine closed down. Now the sea has broken through and the labyrinthine workings are flooded; only the ruined engine-house survives as a reminder of the hive of activity that once employed so many men, every one of whom daily took his life in his hands as he climbed down the cliff face and entered the mine to work out his laborious shift.

There are, however, older features by many centuries than Botallack Mine and its neighbour, Levant Mine, a couple of miles farther up the coast, whose workings are reputed to have run for more than a mile out beneath the sea bed and from which, during less than a hundred years of operating, more than two million pounds' worth of copper and tin were arduously and dangerously extracted. A glance at the Ordnance Survey map shows that this whole Penwith peninsula is strewn with prehistoric and medieval traces—stone circles, hut circles, lone and legendary standing stones, tumuli, cairns, settlements and 'quoits'. One of these last—the word usually indicates the massive stones of a burial chamber—

One of the many disused Cornish mines

can be well seen beside the B 3312 between Penzance and Morvah. Known as Lanyon Quoit, this is a famous survival of megalithic man's work, with three great blocks of granite supporting an enormous oval capstone some eighteen feet in length, almost nine feet wide and a foot and a half thick.

A mile or so to the north, up the slope away from the road and accessible only by way of a rough track, there is a much more unusual relic of prehistoric man—two rough blocks of granite standing one on either side of a hollow stone set on edge between them. And truly a hollow stone it is: not just a block of granite with an orifice but a stone ring nearly a yard in diameter with a hole in it that is almost perfectly circular and wide enough for a child or a very slim adult to wriggle through from one side to the other. This is the Maen-an-tol; and that is about all that can be said about it. What its purpose was has never been established; nor in all probability will it ever be. Obviously, like so many of these mysteriously shaped stones erected by our remotest forbears, it is of ritualistic significance. Fertility rites are the first explanation that come to mind, though maybe local tradition is nearer the mark in insisting that children squeezed through the hole were cured of rickets.

This area of Cornwall, virtually Land's End, is notable too for the proliferation of ancient Cornish crosses. Many of them, it is true, are today little more than rough stumps, and any carving there may have been on them has been near-obliterated by the passage of the centuries since they were erected. Many of them date back twelve hundred years, to the eighth century. You will find them at cross-roads; in the heart of hamlets like St Buryan, where there is a famous example; set up apparently at random along ancient trackways across the moors; in churchyards; and, as it were, 'in the middle of nowhere'.

Most of these crosses are no more than three or four feet high; often they are smaller than this. Some of them still carry the typical and traditional Cornish type 'cross-cum-circle', its edges now blurred and the whole lichen-grown. In some cases only the stump remains, and one must speculate as to why the upper part was broken off, and when this happened. Not one of these ancient crosses, many of them probably established as parish boundary marks, to be seen throughout this tapering end of Cornwall can begin to compare in stature with the one in the churchyard at Mylor, far to the east near Falmouth. This is the giant of them all, standing as it does some ten feet high. It is, in fact, a granite block not far short of twenty feet in length, for cautious excavation has proved that seven feet of it is buried below the surface. Its survival is doubtless in part due to the fact that it was erected in a churchyard instead of merely in open country, as are most of the others.

The Cornish word for cross, variously spelt, or corrupted, since its early Celtic spelling, is Crowz, or Crows, or Crowse. Place-names incorporating this word can be safely assessed as ancient, for they will have sprung up

about such a landmark. An interesting specimen is to be found beside the
A 30 to the north of St Buryan at a place marked as Crows-an-Wra;
translated, this is simply 'Witch's Cross'. Now, what lies behind this
name? Why has an essentially religious symbol come to be associated with
black magic? Did some maleficent woman (or man: it seems that the term
witch can be applied to individuals of either sex) live here? Or was one such
buried here, traditionally at a cross-roads, with a stake through her breast?
No one can say for sure. But witchcraft is implicit; there has been some
interference by the Devil with the sober Cornishman's way of life, at some
date unknown and, it would seem, now no longer remembered. Inquiry
revealed that a Cornish couple who had lived all their lives in St Buryan,
had 'never heard' of 'Witch's Cross'; but they could pin-point Crows-an-
Wra accurately enough. They had no idea what it meant.

The granite of the whole of this region is memorable. And not least in
the walls and in the smaller, less important buildings. This may seem
paradoxical, but it is not. For in a large building—church or manor house,
for example—even the largest blocks of stone may be to some extent
dwarfed by the scope of the whole conception. But when giant stones are
utilised for a cart shed, for a retaining wall, for some otherwise
insignificant structure, the disproportion between the material used and
the final result becomes emphasised. Nowhere is this more in evidence
than it is along a length of the coast road near Morvah, the B 3306.

Where granite has been used in comparatively recent times, and modern
machinery has been available for shaping the blocks, these are often not
much larger than, say, two-pound loaves. But the granite quarried and
hewn in older times is very different from this. These stones are only very
roughly shaped, and often give the impression of having been almost
literally hacked out of the ground and lifted stage by stage into position.
The nearest parallel to the size and distribution of such enormous stones is
to be found in the north-west of Ireland, near the Atlantic coast, where
superhuman agencies would appear to have manipulated them. A similar,
but much more distant, parallel is to be found, for example, at Tiryns,
between Nauplion and Mycenae, where this so-called Cyclopean building
style may be seen at its most spectacular. Here, surely, the Cyclops
themselves must have been at work? Greece, after all, is the legendary
home of many of the most traditional giants. The sheep-folds at Tiryns
have been in use for so many centuries that you will find, on close
inspection, that the inner side of these vast granite boulders, near to
ground level, have been worn silk-smooth by the passage of untold
thousands of woolly coats moving against them under steady pressure
from the rest of the flock contained between them; it is a minor, but a
telling and memorable aspect of the picture.

Examine these Cornish walls closely and you will be impressed by the
fact that the individual stones, many of which must weigh two, perhaps

Herringbone pattern slate walls

three hundredweight and more, are laid apparently haphazard, with little or no attempt at establishing regular courses. The rock is igneous, not sedimentary, therefore there is no need to ensure that the bedding-planes of each block are recognised and allowed for. So, these gigantic blocks may be tilted one against the other, seemingly without design. Yet, there is clearly an overall equilibrium. There must have been; or these walls, often constructed on undulating, steeply-pitched terrain, would never have stood up to the passage of time, and the weight of animals pressed against them in fields and byres and gateways, and the enormous force of the wind sweeping in continuously off the Atlantic, as they so obviously have succeeded in doing. They amply repay close inspection; and incidentally, when the light is right, as was the case with the component rocks of the Dartmoor tors, they amply repay care and patience and the imaginative use of the camera lens. There are rarely any sharp angles to these granite blocks. Whether deliberately rounded by hammer and chisel (which is unlikely), or by natural disposition plus the effect of centuries of abrasive wind and weather, these blocks rarely present anything more angular than a snub nose, a protruding wedge, a rounded minor end to balance the subtler contours of the remainder.

Northwards in Cornwall the granite little by little gives place to that other characteristic stone, Cornish slate. It is different in most respects, save origin, from the familiar slate of Wales, to be seen in a million roofscapes. At Delabole, well up the coastline beyond Wadebridge and Padstow on the seaward side of Camelford, you will come upon the gigantic quarry named Pengelly. This slate is memorable for the colours to be found in it. Few delights are rarer than to watch an expert slate-splitter (and they are all experts at Delabole) splitting a huge block dislodged from the quarry face by explosives and thus releasing the subtle and lovely tones of green and blue and russet and tawny yellow and gold and every conceivable variation of tone among these.

Where slate predominates it is, of course, the raw material of building. As building material it is both lighter to handle and more malleable than granite. Quite apart from buildings which may consist almost wholly of slate, you will see the potential of this material in countless miles of the characteristic and traditional Cornish wall. The style of building these walls varies from district to district, even from parish to parish; but basically it remains the same in concept. The slabs of slate, of varying thickness, will be set in courses, either vertically on edge so that they look like rough books packed close together on invisible shelving, or slanting left and right in alternating courses, herringbone-wise. Earth, not mortar, is the in-filling medium. It seeps gradually downwards between each slate and its neighbour, gripping both by the simple means of increasing the pressure against them. Four, five, six, perhaps eight courses of slate may be ranged one above the other; and over all is the traditional elongated capping of earth and turf that binds the whole assembly together. One of the simplest and most exhilarating of childhood delights was to run along the top of these endless meandering slate-and-turf walls, at very much more than head height above the staider adults walking soberly along the lane below.

The herring-bone pattern is particularly attractive. It imparts a sense of life, almost of movement, to any wall so built. From a distance, in certain conditions of light, such a wall can look like a length of strongly check-patterned tweed. But the older walls, indeed almost all of these slate walls, are often almost completely overgrown by the plants that have seeded themselves naturally over the years and taken firm root and established themselves for all time. A myriad small plants await the eye of the botanist; the casual observer, especially in June and July, will be struck by the vast number of foxgloves which, among the larger plants, seem to be especially attracted by these earth-and-turf-topped walls, often six or eight feet above road level.

Where the slate is used for roofing it seems to be of two types. It may be the heavy slab, that bears downward with immense weight on the rafters beneath, so that most of the older roofs have subsided into gentle undulations now firmly set in their ways. There is a very fine example of this somewhat farther up the coast, in the village with the romantic,

Arthurian name, Tintagel. But where the ordinary thin-split slates are used the Cornish tradition is to set them edge to edge, sealing the near-invisible joins with bitumen or tar as an extra safeguard against the weight and penetrative properties of rain borne in on the prevailing south-westerlies off the boundless Atlantic.

These south-westerlies, of course, produce a feature that is character-istic of Cornwall and increasingly apparent the nearer you find yourself to the coastline. Save in the remoter valleys there are few high-standing, free-growing trees in this county. The salt in the air and the strong, often violent, winds prevent them from growing to the height and girth that would be attained in inland counties. More than this, the trees, most of them stunted, grow to maturity and old age (like Central European peasants, they tend to look older than they really are, thanks to the conditions in which they live) leaning away from the prevailing wind. In particularly exposed areas, for example just inland from the north coast, they can assume fantastic, even monstrous shapes. Their main trunks are strongly curved to leeward; where they have resisted the steady pressure, and in part succeeded, they have assumed contortions that have become established, so that they seem, particularly in the half-light, to writhe almost like human torsos under great stress; they have reached early maturity, let us say, agonised by frustration.

One odd advantage accrues to this general lopsidedness of the Cornish tree, whether it stands isolated in a field or in clusters along a hedge or field boundary. If you were to emerge from a very minor road on to a less minor road and find, for once, that no signpost existed to help you; and if at the same time the sky was overcast and you therefore could not get your bearings from the position of the sun, you could still form a pretty clear idea of north, south, east and west, and so of the direction you must take to reach your desired destination. The trees all about you would, one and all, be sloping generally in a north-easterly direction because the prevailing wind throughout their lifetimes and those of their ancestors had ordained that they should do so. You have, then, simply to orientate yourself in relation to that clear-cut bearing, and there is no further problem!

In fact, there is only one problem that really confronts today's visitor to the Cornish Peninsula: how to savour to the full the manifold resources of this most popular of all counties without being obliged to do this while shoulder to shoulder with a hundred thousand others who have travelled so far with just this objective in mind. There is of course no counsel of perfection. Obviously one should avoid (unless one has a strong predilection for the close-company of one's fellow-men *en masse*) the main resorts, happily sited mainly along the indented coastline. But there is still, even well into the second half of this twentieth century, a great deal of countryside through which the majority of seaside-bound traffic tends to pass swiftly and unheeding.

Index

Entries in italics refer to persons or groups of persons. In the page references, italics refer to illustrations.